Global Management

Global Management
Universal Theories and Local Realities

edited by
Stewart R. Clegg, Eduardo Ibarra-Colado and
Luis Bueno-Rodriquez

SAGE Publications
London • Thousand Oaks • New Delhi

First published 1999

 SAGE Publications Ltd
6 Bonhill Street
London EC2A 4PU

SAGE Publications Inc.
2455 Teller Road
Thousand Oaks, California 91320

SAGE Publications India Pvt Ltd
32, M-Block Market
Greater Kailash – I
New Delhi 110 048

British Library Cataloguing in Publication data

A catalogue record for this book is available
from the British Library

ISBN 0 7619 5814 2
ISBN 0 7619 5815 0 (pbk)

Library of Congress catalog card number 98–61654

Typeset by Mayhew Typesetting, Rhayader, Powys
Printed in Great Britain by The Cromwell Press Ltd,
Trowbridge, Wiltshire

Contents

Notes on Contributors

Richard Badham is Professor of Management in the BHP Institute for Steel Processing and Products at the University of Wollongong. He is the author of numerous publications in the area of technology, politics and work organization. His most recent book, co-authored with David Buchanan, is *Winning the Turf Game* (Chapman–Sage, in press).

John L. Brown is a researcher in The Centre for Professional Service Firm Management in the Faculty of Business at the University of Alberta in Canada, working with the other colleagues there in the world's leading research centre into professional organizations.

Luis Bueno-Rodriquez is a member of the Organization Studies Research Group at the Universidad Autonoma Metropolitana-Iztapalapa in Mexico City. He is one of Mexico's leading organization theorists with a 'Francophone accent'.

Thomas Clarke is the Professor of Corporate Governance at Leeds Business School, in Leeds Metropolitan University, UK. He is well known for earlier work on 'privatization strategies' and on 'industrial relations' and also holds a position in CEIBS – the China Europe International Business School in Shanghai. A forthcoming book with Stewart Clegg on *Changing Paradigms* will be published in 1998.

Stewart R. Clegg is Professor of Management in the Faculty of Business, School of Management, at the University of Technology, Sydney (UTS), in Australia. He is a well-known contributor to sociology, management and organization theory, and recently won the American Academy of Management George R. Terry Award for the 'most outstanding contribution to management knowledge', awarded to the *Handbook of Organization Studies*.

David J. Cooper is a leading member of The Centre for Professional Service Firm Management in the Faculty of Business at the University of Alberta in Canada. Originally from Britain, he is an editor of *Critical Perspectives on Accounting*, the well-respected journal, unusual in that it regularly contains poems among its contributions. Who says accountants have no aesthetic sense?

Paul Couchman is a Principal Research Fellow in the Department of Management at the University of Wollongong, and Coordinator of the Organizational Change and Innovation Research Program in the university's International Business Research Institute. He is an action researcher, with an interest in the organization and management of manufacturing companies.

Richard Dunford, originally from New Zealand, has spent much of his career in Australia, where he recently became Professor at the University of Western Sydney, Macarthur (where he succeeded Stewart Clegg, briefly), before moving on to the Macquarie Graduate School of Management at Macquarie University, also in Sydney.

Bruno Grancelli is a prominent European sociologist (an Italian who is a specialist on the ex-Soviet Union) who researches and teaches at the Universita degli Studi di Trento, Dipartimento di Sociologia e Ricerca Sociale in the north of Italy, in Trento. He is also a keen sailor.

Royston Greenwood is a leading researcher in The Centre for Professional Service Firm Management in the Faculty of Business at the University of Alberta in Canada. Fond of British sitcoms, beer and football, he still maintains many of his English cultural pursuits, but nonetheless finds certain aspects of the Canadian climate more congenial, and has been in Alberta since 1980.

Cynthia Hardy, another migratory Pom, was previously a member of the Faculty of Management at McGill University in Montreal, Quebec, in Canada. In 1998 she took up an appointment at Melbourne University in Australia. With Stewart Clegg she was an editor of the prize-winning *Handbook of Organization Studies*.

Jean Hatfield is a member of the Department of Commerce at Mount Allison University in New Brunswick, Canada. Seventeen years with the airline industry instilled in her the need to make sense of the culture of organizations – which she is currently completing for a thesis in the Department of Behaviour and Organisation at Lancaster University.

Bob Hinings was a founder member of the Aston School and has forsaken both Britain and Aston for the sirens of Canada and institutional theory. Certain friends have never forgiven him the latter. He is the Director of The Centre for Professional Service Firm Management in the Faculty of Business at the University of Alberta in Edmonton, Canada.

Eduardo Ibarra-Colado, also from the Universidad Autonoma Metropolitana-Iztapalapa Organization Studies Research Group in Mexico City, has recently completed a Doctorate on the organization (and re-organization) of the Mexican Higher Education System. He is well known internationally from his participation in fora such as EGOS (European Group for Organization Studies), APROS (Asia Pacific Researchers in Organization Studies, ISA (International Sociological Association) and the American Academy of Management.

Mihaela Kelemen is a member of the Department of Management at Keele University, in the UK. Her Doctorate, recently completed, was a critical analysis of the TQM phenomena and literature.

Thomas B. Lawrence has worked as a Visiting Lecturer the University of St Andrews, and now works as a member of the Faculty of Business in the University of Victoria, in British Columbia, Canada. Tom combines recreational pursuits and research in activities such as whale watching. We anticipate, with interest, where this reflexivity between work and leisure may lead in future.

Frenando Leal is a member of the Centro Universitario de Ciencias Sociales y Humanidades at the Universidad de Guadalajara in Mexico.

James Lowe was, until his recent tragic death, an ESRC Management Research Fellow at Cardiff Business School. His research interests included the roles of supervisors and front-line management, organizational learning in the manufacturing sector and different conceptions of business performance.

Albert J. Mills another migrant to Canada from the UK, is presently employed in the Department of Management, in the Faculty of Commerce at Saint Mary's University in Halifax, Nova Scotia. He is better known for his contribution to the study of gender and organizations in such journals as *Gender, Work & Organisation*, and for his books, including *Gendering Organizational Analysis*, which he co-edited with Peta Trancred.

Luis Montano, from the Universidad Autonoma Metropolitana-Iztapalapa Organization Studies Research Group in Mexico City was also one of the organizers of the Sixth APROS International Colloquium that was held in the beautiful and enchanted city of Cuernavaca at the end of 1995.

Jonathan Morris is Senior Distinguished Fellow at Cardiff Business School, in Cardiff University, Wales. He has published widely in the area of comparative management, including, with Barry Wilkinson and Max Munday, *Working for the Japanese* (1993).

Nelson Phillips works in the Faculty of Management at McGill University in Montreal, Quebec, in Canada, and has made many contributions to the literature in some of the leading journals in North America. Among other interests he shares with Tom Lawrence is whale watching.

Teresa Rose is a recent graduate of the PhD program in the Faculty of Business at the University of Alberta, Edmonton, Canada. Her research builds on, and extends the work done by the Centre for Professional Service Management by focusing on the internationalization processes of the largest accounting and management consulting firms and describing the impact of global clients on these processes.

Graham Sewell left the University of Wollongong Department of Management to join the Department of Management at the University of Melbourne, also in Australia, a long way from his roots in Southend on the Thames estuary in the UK. He is a contributor to leading European as well as North American journals, such as the *Administrative Science Quarterly*. Also, he shares a fascination with one of the editors of this volume in the œuvre of the Simpsons as well as some of the classics of blues, rhythm, and Latin music, as authentic voices of late twentieth-century popular culture.

Victor M. Soria is one of the founder members of the Universidad Autonoma Metropolitana-Iztapalapa Organization Studies Research Group in Mexico City, and widely regarded as one of the foundational Mexican scholars in this area.

Barry Wilkinson is Professor of Management at the University of Bath, England. He has published widely in organizational sociology, including, with Nick Oliver, *The Japanization of British Industry* (1992) and *Labour and Industry in Pacific Asia* (1994).

Preface

Without the existence of a 'virtual organization', APROS (Asia Pacific Researchers in Organization Studies), and a 'real' organization, Universida Autonoma Metropolitana (UAM), Mexico City, this book would never have come into existence. The chapters collected in this book were all first presented at the Sixth APROS International Colloquium, organized by the editors, and held in the beautiful and historic city of Cuernavaca, Mexico, in December 1995. With this conference APROS made its third venture into the eastern Pacific Rim (earlier conferences had been held in Kyoto, Japan, and Hawaii, USA), but its first in Latin America.

The conference was supported by UAM and we wish to thank them for their assistance. Subsequently, editing of the volume took place in three continents. First, Asia, notably in the special Administrative Region of the People's Republic of China (thanks to Hong Kong University and the Hong Kong Baptist University, who both supported Stewart Clegg as he worked on the book at various times). Secondly, Latin America, in Mexico, where Eduardo Ibarra and Luis Bueno worked on it, and, thirdly, Australia, where the book was finally put together when Eduardo Ibarra visited the University of Technology, Sydney (UTS) at the end of 1997 and worked on the penultimate version with Stewart Clegg. Subsequently Stewart edited the entire manuscript. We would like to acknowledge the assistance provided by the School of Management at UTS in the book's final production, especially the assistance of Anne Ross-Smith, Stella Ng, and Cathy Wright.

Stewart Clegg, Eduardo Ibarra-Colado and Luis Bueno-Rodriquez
Sydney

Introduction

Stewart R. Clegg, Eduardo Ibarra-Colado and
Luis Bueno-Rodriquez

Global Myths that Changed the World

Management theory, in the past, has provided a set of fashionable recipes frequently marketed in such a way as to lead one to regard them as the best solution to the problems of how to manage, and how to organize, modern enterprises. Such theories have promoted a series of representations, myths and legends that have pervaded management thought and shaped managers' actions. Managers, above all, are practical people, beset by many contingencies on a daily basis, some routinized, others not. If Mintzberg (1973) is a reliable guide, they need to find solutions to new problems every ten minutes or so. Not surprisingly, they have little time for other than the most local, contextual and bounded of rationalities. Yet, managers, much as any agents in local contexts, do not conceive themselves immaculately: they take their shape from wider, more discursive rationalities that are available to them. While many forms of knowledge may in practice enter their calculations, in formal theoretical terms the chief forms of knowledge among these will be those represented as theories of organizations and management.

Organization theories have provided, as a best solution for the problems of managing modern organizations, a set of recipes. Such knowledge promotes a series of representations of and for management thinking, often used retrospectively to constitute those actions that have already been undertaken as being in accord with some rationality, as being, thus, legitimated. Hence, accounts are not so much causal springs of actions; rather, actions can be brought-off, justified, in terms of the accounts that discursively, legitimately, seem to be available at any time. However, between these 'accounting' solutions, often presented as universal solutions to particular problems, and the pressures of concrete situations, there exists a tension. In this tension is inscribed management and organizational functioning.

One can clarify the tension if one confronts the organizational rationality of the current epoch with the cultural and institutional forms of local and national realities. On the one hand, that an organizational rationality is presented as such, signifies the triumph of fashionable recipe knowledge.

Organizational theory proffers rationalities that can make the particular universal, that can ascribe the particular as an instance of that which is universal, and thus able to pass as if it were universal, while at the same time they are subject to very specific local modes of production. Thus, when we apply these theoretical rationalities, we can never apply them universally: they always finds application in very different settings, in diverse realities, one might say, with quite locally contingent results. Between the universal prescriptions and the discourses that they privilege reside the local realities.

Management and organizational theories constitute grand narratives that exploit fashionable myths associated with signs of success, such as 'competitiveness', 'excellence', and 'quality', for example, for a global industry. The book market has been inundated with best-sellers from the gurus of management (e.g., authorities such as Peter F. Drucker, Tom Peters, Michael Hammer and James Champy, and Peter Senge). In these books the world is informed through logical sequences, simple principles and platitudinous precepts, how to solve local organizational crises and to succeed in an internationally competitive environment. Where the gurus do not persuade, then perhaps war-stories might: there are many manuals that tell one 'how to', based on unique practitioner 'know-how', as well as biographies that celebrate the innovative capacities of their heroes as they fought strategic campaigns.

Consider the scenarios of innovation and change that are confronting organization managers today and the role that such universalizing theories play as practical knowledge in these local scenes. Chart the distance that separates the universal imaginary from the specific realities in which it must find expression, for it is the latter that determine the exact balance between the recipes and the performance. The cultural and institutional diversity of the world confronts universal organizational rationalities common to the representation of each historical epoch; that is to say, while each may be universal, each is so only for an epoch. (Who, for instance, now recalls the fuss about 'informal organization' and hygiene factors that characterized the 1960s?) In the century whose time has just about past, organizational and management representations were invariably cast in terms of universalist themes. After all, universalism, in its eclipse of particularism, was the very hallmark of modernity, according to influential theorists such as Talcott Parsons.

Increasingly, after Burrell and Morgan's (1979) work, this universalism was constructed, platonistically, in paradigmatic terms. Thus, fashionable recipes, when they display family resemblances, assume a certain coherence, usually discussed in terms of their sharing a common paradigm arranged around systems of values that provide an interpretation of the world. Defining the limits of action, such paradigms establish the rules and procedures that all who would be legitimate are entitled to respect. The fundamental ground of all paradigms is constituted by a presumed universalism, a universalism which projects a paradox. The paradox resides in the particularity of the universal: that which is presumed to be universal is only representable as such from the auspices of a position that is already ethnocentric, yet which presumes to project its ethnocentrism – on the whole world! Where does this universalism reside? In a predominantly Anglo-Saxon conception of paradigm universalism (see its representation by Pfeffer, 1993 and Donaldson, 1995.

The major challenge to this universalism arises from the economic success of organizations whose local realities seemed starkly at odds with those assumed by the universalizers: one thinks, for example, of Whitley's (1994) accounts of East Asian business systems, of Redding's (1990) account of the 'Spirit of Chinese Capitalism', of Clegg's (1990) account of 'French Bread, Italian Fashions, and East Asian Enterprise'. Yet, the currency turbulence of 1997–98 threatened the assumption that there might be organizational scope for local realities, local rationalities, that ran counter to the trend of the universalization. Previously the existence of these alternative realities weakened any recourse to a universalizing vision of order and equilibrium, where everything had its place. Now we might propose that the recent disorder of the markets serves to communicate, once more, in a heightened form, the values of a universal order, reasserting the old rationality over and above the local rationalities. Whatever interpretation one might make of the market's judgement of the East Asian economies, it is evident that much has changed organizationally.

Initially, organizational changes are experienced locally: liquidity tightens, credit becomes more expensive, firms go bankrupt, workers are laid off, currencies are devalued. But the effects are not just local: these experiences result in part from the international connectedness of world-wide markets, such that at the close of the twentieth century no market is an island. Information technology connects every local rationality to the expressive essence of universal rationality constructed as the effects of 'buy or sell' decisions made on a few thousand terminals around the world on a 24-hour basis. Speculation translates into life and death judgements, the rationality of the market; at the time of writing, these impact most adversely on those business systems, and their organizations, that do not correspond to the universally accepted economic prescriptions for excellence. What the speculations of 1997–98 demonstrated is that information technology capacities, and the decision-making that they support, have a universal dimension.

The technological advances associated with information technology have transformed the nature of office work and bureaucracies, as well as trans-forming the structure of occupations. Established occupations have been 're-engineered'; new occupations have been born on the back of the new technologies. The old orders have melted away, however solid they might once have seemed. The nature of property conveyancing, for example, once the bread and butter of suburban legal practice, has been transformed from an arcane knowledge of the files to a capacity to access relatively available data-bases. Conveyancing para-legals now do much of the work that solicitors used to do, at a greatly reduced cost to the consumer.

It is not only occupations that have been transformed. New information technologies have relativized the boundaries of organizations to a considerable extent. Once upon a time, at the core of the theory of bureaucracy, was a split between the public and the private spheres. To the one was the world of masculinity, the public space of the office as the workplace, the sphere of the productive economy; to the other was the world of femininity, the domestic space of the household as a haven in a heartless world. Today the spherical separation of the world that Weber (1978) imagined makes little sense. A vignette helps to make this clear.

Imagine a person called Maria. Maria works mostly in cyberspace. Sometimes, physically, she works at 'home' and sometimes she works at 'work'. Mostly she sleeps at home, however, and in the morning, when she wakes up, she switches on the computer in her study, on the way to the espresso machine in her kitchen. As the water forces through the coffee to make the beverage, she taps into her e-mails. Crisis! Overnight, there has been a currency meltdown through the East Asian economies. First, the Thai baht, then the Indonesian rupiah, Korean won, and now the Australian dollar. It is like Mexico in 1994 all over again, but with a domino effect. Rapidly she switches to her market data-base. The slide has not been arrested. Immediately she logs into the remote access to the office and starts a complex series of computer transactions designed to try to cover the debts that she has accumulated overnight in the portfolios that she managers.

Meanwhile the coffee boils away and her children have stirred, wanting breakfast. Abstractedly she dismisses their calls on her attention and stares anxiously at the screen. All her realities are currently embedded there. Her husband, coming home from his night-shift, attends to the children instead. Later in the day, exercising her flexi-time, she leaves for an appointment at the office. On the way she advises the party that she is meeting, using her new mobile phone, that she will be late because of a traffic-accident that has occurred on the Harbour Bridge, causing a gridlock way up into the northern suburbs. During her afternoon tea-break in the office, after her overseas markets are closed, she logs on to the networked game of *Riven* that she is involved in playing, for some relaxation. Later still she returns home to meet her husband heading off to work and the children once more demanding her attention as she settles down in front of the computer to check the opening prices on the FT 100. The evening is almost over, but before bed beckons, there is homework to do for her MBA. She settles down in front of the television with a small glass of tequilla and a pastrami sandwich and switches it on for the Late News as she prepares her term paper in International Management. Prior to the News, as she ponders the question 'How universal are contemporary management theories? Discuss with reference to Foucault's changing accounts of surveillance and governmentality', she catches the end of a documentary about the history of the post-Cold War world, charting its changing fortunes since the collapse of the Berlin Wall. (She thinks 'I would love to visit Germany one day'.) But it is only a momentary thought: other, more reflexive thoughts jostle her attention. It would be surprising, in such a scenario, if Maria were not to be a little reflexive.

Reflexively, the resurgence of neo-liberalism as a form of governmental rationality, rather than as just economic doctrine (an account that she had found in Foucault, 1997 and Rose, 1996), seemed increasingly to be relevant to her life as well as to her paper. She was well aware of how, increasingly, she governed herself in the name of other rationalities, and lived in an increasingly neurotic state of ego-surveillance – where she was doing the surveillance that allowed her to be under surveillance by others (she thought of that e-mail requiring an instant reply that she had received from her 'supervisor' [who couldn't see her] when working at home earlier that week: she was sure it was sent just to check up on whether she was at her work-station.). It wasn't only Foucault that seemed to be connecting her study, her life, and her work in an intricate interlacing of escalating anxiety and enlightenment. There was also the evening's news, she reflected: was the meltdown in East Asia the revenge of universal theories, delivered through the judgements of the markets, on the idiosyncracies of local particularisms out of kilter with the times? Maybe, instead, as one of her tutors suggested, it was just a sign of the hegemonic dominance, premised on both ideological legitimacy and financial power, of one presumed best-way of running the new world order? Yet, how can it be that the very factors that her books told her contributed to the success of these economies were now being hailed as the signs of their weakness?

Absent-mindedly, as she did her nails and continued to watch the television, she thought some more about her MBA. She had spent time at a workshop with her feminist tutor at the university recently, deconstructing the sexist bias of organization theory from Weber to the present day, particularly in its privileging of the public over the private. She, on the other hand, was not sure that these terms meant much to her, and certainly not to her children, anymore. She almost did as much work from home for her employer as she did from work. At least at work she had opportunities for conviviality which were singularly lacking at home. Her husband was rarely there when she was, and they needed the shift-work earnings that he made to pay the mortgage and the child-care costs, which, she speculated, were likely to rise again if the Australian dollar kept declining (interest rates would almost certainly be increased to try to arrest capital flight, according to her finance lecturer). What was private and what was public anymore? She wasn't sure, but having just smeared her varnish, she wasn't in any mood to think about it any further right then.

Later, in bed, with a few minutes to catch up on the back-log of papers, she noticed an article by Adele Horin in the *Sydney Morning Herald* of the 25 October 1997 on a new book. The book was by Arlie Hochschild (1997), called *The Time Bind*, and published by an American company, Henry Holt & Co. Hochschild's argument seemed to be that it was less stressful to be at work than to be at home these days. I hardly know the difference, she thought, as she drifted off to sleep, fretting not only about the markets but also her MBA paper. Could she work Hochschild into it, she wondered? Maybe one of her professors, who she knew was working on a book on 'global management', might be able to advise her?

For Maria, as a student practitioner of the management arts, market turbulence foreshadowed major intellectual as well as practical preoccupations. To what extent were the organization and management theories that she was learning about prepared to change their traditional universalism and recognize the diversity of the world that she moved in, saw on the News, and experienced in her everyday life? What role did universal theories, grand narratives as she had learnt Lyotard (1985) call them, play in the constitution of the many local realities and diversities she had to navigate? Or, to put it slightly differently, what, in the past, had been the symbolic function of universalism? How does it reintegrate diverse worlds? How does it perform the odd trick of being a particular universalism that denies its provenance as it simultaneously seeks to hold sway over all domains, all places, all times? These are not merely academic concerns, as we would have Maria realize. If we could construct the reader as easily as Maria we would have her realize this also.

The institutional spaces within which organizational and management knowledge flourish are dominated by an ethnocentric vision that assumes the a priori of a modernity already installed. It is only within this modernity that we can think in terms of its presumed universalism. Local differences are to be managed from within a logic of development in which everything that does not respect the rule of the grand narrative can only be considered as deviant, as an example of the type of error for which the universal theory serves as a corrective. Universal theory requires local error; without it truth would not be transparent. For this reason, the unique problem for universalism resides in the determination of ways in which problems of organization are constituted as problems outside the norm, outside the rule, outside that which would be universal. Such organizations, to preserve rationality, must be chastened in order to become modern exemplars of the one reality that is universal. In the absence of such retribution they remain an instance of the many realities that must be local, and being so, must be in error, according to the universalistic perspective. Such error defines reality, representing the modern hope either of integrating or containing everything that exists outside its logic of rationalization. That which cannot be integrated or contained must be destroyed. That which remains, appears as the universal logic of the electronic market, especially to those subjected to its dictates. As Morin (1984) suggests, we need a theory of error rather than of order.

The gaze embedded in a vision that locates itself as a universal pinnacle can see only that which is close to it, normatively, however encompassing its viewpoint may be. The 'other' can only be absent, an empty space with no substantive existence, in the face of an overriding presence. The other is only recognizable when its presence is subordinated to the universal gaze; thus, it can only ever attain a subjected position. Any universal gaze of the cultural world must, by definition, be ethnocentric. As such, its gaze ranges across the terrain made visible in any by the 'postmodern', 'post-industrial', 'post-Fordist', 'post-bureaucratic', 'post-masculinist' world, that world of 'post' societies that comprises the imagined societies for certain types of intellectual of the First World, one that sees only those subjects visible and recognizable to the colonizing hero's vision, fixed in the universalizing gaze. The rest of the world, those 'past' societies that are not advanced, not economically rational, not white, and not Western, are only a complement, a domain, a data, an occasion for the market to correct. Error reigns supreme in order to prove truth.

In reality, the problem is complex because a diverse world co-exists simultaneously with an organizational logic that presumes and assumes a universal character, one, however, that can only really find its specific forms in the institutional and cultural contexts of every local reality. As we have already indicated, the contrast between the fashionable recipes and the results of their translation to these diverse locales, establishes the terms of this ambivalence.

The Margins

Our introductory contribution is written from the margins – but these margins differ greatly. One is geographically proximate to the imperium, while culturally distant; the other is culturally proximate, while geographically distant. One uses the colonial language of today; the other finds itself at home in a colonial language of the past: each locale struggles with the ghosts of its colonial past in ways that make the histories still real, still lived, whether by aboriginal people or Zapatistas, seeking land rights and reconciliation with their respective invaders. Thus, both Mexico and Australia are colonial and post-colonial spaces simultaneously, depending on the metric applied. However different their respective sense of place and space may be, the editors share one characteristic: struggling to make sense of organizations and politics in these places and spaces through theories that are overwhelmingly produced and reproduced elsewhere, under different assumptions, from different realities.

For our Latin-speaking contributors, language and culture are a large part of the problem – the two are inexorably intertwined. For the English-speaking authors, the signs of difference are far more elusive, more subtle. So much of their reality is a reality made elsewhere, in the North American core of the USA. None of our contributors occupy this space, although some are, in several senses of the term, peripheral to it. Even in this proximate culture and language, there remains a recognizable sense of difference embedded in a peculiar history and specific institutions. This only reasserts, again, that while universal management practices may often be proclaimed as such, they always have to be implemented through local regimes.

The main contribution of this book lies in exploring the dichotomy between universalism and locality. Organizations and their management are always inscribed in a tension between attempts at universalism, as fashionable recipes and institutionalized knowledge are taken up, and the pull of situational particularisms: locales, places, spaces and times, in which are inscribed specific substantive values. Sometimes these are the stuff that makes organization possible; on other occasions they may be deeply destructive and disorganizing.

Prehistory

Some current fashionable management recipes, such as 'quality', are not as new as many might believe. There has been a concern with related matters from at least the beginning of modern management and organization theory, when Taylor became constituted as the first mythical hero of the new American managerial ideals of progress and prosperity attained through rational efficiency. The application of scientific management principles were the first universal imaginary of management theory. The 'one best way' was the only way to achieve economic successes and social wealth. Time-and-motion studies functioned as a very effective disciplinary practice, because they sought to abstract the 'secrets' of the labour process from workers. The reason was to limit the rationality of workers in favour of the newly prescribed rationality of the surveillance formally embedded as the 'best way' by the new managers of industrial enterprises. The incorporation of new technology to the production process supported a system of ever more deeply differentiated work, imposing new rhythms on to workers who previously had these rhythms in their own hands. The abiding image of Taylor is of a stern and highly disciplined gentleman, surveying the scene with a stopwatch held firmly in his hand, and a slide-ruler not far away. The chronometer symbolically represented the authority of management over workers. All these elements – the corporeal, symbolic and technological dimensions – gave shape to only one disciplinary form that projected an imagery in which the essential properties of the enterprise were in the management and disposition of work-time, especially as it was limited by management authority.

The Ford Motor Company in Detroit, the most powerful USA business firm in the world in the early 1920s, constituted an organizational example for many enterprises to follow. The typical model of organization became represented by rational bureaucracy based on the principles of standardized production and vertical integration. From the 1920s industrial production was organized through the assembly-line, thus facilitating the production of goods 'in series'. The workers increased the intensity of their work-rhythms, yet sought also to reject this productive order through informal norms or rules of behaviour, sometimes in strikes commanded by the union bureaucracies that emerged parallel with the machine-bureaucracies of Fordism; sometimes more spontaneously. Individually, workers resisted Fordism through increasing rates of absenteeism, high turnover, low quality in production, spoiling materials, simulating work, and sabotaging machines.

Taylorism/Fordism, as the first generalized organizational rationality, imposed a new organization structure of work and a new norm of consumption that gave way to a more coherent social organization based on the expansion of markets, through new forms of marketing and credit. However, the specific experiences were very different from the universal imaginary. The recipes that were promoted could never be applied directly to the latter (Nelson, 1979; Williams et al., 1992). Taylorism/Fordism represented an organizational rationality that took a specific form in the institutional and cultural contexts that determined its success or failure.

By the 1970s Taylorism/Fordism was a pervasive failure. The inefficiencies of the standardized systems of fabrication indicated the end of these recipes in the 1970s: unable to survive the conditions of uncertainty associated with dynamic and diversified markets that emerged as the early stages of a global economy, with new technological and institutional conditions within which enterprises were to function, the old certainties were eclipsed in a crisis of management knowledge: first, in consumption, especially in the consumers' rejection of poor-quality products in favour of perceived better-quality goods from Japan; secondly, in the demand for differentiated rather than mass products; thirdly, in the production of knowledge – knowledge of what, for what?

It was during the 1970s that we saw the transition to a new organizational rationality that tried to solve the productive rigidities inherited from the older recipes. New formulas were sought to increase flexibility in production, management and marketing. There is general agreement that the post-1970s conjuncture required flexibility in production and increasing quality. However, the ways chosen have been very diverse; yet, despite the diversity of the solutions (from TQM, through continuous improvement, to business process re-engineering, and beyond), they are always proffered as if they were, in principle, universally generalizable.

Empirical research and comparative studies allow one to grasp that such recipes never applied completely, anyway. The results associated with their translation always left something behind in the specificity of local and cultural contexts. Above all, the recipes were of symbolic value. The initial symbolic referent was the success of Japanese industry (although, more recently, some reference might have been made, at least before the market ruptures of 1997, to leading-edge firms, such as Samsung, in other of the economically powerful countries of East Asia). The question now must be, after the economic calamities afflicting East Asia, including Japan, where will one find the new local recipes that should be generalized universally?

Maybe it is time to go back to the USA, and look at some of the new-fashioned neo-monopolists, such as Microsoft (Clegg and Clarke, this volume)?

New Recipes

The end of the Taylorist/Fordist systems of fabrication gave way to more flexible forms of organization. To solve the rigidities of the previous system, enterprises began to reconvert the old assembly-lines to incorporate numerically controlled machines and robotics, to try to realize the dream of the fully flexible firm. Such projects tried to save time between operations, when the work processes were being re-jigged, tried to balance the differentials between lines and work-stations in production, and thus minimize the need for stores of inventories, raw materials, products-in-process, and finished products. Additionally, advances in electronics and informatics allowed better planning of time and better integration of polyvalent production systems. Instantaneous reprogramming provides an opportunity to respond to the changing necessities of the market as it becomes more segmented and unstable. Japanese models synthesized these new efforts of productive reconversion, basing them on total quality management (TQM) and just-in-time (JIT) production. These new flexible systems of production require a new, more 'social', worker, and also a new model of strategic management, based on the reorganization of labour rules. For example, to recruit workers with higher levels of skill it was necessary to change the idea of internal labour markets, to modify labour legislation, and to eliminate obstacles to productivity. The collective agreements that provided the contractual basis of organization, in employment relations, also required redefinition.

Within work, productivity and quality became associated with new models of participation. These models promoted the identification of the worker with the enterprise, using techniques such as work enrichment, quality circles, and humanization programmes. Such programmes posited a modification of the relational deal that had previously been established between workers and managers. In the past, these relations tended to individualize workers under the gaze of the supervisor. For the future, the transition seemed to be one where the group becomes its own collective supervisor, practising a form of collective self-management.

While the object of self-management may be to create a collectively reflexive and functioning entity, the subjects required to do this frequently remain doggedly individualistic in their historical constitution, present identity, and future possibilities. Translating supervisory vigilance from a superordinate to a collectively group-based and self-reflexive gaze, where the employees apprehend their own defects, rather than have them pointed out subsequently, is the way of the future (Morris, Lowe and Wilkinson, this collection). The pressure is on to create a new type of personality; one that is constantly neurotic as a condition of existence because one knows that however well one had done, one could always do better. Even if the standard is exceeded, it can always be made tougher. In principle, there is no respite from the effects of self-surveillance, as du Gay (1996) recognized.

The limits of the new forms of participation must not be overstepped: they are a necessary security for the continuing control of the enterprise. The new models and their recipes require a specific type of participation, so the question is – participation to what extent? Participation is welcomed when it reduces costs, increases productivity, quality, and innovation. But what of a broader-based participation? In their contributions, Kelemen and Dunford investigate some answers to this question.

The new forms of participation require more co-operation at work if we compare them to the Taylorist/Fordist models of organization. Consequently, participation potentially increases workers' power. Workers now have the capacity to dislocate and disrupt the entire system of work relations in just a few seconds, if they choose. The ties of co-operation and consensus are more fragile than the purely instrumental cash-nexus, because they require active consent, not just passivity, in the face of the organization and its technology. To control against these possibilities being realized, managers provide economic bonuses linked to productivity, and try to recommodify the new emotionalism at the heart of the changed contractual commitments. Management designs a new symbolic architecture and landscape for the organization (Gagliardi, 1990). Ideas that stress the one big 'family' metaphor applied to the work-group and to unity within the enterprise as a 'community' become favoured management rhetoric. The power of these new recipes resides in their capacity to reinforce individualistic and competitive behaviours, but at the same time to appropriate the name of solidarity and unity that in the past characterized resistance to management prerogative rather than its further extension. The new capacity is inverted on the shop-floor as well as being extended into the official ranks of management: witness the discourses of 'excellence' (Peters and Waterman, 1982). From this moment the enterprise becomes preoccupied with corporate culture (Kono and Clegg, 1998). The individual's identity as an employee becomes something that the enterprise seeks to produce as practical autonomy, where work-fulfilment becomes a source of personal fulfilment and identity, in an informal environment of work. Managers and work-groups, in principle, acquire a common sense of identity to orient their thinking, beliefs, and values, as they face work, markets, and competition. Not surprisingly, such messages, filtered through old habits, may well be contradictory, a double-bind of schizoid potential.

According to the flexible recipes, the enterprise will be successful where it realizes a scenario in which the sense that individuals have of themselves accords with that which management would script for them. The problem with this strategy of producing interdependent independencies is that it overstates the possibilities for cultural unity and identity in the first place. The workplace, since at least Taylor, has been a locale of cultural tension:

after all, it was in large part as a result of linguistic heterodoxia that Taylorism first seemed attractive as a way of overcoming the 'Babel' of the workplace composed of multicultural first-generation immigrants. Today's workplaces in the major European, North American and Australasian cities are no less heterodox. When one is a Muslim and the other is a Christian or an adherent of Buddhism or Orthodoxy, one hardly has the basis for familial or cultural solidarity, despite whatever platitudes management might mouth. Western values, such as individualism, leadership, entrepreneurship, competition, initiative, etc., are the terms proffered for cultural and familial incorporation, yet not every culture is as comfortable with these values as the dominant Anglo-Saxon cultures. For many, these terms are as alien as a new language. How these terms resonate, or fail to resonate, with values held dear within one's community, is supremely important. The new recipes may be thought of as a tool used to shape individual and group behaviour. The tool is not innocent or, value-neutral any more than is language. Language projects a social imaginary from which people are supposed to think and act. In fact, the imaginary constitutes discursive strategies, from which, in different cultural contexts (that are both local and national), different cultural identities are tacitly subjugated to the promissory note of a paradoxical cultural universalism (of competition etc.), paradoxical because universalism is the localism of Western economic rationality, the context for globalization today. No wonder that there should be fault-lines, tensions, strains.

Remaking the World Locally

Are organizations that follow universal strategies more successful than others? Are there specific frameworks (such as are addressed in the contribution by Grancelli on Russia) that need to be in place before a universal, market-oriented strategy works? Are there drawbacks of universal strategies that can only be answered by local adaptations or completely different local strategies? The universalisms are many, if sometimes similar. For instance, in the wake of the MIT studies of 'lean production' (Womack et al., 1990), techniques such as TQM, 'continuous improvement', the 'learning' organization, and the importance of 'downsizing' for leanness, have become the very stuff of fashionable management theory. Sandkull (1996) has suggested that these are 'management myths'. They are the presumed universals driving current management theory, manufacturing restructuring, and consultancy advice (Ramsay, 1996), the 'rising sun' that illuminates thoroughly modern management.

The book starts with Sewell's historical study of how such universal strategies developed and continues with an account by Mills and Hatfield of how they have been reinforced and incorporated within the conventional wisdom of successful US textbooks. Mills and Hatfield's contribution is clearly lodged within what has become known as the 'contra', rather than the 'orthodox', camp of organization studies (Marsden and Townley, 1996) and demonstrates how the global agenda of 'organization' and 'management' theories that have been forged in the leading US textbooks display the symptomatic silences and absences of the local times that they sought to chart globally. It moves on to consider some examples of universal strategies and the problems that they present (Dunford, Soria, Grancelli). This first part of the book, through its various historical and comparative strategies, deconstructs the myth of global management universalism that has recently been so much in vogue after the MIT studies, and points to its downside, the dark side that the guru's gloss over.

One of the least studied but most important spheres of organizational action is the global organization of the contemporary era: accomplished by bodies such as the United Nations and its various agencies, and the World Bank. Soria's contribution addresses how the World Bank's organizational paradigm places the following universal values as the prime objectives for social programmes: 'universality of coverage', 'equity', 'efficiency', 'community participation', 'decentralization and municipalization'. It is these values that are located at the centre of the design of organization structures and the development of an 'adaptive' management. Yet, the World Bank is a persistently failing organizational programme. Soria's contribution identifies how the organizational practices that are supposed to deliver a solution remain the problem.

Following on the theme of 'organizational failure' is a contribution that studies a system-wide failure of organization. The failure is that of Russia. Management theorists forget the lessons of Max Weber at their peril. One of the most important of Weber's lessons, little heeded in a context where these things could be assumed, was the importance of a rational state, rational law and rational money as frameworks for capitalist rationality to flourish. The post-Soviet situation in Russia presents a context where Weber's lessons seemingly are being painfully re-learnt, from scratch. The market cannot be created simply by presidential proclamation or consultancy, but depends upon a specific 'economic culture', one in which certain values are well established.

Comparative studies (the contributions by Couchman and Badham, and Morris, Lowe and Wilkinson) establish how, even in the most influential and contemporary of modern management and organization theories, a key role is played by local values that are often more implicit and taken for granted than explicit and acknowledged. Yet, they affect the nature of the theories, their implementation and their effectiveness when put into practice in substantively distinct contexts.

Critiquing the Global World of Management Theories

Total quality management has been the most universally adopted aspect of recent global 'best practice' management. Although its reception has been largely uncritical to present, or critiqued mainly in theoretical terms, Kelemen's contribution systematically deconstructs TQM from a perspective that makes explicit the implicit power relations hidden within the TQM concept. What counts as TQM is constructed and, therefore, contingent upon people's interpretations. Locally, TQM has multiple individual meanings but, ultimately, one account (typically top management's) wins out, often only temporarily, and is taken to be the 'truth'.

The contribution by Clegg and Clarke picks up some themes from the TQM framework, by looking at recent attempts at globalizing a model of intelligent organization as best practice, from the lean production and quality debates of the early 1990s through to the current concern with virtual organizations. It becomes evident that while intelligent organizations require clever countries to make organization learning possible, the conditions for the widespread dissemination of organization learning, at least of an exploitative type, serve to undermine whatever competitive advantages clever countries might enjoy. The implications of this paradox for modes of organization learning are explored.

Total quality management, quality, and intelligent organizations, all function as metaphors. Recently, in the wake of Morgan's (1986) work on the 'metaphors' of organization, it has become easy to accommodate any new perspectives or values in organization and management theory as new metaphors. One thinks, for instance, of Foucault's contribution being attributed to the 'Foucault effect' of the 'disciplinary' metaphor. Metaphors are inherently value-based. To say that one thing is like another thing, in a metaphorical allusion, is to make an implicit value statement. But what do we *do* when we use metaphors in organization theory? According to Montano, we are involved in a seemingly superficial way in some complex methodological, epistemological and ontological work. The use of metaphors will never seem as innocent again.

Rethinking Values, Collaboration and Global Management as Political Practices

Finally, the book opens up new approaches (Leal, Lawrence, Phillips and Hardy, and Greenwood, Rose, Brown, Cooper and Hinings). Leal notes that the existence of different interests and values, as well as conflicts over them, are inherent to any organization. Rather than settle these by managerial fiat, the normal strategy of organizational power, Leal recommends a method of organizational dialogue and collaboration, that is more truly political because it involves mutual negotiation of complementary views of the nature of what is taken to be 'real'. The next contribution is a fascinating case where a conflict of interests, but not of values, in Leal's terms, is turned into practical exemplification of the dialogue that he recommends. Lawrence, Phillips and Hardy focus on the emergence of a theory of collaboration that is essentially a political theory of organizations.

Collaboration does not assume common interests, in Leal's terms, as an a priori, despite the many assumptions in the consulting literature that seem to suggest a contrary view. Uncommon interests may lead, through a value that stresses collaboration, to a political dialogue of the type that Leal recommends.

In terms of global management some collaborations and some political partnerships are more influential than others. At the core of capitalism is the value of double-entry book-keeping, according to Weber (1976), for whom, while this prosaic value had almost a religious quality, and certainly a religious affinity, it always displayed a value of rationality. If Russia is the most spectacular contemporary example of an economy with system-wide organization failure, then the international accounting firms seem to be the very embodiment of that missing rationality. The major league accounting firms are the regulators of the global economy. Chapter 13, by Royston Greenwood, Teresa Rose, John L. Brown, David J. Cooper and Bob Hinings examines how the professional services area, in becoming global, has developed styles of management that are distinctive depending on the national origin of the original form or forms from which the global corporation has emerged. Each accounting corporation offers a similar range of diversified services but each does not offer them similarly. One aspect of a globalized economy is that nationally specific value-differences globalize, not that everything converges on one form. Existing organization theory frameworks have not captured these processes adequately. In an innovative use of developments from institutional theory, the authors develop a theory of archetypes that captures the emergent and hybrid management and organization practices of the 'Big Six' accounting firms. Hence, the contribution concludes by showing how even the architects of the global economy are themselves shaped in their archetypes by the ways in which organizations' local political biographies are constructed.

References

Burrell, G. and Morgan, G. (1979) *Sociological Paradigms and Organizational Analysis*. London: Hutchinson.

Clegg, S.R. (1990) *Modern Organizations. Organization Studies in the Postmodern World*. London: Sage.

Donaldson, L. (1995) *American Anti-management Theories of Organization: a Critique of Paradigm Proliferation*. Cambridge: Cambridge University Press.

du Gay, P. (1996) *Consumption and Identity at Work*. London: Sage.

Foucault, M. (1997) 'The birth of biopolitics', in M. Foucault, *Ethics, Subjectivity and Truth*, edited by P. Rabinow. New York: The New York Press. pp. 73–9.

Gagliardi, P. (ed.) (1990) *Symbols and Artifacts: Views of the Corporate Landscape*. Berlin: de Gruyter.

Hochschild, A.R. (1997) *The Time Bind: When Work Becomes Home and Home Becomes Work*. New York: Henry Holt & Co.

Kono, T. and Clegg, S.R. (1998) *Transformation of Corporate Culture: Experiences of Japanese Companies*. Berlin: de Gruyter.

Lyotard, J.-F. (1985) *The Postmodern Condition: A Report on Knowledge.* Minneapolis: University of Minnesota Press.

Marsden, R. and Townley, B. (1996) 'The owl of Minerva: reflections on theory in practice', in S.R. Clegg, C. Hardy and W.R. Nord (eds), *Handbook of Organization Studies.* London: Sage. pp. 659–75.

Mintzberg, H. (1973) *The Nature of Managerial Work.* New York: Harper & Row.

Morgan, G. (1986) *Images of Organization.* Beverly Hills, CA: Sage.

Morin, E. (1984) 'El error de subestimar el error', in E. Morin, *Ciencia con Consciencia.* Barcelona: Anthropos. pp. 273–89.

Nelson, D. (1979) *Managers and Workers. Origins of the New Factory System in the United States, 1880–1920.* Madison, WI: University of Wisconsin Press.

Peters, T. and Waterman, R. (1982) *In Search of Excellence.* New York: Harper & Row.

Pfeffer, J.(1993) 'Barriers to the advance of organizational science: paradigm development as a dependent variable', *Academy of Management Review,* 18 (4): 599–620.

Ramsay, H. (1996) 'Managing sceptically: a critique of organizational fashion', in S.R. Clegg and G. Palmer (eds), *The Politics of Management Knowledge.* London: Sage. pp. 155–72.

Redding, S.G. (1990) *The Spirit of Chinese Capitalism.* Berlin: de Gruyter.

Rose, N.S. (1996) *Inventing Our Selves: Psychology, Power, and Personhood.* Cambridge: Cambridge University Press.

Sandkull, B. (1996) 'Lean production: the myth which changes the world?', in S.R. Clegg and G. Palmer (eds), *The Politics of Management Knowledge.* London: Sage. pp. 69–79.

Weber, M. (1976) *The Protestant Ethic and the Spirit of Capitalism.* London: Allen and Unwin.

Weber, M. (1978) *Economy and Society: an Outline of Interpretive Sociology* (2 vols), edited by G. Roth and C. Wittich. Berkeley, CA: University of California Press.

Whitley, R. (1994) *Business Systems in East Asia: Firms, Markets and Societies.* London: Sage.

Williams, K., Haslam, C. and Williams, J. (1992) 'Ford versus "Fordism": the beginning of mass production?', *Work, Employment & Society,* (6): 517–55.

Womack, J.P., Jones, D.T. and Roos, D. (1990) *The Machine that Changed the World.* New York: Rawson.

PART 1

GLOBAL MYTHS THAT CHANGED THE WORLD

---

1   How the Giraffe got its Neck: an Organizational 'Just So' Story, or Continuous Improvement and the Limits to Managerial Orthodoxy

Graham Sewell

Although, at one level, this chapter may appear to be both playful in its title[1] and polemical in its content, its intent is very serious – to explore the ways in which contemporary management approaches articulate the idea of 'continuous improvement'. Not that continuous improvement is a new phenomenon – it will become evident later on in this chapter that there has been a preoccupation with this notion throughout the history of management thought. However, with the emerging interest in techniques like 'total quality management' (TQM) and, more recently, 'organizational learning', continuous improvement has been systematically and explicitly integrated into the mainstream of management theory. As a result, it deserves closer scrutiny, especially as prescriptive management tests look towards the emulation of 'best practice' as a key component of continuous improvement. This implies that, first, we can identify best practice as a set of processes or techniques and, secondly, that these can then be transferred to other organizations. Such an assertion opens up two obvious avenues of inquiry – *how* are best practices identified and *how* are they then transferred? Most TQM and organizational learning texts tend to concentrate on the former question, while tending to assume that the emulation of best practice follows on as part of a competitive process. Thus, successful firms are those which, if they are not already pioneers of best practice, can quickly adopt them. This suggests a process of organizational adaptation and, invoking the trope of evolutionary development, implies that the most successful organizations have always been the most adaptable. Although the term 'survival of the fittest' does not appear in the first edition of *The Origin of Species* (Darwin, 1859),[2] its association with evolutionary tropes in the human and social sciences is reflected in management discourse which lionizes the 'fittest' organizations that provide us with edifying examples of best practice. The recent popularity of the notion of the 'learning organization', with Senge's *The Fifth Discipline* (1990) being only the most popular of texts, reflects the long-running concern of management literatures to identify the essence of the adaptive and, thus, enduring organization (although Senge, himself emphasizes the notion of 'generativeness', suggesting simple 'survival' is too negative as a motivational mantra). Refreshingly, Senge's book is less hectoring and rigidly programmatic in tone than other management 'guru' books,[3] but it still contains a highly normative and didactic approach to the transformation of companies that might culminate in the elusive 'learning organization'.[4]

This chapter will not directly attempt a thoroughgoing critique of Senge's work, although his particular approach to continuous improvement is undoubtably an important one. Nevertheless, it is concerned, in the main part, with scrutinizing a narrow area of literature – quality management – that, prima facie, appears to be closely aligned with the organizational learning movement and its attempts to identify the particular organizational forms which best facilitate the adaptability that authors like Senge seek. In order to do this, initially the chapter draws parallels between the development of, on the one hand, social theories influenced by principles of evolutionary biology and, on the other hand, more recent ideas of organizational adaptation. It will then examine how best practice is identified on a day-to-day basis in organizations. Here my focus is that of manufacturing – in particular, the debates that range over, respectively, the micro-level impact of 'quality' management, and the organization of the labour process into teams which possess varied levels of autonomy in relation to the inception and implementation of work. Finally, I will return to the broader issue of organizational adaptation and offer some speculative comments on how the use of biologically-derived tropes may distort our ideas of organizational change in a particularly pernicious manner.

An Excursion through Evolutionary Theory as applied to Organizations

Before embarking upon the substantive discussion contained in this chapter I would like to comment on the common invocations of evolutionary theory found in social science literature. Despite notions of evolution having long since passed into the realm of 'common sense', Darwinian theory is far from being an uncontested terrain. For example, the recent works of Richard Dawkins such as *The Selfish Gene* (1976), *The Blind*

Watchmaker (1986) and *River Out of Eden* (1995) have formed a highly controversial focus for a renewed debate as to the verisimilitude of Darwin's vision of evolution – that is a series of random mutations being naturally selected on the basis of biological functionality and then passed on through genetic reproduction.[5] However, with the emergence of the apparently 'irrefutable' evidence of the Human Genome Project impinging on this debate, vested interests seem prepared increasingly to characterize dissent against Darwinian evolutionary theory as being irrationalist, lumping any criticism of its 'truth' claims in with the fundamentalist rump formed by Creationists.[6] In the light of these developments, some of Dawkins's less guarded pronouncements on Darwinism bear a startling resemblance to 'end of history/ideology' arguments emanating from certain social commentators in the early 1990s. Norris (1993) has convincingly and effectively dispatched such 'end of ideology' delusions (as if anybody really took these ideas seriously) but challenging Science with a capital S is a more troublesome proposition. But have these developments in the biological sciences and genetics increased the legitimacy of the use of the evolutionary trope in contemporary social science?

The deference of social science to evolutionary principles in the desire to validate truth claims has a chequered and ignoble history. Indeed, a brief reflection on the matter does not reveal an auspicious and edifying genealogy. One only has to consider the impact of Social Darwinism and its articulation through the Eugenics movement in the early part of the twentieth century to realize that the use of the evolutionary trope outside the narrow confines of the biological has often been ideologically motivated. Social Darwinism has, thankfully, fallen out of favour with all but the most extreme and self-defeating representatives of racial supremacy. Yet, seeking more sophisticated homologies between the natural and social sciences apparently remains seductive. Reflecting on discernible areas of management discourse, one only has to consider the tenacious influence of the population ecology approach to organizational survival articulated by Hannan and Freeman (1977, 1989) while, at the micro-level, theorists such as Singh and Lumsden (1990) and Burgleman (1991) have attempted to explain how individual organizations develop adaptation and survival strategies. More recently, Baum and Singh (1994a) have assembled an eloquent collection of essays which reflect upon contemporary themes and debates concerning the evolutionary dynamics of organizations. Despite the cautionary comments of Hannan and Freeman (1977) and Singh and Lumsden (1990) that it may not be sensible to develop direct analogies between the natural and organizational worlds, many branches of management 'science' still elevate ecological theory to the level of explanatory organizational theory by identifying a homological relationship,[7] and, in this respect, they are attempting to extend the assimilation of evolutionary principles beyond the realm of the tropical and towards the teleological. This view is reinforced by Van der Ven and Poole (1995) who identify evolutionally-based theories as one of four principal domains in a typology devised to explain processes of development and change in organizations, with each theoretical type being driven by a distinct 'motor of change'.[8] Thus, the evolutionary model of development consists of a

> . . . repetitive sequence of variation, selection, and retention events among entities in a designated population. Competition for scarce resources between entities inhabiting a population generates this evolutionary cycle. (Van der Ven and Poole, 1995: 512)

Hence, in the area delineated by their conception of evolutionary theories, Van der Ven and Poole's concerns lie with the survival of populations, an ebb and flow of teeming 'life' characterized by organizational birth, death and adaptation. What differentiates this from a simple life-cycle conception is the concern with 'populations' and the selection process itself, which they identify as being Lamarckian rather than strictly Darwinian (see also Baum and Singh, 1994b). Lamarck, who published his *Philosophie Zoologique* in 1809 (Lamarck, 1963), some 50 years before Darwin's *Origin of Species*, claimed to have identified the basis of a process of natural selection. Under Lamarck's vision, individual creatures would adapt to changing environmental conditions within a generation by somehow growing new organs or attributes through an act of will before passing them on to their offspring, a process which is still genetic but is based on self-selection of advantages rather than random mutation. A commonly cited example of this principle is the giraffe who, by craning to reach vegetation on the furthest branches of a tree, stretches its neck a little every day, passing on an acquired attribute to its offspring. On reflection, this neatly sums up the message of much of the management 'guru' or 'self-help' authors – that successful companies choose to be 'excellent', 'world class' or 'learning' organizations and that others should seek to emulate them – that is, to crane their necks like the giraffe. If it is not stretching the analogy beyond its limits, then attempts by commentators to identify 'excellent', 'world-class' or 'learning' organizations can be read as the desire to identify superior organizational genotypes while the discourse of organizational adaptation (i.e., much of the management literature and its supporting industry, exhorting companies to 'adapt or die') can be depicted as the embodiment of the genetic code of competitive capitalism.[9]

The idea of a rigorous and coherent teleological theory of organizational survival based on a biological homology would appear to strengthen the claims of management literature to assert the 'truth' about organizational adaptation. However, Van der Ven and Poole's identification of the Lamarckian approach to the acquisition of traits immediately undermines implicit appeals to the 'scientific' legitimacy of much of this literature by introducing notions long since superseded (although not necessarily *completely* discredited) within the biological community,[10] thus relegating evolutionary theories of organizational survival from that of the teleologically explanatory to the *merely* tropological. In the light of this comment, management discourse of this form should be constituted as advocatory narrative which attempts to perform a 'three-card trick' of representing itself as scientific 'truth' through its indirect allusions to contemporary biological theory – in effect, a form of organizational eugenics.

Lamarckian organizational eugenics are evident at two levels of representation. At the macro-level of 'population' they are present through the desire to identify and promulgate 'best practice', and at the micro-level of the organization through the desire to identify continuous improvement. The former would characterize the long history of management guru literature identified by Huczynski (1993) while the latter, as I will argue later, represents a preoccupation to be found in management literature from its earliest days and which is still reflected in areas as diverse as total quality management, systems theory, learning organizations and business process re-engineering. However, before proceeding I would like to mention, in passing at least, two related critiques of the genetic and the socio-biological sciences which challenge the dominance of Darwinism. The first of these is the tautological nature of the term 'the survival of the fittest'. Leith (1982) suggests that it might be more apt to use a term like 'the survival of the survivors'. Under this logic, dinosaurs did not die out due to any genetically derived adaptive deficiencies.[11] Indeed, they were very well equipped to deal with the prerequisites of being a dinosaur until catastrophic events, perhaps climate change, showed that biggest was not necessarily best (Gould, 1990).[12] This could be said to be the worst case of bad luck in the history of the universe and is eerily reminiscent of the experience of that powerful icon of 'excellence', IBM (Peters and Waterman, 1982). That a company like IBM can, within a decade, post the single biggest loss in business history should give the lie to 'best practice' books like *In Search of Excellence* (1982), a point that brings me to a second and more pernicious example of the tautology of Darwinism – that it reflects the 'survival of the fitted' (Leith, 1982; Gould, 1990 – see especially the discussion of Piltdown Man and 'brain primacy'). This view suggests that explanations as to the survival of certain species and the demise of others reflects a *post hoc* rationalization to fit an ideological position, taking us full circle (as tautologies are wont to do) to the ideas of the eugenicists who attributed the dominion of classes or races over others to 'better' breeding (see Galton, 1909). In biology, as in life, organisms and organizations may adapt and change, come and go, but it may not be through following an apparently inexorable and impartial logic contained in a DNA spiral or management books such as *In Search of Excellence* (Peters and Waterman, 1982), *Reengineering the Corporation* (Hammer and Champy, 1993) and *The Fifth Discipline* (Senge, 1990). Thus, although 'best practice' textbooks may contain information that is of immediate *practical* value to a manager, they should be read, at one level at least, as instruments of domination attempting to assert culturally-specific ideals through appeals to a eugenicist consciousness.

But what of the idea of continuous improvement at the level of the organism/organization? What of the giraffe's neck? In the rest of this chapter

I will examine the relationship between quality management and learning by focusing on attempts to define and identify organizational knowledge.

The 'Total Quality' Organization as a 'Learning Organization'

Evolution, innovation and organizational routines

Although the 'Quality Movement' as described by Drummond (1992) is diverse and multi-faceted, it has not escaped commentators that there are strong resonances between conceptions of total quality management (TQM) – especially its central concern with *kaizen* or continuous improvement – and the learning organization literature (e.g., Noori, 1991; Macher, 1992; Wetzel and Yencho, 1992; Dodgson, 1993; Maul and Gillard, 1993; Walker, 1992; Sitkin et al., 1994). Indeed, Hodgetts, Luthans and Lee (1994) argue that a truly world-class organization (i.e., the best in its class or better, at least, than its competitors) must combine the best practice aspects of both TQM and learning organizations. One result of this observation is that a key question arises: how close are the similarities between 'TQM' organizations and 'learning' organizations? Or, to put it another way, are any similarities between the two merely formal or are they *both* reinscriptions of common and perennial concerns related to the organization of the industrial labour process?

The equation between continuous improvement and 'learning' is explicitly stated by Sidney Winter. He also reverts to the trope of evolution, examining the relationship between the quality management movement and his earlier explorations in evolutionary economic theory (on this see Winter, 1964; Nelson and Winter, 1982). Winter (1994) identifies three main elements of this contemporary relationship: (i) corporate 'knowledge', much of which is tacit, is not embodied in an organization at the level of its unitary (legal and economic) entity but is embedded in organizational routines and can be revealed through 'organizational learning'; (ii) 'learning' is achieved through a systematic scrutiny of these existing routines, a process which is likely to turn up major opportunities for improvement; and (iii) firms identify and select new routines, not by dipping into some universal technical handbook, but by focusing on the idiosyncrasies of processes founded on unique aspects of an individual firm's history. For Winter, these elements support an evolutionary perspective in that they force the organization to continue to evolve (and, therefore, survive in a competitive environment) by encouraging it to focus not only on areas of perceived strength but also on areas of perceived weakness, thus reducing the chance of complacency. For Winter, the crucial element in this process of learning is the elicitation and representation of the knowledge embedded in organizational routines and it is his suggestion that quality management provides an effective means of achieving this.

Taylorism and the revelation of knowledge

Winter's concern with knowledge is a contemporary statement of preoccupations characteristic of one of the most important developments in the emergence of management thought – the rise of scientific management or 'Taylorism'. Here I want to explore the objectives of Taylorism with respect to the elicitation of knowledge and relate this to a common concern to be found in much of the quality management literature.

Similarities between quality management and scientific management have been noted elsewhere. For example, it has been claimed that 'stripped of its rhetoric, [TQM] is basically the apotheosis of scientific management' (Drummond, 1995: 68). Webster and Robins (1993) also touch upon the role of quality management in identifying knowledge about the work process through the generation of information. They identify the advent of scientific management or Taylorism as *the* key event in the development of industrial management as a discernible discipline. Taylor's work is presented as the thoughts of the first 'modern' manager, with individuals acting as 'information specialists – ideally monopolists – as close observers, analysts and planners of the production process' (Webster and Robins, 1993: 245). Although this may be a characterization of the *methods* of scientific management, Webster and Robins discuss how the information that concerns them is elicited but contribute little to the debate on how it becomes represented as 'knowledge'. In order to do this I would like to return directly to Taylor himself, especially the first of his four principles of scientific management outlined in his famous testimony to the Congressional Investigative Committee:

> The first of these groups of duties taken over by the management is the deliberate gathering on the part of those on the management's side of all the great mass of traditional knowledge, which in the past has been in the heads of workmen, and the physical skill and knack of the workmen, which they have acquired through years of experience. The duty of gathering in all this great mass of traditional knowledge and then recording it, tabulating it and, in many cases, finally reducing it to laws, rules and even to mathematical formulae, is voluntarily assumed by the scientific manager. . . . The first of these principles, then, may be called the development of a science to replace the old rules-of-thumb knowledge of the workmen; that is, knowledge the workmen had, and which was in many cases, quite as exact as that which is finally obtained by management, but which the workmen nevertheless in nine hundred and ninety-nine cases out of a thousand kept in their heads, and of which there was no permanent or complete record. (Taylor, 1912: 204)

From this pronouncement it is clear that Taylor is mainly interested in identifying what he sees as *knowledge*, knowledge which should be the sole possession and prerogative of management. Webster and Robins suggest that this is the *first* articulation of the desire to concentrate knowledge of the work process in the hands of management. However, a close reading of authors as diverse as Owen (1813), Babbage (1835), Ure (1835) and other studies of the organization of early factories (Roll, 1930; Pollard, 1965; Landes, 1969; Perrot, 1979) reveals a gradual formation of a set of discursive practices delineating managerial knowledge and its boundaries – in effect a management 'science' which attempts to define what managers *can* and *should* know and that sets the conception of work by managers apart from the execution of work by managerial objects – that is those who carry out the formalized and standardized tasks devised by professional managers. In this respect the development of a management science is deeply implicated in other projects of instrumental rationalism, such as those identified by Foucault in *The Archaeology of Knowledge* (1972) – especially those of economics and politics. However, it should be noted that, from a Foucauldian perspective at least, it is less that economic or political moments suddenly 'created' new managerial objects such as the waged labourer and more that they opened up new domains where managers could deploy a management science and management objects could be defined, mapped, measured, compared, enumerated, recorded and subjected to all the other techniques of compartmentalization or judgement. At this level, managerial discourse reflects similar developments in political and economic practices in two significant ways. First, in the form of the status accorded the manager within the institutional relationship between manager and managerial object and the means by which managerial knowledge is accumulated and transferred, between manager and managerial object (i.e., workplace control) and, secondly, between manager and manager (i.e., managerial education). One consequence of taking this position is that it is possible to locate Taylorism not as the unifying force of a previously inchoate discipline of modern management, but as a lucid representation of well-established themes in the continuing development of a discourse, including, *inter alia*, quality management or organizational learning, where managers act as the judges of managerial objects through the exercise of privileged knowledge.

Practically, any reading of Taylor's 'first duty of scientific management' yields his preoccupation with knowledge. However, raw and undifferentiated information does not constitute knowledge *per se*, even in Taylor's crudest sense. For Taylor, obtaining knowledge proceeded through the gathering and systematic analysis of information (generated by subjecting individuals to the closest rationalizing scrutiny), then through reducing it to empirically derived and universal laws. This is a process whereby knowledge, as a complex combination of explicit and tacit elements of human skill and mastery over tasks, becomes abstracted and embodied in the incomplete form of management information – tables, the outcomes of time-and-motion studies, productivity figures, etc. Hence, although Taylor was interested in appropriating knowledge for management, he was also faced with an issue which prefigures the same problems encountered by the 'knowledge engineers' of today's expert systems – the ultimate impossibility of the elicitation and representation of knowledge through a finite number of formal rules and programmes (Searle, 1980; Shaiken, 1985; Collins, 1986; Tenkasi and Boland, 1993). It is my argument that, in its narrow industrial context, Taylorism has increasingly pushed up against the limits of its ability to achieve this very objective (Sewell and Wilkinson, 1992a, 1992b). No matter how tightly monitored and subjected to the rationality of measurement – that is regulated by rules and programmes which approximate to an individual's mastery over a task – Taylorism is unable to elicit fully the knowledge exercised by the industrial worker and, despite management's best efforts to sequester individuals in the workplace by reducing their actions to a minimum set of highly rationalized, tightly regulated and repetitive tasks, cannot entirely eliminate destructive actions like sabotage (Shaiken, 1985) or creative activities like 'Goldbricking' (Roy, 1952) or 'making-out' (Roy, 1969). The latter, creative activities are important to managers because they represent instances where the work force is applying its own expertise or 'knowledge' to make incremental improvements in the production process to their own benefit. Thus, for managers at least, scientific management must at least attempt to identify and appropriate this knowledge for the 'good' of the company through 'continuous improvement'. Taylorism's response to this challenge is to increase the intensity of scrutiny – to gather more information – in the hope that this will 'reveal' the diverse and individualized practices which constitute workers' knowledge, as seen through the eyes of management. However, the constant abstraction of new rules or measurable standards cannot hope to capture fully the fluid ingenuity of workers as they respond to the strictures and possibilities set by previously asserted rules and procedures.

Taylorism reasserted?: Adler's 'learning bureaucracy'

In the light of this intractable problem associated with the methods of scientific management, recent discussions of industrial organization have focused on more sophisticated ways of appropriating knowledge in the pursuit of continuous improvement. One of the richest discussions of the transformation of the contemporary industrial workplace to emerge recently must be that contained in the work of Paul Adler, especially his conception of the 'learning bureaucracy' (Adler, 1993). Adler's depiction of NUMMI – the GM–Toyota joint venture assembly plant in Fremont, California – provides the reader with a vivid representation of the contemporary problems and possibilities of industrial organization. For the purposes of this chapter, I do not wish overly to dwell on Adler's detailed descriptions of the organizational practices to be found in NUMMI, valuable as they are. Rather, I wish to concentrate on Adler's broader discussion of an apparently orthodox, rationalized labour process and its operation under a rubric of organizational learning, especially the way in which it facilitates continuous improvement. Prima facie, the juxtaposition of terms like 'regimentation' and 'standardization' with organizational learning might seem like something of a paradox given the exhortations to empowerment and the devolution of responsibility found in texts like *The Fifth Discipline* (Senge, 1990). Adler suggests that, in the NUMMI case at least, no such paradox exists. His argument is that the configuration of the labour process in NUMMI – a subtle combination of orthodox techniques of work standardization and teamwork – provides a particularly effective means by which continuous improvements can be identified and asserted. Ironically, for Adler, the key to this is standardization and, through a series of reproduced interview transcripts, he maps out a story around this issue. For example, Borton (Stamping Department Manager) was concerned that people at NUMMI should constantly improve upon standardized work as *minimum* performance criteria while Hogan (Manager, General Affairs and Comptroller) saw the role of the team as a vehicle for establishing *new* standards on the basis of improvements made on the shop-floor. In the light of Adler's depiction of work organization at NUMMI, the divergence from orthodox Taylorism in this case is related to the specification of where the eventual responsibility for setting standards resides. Clearly, the team has to assume a degree of responsibility as initial standards are enacted and then improved upon, a view which was in line with Borton's reflection on the inability of Industrial Engineers to come up with a *perfectly* standardized *and* continuously improving programme of work. At the outset, the narrow delineation of tasks allowed by managerially imposed work standards initially determines the domain over which teams are allowed to exercise limited, but highly focused, discretion, reflecting Winter's concerns that the revelation of knowledge 'resides' in organizational routines (Winter, 1994). The acuity of this focus enables the team to concentrate its innovative efforts and problem-solving energies very tightly and provides a means by which crucial operational issues are prioritized.

Although the amount of discretion afforded workers at NUMMI is limited, management must still ensure that any innovations made in the production process are first revealed and then operationalized positively. I have previously identified, courtesy of Clegg (1989), the double-edged nature of discretion as the key problematic of any system of manufacturing which diverges, even slightly, from the formal rationalism of the orthodox bureaucratic form (Sewell, 1992; Sewell and Wilkinson, 1992a, 1992b; Sewell, 1996, 1998). Adler's position on how innovations come to be captured is a little ambiguous, although he seems to rely on his discussion of motivation as the principal causal factor at play here. It is as if discretion is its own reward, a factor which can be attributed to an amelioration of the worst alienating effects of bureaucratic Taylorism. Adler identifies three distinct sources of motivation which are evident in NUMMI: (i) the desire for excellence, the instinct of craftsmanship, and the desire to do a job well done; (ii) based on Freud's 'reality principle', the understanding by psychologically mature workers of the need to protect the plant's competitive position and, thus, jobs by constantly improving its performance; and (iii) the respect and trust that management showed towards workers, reciprocated through the commitment shown in return by those workers (Adler, 1993). According to Adler, all three sources of motivation stem directly from the democratic slant placed on NUMMI's vision of Taylorism. But this begs the question – is it legitimate to characterize the technology of production (in its broadest sense), as it is described by Adler, with its attendant superstructure of rationalization and control, as *either* Tayloristic *or* bureaucratic?

Before responding to the question posed at the end of the previous paragraph I note that the NUMMI regime depicted by Adler bears a striking resemblance to the one found in a plant I studied with my colleague Barry Wilkinson – especially in terms of the alignment of a team-based structure (thus, allowing for the exercise of limited discretion) with a traditional line-based manufacturing approach using standardized work practices (Sewell and Wilkinson, 1992a, 1992b). It was the study of this plant that led me to form the ideas on the relationship between Taylorism and knowledge outlined in the preceding section (see also Sewell, 1996) and I would like to make recourse to this discussion in order to address the rhetorical question concerning the Tayloristic and bureaucratic nature of work at NUMMI.

In ceding even the slightest degree of discretion to work teams at NUMMI the management are effectively acknowledging that they are no longer the sole custodians of 'explicit' knowledge regarding the work process. This is not to say they are giving up their prerogative to appropriate and exercise that knowledge. On the contrary, the discretion ceded to workers provides the 'space' in which tacit knowledge can be identified and then operationalized by management. This is not a fundamental contradiction of Taylorism *qua* its objectives concerning the identification and appropriation of knowledge but it *is* incompatible with its methods. Thus, as with Taylorism, the regime at NUMMI may be an embodiment of the desire to define the managerial object and subsume it under a totalizing rationalism, but it does not do it in the same way that Taylor advocated.

Adler underplays the role of the technology of production (cast in its widest sense to include innovations in social organization) to provide a mechanism by which knowledge is defined, identified and ultimately operationalized. Although this focus on technology to 'capture' innovation may appear to resemble Foucault's Panoptic trope, there are some important differences, most notably in the reversal of the tendency of both Panoptic disciplinary practices and Tayloristic practices to sequester individuals (i.e., to isolate their activities in time and space under the influence of a rationalized set of tasks). I would argue that the key innovation – that of the combination of standardized line-based work with team-based organization – *is* a (modest) reversal of sequestering practices. That is not to say that, in line with Foucault's discussion of Panopticism, where subjects are caught up in relations of domination of which they are themselves the bearers, employees at NUMMI are not incorporated into a power/

knowledge nexus of self-management. Rather, the forces acting on an individual's subjectivity now incorporate a slightly loosened degree of rationalizing scrutiny in combination with the emergent intersubjective relations of a resocialized labour process achieved through the deployment of teams (Sewell and Wilkinson, 1992b; Barker, 1993; Sewell, 1998). The retention of a high degree of standardization and regimentation circum-scribes the domain over which a team exercises influence, thereby focusing efforts on a limited number of aspects of the production process most likely to yield small but cumulative instances of continuous improvement. To be sure, Adler acknowledges the centrality of teams to the productive regime found at NUMMI, especially in terms of the requirement of multi-skilling (essentially a limited opening up of a previously isolating and de-individuating work process) and he also pays attention to the potential problems associated with team work, especially peer-group pressure (Grenier, 1988) and 'management-by-stress' (Parker and Slaughter, 1988). However, Adler's view on this appears to be that such tendencies are simply a dilution or subversion of the democratic principles under which Taylorism has been implemented at NUMMI and should be constituted as peripheral, albeit worrying, problems of implementation to be ironed out in the long run through the good offices of traditional industrial democracy.

My position is contrary to Adler's account of democratic tendencies in that I would assert that the peer-group scrutiny of the team is essential to the successful pursuit of organizational learning as it is conceived at a plant like NUMMI. Not that teams are *necessarily* coercive in their operation and are *always* the forum for unedifying social practices of petty tyranny. Rather, my point is that we must be vigilant in order to prevent this kind of development occurring, even in situations where, rhetorically at least, empowerment, inclusion and commitment are the stated objectives.

Building on many of the ideas developed in the NUMMI study, Adler and Borys (1996) address the issue of coercion *versus* empowerment. They explore the relationship between rule-setting and discretion, reviewing the established literature within organizational theory on standardization and formalization. They identify two main types of rule setting – 'coercive' and 'enabling'. They reflect on how perceptions of 'good' rules and 'bad' rules develop. Enabling formalization occurs when best practice becomes identified and stabilized to allow it to be adopted throughout an organ-ization (Nelson and Winter, 1982; Winter, 1994). In contrast, coercive formalization occurs when procedures are a substitute for, rather than a complement to, commitment. In the case of NUMMI, formalization through rule-setting was seen as distinctly enabling (Adler, 1993; Adler and Borys, 1996). However, in Adler's earlier discussion of NUMMI he seems to underplay the role of technologies in the workplace (again, in the broadest sense) as the embodiment of significant power relations operating in a so-called 'enabling' context. These are evident in two significant areas. First, there is a failure to see systems that might support nominal commitment through standardization and formalization as technologies acting on individual subjectivities (i.e., technologies that not only attempt to normalize behaviour but also contribute to the way in which individuals think of themselves, perhaps as 'good' workers or 'bad' workers in the case of performance measurement). Secondly, there is little discussion of the way in which technologies of standardization and formalization shape the actual practices of continuous improvement to be found in NUMMI. By this I mean the day-to-day shop-floor practices whereby individuals, exercising their skill and ingenuity under conditions of limited autonomy, may identify, and then pass on, innovations in work activity. The interesting research questions here would revolve around how standardized working and peer scrutiny impinge on the operation of individual discretion in a team context.

Despite all the talk of standardization and formalization, Adler still argues that, with the emergence of the limited form of autonomy enjoyed by the employees of NUMMI with respect to innovating around work routines, a degree of empowerment has occurred. However, it is more a matter of the quality rather than the quantity of empowerment that is at question. Thus, 'NUMMI's disciplined production system brought greatly increased technical/positive power for workers' (Adler, 1993: 176) but, with regard to his conception of social power,[13] Adler chooses to concentrate on the role of union participation at the plant level, rather than individual subjects' or even teams' responses to their experiences of work at NUMMI. As a result, he has very little to say about the nature of the empowerment that occurred and how it impacted on the broader play of power relations at the site where they are felt most acutely – the individual and the body.

It is clear that Adler's work contains much to commend. However, I do feel that his term, the 'learning bureaucracy', is unfounded as the configuration of team work and standardized tasks begins to reverse the logic of ever-increasing individuated scrutiny and rationalization characteristic of bureaucracy and Taylorism. In broadening the domain over which employees can exert an influence by just a fraction, the form of labour process described by Adler enables a whole new set of intersubjective relations to emerge which may not have been incorporated in the calculus of industrial production before. Of these, the key innovation of teamwork, while bringing with it allusions to equity, empowerment and inclusion, can also be the vehicle for intense peer-group pressure, normalization and stress. Barker (1993) has already noted this, although he sees this as a means of intensifying the rational control of bureaucracy – tightening the iron cage. However, it should be noted that Weber's use of the term 'iron cage' was consciously ambiguous – a cage not only constrains, it also protects. Weber went to great pains to show that the 'legitimate' authority of bureaucracy protected its members from management by *fiat* or capricious whim (Weber, 1947). In the light of this concern any loosening of the iron cage is to be encouraged, so long as it is not accompanied by new forms of tyranny and domination – perhaps like those enacted, in Barker's terms, through the 'concertive control' of self-managed teams?

Concluding Remarks

In much of this chapter I have explored how projects such as total quality management might contribute to a process of organizational 'learning' through identifying techniques of continuous improvement. Towards this end I have attempted to problematize this process around the elicitation and representation of knowledge within the domain inscribed by the industrial labour process. The tendency towards ever-increasing rationalization and standardization associated with orthodox Taylorism will inevitably push up against limits – Taylorism will never retain the suppleness needed to reveal each new incremental innovation that originates at the heart of the manufacturing process. In this sense, the project of continuous improvement central to quality management, and other management approaches, demands new forms of organization. Adler's identifies such a new form as the 'learning bureaucracy'. Although the form of organization found at NUMMI may be particularly adept at 'learning', I would contend that it cannot be considered as a bureaucracy in the technical sense. It may well formally resemble a bureaucracy but the processes which characterize it, especially those of a limited loosening of the grip of rationalization in combination with team work, set it apart from Weber's ideal type.

I suggested very early on in this chapter that a reconfiguration of the notion of organizational learning around the problem of 'knowledge' can lead us to think of continuous improvement through the trope of Lamarckian evolution – the giraffe craning in an attempt to reach beyond the frustrating limits imposed by its own physiology. Identifying better ways of neck-stretching abound in management literature but I have gone further with the evolutionary trope, suggesting that much of contemporary management discourse can be represented as a project of organizational eugenics – smarter organizations through better breeding. I would not for one moment suggest that authors of 'best practice' and 'how-to-manage-better' texts would in any way consciously subscribe to any concept as crude as eugenics. However, frequently there is an explicit assumption that best practice (which often tends to mean North American practice) can, indeed should, be implemented in any business situation, with any cultural or practical differences only posing small hurdles that can be overcome through 'sensitive' management. This may well be the management consultant's ideal but does it really constitute an imperialistic view of organizational superiority? Well, if anybody was still in doubt over the insidious and covert influence of an eugenicist consciousness in the discourse of management, then one need only reflect on the apparently innocuous stereotype of the Japanese, not as innovators themselves but as highly effective and successful imitators of the fruits of the creativity of others. Singling out quality management, narratives depicting Demming's involvement in the post-war reconstruction of Japanese industry fall comfortably into this worrying pervasive mythology – that is Demming as the prophet of quality management preaching to a receptive audience which listens with rapt attention to the words of the master and then assimilates his ideas into a synthesized but unoriginal approach to manufacturing organization.

If we are to believe certain authors, then this process is still continuing. For example, witness the following comment: 'Even today, as any academic in the West will know, the Japanese remain hungry for new innovative ideas sending their academicians to leading research groups in the West' (Flood, 1993: 8). Here we have a characterization of the Japanese as plundering the 'blue skies' research of the West but offering little in return by way of their own contribution. A reflection upon good business sense on the part of the Japanese perhaps, but hardly a pernicious and ideologically motivated view. Perhaps . . . until we reflect upon the story of Dr John Langdon Haydon Down (Gould, 1990). Down, the superintendent of the *Earlswood Asylum for Idiots* in Surrey, England during the mid-nineteenth century, was by all accounts a fairly progressive psychiatrist, for the time, who had the best interests of his wards (presumably 'idiots') at heart. He was also an avowed Darwinian who accepted that apes and men had a common ancestor. Down was convinced that, after the split with this common ancestor, the races of *Homo sapiens* had developed at different rates and he was equally sure that their advancement to higher stages of evolution, and hence intelligence, could be determined by the average size of the brains of different groups. On the basis of his measurements, Down felt no compunction in stating that men possessed superior intelligence to women, white Europeans possessed superior intelligence to black Africans, and so on, until he was able to construct a general and causal classification of racial mental superiority, all by dint of brain size. We may not have heard much more of Down in this context after such ideas had fallen into widespread disrepute except for his concern to equate mental deficiencies with racial 'failings', but he is not without record in the annals of medical science. In 1866 Down described a common set of physiological and behavioural characteristics associated with the chromosomal disorder, trisomy-21 – now commonly known as Down's syndrome. Lest we forget, Down's Syndrome is a contemporary euphemism for what used to be called Mongolism. But why the term Mongolism? Down was convinced that mental disorders of a genetic nature were caused by instances of atavism – a case of arrested development or a throwback to the level of a less intelligent 'lower' race. This led Down to look for a race which, to his way of thinking, had characteristics closely resembling those displayed by people with trisomy-21. Here he used the German naturalist Blumenbach's classification of racial superiority – in descending order, the 'Caucasian' variety, the 'Mongolian' variety, the 'Ethopian' variety and the 'American' variety. But Down was not only concerned with physical characteristics, although in the case of trisomy-21 these can hardly be described as being typical of the people of Mongolia, either then or now. He noted that 'Mongolian idiots' have 'considerable power of imitation, even bordering on being mimics' (quoted in Gould, 1990: 137). The identification of Orientals as mimics is significant because,

> [T]he sophistication and complexity of oriental culture proved embarrassing to Caucasian racists, especially since the highest refinements of Chinese society had arisen when European culture still wallowed in barbarism. . . . Caucasians solved this dilemma by admitting the intellectual power of orientals, but attributing it to a facility for imitative copying, rather than innovative genius. (Gould, 1990: 137).

Here, Down was equating the behavioural characteristics of the trisomy-21 condition with those he considered to be displayed by oriental races – that is mimicry and imitation.[14,15] His conclusion was that Mongolism was caused by a genetic throwback to these 'less developed' races of *Homo sapiens*. Thus, when we next hear the Japanese described as good imitators but poor innovators or read in the quality management literature of how the Japanese merely copied the best practices of the West, remember Dr Down and his syndrome. I hope this final comment is not taken to be flippant or trivial for I strongly believe that we need radically to reassess our ideas about best practices in business, not only concerning how they are identified but also how they are passed on. This is particularly pressing if we are seduced by the apparently 'scientific' and 'impartial' nature of TQM, organizational learning and emergent approaches which adopt an ecological approach to organizational adaptation and, thereby, fail to recognize that these approaches to management can also be used to rationalize organizational developments motivated by ideology or even by ideas of cultural and racial superiority.

Notes

1. The title alludes to the 'Just So' stories of Rudyard Kipling – tall tales explaining 'How the Elephant got his Trunk', 'How the Tiger got his Stripes', etc. There is a conscious irony in choosing this title as Kipling was a bastion of the British Empire and one of the most vociferous defenders of imperialism.
2. The first use of the term in reference to Darwin's theory of evolution is normally attributed to Herbert Spencer who was attempting to assimilate Darwinism into his own view of political economy. It is only after its entry into common parlance in the context of evolutionary theory that Darwin felt compelled to use the phrase himself (Burrow, 1985).
3. The 'New Age' feel of many of Senge's exhortations sets it apart from most of the more 'macho' examples of the guru business. For a concise summary of Senge's position, see Kofman and Senge (1993).
4. It is by no means obvious what a 'stupid' (i.e., non-learning organization) would look like prior to this transformational process.
5. Dawkin's work is controversial because he argues that the fundamental 'unit' of natural selection is at the level of individual genes rather than at the level of the

organism. Others, like Wynne-Edwards have argued that the unit of selection should be at the level of the population.

6. This is not to say that there is no disagreement over specific interpretations of Darwinian evolution – for example, the 'Punctuated Equilibrium' theory (Gould, 1989, 1990).

7. In genetic biology a homologous relationship indicates that two sets of genes may exhibit similarities in relation to their position and structure but not in their function. In the same way, organizational evolution appeals directly to biology in suggesting that, although organizational and biological functions are not identical (a very obvious statement), some processes are similar.

8. In addition to the 'evolutionary', Van der Ven and Poole include the 'teleological', along with the 'dialectic' and the 'life-cycle', as self-contained, although not mutually exclusive, explanatory models. However, I would suggest that Van der Ven and Poole's whole enterprise is, in itself, broadly teleological in its scope.

9. In *Fatal Strategies* (1990), Baudrillard also uses the metaphor of genetic codes to articulate his position on the development of theory.

10. Leith (1982) notes that a failed attempt has been made to revive Lamarckian ideas in modern biology (e.g., Steele and Gorczynski, 1980).

11. How often have we heard 'old-fashioned' large-scale organizations described as 'dinosaurs'?

12. The recent work of Peter de Menocal of Columbia University has supported a similar view in terms of the rise to dominance of *Homo Sapiens'* ancestors over other hominids.

13. '[This] assessment of workers' power focuses directly on social power, which, as all the classical definitions suggest, is fundamentally negative – the capacity of one actor to impose their will on another' (Adler, 1993: 176).

14. The attribution of mimicry as a characteristic of 'other' races is still apparent (see Turner, 1994).

15. According to Aristotle, the propensity to mimic others is the quality which most sets humans apart from other animals. This classical view is revisited by Olsson (1991) who sees 'mimeticism' as means for the ironic assertion of difference through sameness, a mechanism for assimilating the desire of others as one's own.

References

Adler, P.S. (1993) 'The "learning bureaucracy"': New United Motor Manufacturing, Inc.', *Research in Organisational Behaviour*, 15: 111–94.

Adler, P.S. and Borys, B. (1996) 'Two types of bureaucracy: enabling and coercive', *Administrative Science Quarterly*, 41: 61–89.

Babbage, C. (1835) 'On the economy of manufactures'. Reprinted in M. Berg (ed.) (1979) *Technology and Toil in Nineteenth Century Britain*. London: CSE Publishers.

Barker, J.R. (1993) 'Tightening the iron cage: concertive control in self-managing teams', *Administrative Science Quarterly*, 38: 408–37.

Baudrillard, J. (1990) *Fatal Strategies*. New York: Semiotext(e).

Baum, J.A.C. and Singh, J.V. (eds) (1994a) *Evolutionary Dynamics of Organizations*. Oxford: Oxford University Press.

Baum, J.A.C. and Singh, J.V. (1994b) 'Organizational hierarchies and evolutionary processes', in J.A.C. Baum and J.V. Singh (eds), *Evolutionary Dynamics of Organizations*. Oxford: Oxford University Press.

Burgleman, R.A. (1991) 'Interorganizational ecology of strategy making and organizational adaptation: theory and field research', *Organization Science*, 2: 29–34.

Burrow, J.W. (1985) 'Editor's introduction' to C. Darwin, *The Origin of Species by Means of Natural Selection*. Harmondsworth: Penguin.

Clegg, S.R. (1989) 'Radical revisions: power, discipline and organizations', *Organizational Studies*, 10: 97–116.

Collins, H. (1986) 'Expert systems: artificial intelligence and the behavioural coordinates of skill', in B. Bloomfield (ed.) *The Question of Artificial Intelligence*. London: Croom Helm.

Darwin, C. (1859) *The Origin of Species by Means of Natural Selection*. London: John Murray.

Dawkins, R. (1976) *The Selfish Gene*. Oxford: Oxford University Press.

Dawkins, R. (1986) *The Blind Watchmaker*. London: Longman.

Dawkins, R. (1995) *River Out of Eden: A Darwinian View of Life*. London: Weidenfeld and Nicolson.

Dennis, D. (1993) 'License and commodification: the birth of an information oligarchy', *Humanity and Society*, 17: 48–69.

Dennis, D. (1995) 'Evocations of empire in a transnational corporate age: tracking the sign of Saturn', *Postmodern Culture*, 5 (2): no page numbers – electronic journal.

Dodgson, M. (1993) 'Organizational learning: a review of some literatures', *Organization Studies*, 14: 375–94.

Drummond, H. (1992) *The Quality Movement: What Total Quality Management is Really all About*! London: Kogan Page.

Drummond, H. (1995) 'Beyond quality', *Journal of General Management*, 20 (4): 68–77.

Flood, R.L. (1993) *Beyond TQM*. Chichester: John Wiley.

Foucault, M. (1970) *The Order of Things*. New York: Random House.

Foucault, M. (1972) *The Archaeology of Knowledge*. London: Tavistock Publications.

Foucault, M. (1977) *Discipline and Punish*. London: Allen Lane.

Galton, Sir F.G. (1909) *Essays in Eugenics*. London: The Eugenics Education Society.

Gillespie, R. (1991) *Manufacturing Knowledge: A History of the Hawthorne Experiments*. Cambridge: Cambridge University Press.

Gould, S.J. (1989) 'Punctuated equilibrium in fact and theory', *Journal of Social and Biological Structures*, 12: 117–36.

Gould, S.J. (1990) *The Panda's Thumb*. Harmondsworth: Penguin.

Grenier, G.J. (1988) *Inhuman Relations: Quality Circles and Anti-Unionism in American Industry*. Philadelphia: Temple University Press.

Hammer, M. and Champy, J. (1993) *Reengineering the Corporation*. New York: HarperCollins.

Hannan, M.T. and Freeman, J. (1977) 'The population ecology of organizations', *American Journal of Sociology*, 82: 929–64.

Hannan, M.T. and Freeman, J. (1989) *Organizational Ecology*. Cambridge, MA: Harvard University Press.

Hodgetts, R.M., Luthans, F. and Lee, S.M. (1994) 'New paradigm organizations: from total quality to learning world-class', *Organizational Dynamics*, 22 (3): 5–19.

Huczynki, A. (1993) *Management Gurus*. London: Routledge.

Kofman, F. and Senge, P.M. (1993) 'Communities of commitment: the heart of the learning organization', *Organizational Dynamics*, 22 (2): 5–23.

Lamarck, J.B. (1963) *Zoological Philosophy*. New York: Hafner.

Landes, D. (1969) *The Unbound Prometheus: Technological Change and Industrial*

Development in Western Europe from 1750 to the Present. Cambridge: Cambridge University Press.

Leith, B. (1982) *The Descent of Darwin*. London: Collins.

Macher, K. (1992) 'Organizations that learn', *Journal for Quality and Participation*, 15 (7): 8–11.

Maul, G.P. and Gillard, J.S. (1993) 'Training today's managers to effectively use TQM', *Industrial Engineering*, 25: 49–50.

Nelson, R.R. and Winter, S.G. (1982) *An Evolutionary Theory of Economic Change*. Cambridge, MA: Harvard University Press.

Noori, H. (1991) 'TQM and its building blocks: learning from world-class organizations', *Optimum*, 22 (3): 31–8.

Norris, C. (1993) *The Truth about Postmodernism*. Oxford: Blackwell.

Olsson, G. (1991) *Lines of Power/Limits of Language*. Minneapolis: University of Minnesota Press.

Owen, R. (1813) 'To the superintendents of manufactories'. Reprinted in M. Berg (ed.) (1979) *Technology and Toil in Nineteenth Century Britain*. London: CSE Publishers.

Parker, M. and Slaughter, J. (1988) *Choosing Sides: Unions and the Team Concept*. Boston, MA: South End Press.

Perrot, M. (1979) 'The three ages of industrial discipline in nineteenth century France', in J.M. Merriman (ed.), *Consciousness and Class Experience in Nineteenth Century Europe*. London: Holmes and Meier.

Peters, T. and Waterman, R.H. (1982) *In Search of Excellence*. New York: Harper & Row.

Pollard, S. (1965) *The Genesis of Modern Management*. London: Arnold.

Roll, E. (1930) 'An early experiment in industrial organisation: Boulton and Watt 1775–1805'. Reprinted in M. Berg (ed.) (1979) *Technology and Toil in Nineteenth Century Britain*. London: CSE Publishers.

Roy, D. (1952) 'Quota restriction and goldbricking in a machine shop', *American Journal of Sociology*, 57: 427–42.

Roy, D. (1969) 'Making out: a workers' counter-system of control of work situation and relationships', in T. Burns (ed.), *Industrial Man*. Harmondsworth: Penguin.

Searle, J. (1980) 'Minds, brains and programs', *The Behavioural and Brain Sciences*, 3: 417–24.

Senge, P.M. (1990) *The Fifth Discipline: The Art and Practice of the Learning Organization*. New York: Doubleday.

Sewell, G. (1992) '(In)Information we trust(?)'. Paper presented at the MERIT 10th Anniversary Conference, Maastricht, 10–12 December.

Sewell, G. (1996) 'Be seeing you: a rejoinder to Webster and Robins and to Jenkins', *Sociology*, 30: 785–97.

Sewell, G. (1998) 'The discipline of teams: then control of team-based industrial work through electronic and peer surveillance', *Administrative Science Quarterly*, 43.

Sewell, G. and Wilkinson, B. (1992a) 'Someone to watch over me: surveillance, discipline and the just-in-time labour process', *Sociology*, 26: 271–89.

Sewell, G. and Wilkinson, B. (1992b) 'Empowerment or emasculation?: shop floor surveillance in a total quality organisation', in P. Blyton and P. Turnbull (eds), *Reassessing Human Resource Management*. London: Sage.

Sewell, G. and Wilkinson, B. (1993) 'Human resource management in "surveillance" companies', in J. Clark (ed.), *Human Resource Management and Technical Change*. London: Sage.

Shaiken, H. (1985) *Work Transformed: Automation and Labour in the Computer Age*. New York: Holt, Rinehart and Winston.

Singh, J.V. and Lumsden, C.J. (1990) 'Theory and research in organizational ecology', *Annual Review of Sociology*, 16: 161–95.

Sitkin, S.B., Sutcliffe, K.M. and Schroeder, R.G. (1994) 'Distinguishing control from learning in total quality management: a contingency perspective', *Academy of Management Review*, 19: 537–64.

Steele, E.J. and Gorczynski, R. (1980) 'Somatic selection and adaptive evolution', *Proceedings of the National Academy of Science*, 77: 2871–92.

Taylor, F.W. (1912) 'General principles of management'. Extracts from the testimony of Frederick W. Taylor, Hearings Before the Special Committee of the House of Representatives to Investigate the Taylor and Other Systems of Shop Management. Reprinted in D.S. Pugh (ed.) (1990) *Organization Theory*. Harmondsworth: Penguin.

Tenkasi, R.V. and Boland, R. (1993) 'Locating meaning making in organisational learning: the narrative basis of cognition', in R. Woodman and W.A. Passmore (eds), *Research in Organizational Change and Development*. Greenwich, CT: JAI Press.

Turner, B.S. (1994) *Orientalism, Postmodernism and Globalism*. London: Routledge.

Ure, A. (1835) 'The philosophy of manufactures'. Reprinted in M. Berg (ed.) (1979) *Technology and Toil in Nineteenth Century Britain*. London: CSE Publishers.

Van der Ven, A.H. and Poole, M.S. (1995) 'Explaining development and change in organizations', *Academy of Management Review*, 20: 510–40.

Walker, T. (1992) 'Creating total quality improvement that will last', *National Productivity Review*, 11: 473–8.

Weber, M. (1947) *The Theory of Social and Economic Organizations*. New York: The Free Press.

Webster, F. and Robins, K. (1993) 'I'll be watching you: comment on Sewell and Wilkinson', *Sociology*, 27: 243–52.

Wetzel, C.F. and Yencho, N.M. (1992) 'Taking quality beyond the awareness stage', *Journal for Quality and Participation*, 15 (1): 36–41.

Winter, S.G. (1964) 'Economic "natural selection" and the theory of the firm', *Yale Economic Essays*, 4: 225–72.

Winter, S.G. (1994) 'Organizing for continuous improvement: evolutionary theory meets the quality revolution', in J.A.C. Baum and J.V. Singh (eds), *Evolutionary Dynamics of Organizations*. Oxford: Oxford University Press.

2   From Imperialism to Globalization: Internationalization and the Management Text

Albert J. Mills and Jean Hatfield

In North America the business student's first introduction to the study of management and organization is normally through a textbook. As such, the business textbook occupies an important position in the introduction of the theory of management to new generations of managers. The typical textbook introduces the student to an understanding of individual behaviour in the workplace, motivation, perception, learning, organizational power and politics, leadership, communication, decision-making, group dynamics, organizational change, organizational structure and design, and a number of other seemingly important skills and techniques of managing. On the surface such texts appear to offer useful insights into the art and science of management and managing: closer analysis reveals a different story. The typical text – as we shall show – is reflective of a limited narrative which presents such a distorted, ethnocentric view of reality that, even in its own terms, it is unable to be of much use to the development of future managers or 'organic leaders' (Gramsci, 1978). As Fineman and Gabriel have noted:

> The textbook, as a rhetorical device, does not seduce. Nor does it persuade through argument. It comforts and reassures. It 'asserts' and it 'infuses' to a relatively passive, but normally willing, recipient. (1994: 385)

Based on content analysis of 107 widely used North American business texts published between 1959 and 1996 (see Appendix at the end of the chapter), we shall argue that the typical business or management text constitutes a narrative that is built around a white, male, liberal American view of reality. It is a narrative lacking in dynamism due to an extensive process of theory dilution, mimicry and political timidity. If it is 'successful' at all, it is in its ability to encourage an anti-intellectual approach to the study of management, to excise theory from practice, and to legitimize a particular view of the business world.

The Management Text and the Cold War

Persons born prior to 1974 will have spent between 15 and 45 years their life under the shadow of the 'Cold War'. We may not have understood its origins and we may not have fully understood what the term referred to, but most of us knew that it spelt danger. The Cold War was one of the most powerful discourses of the twentieth century and its influence reached deep into everything we did and felt.

At the most basic level the Cold War evoked an image of deadly competition between two powerful forces – communism (in the shape of the USSR) and capitalism (in the shape of the USA). Antagonism between 'the forces of communism' and 'the forces of capitalism' has a long history that was only temporarily suspended during the course of the Second World War. Almost immediately following the end of that war the old antagonism resurfaced. By the late 1940s those antagonisms were beginning to be understood through the development of a discourse of a 'Cold War' – a discourse which was to shape and be shaped by events over the next 40 years.

Apart from the central protagonists and their respective ideologies, the Cold War became associated with a series of events (e.g., the Korean War, the Chinese Revolution), policies (e.g., the Truman Doctrine, Marshall Aid), socio-political practices (e.g., McCarthyism, Stalinism) and institutions (e.g., the Warsaw Pact, NATO). These factors were to have a profound influence on business and other social institutions. For one thing it led to the establishment of numerous organizations dedicated to the pursuit of the Cold War. These included the proliferation of businesses associated with the production of military weapons, vehicles, communications, and various other activities associated with war preparations that was so extensive that by 1960 President Eisenhower was referring to it as 'the military-industrial complex' (Hobsbawm, 1994). A vast number of organizations became redefined and refocused on Cold War issues: the Federal Bureau of Investigators (FBI), for one, turned much of its attention on the activities of communists and so-called communist sympathizers within the USA (Fast, 1990). So did the House Un-American Activities Committee (HUAC) which had originally been established to investigate the activities of the Ku Klux Klan.

The Cold War influenced business organizations in at least three major ways:

1 The effect of the Cold War was felt through a series of laws and actions which purged communists and left-wing sympathizers from the trade unions. The Taft–Hartley Act (1947), for instance, denied the benefits of legal protection to any trade union unless each officer of the union and its affiliates filed an affidavit stating that,

he is not a member of the Communist Party, or affiliated with such party, and that he does not believe in or teach the overthrow of the United States government by force or by any illegal or unconstitutional means. (Quoted in Goldstein, 1978: 291)

The law was so effective that by 1954 40 unions with six million members barred communists from membership, while 59 unions with ten million members barred communists from holding office (Goldstein, 1978: 365). These activities were not restricted to the few who happened to be in or associated with the Communist Party of the United States (CPUSA). Tens of thousands of individuals came under suspicion of having communist sympathies or tendencies – a broad-brush characterization that placed many people at the mercy of employers, unprotected by trade unions anxious to distance themselves from the taint of communism.

2   In the shadow of HUAC and the newly formed Senate Internal Security Subcommittee (SISS) employees in many industries were required to sign 'loyalty oaths', swearing allegiance to the USA and denying communist associations. Across a number of industries employees lost their jobs if their employer deemed that he or she was less than an 'ideal citizen'. This was an atmosphere that affected the post-war era until the early 1960s and was felt primarily in the movie industry, the Federal Civil Service, the trade unions, state and city government, the press, the libraries, schools and in the universities (Caute, 1979).

3   International trade was profoundly influenced by the Cold War. '[I]t had entirely eliminated, or overshadowed, all but one of the rivalries and conflicts that shaped world politics before the Second World War' (Hobsbawm, 1994: 252). The Cold War agreement was built on a wartime agreement between the USA, Britain and the USSR which divided the world into spheres of influence. Thus, for the USA a major part of its trading policy was aimed at doing business with allied nations and, on differing occasions, placing embargoes prohibiting trade with countries deemed 'communist' or allied to the communist bloc.

Image and reflection: inside the management text

The Cold War went through at least three major phases. The first phase was perhaps the most tense and repressive and lasted from about 1947 to the early 1960s. The second phase, which came to be termed 'the era of *détente*', saw an easing of tension and limited arms control agreements and lasted until the mid-1970s. The third phase became known as 'the Second Cold War', involving as it did a new revival of international tensions and military rivalry between the USA and the USSR: this period ended with the Reagan–Gorbachev summits in 1986 (Reykjavik) and 1987 (Washington) (see Hobsbawm, 1994: 225–56).

TABLE 2.1 *Contrasting images of industrial relations in the Cold War era*

Inside the Cold War organization	Inside the management text
The witch hunt	*Controls in wage administration*
The violent epicenter of the anti-Communist eruption in postwar America was the steel city of Pittsburgh. . . . [The] *Pittsburgh Press,* Hearst's *Pittsburgh Sun-Telegraph,* the *Pittsburgh Post Gazette* and other local newspapers joined in the witch hunt by blazoning the names, addresses and employers of [suspected communists. In 1950 alone] nearly one hundred people lost their jobs . . ., notably at U.S. Steel, Etna Steel, and the Crucible Steel Company. . . . Many workers were ostracized, were refused credit at local stores, saw their kids abused or attacked at school, were denied state welfare benefits, or were threatened with denaturalization or deportation. As this steel city began to boom with the Korean war orders, the fever rose: perhaps two hundred people had to leave town. A number of men . . . were expelled from their unions. (Caute, 1979: 216–17)	In one sense an appreciable proportion of the long-term employees of major companies already enjoy an annual guarantee through the operation of seniority provisions when the United Auto Workers and the large automobile manufacturers agreed to an unemployment-compensation supplement and the Steelworkers were granted an employment or wage guarantee in 1955 negotiations. (Bethel et al., 1959: 379)

At the height of the first phase of the Cold War it is quite remarkable that any text on management could leave the issue out of the account, yet, as our review suggests, many did. In the *Essentials of Industrial Management,* for example, Bethel, Atwater, Smith and Stackman (1959) make extensive reference to the 'principles' and 'administration' of industrial relations. In the process they discuss a large number of union organizations, including the American Federation of Labor (AFL), the Steelworkers Union, the United Auto Workers (UAW), the United Mine Workers, and the United Textile Workers. They fail to mention a single detail about the anti-communist struggles within those unions and how they affected management within individual organizations: Table 2.1 provides contrasting images of industrial relations in the Cold War era.

In a similar way Bethel, Atwater, Smith and Stackman (1959: 344) refer to the Taft–Hartley Act (1947) without mention of its impact on organizations in general and industrial relations in particular. The sole reference states that: 'Management actions in labor relations are also greatly influenced by a score or more of labor laws . . . [including] Taft–Hartley, 1947.' Likewise, the discussion of the management policies of selected major companies excludes reference to their widespread Cold War practices. Thus, the reader is informed by Bethel et al. that: 'Many of the larger companies, such as General Electric, Bell Telephone, General Motors, Ford, etc., have established full-blown management schools or institutes (1959: 337). What the reader is not informed about is that at least 1.5

million employees in private industry were subjected to security pro-
grammes and that Bell Telephone accounted for 780,000 and General
Electric for 280,000 of such company-instituted security checks. Or that in
Michigan the large automobile companies of Ford, General Motors and
Chrysler all made extensive use of local police departments to spy on and
police their employees. Ford went further by employing the former head of
the FBI's Detroit Bureau, John Bugas, to spy on company employees.
Other companies, including GE, Honeywell, Stewart-Warner, Motorola,
Lockheed Aircraft Corp., US Steel and the Emerson Electric Company,
employed the American Security Council (ASC), prominently staffed by
ex-FBI agents, to list, monitor and exercise surveillance over suspected
radicals among their employees (Caute, 1979: 370–2). In the sanitized
world of Bethel et al. (1959) there is no mention of communism or
capitalism, socialism or free enterprise, international trade or trading blocs.
Indeed, there is no mention of the USSR or any of the 'Eastern Bloc'
countries. Nor is there mention of power politics and conflict in regard to
the workplace.

The work of Bethel et al. (1959) was not untypical. A key symposium
convened by the Foundation for Research on Human Behavior was held at
Ann Arbor, Michigan, in February 1959 and brought together many of the
leading theorists in the field of organizations. The papers were published as
a collection under the title *Modern Organization Theory* and edited by
Mason Haire (1967). None of the illustrious authors, who included
Richard Cyert and James March, Christopher Argyris, William Foote
Whyte, Renis Likert and Dorwin Cartwright, make any reference to key
contours of the Cold War.

In the following year the edited collection of Heckmann and Huneryager
(1960) made vague and tentative references to the Cold War. This
collection again included well-known luminaries such as Likert, Whyte and
Argyris, joined by Fritz Roethlisberger, Douglas McGregor, Robert
Tannenbaum, Abraham Maslow, Carl Rogers and others. Introducing the
collection, Heckmann and Huneryager allude to the fact that capitalism
has been reformed:

> Obviously, certain relationships have always existed between employer and
> employee. . . . It was not, however, until the latter part of the nineteenth century
> that much attention was given to the human element in business. Previous to
> this, the era of the corporate mogul held forth, with the principal approach to
> labor being that of the commodity concept of earlier economists, namely, that
> workers were something to be bought and sold in the market place with only
> isolated attention being given to them as human beings. (Heckmann and
> Huneryager, 1960: 2)

Within this context they raise the issue of trade union militancy but as
something belonging strictly to the pre-Second World War era: 'Today
management is explained as being in part a social process – a process of

combining techniques with men for the mutual benefit of both' (Heckmann and Huneryager, 1960: 4).

In a section of the book devoted to motivation, Ross Stagner – in an article reproduced from 1950 – states approvingly that 'Capitalism strengthens ego motives' and argues that industrial conflict is actually rooted in deeper 'psychological aspects' of personality. For example, says Stagner, in the late 1940s there were 'strikes by "workers" receiving an average pay of $10,000 or more per year (airline pilots, Hollywood script writers). To imply that these are economically motivated, merely because pay increases were demanded, is to be very naive about human nature' (ibid.: 158). In Stagner's view 'the workers first get angry and go on strike, then look around for something to demand' (ibid.: 156). Stagner failed to say that at the time of the script writers strike the Screen Writers' Guild (SWG) had, since 1947, been facing the brunt of the anti-communist attacks on the movie industry. In September 1947 HUAC turned its attention on the movie industry, subpoenaing 41 witnesses, including 19 'unfriendly witnesses' of whom 13 were script writers. More than half of this latter group, to become known as 'The Hollywood Ten', was eventually jailed for 'contempt' of Congress (Goldstein, 1978; Caute, 1979).

In a rare comment on the existence of communist theory, Robert N. McMurray – in an article reprinted from 1953 – plugs into that aspect of Cold War discourse which hinted at a communist conspiracy, arguing that communist thought in the USA was only kept alive by 'Communist propaganda circles':

> The old stereotype of the capitalist as a hard-eyed, blood-sucking leech, mercilessly exploiting the helpless proletariat, has been relegated chiefly to Communist propaganda circles. Most employees are sufficiently sophisticated to know that top and middle management is composed of hired hands whose positions are fundamentally no different from theirs, except that the pressures are greater. (Heckmann and Huneryager, 1960: 592)

Communist conspiracy raises its head yet again in a collection of readings by Davis and Scott (1964). A study of a 1948 strike of meat packers in a (1954) reading by Purcell sets out to analyse the degree to which employees can have a 'dual allegiance to company and union'. Concluding that 'rank-and-file workers want *both* their company and union to coexist' (Davis and Scott, 1964: 333), Purcell's only reference to the impact of the Cold War is to Communist party control of the union local during the strike. Using the following selected comments from employees five years after the ending of the strike, Purcell suggests that

> the 'communist' leadership of the local 'forced (workers) into a strike they did not want . . . were excessively anti-company in their policies and acts . . . [and] they were too militant on Negro rights'.

The strike shouldn't have been. . . . The people didn't want to go out. . . . They're biting the hand that feeds us. . . . The District is run by Moscow. . . . It's definitely red. . . . The union ought to confine their business to the union and leave out interracial housing. (Davis and Scott, 1964: 331, 331–2)

In contrast to the normal avoidance of the issue, the 1962 business text by Bayard O. Wheeler embraces the rhetoric of the Cold War. Wheeler makes it clear from the beginning that he is committed to a form of pro-Americanism that sees 'free enterprise' as a value to be defended against the evils of communism. For Wheeler, the USA 'leads the world in productive capacity and output' with a 'long-term growth unparalleled in the history of mankind':

In essence the American business system is both *democratic* and *capitalistic*. Democracy is evident in the various rights and freedoms granted to individuals. No less important are the economic freedoms which support private enterprise in business. . . . In short, we have a bundle of rights and freedoms which marks our system as capitalistic rather than socialistic or some other form. (Wheeler, 1962: 7–10)

Socialism is characterized as a system opposed to 'rights and freedoms', and, clearly utilizing a Cold War framework, Wheeler loses little opportunity to contrast the 'achievements' of capitalism with the 'evils' of communism.

Our combination of democracy and capitalism is a leading clue to the world leadership of American business. Other political and legal systems such as communism and socialism limit the scope of man's individual enterprise. (Ibid.: 12)

The Russian political and legal system, in contrast to that of the United States, grants little, if any, personal freedom to own or invest in business enterprise. . . . Private property rights in basic industries are nonexistent, and, of course, political democracy with free elections as practiced in our country is not followed. (Ibid.: 30)

The freer atmosphere after World War II was soon dispelled by the threat of world communism, the war in Korea, and the continuing international tensions of today. (Ibid.: 68)

Wheeler brings his Cold War framework to bear on the labour front. Far from avoiding discussion of the Taft–Hartley Act (1947) Wheeler refers directly to its 'anticommunist' provisions but states that it 'corrected some of the labor abuses which had sprung up' (ibid.: 517–18). When it comes to the issue of unions, Wheeler is firmly of the belief that communist views are alien and, by implication, un-American:

The union movement in the United States has been evolutionary, rather than revolutionary, in seeking its aims. Except for a few unions with communist or alien attitudes and leadership, unions have worked to fulfill their objectives through democratic processes within the framework of our constitutional government and consistent with our institutions and traditions. (Ibid.: 510)

In regard to international trade, Wheeler clearly identifies some of the Cold War elements involved:

> Today, American business, along with other elements of society, faces increasing dependence and responsibilities in international relations. We have become acutely conscious of the world balance of power between communism and the western world, with substantial amounts of our resources being deployed throughout the world to win the support of uncommitted nations. (Ibid.: 62)

> Under our postwar program of economic aid to the Free World, and through our military expenditures abroad, substantial amounts of dollar exchange have been made available to foreign countries in the past to pay for our exports. (Ibid.: 289)

From exclusion to rhetoric: institutional isomorphism and the Cold War on campus

The Cold War in action had a tremendous impact on societies across the globe. A powerful discourse, supported and reproduced through a series of discursive practices throughout institutions, the Cold War reached into most aspects of social life. How this phenomenon came to be either missing from many of the business texts of the late 1950s and early 1960s, or represented in only a crude, belligerent form, needs some explanation.

Part of the explanation can be drawn from the work of the new institutionalism and analyses of the structural forms of educational organizations. In the seminal work by DiMaggio and Powell (1991: 64, 66) it is argued that a 'startling homogeneity of organizational forms and practices' is due, in large part, to a process of 'isomorphism' – 'a constraining process that forces one unit in a population to resemble other units that face the same set of environmental conditions'. In particular 'institutional isomorphism' refers to 'forces pressing communities towards accommodation with the outside world'. DiMaggio and Powell go on to detail three types of 'institutional isomorphic change':

> (1) *coercive* isomorphism that stems from political influence and the problems of legitimacy; (2) *mimetic* isomorphism resulting from standard responses to uncertainty; and (3) *normative* isomorphism, associated with professionalization. (DiMaggio and Powell, 1991: 67)

We will argue that all these processes go a long way to explaining the development of a particular form of the business textbook. In an analysis of the structure of educational organizations Meyer and Rowan (1983) argue that educational organizations are order-affirming as opposed to task-performing and that educational bureaucracies:

1 are personnel-certifying agencies in modern societies (p. 72);
2 function to maintain the societally agreed-on rites defined in societal myths (or institutional rules) of education (p. 76);
3 are formed to instruct and socialize (p. 78);
4 produce education for society, not for individuals or families (p. 82);
5 become the central agency defining personnel – both citizen and elite – for the modern state and economy (p. 83);
6 have come to be increasingly structured by centers of political authority (p. 83);
7 incorporate citizens into the political, economic, and status order of society (p. 83);
8 consist of a set of standardized public credentials used to incorporate citizen personnel into society (p. 83).

The role of the modern university (and other educational institutions), according to Meyer and Rowan (1983), is the 'tight control of ritual classifications':

> The growth of corporate control of education has major implications for educational organizations. As citizen personnel are increasingly sorted and allocated to positions in the social structure on the basis of classified or certified educational properties, the ritual classifications of education – type of student, topic, teacher, or school – come to have substantial value in what might be called the social identity 'market'. A workable identity market presupposes a standardized, trustworthy currency of social typifications that is free from local anomalies. (Meyer and Rowan, 1983: 83)

In contrast to the control of ritual classifications, the classroom is managed through 'the logic of confidence'. Such a logic is a taken-for-granted, good-faith assumption that, by dint of his or her qualifications, the individual teacher can be relied on to do a good job without interference. In this way the institution is able to engage the commitment of participants:

> the avoidance of close inspection, especially when accompanied by elaborate displays of confidence and trust, can increase the commitments of internal participants. The agreement of teachers to participate actively in the organized social reality of the ritual classifications of education is crucial, and an administrator can trade off the matter of conformity to the details of instruction and achievement in order to obtain teachers' complicity and satisfaction. (Meyer and Rowan, 1983: 88)

What does any of this have to do with the Cold War and the business textbook? Four key points can be made:

1 It can be argued that the Cold War played a crucial and direct role in shaping and determining the legitimacy of universities.

2 Within the framework of the Cold War discourse the legitimacy of business study was narrowly defined.
3 The process of ritual classification involved the segregation of business study into diverse units of study (e.g., the splitting of organizational studies into Organization Theory and Organizational Behaviour – see Marsden and Townley, 1996).
4 The development of business and management texts – within the general framework of university and business legitimacy – set a narrow tone of isomorphic influence for future textbook production.

The Cold War on campus

McCarthyism is often associated with an anti-communist attack on freedoms within the movie industry but one of the first industries to come under investigation was education. In universities, colleges and schools throughout the USA a series of actions were taken to restrict certain freedoms. Numerous professors and teachers were forced to appear before HUAC to answer charges that they had communist affiliations, associations or sympathies: HUAC's definition of 'communist activities or sympathies' was known to encompass a wide range of opinions. In many cases persons subpoenaed to appear before HUAC ended up being dismissed from their educational institution (Goldstein, 1978; Caute, 1979). Communists and former communists called to appear before HUAC were placed in an impossible situation, facing dismissal from their university if they admitted membership of the CPUSA, if they pleaded the Fifth Amendment (i.e., refused to say anything on the grounds that it may be self-incriminating), or if they refused to provide HUAC with the names of suspected communists. At Harvard, for example, Helen Deane Markham, an assistant professor of anatomy, pleaded the Fifth Amendment before HUAC in 1953 and was subsequently informed by the university that she would not be re-appointed (Caute, 1979: 411).

Direct government influence was also exerted on educational establishments. In June 1949, for example, HUAC wrote to 81 colleges and high schools demanding lists of textbooks in use in the fields of literature, economics, government, history, political science and geography. The military, in a similar vein, demanded the right to scrutinize the curricula of about 200 colleges engaged in classified work under military contract. Indeed, in 1953 the US Armed Forces Institute (USAFI) added a clause to its university contracts, endowing itself with the power to veto faculty members conducting correspondence courses under the scheme: only 14 of 46 universities refused to renew their contracts with the USAFI (Caute, 1979: 404).

In several cases university administrations did not wait for government intervention, preferring to demonstrate their own loyalty and, thus, educational legitimacy. At the University of Washington, for example, the Board of Regents determined that membership of the CPUSA violated

TABLE 2.2 *Selected US universities and scholarly bodies experiencing prominent cases of Cold War intervention**

American Council of Learned Societies	Queens College
American University	Reed College
Carnegie Foundation	Rockefeller Foundation
CCNY (City College of New York)	Rutgers University
Columbia University	San Diego State College
Cornell University	San Francisco City College
Council on Foreign Relations	San Francisco State College
Dickenson College	Social Science Research Council
Evansville College, Indiana	State University, Brockport, New York
Fairmont State College, Virginia	UCLA (University of California at Los Angeles)
Far Eastern Association	
Fisk University, Nashville, Tennessee	University of Chicago
Foreign Policy Association	University of Colorado
Fund for the Republic	University of Florida
Guggenheim Foundation	University of Idaho
Harvard University	University of Kansas City
Kansas State College at Emporia	University of Michigan
MIT (Massachusetts Institute of Technology)	University of Minnesota
	University of Oklahoma
National Education Association	University of Vermont
New York City municipal colleges	University of Washington
New York University (NYU)	University of Wyoming
Ohio State University	Wayne State University
Oregon State College	Wayne University

* Compiled from Goldstein (1978) and Caute (1979): interventions include loyalty-oath requirements, the firing of professors, the banning of campus speakers and other activities (e.g., art exhibitions), etc.

the University's Administrative Code because it involved (a) incompetence, (b) neglect of duty, and (c) dishonesty or immorality (quoted in Caute, 1979: 408). Using the edict, the administration immediately fired a philosophy professor and a professor of English. At the University of Colorado the Regents hired two former FBI agents to root out suspected communists on the campus. In 1949 the Regents of the University of California voted to impose a private loyalty oath on the faculty: each member of the faculty was expected to sign an oath which declared that he or she was 'not a member of the Communist Party or any other organization which advocates the overthrow of the Government' (quoted in Caute, 1979: 423). Other actions by university administrations included such things as the banning of an art exhibition due to 'the use of communist symbols' (UCLA), the banning of speakers from the campus (e.g., the University of Washington banned J. Robert Oppenheimer from addressing the faculty and students), as well as various forms of pressure on faculty suspected of leftist sympathies. There was hardly a university, educational body, or even funding agency that was left untouched by the process (see Table 2.2).

Certainly the Cold War was dictating what was to be considered legitimate on university campuses but the legitimacy argument alone does not explain the zeal with which some administrators adopted anti-communist and anti-liberal measures. As Caute explains it:

> Schools and colleges were governed very rarely by educators, but more commonly by businessmen, bankers, lawyers and, in the case of state universities, by politicians. By 1950 such people accounted for about 80 percent of university trustees or regents. . . . For example, the trustees of the University of Washington at the time of the 1948–49 purge were seven in number: two attorneys, two major industrialists, an investment broker, the corrupt vice-president of the Teamsters . . . and a solitary liberal educator. The Board of Regents of the University of California at the time of the loyalty-oath calamity included an osteopath who specialized in property deals, a lawyer who sold his interest in a gold mine for $325,000, two prominent members of Associated Farmers employing sweated Mexican labor and the president of the largest bank in the world, the Bank of America, who declared, 'I feel sincerely that if we rescind this oath flags will fly in the Kremlin'. (Caute, 1979: 404–5)

Caute goes on to draw the conclusion that: 'Whereas in Britain the universities have been carefully shielded from transitory public pressures, the heads of American colleges have had to face the rude winds of populist intolerance' (1979: 405). It is perhaps not surprising that, with this kind of political structure and pressure, notions of legitimacy in American universities were narrowly interpreted from the top down during this period.

Cold War rhetoric and the business curriculum

A central theme of the rhetoric of the US Cold War warrior is the continual reference to 'democracy' and 'free enterprise', terms which are almost always contrasted with 'totalitarianism' and 'state ownership and control of industry' within the Soviet Union (see Wheeler, 1962). The notion of state ownership of property was seen by the American Cold War warrior as a threat to business and the freedom of the business owner to develop and profit. It is certainly no surprise that, in the USA, the business community has been among the most vociferous pursuers of the Cold War (see Chomsky and Herman, 1979; Hobsbawm, 1994). It would have been unthinkable to employ anyone in the field of business and management study who appeared to question the basic tenets of free enterprise. It has been well documented elsewhere that, until quite recently, the legitimate study of business within the university community was restricted to those with a fundamental commitment to a managerialist or, at least, broadly functionalist approach (Burrell and Morgan, 1979; Clegg and Dunkerley, 1980).

In an atmosphere where, at many of the top universities, established professors of science, literature and social studies were being penalised for their beliefs, it is not surprising that business professors were either silent on the issue of the Cold War,[1] or, as in the case of Wheeler (1962), wholeheartedly committed to its pursuance.

Ritual classification and the divisionalization of management and organizational study

Until the late 1950s the study of business had already divided into the study of management (analysis of the internal operation of the firm) and the study of business (analysis of the relationship of the firm to its general environment). The study of management itself was already being divided into management and organizational specialisms, and the latter was beginning to experience a further split into organization theory and organizational behaviour.[2] Such divisions legitimize the academic pursuit of a narrow focus to the exclusion of broader concerns such as the political economy of organizational behaviour and structure.

The business textbook and the social identity market

The developing business text of the era established a narrow focus of analysis which has served as the model for future years. That focus generally excluded consideration of broad and specific political and socio-economic influences on the development of organizations and behaviour within those organizations.[3] By removing the organization from its context what was left was a focus on the organization as an individual *unit* of study. Devoid of broader constraints, it was relatively easy to focus on a supposed underlying rationality and a need for organizational efficiency.[4] Within the framework of the single organization the notion of the individual takes on a peculiar meaning: the developing study of 'organizational behaviour' was beginning to carve out an interest in how the individual can be motivated, led, communicated with, organized, encouraged to participate, counselled and changed *within* the organization.[5]

We are not arguing that a closed system model of organizations developed as a result of a generalized Cold War mentality. However, we are suggesting that such a mentality strengthened any tendency to avoid a concern with broader socio-political issues. At the very least, the Cold War mentality would have ensured that the evolving organization and management disciplines were confined to analyses which did not question the legitimacy of business in general or organizational power and control in particular.

Organizational Culture and Imperialism

Edward Said (1993) has discussed at length the relationship between literature and imperialism. The business text, we would argue, is but a newer form of fiction and, by its direct relationship to business enterprise, more likely to reveal traces of the imperialism noted by Said. In this section we examine the social construction of international organizational links and of race in the business text.

The decades 1955 to 1985 saw momentous changes in the world, including the independence of most of the remaining colonies of France, Britain and Holland; the Cuban (1959), Portuguese (1974), and Nicaraguan (1979) revolutions; the election of Salvador Allende's Popular Unity Government in Chile in 1970; the death of Stalin and the revelations of the 20th Congress of the Communist Party of the Soviet Union; the Hungarian Uprising (1956), the Prague Spring (1968), and the Gdansk strikes (1980); the widespread unrest in France in 1968; the Vietnam War; and the establishment of the European Economic Community (EEC). In all cases the USA perceived a national interest and acted in numerous ways to protect or advance that interest – in some cases establishing 'client state' relations with various countries throughout the Americas, Asia, and the Middle East (see Chomsky and Herman, 1979); in some cases using direct (the Vietnam War; the Bay of Pigs) and indirect (the overthrow of Allende) force; and in some cases using political channels (e.g., NATO involvement). On the domestic front the USA was confronted with numerous race riots, freedom marches, and anti-Vietnam War demonstrations throughout the middle part of the era.

Over the same period, with few exceptions, the reviewed texts had nothing to say about the relationship between organizations and the international environment.[6] Among the exceptions the Davis and Scott (1964) text is unusual in its direct reference to the Cold War and a detailed discussion of national cultural differences. In a reading on 'industrialization, ideologies and social structure' the sociologist Reinhard Bendix argues for 'the comparative study of ideologies of management' in the context of the Cold War. In a detailed and complex reading on 'intercultural communication' sociologists Edward T. Hall and William Foote Whyte attempt to assist the American manager to deal 'with people of another culture' through a comparison of broad national cultural mores.

Texts by Newman, Summer and Warren (1972) and Huse and Bowditch (1977) were ahead of their time in their, respective, references to 'international management' and the 'internationalization of business'. While Huse and Bowditch barely devote a page to the issue, Newman et al. devote an entire chapter, noting that:

> A growing number of companies based in the United States are conducting operations abroad. Foreign-based companies, likewise, are opening branches in the United States. . . . Many more firms in all parts of the world exchange technical and management know-how. Day be day the pace of this internationalization is accelerating. (Newman et al., 1972: 711)

Ostensibly concerned with the issue of 'culture and the transfer of management know-how', Newman et al. devote a chapter to developing the notion of the 'American manager' and how 'he' compares with his foreign counterparts (see Table 2.3). Unlike the complex images of the earlier work by Hall and Whyte (1964), Newman et al.'s picture of the ideal typical

TABLE 2.3   *Characteristics and beliefs of the American and the 'foreign' manager*

The American manager	The 'foreign' manager
• self-determined	• driven by mysticism or fatalism (e.g., 'some Moslem countries')
• has realistic objectives	• taken to flights of fancy
• achieves objectives through hard work	• curries favour to achieve objectives
• ethically obliged to fulfil commitments	• inconsistent commitment
• time is a crucial aspect of performance	• relaxed attitude to time ('part of the charm of our Latin American friends')
• primary obligation to the enterprise	• primary commitment to extended family
• gives undivided attention to the company	• sometimes takes bribes
• respects company rules and regulations	• lacks respect for formal rules (e.g., 'the Arab')
• appoints the 'best man' for the job	• uses nepotism to hire employees
• fires 'second raters'	• is influenced by family, personal, and political ties to keep certain people employed
• has unlimited upward mobility	• is restricted by class and other non-work considerations
• is free to move horizontally	• is loyal to a single company (e.g., Japan)
• egalitarian	• unconcerned with egalitarian principle
• rational decision-maker	• irrational, emotional decision-maker
• frank and open	• polite but deceiving (e.g., Far Eastern cultures)
• ambitious	• lacking in ambition
• respects all kinds of work	• won't take work 'below his dignity'
• accepts change	• resists change
• results oriented	• concerned with appearances (e.g., Latin America)

Source: Newman et al., 1972

American manager is that of someone with drive and integrity who manages to achieve what he sets out to achieve; someone who is different from and, by implication, superior to those less fortunate enough to be born in another culture. The image – like the one by Hall and Whyte (1964) – is decidedly male and decidedly white. In addition to the exclusive use of the masculine pronoun, the characteristics of the American manager conform to a specific view of masculinity (e.g., references to rationality, primary and undivided commitment to the company, etc. – see Ferguson, 1984). In a similar vein the images draw on stereotypes more associated with white males than people of colour and all the contrasting images of 'foreigner' are of non-white individuals.

International trade and the discourse of globalization

By the mid-1980s authors of management textbooks were beginning to note a phenomenon that they tagged 'globalization'. Pucik (in Fombrun et al., 1984), for example, comments that:

> From a corporate perspective the dominant feature of today's world economy is the increasing globalization of market competition. Formerly isolated geographically bounded markets are being transformed, if not always into a global market, then into a set of interconnected markets. (Pucik, in Fombrun et al., 1984: 403)

Such commentators were correct in sensing that dramatic changes were occurring in the conduct of international trade. In sheer volume, the world economy was growing at an explosive rate, with the world output of manufactures quadrupling between 1950 and 1970 and world trade in manufactured products growing tenfold over the same period (Hobsbawm, 1994: 261). In terms of political change, there was a substantial restructuring and reform of capitalism (e.g., the development of 'mixed' economies, and commitments to full employment and social welfare) which encouraged the growth of mass consumer markets in the capitalist states (Hobsbawm, 1994: 269). Also, there was a widespread process of decolonization which had enabled rapid industrialization throughout the so-called 'Third World'; technologically a revolution in transportation and communication 'made it possible and economically feasible to split the production of a single article between' several geographical, national locations (Hobsbawm, 1994: 280; Laxer, 1995: 290).

The *extent* of recent changes has encouraged some business textbook writers to confuse the growth of internationalization with its advent: as Laxer (1995) points out 'globalization is not new'; for instance, compare the description of Marx and Engels (1848) with that of Pucik (in Fombrun et al., 1984) quoted above:

> The need of a constantly expanding market for its products chases the bourgeoisie over the whole surface of the globe. . . . The bourgeoisie has through its exploitation of the world market given a cosmopolitan character to production and consumption in every country. (Quoted in Laxer, 1995: 289)

A focus on the *extent* of world trade allows the textbook author to overlook the character (and associated problems) or the *new forms* of globalization. Whereas in Marx's time trade was opened up through the process of imperialism, today the transnational corporation plays a central role:

> [An increasingly *transnational* economy began to emerge, especially from the 1960s on, that is to say, a system of economic activities for which state territories and state frontiers are not the basic framework, but merely complicating factors. . . . Three aspects of this transnationalism were particularly obvious: transnational firm . . ., the new international division of labour and the rise of offshore finance. The last of these was not only one of the earliest forms of transnationalism to develop, but also the one which demonstrates most vividly the way in which the capitalist economy escaped from national, or any other control. (Hobsbawm, 1994: 227)

A key difference between 'imperialism' and 'globalization' is that the former had at its heart national interests (the interests of the imperial power), while the latter is centred on organizational interests:

> A multinational enterprise is very different from simply a transmitter of capital. A multinational enterprise transmits management, it transmits knowledge of a product, knowledge of how that produce is made, how that product is marketed – an entire organization. (Mira Wilkins, quoted in Laxer, 1995: 291)

As Laxer has commented, 'the transnationals' ability to determine events results from this organizational power' (1995: 291).

In its heyday imperialism involved the conquest of groups of people by the imperial nation state. The state maintained order and controlled by force (e.g., armies, police) and ideology (e.g., missionaries, rudimentary education, etc.). By contrast, the transnational corporation exerts controls through economic sanctions[7] and the ideology of management training and practice: both forms of control are, of course, fictions. Unfettered by purely national interests, the transnational has, quite literally, managed – where Imperialism failed – to create a particular view of Enlightenment thinking over a substantial part of the globe:

> In other words, 'globalization' carries much freight. How prophetic – or should that be 'how convenient'? – that this freight is the heart of the capitalist Enlightenment project of the past two centuries, with its emphasis on universalism, scientism, rationality, private property rights, liberalism and individualism. (Laxer, 1995: 288)

By the late 1980s there were approximately 20,000 transnationals in the world, accounting for 25–30 per cent of the gross domestic product of the world's market economies, controlling 80 per cent of the world's land cultivated for export crops, and 'the lion's share of the world's technological innovations' (Laxer, 1995: 291). Most of the transnationals are based in the major capitalist states, with 85 per cent of the top 200 based in the USA, Japan, the UK and Germany: in terms of the USA, those transnationals accounted for approximately 75 per cent of the nation's exports and almost 50 per cent of its imports (Hobsbawm, 1994: 279). Yet, in many respects, the national or home base of the transnational is only partially relevant. As one commentator has argued, 'it is doubtful whether any of them, except the Japanese and some essentially military firms, could be confidently described as identified with their government's or nation's interests. . . . [Indeed] the most convenient world for multinational giants is one populated by dwarf states or no states at all' (Hobsbawm, 1994: 279, 281).

That globalization is arguably about the unfettered pursuit of profit (Hobsbawm, 1994), the decline of social reform (Teeple, 1995; McMurtry,

1996), and an attack on democracy and social solidarity (Laxer, 1995) is barely, if at all, considered in the pages of the business textbook. Instead, the business textbook writer has contributed to the growth of a discourse of globalization which images a 'brave new world' of borderless trade (Higgins, 1991), in which global 'democratization' (Schermerhorn et al., 1991) and 'technological progress and innovation' (Bateman and Zeithaml, 1990) go hand in hand. The emphasis here is not on the world *per se* but on the corporate world and how corporate opportunities, trade 'restrictions' (Baird et al., 1990) and cultural diversity (Moorhead and Griffin, 1992) can be managed in a changing world.

Race, gender and the ideal-typical organizational actor

In the USA, 1955 to 1985 marked an era of tremendous human rights challenge and change that saw the 1950s desegregation movement led by Martin Luther King, the 1963 March on Washington, the 1967 race riots, the advent of the Black Power movement (Malcolm X, the Nation of Islam, the Black Panthers, etc.), the movement for women's liberation, numerous anti-Vietnam War demonstrations, and the advent of civil rights, equal pay, and equal employment opportunities legislation. That none of these challenges or changes found their way into the business text is not only remarkable, it is implausible!

From the early texts (1959–67) until very recently there develops an image of the ideal-typical employee who is decidedly white, liberal, male and American. Heckmann and Huneryager, for example, referring to 'the worker as a *whole man*', state that:

> No longer is he viewed solely as an economic tool, but rather as a human being, driven and controlled by diverse elements of society, with fears and frustrations, expectations and desires – all a part of his total make-up. How he performs on his job – his efficiency and productivity – are dependent as much, if not more, on the external aspects surrounding his work place as on the tools and materials he uses. Therefore, it must be recognized that man as a worker is unique compared to other productive factors. He alone must be *motivated*, not only to do his job, but to strive constantly to improve his performance. This, then, remains the cardinal objective of the human relations function: to discover newer and better ways of understanding man and his relation to his work, of motivating him to higher standards of workmanship, and of helping as many people as much as possible to realize their maximum potential. (Heckmann and Huneryager, 1960: 5, original emphasis)

Predating Newman et al. (1972) (see Table 2.3), Heckman and Huneryager introduce stereotypical American values into the image of the ideal worker:

> Those of us fortunate enough to have been born and raised in the democratic atmosphere of the United States have gone through a long process of inculcation in democratic processes. Consequently, we expect to have something to say about

actions and plans that affect our way of life in industry and society. If others attempt to deprive us of this right, we will do all in our power to do something about it. (Heckmann and Huneryager, 1960: 349)

In their discussions of people in organizations very few business texts make any significant references to gender or race.

Gender

Of the 107 texts reviewed, the overwhelming majority – including 18 published in the 1990s – have little (65) or nothing (37) to say about women, gender or even sex differences.[8] Only five texts – Hellriegel et al., 1995; Moorhead and Griffin, 1995; Nelson and Quick, 1995; George and Jones, 1996; and Greenberg et al., 1996 – discuss the issue of gender in any depth.

At times the avoidance of gender appears to have been almost difficult to achieve. Filley and House (1969), for example, discuss 'stereotypes' without any mention of gender or race while Huse and Bowditch (1977) devote four paragraphs to 'the changing composition of the labor force' and manage to say nothing about race or gender.

The majority of references to gender differences are introduced by way of discussion of employment equity legislation or the 'growing number of women in the work force' – with women being depicted in each case as a departure from the male work norm; something of note for male managers. Bethel et al. (1959), for example, are clearly writing in a male voice and for a male audience when they speak about, respectively, 'women in industry' and 'the woman executive':

> The desire for supplemental family income to support a higher standard of living, the greater social independence of women, and shortages of workers at the skill level and at the wage scale women represent are some of the chief factors accounting for the increasing employment of women in the economy. (Bethel et al., 1959: 310)

> Inasmuch as women are entering business in increasing numbers with superior education and with the common advantage of daily confidential contact with real executive problems at the clerical level, it is not surprising that some of them advance to executive jobs. (Ibid.: 312)

Even in some of the recent texts gender is discussed only in passing. The only reference to gender in Randolph and Blackburn, for example, is by way of an exercise which tests 'attitudes people have about women in business' (1989: 155–7). We can hear the male voice in the exercise's 'learning message' which concludes that:

> The scores . . . will provide some indication of how comfortable a person is with women in managerial positions. Since women are entering management in

greater numbers, attitudes about them as managers are important and should be understood.

While the majority of new (post-1990) texts include a fuller discussion of gender, they fail to discuss the implications for understanding organizational behaviour (e.g., the effect of gender on culture, motivation, stress, communication, etc.). And even among the better texts gender – along with race, age, sexual preference, and ethnicity – is becoming subsumed under 'diversity' and problematized anew (Prasad and Mills, 1997).

Race

Not until the mid-1980s do we find more than a passing reference to race in any of the texts reviewed: prior to this point only seven of 33 texts *mention* race. Bethel et al. (1959) devote only 15 words (approximately 0.007 per cent of the total) to a discussion of white fears about the 'racial integration' of trade unions; one of 55 readings in Davis and Scott (1964) compares 'negro' to 'white' attitudes to 'trade union allegiance'; Newman et al. (1972) spend less that 60 words (0.02 per cent of the book) on 'racial issues', arguing that 'management must deal with new emphases, including . . . race and urban problems'; Luthans (1977 and 1981) devotes, respectively, 0.15 per cent and 0.19 per cent of his textbooks to the issue of race, focusing on the existence of the Equal Employment Opportunity Commission (EEOC) and the impact of the Civil Rights Act, 1964 and racial discrimination on psychological testing;[9] and, in a similar vein, Dessler (1983a) and Fombrun et al. (1984) introduce the notion of race through a general reference to equal rights legislation, devoting, respectively, less than 0.11 per cent and 0.15 per cent of the text to the issue. In each case the starting point for discussion of race is a departure from a perceived white norm, with the black worker depicted as a problem or a curiosity for the white manager.

Remarkably, this limited form of referencing has continued through to the present: Hodgetts (1990), for example, devotes only 0.07 per cent of his text to a discussion of 'minorities'; Schermerhorn, Hunt and Osborn (1991 and 1995) argue that 'by the year 2000 ethnic minorities will be a majority of the American workforce' yet they only devote, respectively, 0.17 per cent and 0.09 per cent of their textbooks to discussion of race and ethnicity; and the Van Fleet (1991) and Cherrington (1994) texts, respectively, devote only 0.02 per cent and 0.16 per cent to discussions of 'racial discrimination'. Of the 71 post-1985 texts reviewed, 27 have nothing to say about race and 37 deal with the issue in a cursory way.

The following quotes from Nickels et al. (1994) are prime examples of the way that race and gender continue to be problematized from a white, male perspective; in a context where very little else is said, some of the asides and comments suggest that the hiring of people of colour may even be detrimental to an organization:

Problems being encountered in the human resource area include:

- A complex set of laws and regulations involving hiring, firing, safety, unionization, and equal pay that *limits organizations' freedom to create an optimum labour force.* For example, *it is becoming very difficult to fire an inefficient or ineffective worker.* (Nickels et al., 1994: 474, our emphasis)

[R]ecruitment has become very difficult for several reasons:

- Legal restrictions, such as the Charter of Rights & Freedoms, make it necessary to consider the proper mix of women, minorities, people with disabilities, and other qualified individuals. *Often people with the necessary skills are not available, so others must be hired and trained internally.*
- Firing unsatisfactory employees is getting more difficult to justify legally. *This is especially true of discharges involving possible discrimination by age, sex, sexual preference or race.* (Ibid.: 477, our emphases)

Only seven of the 107 reviewed texts deal with race and ethnicity at a substantial level. Two 1985 texts, by Davis and Newstrom and Douglas, Klein and Hunt, move beyond a cursory reference to explore the issue of race in more depth, devoting, respectively, 0.77 per cent and 1.02 per cent of the book to the issue. Both texts, however, confine discussion to the need to address inequities in the workplace and neither examine behaviour in the workplace from a multi-ethnic perspective: issues such as 'individual behaviour', 'motivation', 'groups dynamics' and 'culture' are all considered from an ethnocentric/eurocentric perspective. The Douglas et al. (1985) text details the growth of 'minorities' in the workplace, arguing that:

> An organization must recognize that there is a potentially large number of people with diverse expectations in terms of work, the workplace, incentives, and the type of leadership to which they respond. It would follow that the people with these different values would place different demands on managers, and traditional practices may no longer by expected to bring traditional results. (Douglas et al., 1985)

But despite this observation the book fails to examine how a focus on race/ ethnic differences would alter traditional ways of understanding organizational behaviour. Davis and Newstrom devote a small section of a chapter on 'Equal Employment Opportunity' to 'race, color, and national origin', framing the discussion with a eurocentric, assimilationist perspective:[10]

> The United States historically has been called a 'melting pot' of people from all parts of the world, so it is important to give *these people* equal access to jobs regardless of their backgrounds. In this way they have a fair chance to *earn their way* into the *mainstream of society* and become self-sufficient. (Davis and Newstrom, 1985: 406, our emphasis)

Five texts that deal substantially with race and ethnicity have all been published since 1995 (Hellriegel et al., 1995; Moorhead and Griffin, 1995; Nelson and Quick, 1995; George and Jones, 1996; and Greenberg et al.,

1996). The best of these argues that 'managing a diverse workforce is not as simple as it was once thought to be':

> Rather than a melting pot, the workplace now resembles a tossed salad of different flavors, colors, and textures. Rather than assimilate those who are different into a single organizational culture, the current view is that organizations need to celebrate the differences and use the variety of talents, perspectives, and backgrounds of all employees. (Moorhead and Griffin, 1995: 523)

Although this text introduces the notion of 'diversity' – 'all of the ways that employees differ' – and includes a 'Diversity in the Workplace' section in some chapters of the book, at the heart of the argument is the ultimate white, male voice and bottom-line considerations. As the authors themselves state, 'valuing diversity is not just the right thing to do for workers, it is the right thing to do for the organization, financially and economically' (Moorhead and Griffin, 1995: 526).

The most recent texts would seem to be an advance on what has gone before but, as has been argued elsewhere, there is a concern that the emerging 'diversity management' is a newer, more subtle, form of cultural imperialism:

> Despite the widespread rhetoric of diversity and multiculturalism, organizations are, in fact, extraordinarily monocultural entities. In other words, the premises undergirding organizational functioning are largely monocultural, comprising a generic set of norms, values and cultural preferences. . . . More often than not, these norms and values do not easily accommodate multicultural preferences over a number of issues including the boundaries between work and home, the role of work in society, and the conduct of interpersonal relationships within organizations. . . .
>
> We are therefore, also suggesting that even while the representation of diverse groups in the workplace may have improved, formal and informal organizational rules have hardly kept pace with the diversity of organizational membership. . . .
>
> More than anything, organizational monoculturalism leads to *institutional resistance* against workplace diversity. *Institutional* resistance can be distinguished from *individual* resistance by the structural potency of the problem. Organizational monoculturalism therefore results in innumerable routine workplace processes (such as reward systems) that are systematically hostile to the cultural values and lifestyles of different groups. The ultimate result is a structural failure to accommodate difference at the workplace. (Prasad and Mills, 1997: 15–16)

It can be argued that this latest form of cultural dominance is being achieved through a process of 'showcasing' which plays down or papers over the 'shadows' or 'dilemmas of workplace diversity':

> A showcase is defined as a setting that facilitates the most advantageous arrangement and display of certain objects. Organizational efforts at implementing workplace diversity have predominantly been showcased in the

literature. In other words, workplace diversity has received enormously positive publicity in the literature, which has showcased it by highlighting its more striking accomplishments and attractive features. The showcasing of workplace diversity takes different forms and is accomplished in different ways. . . . *The Economic Showcase* [where] managing diversity is frequently represented as a viable long-term strategy likely to yield the firm some crucial economic benefits. . . . *The Showcase of Guidelines* [where the] diversity literature also showcases ways in which managers can effectively introduce diversity into organizations. [And] *The Showcase of Exemplars* [where] the literature showcases the 'successes' of workplace diversity by publicizing individual organizational attempts at incorporating difference into the workplace.

It is our contention that the elaborate showcasing of the diversity movement has severely limited our understanding of the more problematic aspects of multiculturalism at the workplace. A host of gender conflicts, race tensions and cultural frictions lie hidden behind the shadows of the showcase. (Prasad and Mills, 1997: 8–12)

The emerging character of 'diversity management' raises numerous concerns:

[There is] evidence of the frustration experienced by women and minority groups regarding persistent obstacles to career advancement . . . and the unchanging hostility of workplace cultures. . . . Experiences of marginalization, condescension, contempt, exclusion etc. continue to surface in personal accounts of women, African-American and Asian organizational participants. Clearly, diversity programs are not having the far-reaching impacts they were meant to. This brings us to some troubling questions. Are diversity programs organizational smoke screens concealing enduring patterns of discrimination and prejudice? Or, are they merely enjoyable training interludes, after which managers return to unchanging realities of race hostilities and gender tensions in the workplace? (Prasad and Mills, 1997: 14)

It can be concluded that:

. . . the concept of 'workplace diversity' itself may not hold uniform connotations, and may signify different things to different groups and individuals within organizations and society. To some, diversity may be little more than proportional representation of various demographic and social groups in the workplace. To others, it may involve overcoming cultural prejudice and instilling new values about difference in the organization. To still others, it may connote changing the very fabric of work practices in keeping with the cultural influences of different social groups. At any rate, this more problematic reading of diversity deserves a closer examination by organization and management scholars. (Prasad and Mills, 1997: 13)

Conclusion

On a number of fronts the business textbook has failed to reflect some of the key trends of the time: from the Cold War to dramatic changes in international business, and from race to gender, the business text has been silent. While some texts are beginning to deal with these changes, the process has been slow and discussion is restricted to narrow frameworks, for example 'globalization', 'diversity management'.

What are we to conclude from all this? Clearly some explanation is required as to why the business textbook has been so insular. New institutional theory, through the concept of 'institutional isomorphism' (DiMaggio and Powell, 1991), offers some insights. However, we would contend that new institutionalism underplays the role of social and institutional *power*. Marsden and Townley, in our view, come closest to suggesting a way forward through an integration of the work of Foucault, Weber and Marx:

> We should adopt an 'ascending' analysis. Starting with the infinitesimal mechanisms of power and showing how they have been incorporated and colonized by more general, state mechanisms and cloaked in its theory of power and system of rights. Thus we should study techniques rather than institutions; practices rather than intentions; webs of power rather than classes or groups; knowledge rather than ideology. (Marsden and Townley, 1996: 669)

We should be asking such questions as, how do people get drawn into textbook writing? How do publishers choose their authors? To what extent is the textbook author required to write to a formula? What discourages authors from incorporating more radical developments? What factors influence classroom instructors to choose one text over another? What constraints are they working within? What institutional factors encourage the adoption of certain texts to the exclusion of others?

These are not idle questions. The textbook has become the *primary* means through which business education is taught in North America and, increasingly, in other parts of the world. What are the implications for us as teachers? Fineman and Gabriel contend that 'the pedagogical implications are problematic – though not insurmountable' (1994: 395). We agree to a point. Clearly improvement in the *style* and *content* of the business textbook is not insurmountable but we would question whether the character of the textbook, as a genre of learning, can be meaningfully improved. Despite the development, in recent years, of competing management paradigms (Burrell and Morgan, 1979) the business textbook presents a single – managerialist – worldview. Tracking developments over time one can see that the content of the average business textbook has become increasingly simplistic – reducing selected segments of (managerialist) ideas into more simplistic notions which are then often further simplified by a multitude of hardworking classroom instructors. The process is confounded by a substantial time-lag whereby selected research findings take from five to ten years to find their way into a new text.

What is to be done? Four strategies have appeared in recent years:

1 *Ignore or marginalize the use of the textbook – this is increasingly unlikely.* Institutional and student expectations, course co-ordination and examination strategies, and increasing workloads are all constraints on the classroom lecturer. The use of a textbook frames the teaching experience throughout university courses and plugs into the expectations of students and department alike, and it helps the overworked lecturer to cut corners, especially with the increasing reliance on teacher's aids, such as prepackaged overhead-transparencies and examinations. Nonetheless, divorcing the teaching process from reliance on a textbook should be a long-term strategy of business educators.

2 *Supplement the textbook with a series of readings.* This strategy is problematic in that the modern business student has become dependent on the textbook as the key learning instrument: lecturers who introduce extra readings often find that their student evaluations are lowered when compared to lecturers who rely on less materials. Nonetheless, this is a worthwhile compromise and can serve to encourage students to 'read' the textbook in a more critical fashion.

3 *Use an alternative textbook.* This strategy is currently limited in a number of ways. First, there are very few alternative textbooks: Clegg and Dunkerley (1980) remain one of the few alternative textbooks in existence. Secondly, alternative 'reads' tend to be either restricted to a particular frame of reference (e.g., Boje and Dennehy, 1992) or a specific aspect of organizational behaviour (e.g., Wilson, 1995). Thirdly, institutional constraints conspire to force the teaching of specific subject areas, in specific ways. And, fourthly, the form of the textbook is so entrenched that even alternatives cannot but help to reference a particularly restricted way of thinking. Nonetheless, this is also a valuable strategy, when combined with the use of mainstream texts. Faced with two texts, we can encourage in our students a dialogue between competing frames of reference. To be successful, however, critical thinkers have to be prepared to put the time and effort into the development of alternative textbooks.

4 *The injection of critical ideas into an existing textbook framework.* That is, the involvement of critical thinkers in mainstream textbook production. This is the least developed strategy and the one involving the most risk – for both the author and the project. Yet we believe that this may be a useful strategy to develop, the idea being that students are confronted with a dialogue within the confines of a single text. In this way the radical thinker can work within different paradigms and different discourses to alter the processes of teaching.[11]

Notes

1. It is unlikely that the authors of the previewed early (pre-1965) textbooks were unaware of the Cold War activities on campus: based at the State University

of New York, the University of Illinois, Kansas State University, Berkeley and the University of Washington, these authors, respectively, could not have been unaware of the situation throughout the New York University, City College of New York (CCNY) and the New York City municipal colleges; at the University of Michigan; at Kansas State College at Emporia and at the University of Kansas City; at the University of California and San Francisco City and State Colleges; and at the University of Washington (see Table 2.1).

2. In 1959 E. Wight Bakke noted the emergence of (what 'is beginning to be called') organizational behaviour as a subject that, unlike organization theory, has 'a relatively small concern with the . . . structure of a social organization' (quoted in Haire, 1967: p. 16).

3. The Wheeler (1962) text differs only in the use of Cold War rhetoric but it does nothing to reveal how its application influenced organizational structure and behaviour.

4. In the Haire (1967) text, for example, one of the contributors (Dubin) focuses on the 'stability of human organizations', another (Marschak) is interested in 'efficient and viable organizational forms', while Haire himself draws on a biological metaphor to describe 'the organization'.

5. In the Heckmann and Huneryager (1960) text four chapters are given over to leadership, five to organization, six to communication, five to participation, six to resistance to change, and four to counselling.

6. The texts by Herbert (1976 and 1981), Klein and Ritti (1980) and Steers (1981) all make fleeting references to workplace experiments in Norway and Sweden (SAAB and Volvo), and all but the 1976 edition of Herbert make a brief reference to Janis's (1996) notion of groupthink and the Bay of Pigs incident.

7. While some commentators have argued that the interests of the transnational company no longer coincide with the interests of its country of origin, such companies have not been above using political (e.g., United Fruit Company and the US embargo of Cuba in the 1960s) and military (e.g., ITT in Chile, 1973) pressure to achieve their ends.

8. Indeed, very few of the texts were even authored by women: of the 107 texts only seven have a woman author (Gordon, 1993) or co-author (Fombrun, Tichy and Devanna, 1984; Northcraft and Neale, 1990; Nickels et al., 1994; Greenberg et al., 1996; Nelson and Quick, 1995; George and Jones, 1996).

9. Curiously, in his later, 1989, edition Luthans drops all references to race.

10. This perspective is still evident in recent texts. Luthans (1995: 58), for example, writes from the viewpoint of the white manager when he states: 'Many managers are often unprepared to deal with diversity. . . . To better prepare themselves managers must work hard to learn and experience as much as they can about developing appropriate behavior.'

11. We are currently involved in the latter two strategies: (i) alongside a mainstream text we use a critical text – Mills and Simmons (1998); and (ii) we are in the early stages of writing an organizational textbook – *Understanding Organizations in Context: an Introduction to Behaviour, Structure and Action in Organizations* – for an alternative, left-wing press, Garamond Press.

References

Boje, D.M. and Dennehy, R.F. (1992) *America's Revolution against Exploitation: the Story of Post-modern Management.* Dubuque, IA: Kendall/Hunt Publishing.

Burrell, G. and Morgan, G. (1979) *Sociological Paradigms and Organizational Analysis.* London: Heinemann.

Caute, D. (1979) *The Great Fear. The Anti-Communist Purge under Truman and Eisenhower.* New York: Touchstone.

Chomsky, N. and Herman, E.S. (1979) *The Washington Connection and Third World Fascism. The Political Economy of Human Rights.* Boston, MA: South End Press.

Clegg, S. and Dunkerley, D. (1980) *Organization, Class and Control.* London: Routledge and Kegan Paul.

DiMaggio, P.J. and Powell, W.W. (1991) 'The iron cage revisited: institutional isomorphism and collective rationality in organizational fields', in W.W. Powell and P.J. DiMaggio (eds), *The New Institutionalism in Organizational Analysis.* Chicago: University of Chicago Press. pp. 63–82.

Fast, H. (1990) *Being Red. A Memoir.* Boston, MA: Houghton Mifflin.

Ferguson, K.E. (1984) *The Feminist Case against Bureaucracy.* Philadelphia, PA: Temple University Press.

Fineman, S. and Gabriel, Y. (1994) 'Paradigms of organizations: an exploration of textbook rhetorics', *Organization,* 1 (2): 375–99.

Goldstein, R.J. (1978) *Political Repression in Modern America, 1870 to the Present.* New York: Schenkman.

Gramsci, A. (1978) *The Modern Prince and Other Writings.* New York: International Publishers.

Hall, E.T. and Whyte, W.F. (1964) 'Intercultural communication: a guide to men of action', in K. Davis and W.G. Scott (eds), *Readings in Human Relations.* New York: McGraw-Hill. pp. 167–84.

Hobsbawm, E. (1994) *Age of Extremes.* London: Michael Joseph.

Laxer, G. (1995) 'Social solidarity, democracy and global capitalism', *The Canadian Review of Sociology and Anthropology,* 32 (3): 287–313.

Marsden, R. and Townley, B. (1996) 'The Owl of Minerva: reflections on theory in practice', in S.R. Clegg, C. Hardy and W. Nord (eds), *Handbook of Organization Studies.* London: Sage.

McMurtry, J. (1996) *The Global Market as an Ethical System: an Introduction.* Toronto: Garamond Press.

Meyer, J.W. and Rowan, B. (1983) 'The structure of educational organizations', in J.W. Meyer and W.R. Scott (eds), *Organizational Environments. Ritual and Rationality.* Beverly Hills, CA: Sage. pp. 71–97.

Mills, A.J. and Simmons, T. (1998) *Reading Organization Theory.* Toronto: Garamond Press.

Prasad, P. and Mills, A.J. (1997) 'Managing the organizational melting pot: dilemmas of diversity at the workplace', in P. Prasad, A.J. Mills, M. Elmes and A. Prasad (eds), *Managing the Organizational Melting Pot: Dilemmas of Workplace Diversity* Newbury Park, CA: Sage. pp. 3–27.

Said, E.W. (1993) *Culture and Imperialism.* New York: Vintage.

Teeple, G. (1995) *Globalization and the Decline of Social Reform.* Toronto: Garamond Press.

Wilson, F.M. (1995) *Organizational Behaviour and Gender.* London: McGraw-Hill.

Appendix: Textbooks Reviewed

Altman, S., Valenzi, E. and Hodgetts, R.M. (1985) *Organizational Behavior: Theory and Practice.* Orlando, FI: Academic Press.

Baird, L.S., Post, J.E. and Mahon, J.F. (1990) *Management. Functions and Responsibilities.* New York: Harper & Row.

Bateman, T.S. and Zeithaml, C.P. (1990) *Management. Function and Strategy.* Homewood, IL: Irwin.

Bedeian, A.G. (1984) *Organizations: Theory and Analysis.* New York: The Dryden Press.

Bethel, L.L., Atwater, F.S., Smith, G.H.E. and Stackman, H.A. (1959) *Essentials of Industrial Management* (2nd edn). New York: McGraw-Hill.

Certo, S.C. and Appelbaum, S.H. (1986) *Principles of Modern Management. A Canadian Perspective.* Dubuque, IA: Wm.C. Brown.

Champoux, J. (1996) *Organizational Behavior.* New York: West.

Cherrington, D.J. (1989) *Organizational Behavior. The Management of Individual and Organizational Performance.* Boston, MA: Allyn and Bacon.

Cherrington, D.J. (1994) *Organizational Behavior. The Management of Individual and Organizational Performance.* (2nd edn). Boston, MA: Allyn and Bacon.

Coffey, R.E., Cook, C.W. and Hunsaker, P.L. (1994) *Management and Organizational Behavior.* Burr Ridge, IL: Irwin.

Cohen, A.L., Fink, S.L., Gadon, H. and Willits, R.D. (1976) *Effective Behavior in Organizations.* Homewood, IL: Irwin.

Cohen, A.R., Fink, S.L., Gadon, H. and Willits, R.D. (1988) *Effective Behavior in Organizations.* (4th edn). Homewood, IL: Irwin.

Daft, R.L. (1986) *Organization Theory and Design* (2nd edn). St Paul, MN: West.

Daft, R.L. (1992) *Organization Theory and Design* (4th edn). St Paul, MN: West.

Daft, R.L. and Steers, R.M. (1986) *Organizations. A Micro/Macro Approach.* Glenview, IL: Scott, Foresman and Co.

Das, H. (1990) *Organization Theory with Canadian Applications.* Toronto: Gage.

Davis, K. and Newstrom, J.W. (1985) *Human Behavior at Work: Organizational Behavior* (7th edn). New York: McGraw-Hill.

Davis, K. and Scott, W.G. (1964) *Readings in Human Relations* (2nd edn). New York: McGraw-Hill.

Dessler, G. (1983a) *Applied Human Relations.* Reston, VA: Prentice-Hall.

Dessler, G. (1983b) *Improving Productivity at Work.* Reston, VA: Prentice-Hall.

Donnelly, J.H., Gibson, J.L. and Ivancevich, J.M. (1987) *Fundamentals of Management* (6th edn). Plano, TX: Business Publications.

Douglas, J., Klein, S. and Hunt, D. (1985) *The Strategic Managing of Human Resources.* New York: Wiley.

Duncan, W.J. (1978) *Organizational Behavior.* Boston, MA: Houghton Mifflin.

Field, R.H.G. and House, R.J. (1995) *Human Behavior in Organizations. A Canadian Perspective.* Scarborough, Ont.: Prentice-Hall.

Filley, A.C. and House, R.J. (1969) *Managerial Process and Organizational Behavior.* Glenview, IL: Scott, Foresman and Co.

Filley, A.C., House, R.J. and Kerr, S. (1976) *Managerial Process and Organizational Behavior.* Glenview, IL: Scott, Foresman and Co.

Fombrun, C., Tichy, N.M. and Devanna, M.A. (1984) *Strategic Human Resource Management.* New York: Wiley.

Fuhrman, P.H. (1995) *Business in the Canadian Environment.* Scarborough, Ont.: Prentice-Hall.

George, J.M. and Jones, G.R. (1996) *Understanding and Managing Organizational Behavior.* Reading, MA: Addison-Wesley.

Gerloff, E.A. (1985) *Organizational Theory and Design. A Strategic Approach for Management.* New York: McGraw-Hill.

Gibson, J.L., Ivancevich, J.M. and Donnelly, J.H. (1985) *Organizations, Behavior, Structure, Processes* (5th edn). Plano, TX: Business Publications.

Gordon, J.R. (1993) *A Diagnostic Approach to Organizational Behavior* (4th edn). Boston, MA: Allyn and Bacon.

Gram, H.A. (1986) *The Canadian Manager. An Introduction to Management.* Toronto: Holt, Rinehart and Winston of Canada.

Gray, J.L. and Starke, F.A. (1977) *Organizational Behavior. Concepts and Applications.* Columbus, OH: Charles E. Merrill.

Gray, J.L. and Starke, F.A. (1988) *Organizational Behavior. Concepts and Applications* (4th edn). Columbus, OH: Charles E. Merrill.

Greenberg, J. (1996) *Managing Behavior in Organizations.* Upper Saddle River, NJ: Prentice-Hall.

Greenberg, J. and Baron, R.A. (1993) *Behavior in Organizations* (4th edn). Boston, MA: Allyn and Bacon.

Greenberg, J., Baron, R.A., Sales, C.A. and Owen, F.A. (1996) *Behavior in Organizations* (Canadian edn). Scarborough, Ont.: Prentice-Hall.

Griffin, R.W. and Moorhead, G. (1986) *Organizational Behavior.* Boston, MA: Houghton Mifflin.

Griffin, R.W., Ebert, R.J. and Starke, F.A. (1996) *Business Behavior* (2nd Canadian edn). Scarborough, Ont.: Prentice-Hall.

Haire, M. (ed.) (1967) *Modern Organization Theory* (5th edn). New York: John Wiley and Sons.

Hampton, D.R., Summer, C.E. and Webber, R.A. (1978) *Organizational Behavior and the Practice of Management.* Glenview, IL: Scott, Foresman and Co.

Heckmann, Jr, I.L. and Huneryager, S.G. (1960) *Human Relations in Management.* Cincinnati, OH: South-Western Publishing Co.

Hellriegel, D. and Slocum, J.W. (1976) *Organizational Behavior. Contingency Views.* St Paul, MN: West.

Hellriegel, D., Slocum, J.W. and Woodman, R.W. (1989) *Organizational Behavior* (5th edn). St Paul, MN: West.

Hellriegel, D., Slocum, J.W. and Woodman, R.W. (1995) *Organizational Behavior* (7th edn). St Paul, MN: West.

Heneman, H.G., Schwab, D.P., Fossum, J.A. and Dyer, L.D. (1986) *Personnel/ Human Resource Management* (3rd edn). Homewood, IL: Irwin.

Herbert, T.E. (1976) *Dimensions of Organizational Behavior.* New York: Macmillan.

Herbert, T.E. (1981) *Dimensions of Organizational Behavior.* New York: Macmillan.

Hersey, P. and Blanchard, K.H. (1972) *Management of Organizational Behavior. Utilizing Human Resources* (2nd edn). Englewood Cliffs, NJ: Prentice-Hall.

Hersey, P. and Blanchard, K. (1977) *Management of Organizational Behavior* (3rd edn). Englewood Cliffs, NJ: Prentice-Hall.

Higgins, J.M. (1991) *The Management Challenge.* New York: Macmillan.

Hitt, M.A., Middlemist, R.D. and Mathis, R.L. (1989) *Management. Concepts and Effective Practice* (3rd edn). St Paul, MN: West.

Hodge, B.J. and Anthony, W.P. (1991) *Organization Theory. A Strategic Approach* (4th edn). Boston, MA: Allyn and Bacon.

Hodgetts, R.M. (1990) *Modern Human Relations at Work* (4th edn). Chicago: The Dryden Press.

Hodgetts, R.M. (1991) *Organizational Behavior. Theory and Practice.* New York: Macmillan.

Huse, E.F. and Bowditch, J.L. (1977) *Behavior in Organizations: a Systems Approach to Managing* (2nd edn). Reading, MA: Addison-Wesley.

Ivancevich, J.M. and Matteson, M.T. (1990) *Organizational Behavior and Management* (2nd edn). Homewood, IL: Irwin.

Janis, I.L. (1996) 'Groupthink: the desperate drive for consensus at any cost', in J.S. Ott (ed.), *Classic Readings in Organizational Behavior* (2nd edn). Belmont, CA: Wadsworth.

Jenks, V.O. (1990) *Human Relations in Organizations.* New York: Harper & Row.

Johns, G. (1983) *Organizational Behavior. Understanding Life at Work.* Glenview, IL: Scott, Foresman and Co.

Johns, G. (1988) *Organizational Behavior. Understanding Life at Work* (2nd edn). Glenview, IL: Scott, Foresman and Co.

Johns, G. (1992) *Organizational Behavior. Understanding Life at Work* (3rd edn). New York: HarperCollins.

Johns, G. (1996) *Organizational Behavior. Understanding and Managing Life at Work* (4th edn). New York: HarperCollins.

Jones, G.R. (1995) *Organizational Theory*. Reading, MA: Addison-Wesley.

Klein, S.M. and Ritti, R.R. (1980) *Understanding Organizational Behavior*. Boston, MA: Kent Publishing.

Luthans, F. (1977) *Organizational Behavior* (2nd edn). New York: McGraw-Hill.

Luthans, F. (1981) *Organizational Behavior* (3rd edn). New York: McGraw-Hill.

Luthans, F. (1985) *Organizational Behavior* (4th edn). New York: McGraw-Hill.

Luthans, F. (1989) *Organizational Behavior* (5th edn). New York: McGraw-Hill.

Luthans, F. (1995) *Organizational Behavior* (7th edn). New York: McGraw-Hill.

McShane, S.L. (1992) *Canadian Organizational Behavior*. Homewood, IL: Irwin.

McShane, S.L. (1995) *Canadian Organizational Behavior*. Toronto: Irwin.

Middlemist, R.D. and Hitt, M.A. (1988) *Organizational Behavior. Managerial Strategies for Performance*. St Paul, MN: West.

Milkovich, G.T. and Glueck, W.F. (1985) *Personnel/Human Resource Management. A Diagnostic Approach* (4th edn). Plano, TX: Business Publications.

Milkovich, G.T., Glueck, W.F., Barth, R.T. and McShane, S.L. (1988) *Canadian Personnel/Human Resource Management*. Plano, TX: Business Publications.

Moorhead, G. and Griffin, R.W. (1992) *Organizational Behavior. Managing People and Organizations* (3rd edn). Boston, MA: Houghton Mifflin.

Moorhead, G. and Griffin, R.W. (1995) *Organizational Behavior* (4th edn). Boston, MA: Houghton Mifflin.

Nelson, D.L. and Quick, J.C. (1995) *Organizational Behavior. Foundations, Realities, and Challenges*. St Paul, MN: West.

Newman, W.H., Summer, C.E. and Warren, E.K. (1972) *The Process of Management. Concepts, Behavior, and Practice* (3rd edn). Englewood Cliffs, NJ: Prentice-Hall.

Nickels, W.G., McHugh, J.M., McHugh, S.M. and Berman, P.D. (1994) *Understanding Canadian Business*. Burr Ridge, IL: Irwin.

Northcraft, G.B. and Neale, M.A. (1990) *Organizational Behavior. A Management Challenge*. Chicago: The Dryden Press.

Randolph, W.A. and Blackburn, R.S. (1989) *Managing Organizational Behavior*. Boston, MA: Irwin.

Robbins, S.P. (1976) *The Administrative Process*. Englewood Cliffs, NJ: Prentice-Hall.

Robbins, S.P. (1983) *Organization Theory. The Structure and Design of Organizations*. Englewood Cliffs, NJ: Prentice-Hall.

Robbins, S.P. (1988) *Essentials of Organizational Behavior* (2nd edn). Englewood Cliffs, NJ: Prentice-Hall.

Robbins, S.P. (1989) *Organizational Behavior. Concepts, Controversies, and Applications* (4th edn). Englewood Cliffs, NJ: Prentice-Hall.

Robbins, S.P. (1996) *Organizational Behavior. Concepts, Controversies, and Applications* (7th edn). Englewood Cliffs, NJ: Prentice-Hall.

Robbins, S.P. and Stuart-Kotze, R. (1986) *Management, Concepts and Practices* Canadian edn). Scarborough, Ont.: Prentice-Hall.

Robbins, S.P. and Stuart-Kotze, R. (1990) *Management* (2nd edn). Scarborough, Ont.: Prentice-Hall.

Schermerhorn, J.R. (1986) *Management for Productivity* (2nd edn). New York: Wiley.

Schermerhorn, J.R., Hunt, J.G. and Osborn, R.N. (1982) *Managing Organizational Behavior*. New York: Wiley.

Schermerhorn, J.R., Hunt, J.G. and Osborn, R.N. (1985) *Managing Organizational Behavior* (2nd edn). New York: Wiley.

Schermerhorn, J.R., Hunt, J.G. and Osborn, R.N. (1988) *Managing Organizational Behavior* (3rd edn). New York: Wiley.

Schermerhorn, J.R., Hunt, J.G. and Osborn, R.N. (1991) *Managing Organizational Behavior* (4th edn). New York: Wiley.

Schermerhorn, J.R., Hunt, J.G. and Osborn, R.N. (1994) *Managing Organizational Behavior* (5th edn). New York: Wiley.

Schermerhorn, J.R., Hunt, J.G. and Osborn, R.N. (1995) *Basic Organizational Behavior*. New York: Wiley.

Starke, F.A. and Sexty, R.W. (1995) *Contemporary Management in Canada* (2nd edn). Scarborough, Ont.: Prentice-Hall.

Starke, F.A., Owen, B.E., Reinecke, J.A., Dessler, G. and Schoell, W.F. (1990) *Introduction to Canadian Business* (4th edn). Scarborough, Ont.: Allyn and Bacon.

Steers, R.M. (1981) *Introduction to Organizational Behavior*. Santa Monica, CA: Goodyear Publishing.

Steers, R.M. and Porter, L.W. (1987) *Motivation and Work Behavior* (4th edn). New York: McGraw-Hill.

Stuart-Kotze, S. (1980) *Introduction to Organizational Behavior. A Situational Approach*. Reston, VA: Prentice-Hall.

Tosi, H.L., Rizzo, J.R. and Carroll, S.J. (1990) *Managing Organizational Behavior* (2nd edn). New York: Harper & Row.

Van Fleet, D.D. (1991) *Behavior in Organizations*. Boston, MA: Houghton Mifflin.

Vecchio, R.P. (1988) *Organizational Behavior*. Chicago: The Dryden Press.

Vecchio, R.P. (1991) *Organizational Behavior* (2nd edn). Chicago: The Dryden Press.

Wheeler, B.O. (1962) *Business. An Introductory Analysis*. New York: Harper & Row.

3 'If You Want Loyalty Get a Dog!': Loyalty, Trust and the New Employment Contract

Richard Dunford

Organizational restructuring is having a significant impact on management careers, both in terms of redundancies and in terms of the reconstituted concept of career. An important question that follows from this is what effect these changes have on the way managers see the relationship between themselves and their organization because of the potential for this to impact on organizational performance. This chapter seeks to encourage discussion of this issue by presenting the arguments of two contrasting positions. The first voices concern at what it sees as the destruction/ breaking of the 'psychological contract' between manager and employer; the second heralds the dawning of a new maturity in the employment relationship through the demise of paternalism. The chapter also locates this issue within a consideration of the ways of organizing that are being advocated for new organizational forms (virtual organizations/networks).

Organizational Restructuring

Organizational restructuring has been a common response to an environment increasingly characterized by deregulation – which has blurred market boundaries and produced new competitors – global competition and pressure for short-term results especially from institutional investors (Frohman and Johnson, 1993). Benchmarking against competitors has provided a basis for consolidating a belief that various business units need to reduce costs to remain competitive (Cascio, 1993), while a recurrent theme in the 'popular management' literature has been the need for 'lean', 'focused', 'flexible', 'responsive' organizations (e.g., Peters, 1992, 1994).

1   A reduction in the number of staff employed to carry out the organization's existing activities. This may involve either (i) an across-the-board cut based on achieving specific cost reductions or a set percentage reduction in staff, or (ii) a reduction in staff involved in specific activities believed to be over-staffed.

2   The centralization of some or all of the components of infrastructural functions such as administration, human resource management, public relations, information and accounting.

3   The reduction in the number of levels in the organization (delayering).

4   The redesign of the core business processes underpinning the organization's operations.

5   The out-sourcing of some of the activities previously carried out by employees of the organization. Market relationships replace hierarchical ones. This may involve a reduction in the vertical integration of the organization, by identifying and focusing on 'core competencies' and contracting-out other functions. For example, in a clothing manufacturer that sees its core competencies as product design and marketing, other functions such as manufacturing and distribution may be out-sourced.

6   A reduction in the degree of horizontal integration (diversification) of the organization. That is, a decision is made to focus on consolidating 'core businesses' (Davis et al., 1994).

One of the striking characteristics of this restructuring is the extent to which it has affected the employment of managers. While middle managers make up only five to eight per cent of the US work force, they accounted for 17 per cent of all layoffs between 1989 and 1991 (Cascio, 1993: 95). The relative isolation of middle management from earlier periods of labour cost-cutting, have made them especially at risk (Cameron et al., 1991) and they have often been specifically targeted and labelled by leading management 'gurus' such as Tom Peters (1992, 1994) as a 'non-value-adding' stratum of organizations. For example, Tom Peters proclaims that 'middle management . . . is dead. . . . It's over, d'ya hear? Over. Over. Over' (1992: 758–9). Academic research, by comparison, supports a less extreme scenario (e.g., Storey, 1992; Dopson and Stewart, 1993).

The significance of such 'downsizing' for the employment of managers is due to its application in contexts of both decline and growth (Freeman and Cameron, 1993). The term 'downsizing' is only one of a number of euphemisms. Alternatives include 'decluttering', 'streamlining', 'refocusing', 'decruiting', 'demassifying', 'reduction in force', 'reduction in headcount', 'skinnying down', 'becoming lean', 'work force rebalancing', 'work force transitioned' and 'rightsizing', although, as Hamel and Prahalad (1994: 124) comment, why is the right size always smaller? That is, it is not restricted to being a recession-driven response of debt-burdened corporations; it is also a pre-emptive strategy to improve competition position. Heckscher (1995) argues that the current restructuring is not a crisis response to competitive conditions, because (i) companies have been in trouble before and not resorted to this response, and (ii) the restructuring has spread way beyond companies with any performance problems. Even corporations with record profits have downsized 'in anticipation of a continuing intensely competitive market' (Cascio, 1993: 102). A survey of 800 corporations by the American Management Association revealed that almost half of the downsizing programmes planned for 1993 would be for 'strategic rather than recession-driven reasons' (Greenberg, 1993: 6). In the UK, it has been estimated that the recession-related redundancies may be as little as 20–25 per cent (Syedain, 1991: 46). Correspondingly, the various rationales for downsizing include to cut costs, to improve key financial indicators, to improve productivity, to refocus the organization on core areas of business, to produce a more flexible, responsive organization, to empower employees, and to speed and otherwise improve communication flow (Peters, 1992, 1994; Hamel and Prahalad, 1994).

There is mounting evidence that despite its widespread utilization, downsizing often fails to achieve intended outcomes. Key financial indicators often do not improve (Cameron et al., 1993; Cascio et al., 1997; Tomasko, 1993). A study of changes to the share prices of downsized companies found that they out-perform the Standard and Poor's 500 index only during the six months following news of their restructuring; three years later they lag (*The Economist*, 1994: 63). A study by the American Management Association found that fewer than half of the firms that have downsized in the past five years subsequently raised their profits, and only one-third reported higher productivity (*The Economist*, 1994). Quality and innovation often decline (Kanter et al., 1992; Cascio, 1993; Dougherty and Bowman, 1995). A growing number of studies have identified effects on remaining staff, including anxiety, guilt, reduced morale, and risk-averseness which collectively have become known as the 'survivor syndrome' (Brockner et al., 1987; Brockner, 1988, 1992; Henkoff, 1990; Bennett, 1991; Brockner and Wiesenfeld, 1993).

Managers are thus at the confluence of a number of mutually reinforcing influences that impinge upon their employment relationship within any given organization. Restructuring, and delayering in particular, has reduced the number of positions to which managers can aspire, while the emphasis on 'flexibility' and 'market responsiveness' has moved organizations increasingly towards a contractual/impermanent employment relationship with managers. Various forms of past, present and prospective organizational restructurings are affecting the 'traditional' managerial employment relationship, with as yet uncertain consequences. The objective of this chapter is to map out some of the alternative interpretations of this phenomenon.

Playing with Fire

Disoriented, disempowered, betrayed, scared, cynical, defensive, resentful. Words such as these have been used in a developing discourse within the popular management literature. They are found not so much within the pages of the best-sellers of the 'gurus' (e.g., Kanter, Peters), but rather in journalistic pieces within various magazines. For example, Caulkin, in

Management Today, refers to 'the seething heap of managerial fear and loathing' (1995: 27) that exists as a result of the upheaval in the conditions of management employment. For Caulkin 'beneath the enthusiastic whitewash of the human resources specialists ("empowerment", "team-work", "alignment") dysfunctionalities abound' (1995: 27).

The decline in career prospects for managers may have significant implications given that this has traditionally been assumed to be a core component of the primary labour market to which managers belong (Kramar, 1990) and a key basis for the commitment by, and control over, managerial employees (Edwards, 1979). This is likely to be particularly so in those organizations with internal labour markets. Studies throughout the 1970s and 1980s (e.g., Sofer, 1970; Pahl and Pahl, 1971; Schein, 1978) showed how central careers were to managers' sense of identity. Being on a career path provided a visible symbol of success and psychological rewards were attached to the attainment of stages in the hierarchical career progression. Even where a manager's job becomes more challenging as a result of restructuring, this will not necessarily be seen as compensating for reduced career prospects (Dunford and Heiler, 1994a, 1994b). For Burrell and Scarborough the 'almost fetishistic importance that [career] holds for individual managers can hardly be overstated' (1993: 3).

Goffee and Scase (1992), in a study of 374 managers across six large organizations from six different sectors, found the discrepancy between career aspirations and available opportunity to be the most dissatisfying aspect of the manager's job. A range of responses to this situation were identified, including insomnia, alcohol addiction, marital strife, disengaging from the workplace in terms of their investment of creative energy, development of an 'anti-organizational' attitude, and resisting or at least undertaking tasks only at a minimum acceptable standard. These responses are more likely in the more traditional, bureaucratic organizations where career structures follow a formal, vertical path and where the 'withdrawal of commitment' is tolerated more than in flexible work structures. Also, in flexible organizations the opportunity for 'self-development within jobs' is likely to be greater (Goffee and Scase, 1992). The overall picture Goffee and Scase deduce from their research is one of managers with a more instrumental attitude to their work than their predecessors. They argue that:

> by deliberately cultivating personal identities that are separate and removed from organizational demands, they could be better equipped to cope with work related stresses and to withstand the psychological challenges that can be posed by threats of redundancy and unexpected career challenges. Accordingly managers may cease to be psychologically immersed in their work roles and become less committed to their employing organizations. To do otherwise in the light of increasing uncertainties would be to make themselves more emotionally and psychologically vulnerable. (Scase and Goffee, 1989: 13)

Loyalty may be seen as counter-productive in that it develops bonds/attachments that are unwise given the likely severing of the relationship.

This suggests that downsizing and delayering may constitute a significant challenge to the 'psychological contract', that is, the deeply embedded beliefs that employees have as to the reciprocal obligations involved in their employment relationship. This contract includes what they believe they are entitled to receive, including how they expect to be treated, in return for their contribution to the organization (Rousseau and Parks, 1992). The actions of senior management may be seen by middle managers as inconsistent with their rhetoric. This is most likely to occur in those organizations where senior management have promulgated an image of themselves as being committed to 'core values', such as 'respect for the individual', 'participation', 'open communication', 'family' and 'teamwork'. If, as Keenoy and Anthony (1992: 238) argue, the purpose of a managerial emphasis on such values is 'to transform, to inspire, to motivate and above all, to create a new reality', this purpose is likely to be threatened by practices which are seen as inconsistent with this rhetoric. What may happen is that: 'What employees hear is that "people are our most important asset". What they see is that people are the most expendable asset' (Hamel and Prahalad, 1994: 125).

Senior management may find their own rhetoric thrown back at them. for example, when they seek to explain downsizing as a strategically-driven imperative it is not surprising that they find the argument 'employees are our most valued assets' appears as a central motif in employee responses. A degree of cynicism about pronouncements of 'core values' may develop. In an organization studied by Dunford and Heiler (1994a, 1994b) senior management handled their downsizing in a way consistent with 'best practice' (Brockner, 1992) yet many staff still saw it as contradicting the core values that had a high profile within that organization. Smith (1994) notes that senior managers are often aware of the contradictory roles in which they find themselves: on the one hand they have been told that the management style for the 1990s is to think of themselves as part of a team; on the other hand they may have to play the role of 'executioner' and that 'the strain of reconciling these personas fans the flames of stress and resentment' (Smith, 1994: 52).

The importance of commitment has been a recurring theme in management literature, reflecting a view that it is an important basis for organizational performance. For example, Hecksher (1995) argues that it is managers' commitment that enables them to take actions, to the benefit of the organization, that would otherwise not occur as they are not prescribed in formal rules and regulations. That is, loyalty is 'the force that keeps people using their intelligence in the service of the company even when no-one can scientifically measure performance and enforce conformity' (Hecksher, 1995: 18). Heckscher (1995: 25) identifies seven factors in his managers' descriptions of the causes of loyalty: career advancement, dependence and fear, pride in association with the company, gratitude and sense of obligation, psychological investment, shared values, and personal friendships and contacts. Invoking a well-worn metaphor, he summarizes his position: '*an effective organization must be a community*' (Heckscher, 1995: 31, original emphasis).

From this perspective, 'an employer that signals through word and deed that its employees are dispensible is not likely to generate much loyalty, commitment, or willingness to expend extra effort' (Pfeffer, 1995: 58). This position is consistent with the research of Gaertner and Nollen (1989) which found that employees with favourable perceptions about internal mobility, training and employment security are more psychologically committed to the organization. Where managers feel that the implicit contract has been breached, they may feel betrayed and reject overtures for commitment: 'If you want loyalty, get a dog!' (This expression is a quote from a manager cited in Caulkin, 1995.)

The Flowering of the Free Agent

Challenging, mature, free, creative. These words express the alternative interpretation to that presented above and they come in mild and strong flavours. The mild form is represented by the view that middle manage-ment, through being reshaped, is becoming more challenging (e.g., Dopson and Stewart, 1993; Frohman and Johnson, 1993). The majority of managers in a study by Dopson and Stewart (1993) felt that the changes to middle management were positive, citing closer access to top management, clearer areas of responsibility, more control over resources, freedom to broaden expertise, freedom to innovate and freedom to take on new chal-lenges as reasons for this. A study by Dunford and Heiler (1994a, 1994b) also revealed a situation where the managers believed that their jobs had become more challenging as a result of delayering and downsizing. There was also no evidence of a more instrumental orientation developing, despite the recognition that promotion in the traditional sense was less likely and that high individual performance no longer guaranteed a career in the company. What was consistently described by staff was the greater degree of involvement with the company in both time and psychological terms.

The strong version of this interpretation of the effect on management is much more assertive as to the magnitude of the changes and their benefits. Community is a concept that has diametrically opposed connotations: it is warm, nurturing and supportive, the site of authentic human relationships; it is closed, narrow-minded and oppressive. Similarly, loyalty can have negative connotations, suggesting a less-than-mature stage of individual development. Noer (1993) describes the traditional employment relation-ship as one of 'co-dependency' in which individuals 'enable the system to control their sense of worth and self-esteem' and in so doing 'make them-selves into permanant victims' (1993: 136–7). He argues that 'organizations that are free of co-dependency are vibrant, open and productive' (ibid.: 137). In such a context survivors are 'largely immune to survivor sickness because the survivors do not index their self-esteem and sense of personal worth to the organization, but to their own good work' (ibid.: 137). He further argues that this immunity reduces the likelihood of layoffs because it 'frees up employee energy and creativity' (ibid.: 137).

In a similar vein, Hecksher (1995) argues that the traditional emphasis on corporate loyalty was typically associated with an emphasis on conformity which often manifested itself as an inflexibility towards diversity, for example, in regard to the work patterns of those (women in particular) who were trying to balance family and career commitments. The new employment relationship is presented as involving a greater openness to diversity (see, e.g., Hecksher, 1995).

This strong version sees a new era of 'mature' relationships, characterized by the decline of paternalism and co-dependency. The new employment relationship presents the individual manager as an autonomous being, able to negotiate a mutually beneficial contract between equals. Thus, while the exhortation, 'if you want loyalty, get a dog!' may be a response to a perceived betrayal of trust, it may also be used to express the view that loyalty is a concept whose time has passed, and an inappropriate basis for a 'mature' relationship.

If career systems are being radically changed, what is to be put in their place? The answer, according to Waterman, Waterman and Collard, is to enter into 'a new covenant under which the employer and the employee share responsibility for maintaining, even enhancing, the employee's employability inside and outside the company (1994: 87–8). Under such an arrangement, the employee is expected to be committed to a process of continuous learning; the responsibility of the employer is to provide the environment and opportunity for this to occur. The predicted outcome is an adaptable, skilled work force that is simultaneously providing enhanced value to its current organization and increasing their attractiveness in the broader job market. In a similar vein, Kanter advocates 'employability security', that is, 'the knowledge that today's work will enhance the person's value in terms of future opportunities' (1995: 157). From this perspective, the new employment contract involves individuals taking responsibility for their careers by seeking opportunities to enhance their transferable skills and reputation, and employers providing such 'learning opportunities' (Kanter, 1995: 157).

Peters (1994) says 'forget loyalty'. He advocates the model of the independent contractor, 'who lives by the seat of the pants; whose professional existence depends on word of mouth endorsements from clients; who regularly adds to her portfolio of marketable skills; who routinely delivers on time, creatively, for a competitive price (or else)' (Peters, 1994: 95–6). This involves what Peters calls 'the new loyalty', that is, one in which employees seek, and employers support, 'always grasping for a new learning experience, one that allows you to develop or maintain or enhance skills, your network, and ultimately your labor-market edge' (1994: 113).

Arthur, Claman and DePhillipi (1995) contrast the 'new career paradigm' with the 'old career paradigm' in terms of five factors:

1   Discrete exchange versus the mutual loyalty contract, which contrasts the explicit exchange of market-value-based rewards in return for task performance with the implicit trade of compliance for security.
2   Occupational excellence versus the one-employer focus, which contrasts mobile, occupation-based, development of expertise with reliance on the firm to specify jobs and appropriate training.
3   Organizational empowerment versus the top–down firm, which contrasts widespread involvement with strategic issues with strategy as something reserved for only those 'at the top'.
4   Regional advantage versus the fortress firm, which contrasts the encouragement of inter-firm mobility and interaction with the discouragement of such actions.
5   Project allegiance versus corporate allegiance, which contrasts the orientation of the employment relationship to successful project completion with that to organizational membership.

The result, of this new approach according to Waterman et al. (1994) is the 'career-resilient workforce', in which high levels of commitment exist for the period of the mutually beneficial relationship, and in which inter-organizational mobility – initiated by either party – is expected to occur rather than being seen as disloyalty or betrayal. In this 'boundaryless career', the employment relationship is presumed to simultaneously serve the career interests of individuals and the strategic interests of the employing organization (Arthur, 1994). Hecksher describes the emerging employment relationship as follows:

> In this conception, to sketch its ideal form, individuals are not committed to any company as such, but to a personal set of skills, goals, interests and affiliations. The company offers them not permanent employment, but challenges that give them an opportunity to develop their interests, and a promise of mutual dialogue and openness to manage the two sets of needs. When the two are synchronized, the employees become dedicated to accomplishing the current mission, working with others who are similarly dedicated. They offer not obedience, but intelligence: they will not do whatever they are asked, but they will do whatever they can to further the mission. The relationship lasts as long as the organizational vision and the individual contributions are close enough to lead to a sense of mutual contribution. (Hecksher, 1995: 145–6)

Hecksher argues that this relationship 'does what all forms of community must do: it lays the moral basis for mutual obligations and stable relationships, and therefore for cooperation' (1995: 146).

New Forms, Trust and Commitment

Virtual, boundaryless, horizontal, learning, intelligent, network. In parallel with the announcement of the age of the new employment contract, is the

burgeoning literature on new organizational forms. The 'virtual organization' is described as one which

> will appear almost edgeless, with permeable and continuously changing interfaces
> between company, supplier, and customers; . . . operating divisions [will be]
> constantly reforming according to need [and] job responsibilities will regularly
> shift, as will lines of authority – even the very definition of employee will change,
> as some customers and suppliers begin to spend more time in the company than
> will some of the firm's own workers. (Davidow and Malone, 1992: 5–6)

The means of organizing involved in networks/relationships, many of
which by definition extend beyond the boundaries of any given organization, place a premium on co-operative activities. Although there are
many determinants of co-operation, 'virtually all scholars have agreed that
one especially immediate antecedent is trust' (Smith et al., 1995: 10–11).
The new organizational forms have often been presented as depending even
more than past forms on relations of common understanding and trust.
Peters (1994: 145), for example, has referred to trust as 'the oft-ignored
glue that holds the new-fangled virtual organization together'. Trust is a
key aspect of the way new organizational forms are supposed to work
(Miles and Snow, 1995). Similarly, Handy, in the context of a discussion of
the functioning of virtual organizations, argues that they require trust to
make them work and that trust 'inevitably requires some sense of
mutuality, of reciprocal loyalty' (Handy, 1995: 48).

Barney and Hansen (1994) address trustworthiness as a source of competitive advantage. In this context, trustworthiness is an assessment made
of the exchange relationship between firms; trust means not taking advantage of another's exchange vulnerabilities. They identify three forms of
trust: weak, semi-strong and strong. Weak forms of trust exist where there
are minimal vulnerabilities and therefore few reasons for opportunism.
Semi-strong forms of trust occur if parties to an exchange are protected
through governance devices which mean that rational actors find it in their
interest, for either economic or social reasons, not to behave oppor-
tunistically. In strong forms of trust, trust exists because opportunistic
behaviour 'would violate values, principles and standards of behavior that
have been internalized by parties to an exchange' (Barney and Hansen,
1994: 179).

However, the three forms of trust are not equally likely to be sources of
competitive advantage. Weak forms of trust do not offer much potential
for the development of competitive advantage because their existence is
predicated upon there being minimal vulnerabilities to exploit. In semi-
strong forms of trust the competitive advantages only exist if some
exchange partners have been able to establish more efficient governance
practices which are also difficult to copy. Barney and Hansen (1994) argue
that strong-form trust offers the greatest potential for competitive advantage because it makes unnecessary expenditure on the establishment of

governance mechanisms. This holds true as long as the combined cost of maintaining (or establishing) strong-form trust within an organization and identifying strong-form exchange partners is less than that of maintaining (or establishing) governance devices. The cost advantage of the former is most likely where strong-form trust is embedded in the organizational culture (or at least within critical individuals within the organization) and will magnify as exchange vulnerabilities increase because of the additional complexity (and cost) of developing governance methods to cope with this. Barney (1986), Barney and Hansen (1994) and Pfeffer (1994) argue that organizational culture can be a sustainable source of competitive advantage because of the difficulty of imitation of such a 'socially complex' phenomenon (Barney and Hansen, 1994: 188). This raises some fundamental questions as to the compatibility of the new employment contract with the maintenance of these cultures. Is the 'employability' relationship sufficient to sustain a high trust culture?

The answer rather depends on what is meant by trust. McAllister (1995) notes the importance of both cognition-based trust and affect-based trust. Cognition-based trust derives from an assessment of an individual's past performance, cultural similarity and qualifications. Affect-based trust is based on the demonstration of interpersonal care and concern. This distinction focuses attention on the idea that generic 'trust' may be composed of various constituent elements. From this, it may follow that a given development may diminish one basis for trust while enhancing another. In the situation where people have worked closely and regularly over a number of years a form of trust develops that allows formal organizations, supposedly operating along classic bureaucratic lines, to accomplish much through informal linkages (Hecksher, 1995). Similarly, one reading of the 'trust-effect' of the joint impact of the new career paradigm and new organization forms would be that the decreased emphasis on corporate loyalty reduces the familiarity basis for trust, but that the confidence that they are dealing with skilled individuals increases an alternative basis for trust.

Discussion

The long-term effects of the changes to the nature of the management employment relationship are (by definition) yet to be revealed, but the stakes are high. With the predicted increase in the utilization of the 'new organizational forms', the role of trust increases rather than diminishes in importance. A crisis of commitment is not an attractive prospect. For example, Waterman et al. ask: 'How can an enterprise build capabilities, forge empowered teams, develop a deep understanding of its customers – and most important – create a sense of community and common purpose unless it has a relationship with its employees based on mutual trust and caring?' (1994: 87). Hecksher asks 'is it better to rely on the loyalty of a traditional organization or the rational self-interest of a free-agent system?' (1995: 13). The following discussion picks up some of these issues.

First, the organizational commitment of managers who remain after restructuring – the so-called 'survivors' – is affected by whether they believe the layoff process to have been 'fair' (Brockner, 1992; Brockner and Wiesenfeld, 1993; Dunford and Heiler, 1994a, 1994b). The judgement of survivors as to the fairness of the layoff process is a composite picture formed on the basis of their perceptions as to whether the following are true: the practice of laying-off staff is consistent with the corporate culture, ample notice was given, those laid off were treated with respect, a clear and adequate explanation was given for the layoffs, cut-backs have been shared at higher managerial levels, the decision rule determining who was laid off was both fair and fairly applied, assistance has been provided to those laid off, and employees were involved in the layoff decision process (Brockner, 1992). Commitment is detrimentally affected where there is a perception that layoffs were unfair.

An intervening variable determining the magnitude of this effect is the level of commitment to the organization prior to the layoffs. The commitment of those with a stronger pre-downsizing commitment drops more significantly than that of those with a weaker pre-downsizing commitment (Brockner et al., 1993). This has important implications for the management of the aftermath because it means that senior management may find, in trying to deal with the effect of a perception that there was inequality in the layoff process, that those it may have expected to be its 'front line' in implementing its 'solution' may turn out to be key elements of the problem that has to be addressed. Survivors' 'job attitudes and behaviours' are also affected by whether they believe their jobs have become more interesting as a result of the restructuring (Brockner and Wiesenfeld, 1993). However, the magnitude depends significantly on the nature of contextual factors such as the perceived fairness of layoffs and the reaction of fellow survivors (Brockner et al., 1993).

Secondly, regardless of how the restructuring is handled, the changed career situation remains. In this regard, the response of a manager may depend on the particular orientation to employment that he or she holds. In his research, based on interviews with 250 managers in eight companies, Heckscher (1995) classifies managers into two groups. The first, and largest, group is the 'loyalists', comprising managers who have a strong company orientation and for whom the employment relationship involves mutual loyalty and commitment. The second group, the 'professionals', comprises managers who have a commitment to a mission or task rather than to a company. He found that the managers with the most positive views on their personal future, and that of their organization, were those operating with a 'professional' framework. However, the loyalist response is a reality that needs to be managed on both moral and practical grounds.

The response of many loyalists is ambiguous, in the sense that they can espouse both a sense of betrayal and ongoing commitment. They experience 'a cauldron of contradictory feelings' (Hecksher, 1995: 39). Research in the USA (Hecksher, 1995) and the UK (Watson, 1994) has provided cases where, even in the aftermath of restructuring involving managerial redundancies and increased job insecurity, expressions of commitment and loyalty continue. Heckscher (1995: 26) found that 'despite the destruction of the pillar of the traditional employment relation, the fundamental sense of attachment remained solid, if anguished' and argues that this indicates that loyalty 'is supported by a deeper psychology: it is internalized in the motivations and self-images of managers, and therefore cannot be easily abandoned even when the conditions change' (1995: 26). He turns a common argument on its head when he concludes that the problem is the tenacity of the loyalist stance rather than its destruction. A new generation of young managers may not want traditional loyalty and commitment even if it is on offer, but in the meantime there is a transitional phase in which the embedded loyalist relationship needs to be managed (1995: 11).

Hecksher (1995), while critical of the stance of the 'loyalists', makes it clear that his data do not support the idea that we should rush to the other end of the continuum. The organizations he labelled 'dynamic', as opposed to 'troubled', 'rejected an environment of rapid turnover and short-term focus because it disrupts people's ability to work together' (1995: 149). Managers in these organizations did not see themselves as 'free agents', seeking the best offer; rather, they were strongly committed to the organization and expected to stay as long as they could contribute effectively to the company's mission. Hecksher explains their lack of support for the free-agent relationship as due to the cumbersomeness of a system based on needing to design contracts for different situations as they develop and the advantages of conscious co-operation that follows the general commitment of a group of people to work together. His conclusion is that the relationship of manager to organization involves 'a far more contingent and voluntarist form of community than the old' (1995: 12), but it is not 'pure untrammeled individualism' (ibid.: 11). Handy (1995) suggests that for a small core of managers there should be a 'membership contract' rather than an 'instrumental contract', a sense of 'belonging to a community' although 'trust is tough' and incompatible with any promise of a job for life, so 'core commitments' are restricted to a small group of 'trusties'. A core–periphery model of the managerial labour market is produced.

A critical issue to investigate will be the long-term effects on organizational performance. Does the project-focused professional contribute to a sustainable corporate ethos/philosophy that provides a framework for strategic action? Collins and Porras (1995) provide research-based evidence of the role of a strong corporate culture and internal labour markets in the success of large corporations over the previous decades in this century. Consistent with this has been a decade of work extolling the virtues of a move 'from control to commitment' as the preferred mode of managing (see, e.g., Walton, 1985). However, if we are in the era of transitory organizations and increased interaction via networks, perhaps the notion of a strong corporate culture as a basis for competitive advantage is redundant? If the future is to be a series of networked performances where the notion of corporate longevity is an anachronism, then the sort of commitment to core values that Collins and Porras (1995) cite, may be an historical artifact of little continuing relevance.

A key determinant of the success of the new employment contract will be whether those organizations seeking to operate in this way implement the 'whole package' – the human investment philosophy articulated by Miles and Snow (1995). That is, the new employment contract relies on managers feeling that their current position is providing the opportunity for them to be involved in interesting and 'portfolio developing' activities. Will more than a few widely cited examples do this? A lesson from the implementation of management philosophies in the past (e.g., scientific management) is that some organizations will apply associated techniques without the core philosophy. If this happens, the new contract will be seen as breached. In such a situation, the new managers will either utilize their propensity to mobility or, if stymied in this regard, remain but with a jaundiced outlook on the contract they have entered. It is important that the contract labelled paternalism is not replaced by one that comes to be viewed as cynical disregard.

References

Arthur, M.B. (1994) 'The boundaryless career: a new perspective for organizational inquiry', *Journal of Organizational Behavior*, 15: 295–306.

Arthur, M.B., Claman, P.C. and DePhillipi, R.J. (1995) 'Intelligent enterprise, intelligent career', *Academy of Management Executive*, 9 (4): 1–15.

Barney, J.B. (1986) 'Organizational culture: can it be a source of sustained competitive advantage?', *Academy of Management Review*, 11: 656–65.

Barney, J.B. and Hansen, M.H. (1994) 'Trustworthiness as a source of competitive advantage', *Strategic Management Journal*, 15: 175–90.

Bennett, A. (1991) 'Downsizing doesn't necessarily bring an upswing in corporate profitability', *Wall Street Journal*, 6 June, B1.

Brockner, J. (1988) 'The effects of work layoffs on survivors: research, theory and practice', *Research in Organizational Behaviour*, 10: 213–55.

Brockner, J. (1992) Managing the effects of layoffs in survivors', *California Management Review*, Winter: 9–28.

Brockner, J., Grover, S., Reed, T., Dewitt, R. and O'Malley, M. (1987) 'Survivors' reactions to layoffs: we get by with a little help from our friends', *Administrative Science Quarterly*, 32: 526–41.

Brockner, J., Tyler, T.R. and Cooper-Schneider, R. (1992) 'The influence of prior commitment to an institution on reactions to perceived unfairness: the higher they are, the harder they fall', *Administrative Science Quarterly*, 37: 241–61.

Brockner, J. and Wiesenfeld, B. (1993) 'Living on the edge (of social and organizational psychology): the effect of job layoffs on those who remain', in J.K. Murnighan (ed.), *Social Psychology in Organizations: Advances in Theory and Research*. Englewood Cliffs, NJ: Prentice-Hall. pp. 119–40.

Brockner, J., Wiesenfeld, B., Reed, T., Grover, S. and Martin, C. (1993) 'The interactive effect of job content and context on the reaction of layoff survivors', *Journal of Personality and Social Psychology.*

Burrell, G. and Scarborough, H. (1993) 'Knowledge of, in and for management'. Paper presented at the 11th EGOS Colloquium, ESCP, Paris, 6–8 July.

Cameron, K.S., Freeman, S.J. and Mishra, A.K. (1991) 'Best practices in white-collar downsizing: managing contradictions', *Academy of Management Executive,* 5 (3): 57–73.

Cameron, K.S., Freeman, S.J. and Mishra, A.K. (1993) 'Downsizing and redesigning organizations', in G.P. Hubert and W.H. Glick (eds), *Organizational Change and Redesign.* New York: Oxford University Press. pp. 19–65.

Cascio, W.F. (1993) 'Downsizing: what do we know? What have we learned?', *Academy of Management Executive,* 7 (1): 95–104.

Cascio, W., Young, C.E. and Morris, J.R. (1997) 'Financial consequences of employment-change decisions in major US corporations', *Academy of Management Journal,* 40: 1175–89.

Caulkin, S. (1995) 'Take you partners', *Management Today,* February: 26–30.

Collins, J.C. and Porras, J.I. (1995) *Build to Last: Successful Habits of Visionary Companies.* London: Century.

Davidow, W.H. and Malone, M.S. (1992) *The Virtual Corporation.* New York: HarperCollins.

Davis, G.F., Diekmann, K.A. and Tinsley, C.H. (1994) 'The decline and fall of the conglomerate firm in the 1980s: the deinstitutionalization of an organizational form', *American Sociological Review,* 59: 547–70.

Dopson, S. and Stewart, R. (1993) 'Information technology, organizational restructuring and the future of middle management', *New Technology, Work and Employment,* 8 (1): 10–20.

Dougherty, D. and Bowman, E.H. (1995) 'The effects of organizational downsizing on product innovation', *California Management Review,* 37 (4): 28–44.

Dunford, R. and Heiler, K. (1994a) 'Corporate restructuring through delayering and downsizing'. Paper presented to the Association of Industrial Relations Academics of Australia and New Zealand, Annual Conference, Sydney, 10–12 February.

Dunford, R. and Heiler, K. (1994b) 'Human resource management and downsizing: managing the tensions'. Paper presented to the Fourth Annual Conference on International Human Resource Management, Gold Coast, 5–8 July.

Edwards, R.C. (1979) *Contested Terrain: The Transformation of the Workplace in the Twentieth Century.* New York: Basic Books.

Economist, The (1994) 'When slimming is not enough', 3 September: 63–4.

Freeman, S.J. and Cameron, K.S. (1993) 'Organizational downsizing: a convergence and reorientation framework', *Organization Science,* 4 (1): 10–29.

Frohman, A.L. and Johnson, L.W. (1993) *The Middle Management Challenge: Moving from Crisis to Empowerment.* New York: McGraw-Hill.

Gaertner, K.N. and Nollen, S.D. (1989) 'Career experiences, perceptions of employment practices, and psychological commitment to the organization', *Human Relations,* 42 (11): 975–91.

Goffee, R. and Scase, R. (1992) 'Organizational change and the corporate career: the restructuring of managers' job aspirations', *Human Relations,* 45 (4): 363–85.

Greenberg, E.R. (1993) 'Upswing in downsizings to continue', *Management Review,* 82 (2): 6.

Hamel, G. and Prahalad, C.K. (1994) 'Competing for the future', *Harvard Business Review,* July–August: 122–8.

Handy, C. (1995) 'Trust and the virtual organization', *Harvard Business Review,* May–June: 40–50.

Hecksher, C. (1995) *White Collar Blues: Management Loyalties in an Age of Corporate Restructuring.* New York: Basic Books.

Henkoff, R. (1990) 'Cost cutting: how to do it right', *Fortune*, 9 April: 40–6.

Hirsch, M. (1995) 'Slice, cut, slash', *The Bulletin*, 7 February: 66–72.

Kanter, R.M. (1995) *World Class: Thriving Locally in the Global Economy*. New York: Simon and Schuster.

Kanter, R.M., Stein, B.A. and Jick, T.D. (1992) *The Challenge of Organizational Change*. New York: The Free Press.

Keenoy, T. and Anthony, P. (1992) 'HRM: metaphor, meaning and morality', in P. Blyton and P. Turnbull (eds), *Reassessing Human Resource Management*. London: Sage. pp. 233–55.

Kramar, R. (1990) *Managers in Australia: Changes in Internal Labour Markets and Employment Policies in the 1980s*. Industrial Relations Research Centre Monograph. Sydney: UNSW.

McAllister, D.J. (1995) 'Affect- and cognition-based trust as foundations for interpersonal cooperation in organizations', *Academy of Management Journal*, 38 (1): 24–59.

Miles, R.E. and Snow, C.C. (1995) 'The new network firm: a spherical structure built on a human investment philosophy', *Organizational Dynamics*, Spring: 5–18.

Noer, D.M. (1993) *Healing the Wounds*. San Francisco: Jossey-Bass.

Pahl, J.M. and Pahl, R.E. (1971) *Managers and their Wives*. Harmondsworth: Penguin.

Peters, T. (1992) *Liberation Management*. London: Macmillan.

Peters, T. (1994) *The Tom Peters' Seminar*. London: Macmillan.

Pfeffer, J. (1994) *Competitive Advantage through People*. Boston, MA: Harvard Business School Press.

Pfeffer, J. (1995) 'Producing sustainable competitive advantage through the effective management of people', *Academy of Management Executive*, 9 (1): 55–69.

Purcell, T.V. (1954) 'Duel allegiance to company and union packinghouse workers: a swift-UPWA study in a crisis situation, 1949–52', *Personnel Psychology*, 48–58.

Rousseau, D.M. and Parks, J.M. (1992) 'The contracts of individuals and organizations', *Research in Organizational Behavior*, 15: 1–43.

Scase, R. and Goffee, R. (1989) *Reluctant Managers*. London: Unwin Hyman.

Schein, E.H. (1978) *Career Dynamics: Matching Individual and Organizational Needs*. Reading, MA: Addison-Wesley.

Smith, K.G., Carroll, S.J. and Ashford, S.J. (1995) 'Intra- and inter-organizational cooperation: towards a research agenda', *Academy of Management Review*, 38 (1): 7–23.

Smith, L. (1994) 'Burned-out bosses', *Fortune*, 25 July: 44–52.

Sofer, C. (1970) *Men in Mid-career: a Study of British Managers and Technical Specialists*. Cambridge: Cambridge University Press.

Storey, J. (1992) *Developments in the Management of Human Resources*. Oxford: Blackwell.

Syedain, H. (1991) 'Middle managers: a species endangered', *Management Today*, May: 46–50.

Tomasko, R.M. (1993) *Rethinking the Corporation*. New York: AMACOM.

Walton, R.E. (1985) 'From control to commitment in the workplace', *Harvard Business Review*, March–April: 76–84.

Waterman, R.H. Jr., Waterman, J.A. and Collard, B.A. (1994) 'Towards a career-resilient workforce', *Harvard Business Review*, July–August: 87–95.

Watson, T. (1994) *In Search of Management: Culture, Chaos and Control in Managerial Work*. London: Routledge.

PART 2

REMAKING THE WORLD LOCALLY

---

4   The Regulation of Poverty: the Failure in the Official Program against Poverty in Mexico – a Modern/Postmodern Approach

Victor M. Soria

Capitalism's new flexibility – in the production process, the market, geographical distribution of production as well as the wage relationship – has been postulated as its entrance into postmodernity. Since the 1973–75 depression, capitalism has started a significant restructuring. There has been an intensification of competition among production centres, both domestically and internationally. Production's geographical distribution, including parts and components, has grown considerably. An increasing internationalization of commodity trade, even with low value products (e.g., beer), has occurred, as has the development of highly volatile financial markets, whose destabilizing power has accelerated with the liberalization and de-regulation of these markets. At the micro-economic level, with a recursive relation to the macro-phenomena, the big corporation redoubled their pace of technological change (computerization, telecommunications), reorganized their production techniques (JIT systems), restructured the financial area, emphasized product innovation, and pushed for a massive expansion of image and cultural production. All these had radical implications for the functioning of labour markets, work styles and skills development as well as for the quality of life and consumption patterns (Harvey, 1991: 66–7).

Postmodernism seeks to outdo the scientific discourse of modernism, posing 'an open horizon of all interpretation as a principle, as well as the impossibility of closure' (Clegg, 1990; exhibit 6), underlying the components of irrationality, disorder, and instability in organizational processes. Lyotard (1979) has postulated that the postmodern vision has left behind such meta-narratives 'as the dialectics of Spirit, the hermeneutics of meaning, the emancipation of the rational or working subject, or the creation of wealth' (quoted by Callinicos, 1989: 3). Postmodern approaches see the stability of organization as a myth because of the power relationships that weaken its life. They stress the small-scale informality, as well as the structural multiplicity, of the organization. Postmodern theories suggest that bureaucracy is being substituted by an industrial democracy in postmodern organizations that emphasize creative, expanded, self-controlled and motivated work, that show pluralistic structures, flexibility and ambiguous power centres. Such theories have advanced a characterization of the post-industrial society in which the role of social classes and salaried work have been receding in importance, while consumption is being constituted as a preponderant form of postmodern sociality (Bauman, 1982).[1] Class struggle gives up its place to new social movements against oppression, in which class origins are diluted.

Postmodernism, however, does not escape from an ideological bias derived from simultaneous economic and political change. Thus, in spite of their differences, both Harvey and Callinicos 'agree that the attractions of post-modernism qua ideology relate to what Davis (1985) called the "pathological prosperity" of the consumption booms of the 1980s and the associated hyper-mobility of financial capital' (Bromley, 1991: 139). The acceptance of postmodernism also relates to class alignments and political changes coming from the 1968 revolts that prompted the idea of a postmodern epoch in the 1980s (ibid.: 140). Scepticism towards grand narratives is as old as Enlightenment, and the emphasis upon the informal, the small, the component of irrational behaviour in organizations and in everyday life, etc. is anchored in, and comes from, modernist analysis. It is not true, points out Callinicos (1989) that we are living in postmodern societies as postulated by the 'core thesis'. Rather, we are observing a radicalization of modernity. The relative contraction of unemployment should not be confused with the abolition of capitalism. The decline of peasant agriculture, together with women's entrance into the labour market, show, rather, that salaried work has increased in importance. It is true that services and information play a larger role in advanced capitalism. However, this is part of a continuum of scientific and technological progress as well as economic transformations that are not new at all.

Postmodernity, it can be said, has but partly arrived in Mexico in the form of new foreign cultural events that touch only the select few, and a few isolated cases of postmodern industrialized plants, mainly in the northern part of the country. Very few of the big, private national firms have any tinge of postmodernism, and most government institutions are still trapped in the 'iron cage' of bureaucracy, regardless of whether some of their agencies are termed 'political' and others 'technical'. Most indigenous communities still live in archaism, and peasant mestizo communities live a pre-modern existence with some cultural exchange of semi-modern practices, while a good proportion of black-market workers try to survive in pre-modern conditions in the midst of a heterogeneous semi-modern world.

As to the theme of poverty, it must be said that postmodernity studies are rarely focused on this problem,[2] which capitalist re-composition has reintroduced recently in advanced countries and radicalized in under-developed ones. The economic crisis which poor countries were living through at the end of the 1970s was aggravated in Mexico by the monetarist shock of the Reagan administration in 1981. It was this that catalysed the advent of the external debt crisis and the neo-liberal economic adjustment policies, promoted both by the International Monetary Fund (IMF) and by the World Bank, in search of creditors' protection. Within this context, the production of poverty, brought about by the neo-liberal capital accumulation pattern, has continued to be more vigorous than the social policies designed to combat it.

In order to evaluate the Mexican anti-poverty programme (1988–94), this chapter takes a modernist non-conventional approach. Nonetheless, as long as these theories leave gaps in explaining the state of affairs of current organizations, it is necessary, as Clegg (1990) points out, to complement them with some concepts and methodological emphasis of postmodernism.[3] To this end, this chapter will study the 'modes of rationality' – a concept proposed by Clegg himself – which are behind the National Solidarity Program (Pronasol), a transitory institutional form (IF) built by the Carlos Salinas de Gortari's (SALINAS) administration to combat poverty. As long as Pronasol tries to substitute its effectiveness for the traditional bureaucratic structure applied by social protection organizations, will it also utilize some of the criteria proposed by Clegg? The question is: whether or not this programme incorporates any postmodern features? Notions developed by the regulation theorists of the Paris School will be utilized, as well as the concept of agency as developed by Jensen and Meckling (1976).

Modes of Rationality, Institutional Forms and Agency

According to Clegg and Rouleau (1992) 'the "modes of rationality" approach seeks to fuse elements both of "power" and the "institutions perspective"'. Rationality – together with power relationships – is fundamental in explaining both the direction and the results of collective action on the part of organized bureaucracies. The modes of rationality (MR) notion is an intermediate concept that moves on to the empirical study of concrete organizational realities.[4] In other words, MR are not studied in abstract ways; they can be linked to the concepts of institutional forms (IFs) and agency through the study of the activities of social actors. The IFs are the concrete forms taken by social relationships of production that constitute the cement – whether coercive and/or consensual – that helps to regulate collective action – always in a contradictory and temporary fashion.[5] Agency represents the possibility of establishing not only the calculation mechanisms but also the interpretation criteria of action.[6] In this light, agency becomes the core of analysis that permits the rejection of the construction of closed objects in social theory and at the same time allows the redefinition of theoretical frontiers different from those observed empirically (Montano, 1992: 3). Institutional forms correspond to the concept of organization but agency does not necessarily correspond to IFs; agency could establish itself as a guide to social behaviour, whether at the level of the individual, of both the IF and organization levels, as a part of it, or within a wider social group.

Culture acquires a new status in social action; it does not necessarily represent the starting point from which to identify national variations in organization, but relates to a complex web of power relationships. As Montano points out, 'corporate culture as an expression with more than just a pretence of managerial strategic voluntarism inhering in it, becomes inscribed in a manipulating game, rather than in the production of new values to explain, outdate, and to give direction to collective action' (1992: 4–5).

Before analysing the organization and operation of Pronasol, a brief overview of the evolution of poverty will be given, as well as a synthesis of the role of the accumulation pattern by import substitution, and the bureaucratic-corporate mode of regulation regarding the continuation of poverty.

Regime of Accumulation, Mode of Regulation and the Continuation of Poverty in Mexico

A long-term general outlook in regard to the evolution of poverty in Mexico is not promising for most of the Mexican people. Even though the economy grew steadily for 37 years (1934–70) without any structural crisis, it was not able to deal with absolute poverty. Since 1977, the country had oil exports as an alternative to sustain investment and growth. However the surplus was dissipated by both the public and private sectors, in part because of the political confrontation between these sectors with the onset of structural crisis at the beginning of the 1970s. Paradoxically, both absolute and relative poverty tended to decline during the petroleum boom (1977–81). However, at the end of that period the economy fell into such a profound financial crisis (dating from early 1982) that welfare declined to the proportions of the 1960s. The financial crisis that started in December 1994 will probably take poverty still further back, perhaps even to the 1950s levels.

The logic of the regime of accumulation by import substitution, which caused income to become concentrated in the hands of the few and totally excluded many people from economic opportunities, was upheld by a mode of regulation that this chapter calls corporate-bureaucratic[7] with a populist-developmental ideology. It was this conjunction that helped the incorporation of a substantial part of the labour force into modern sectors, but left an increasing body of excluded people in poverty. The explosions of crisis in 1976 and 1982, together with the globalizing trends of the world economy and North American pressure, gave birth in 1983 to a new accumulation regime, oriented towards exports, that up to now has not been consolidated. This new regime pledges to be still more exclusive and concentrated; it rests on a higher degree of regulation by the market, and on orthodox monetary and fiscal policies, which will probably lead to a higher degree of impoverishment than in the past.

Mexican capitalists were linked to the bureaucratic state on two levels. At a higher level through the 'revolutionary coalition' (formed by the president in office, the Cabinet members, the living ex-presidents, the military cupola, and the top trade union leaders) and its links with the entrepreneurial elite. At a lower level the linkages were implemented by administrative bureaucracy which was designed to control small and medium-sized businesses through the Commercial and Industrial Chambers.

Trade unions, as basic organizations for working people, have a double disadvantage in Mexico because they not only constitute a 'secondary' organization,[8] but in addition they have been organized in a corporate fashion by the state, that is, they have become 'dependent' within the corporate-bureaucratic mode of regulation. The centralization of the Mexican political system (MPS) does not admit competition or threat from independent worker and peasant organizations. Thus, for example, the Ministry of Labour and Social Provision denies the registration of independent unions as legal entities, qualifies the 'legitimacy' of strikes, and fixes a series of corporate practices that set aside any independent organization not in sympathy with government policy.[9]

The regulation of the capital–labour relationship, or 'wage relationship',[10] evolved from a semi-competitive form to a monopolistic one. The former was developed from 1934 to 1961 and was characterized by an ample hierarchy of wages and an industry-by-industry bargaining process; the latter was in operation between 1962 and 1982, when the negotiation process was increasingly effected on a national level through central trade unions and the Labour Congress, as well as the National Minimum Wage Commission giving way to a rationalization of wages.

In 1968 crisis hit the MPS in view of its lack of ability to comply peacefully with demands coming from the citizenry. The political IFs were weakened. Thus, 'presidentialism' began to be questioned by big business in early 1970, with the arrival in office of President Luis Echeverría who tried to make reforms to the educational, health and fiscal systems. Within this context, business organizations representing big capital, such as the National Confederation of Enterprise Owners of the Mexican Republic (COPARMEX is the Spanish acronym) and the Enterprise Co-ordination Council, in collusion with the American Chamber of Commerce, started a struggle against the government's economic and social policy, centred on a type of 'investment strike' as a result of a 'confidence crisis' which had become recurrent at the end of each government administration.

From 1970 to 1976 inflation and speculation were rife. However, the regulation of the wage relationship was reinforced by means of periodic wage increases and by public investment designed to create employment, though it was achieved through a substantial increase in external debt. Nonetheless, the sectorial inequalities, the fiscal crisis, the external sector's vulnerability and inflation all aggravated by the confrontation between government and the private sector, resulted in a flight of capital and speculation, and finally in a currency devaluation and the generalization of crisis in 1976. The IMF's entry on to the scene that year marks the beginning of the fall of monopolistic regulation of the wage relationship, and of the general corporate-bureaucratic mode of regulation.

The oil exports alternative also failed in the revamping of the import substitution accumulation regime. Although the levels of employment increased, wages began to be regulated by ceilings recommended by the IMF, and the distributive conflict ensued both because of the increase of business and banking levels of concentration, and because of the extraordinary increase of corruption. José López Portillo's administration tried to improve the relationship with big capital, though the meagre business confidence gained ended in 1981 with the fall of the internal oil price.

The next big crisis was incubating in the entrails of manufacturing industry, given that amid the petroleum boom, industry had been showing signs of stagnation. Directing oil profits towards private enterprise by means of high subsidies and government contracts had been useless, because the profit was taken out of the country in the heat of the crisis. Although sectorial inequalities continued and external vulnerability increased with import liberalization, which was advised by the IMF, the 1981 fall in the international oil price sparked the worst financial crisis up to that time.

The bureaucratic-corporate mode of regulation started breaking up at the beginning of the 1982 crisis. However, the political monopoly around the Republic's Presidency, with the PRI (Partido Revolucionario Institucional) still refusing to share power instead of proposing political change, framed a profound change of the economic system. During Miguel de la Madrid's administration (1982–88) the wage curve went down to the levels of the early 1960s, that is wages had lost about 55 per cent of their value between 1983 and 1987; the economic surplus was redirected to servicing the foreign debt, by drastically cutting public investment and social development expenditure as well as by an increase in domestic debt; the currency was devalued several times to maintain an under-valued exchange rate in order to promote exports, cut imports and use the surplus to service the foreign debt.

In 1983 there emerged a new accumulation regime oriented to exports for whose reinforcement several important structural changes were made: the entrance to GATT, the lowering of tariffs and non-tariff barriers as well as the relaxation of foreign direct investment (FDI) controls. These measures led to a rapid opening of the economy to foreign competition (1985 to 1989) and to the bankruptcy of thousands of small and medium-sized businesses. On the domestic side, the nationalized banking system was re-privatized to the amount of one-third of its capital, and a brokerage system was established for the placement of domestic public debt, which served to redirect massive amounts of real interest payments into the hands of the newly rich. That, together with old capital, constituted a new com-mercial–industrial–financial elite ready to support the emerging accumula-tion regime.

The prolonged crisis period from 1982 to 1988 had its impact upon the MPS in terms of a punishment vote for the PRI and the candidacy of Carlos Salinas de Gortari (CSG), whose triumph in the 1988 election is still open to question but was nevertheless sustained by presidential authori-tarianism, fraud and the government's repressive forces, a situation that aggravated the political crisis. In spite of the need for substantial changes in the MPS, the Salinas administration gave priority to economic policy (very similar to that of the former government), with the implicit hypo-thesis that economic growth would make slow, cosmetic political changes palatable. However, the economy had a short-lived economic recovery, lapsing again into political crisis at the beginning of 1994, which gave way to economic crisis at the end of that same year.

The Salinas government deepened structural reforms, such as financial liberalization, by opening the Mexican Stock Exchange to foreign capital, by privatization of the main public-sector industries and the commercial banks,[11] and by the negotiation of the North American Free Trade Agreement (NAFTA) with Canada and the USA. Even though CSG's administration built two transitory IFs, one for the regulation of prices and wages (through a pact with workers and companies[12]) and the other to combat poverty (the National Solidarity Programme that will be examined in the next section), they were only in force up to 1993. The first was effective in controlling inflation, but still more effective in keeping wage increases below the rate of inflation, and the second, as will be seen, accorded with political goals but did not reduce poverty.

Ernesto Zedillo, the current president, inherited an explosive political and economic situation. That, combined with his political weakness and his stubborn attachment to neo-liberalism, took the country into a severe financial crisis one month after he took office. Instead of depending on the workers to gain political strength in order to deal with old power groups (the PRI 'dinosaurs') and to negotiate with the USA, Zedillo has yielded to both forces, preferring to execute a criminally severe adjustment pro-gramme that will destroy the already decimated middle class and push poverty to the extreme.

In synthesis, the evolution of poverty during the period of 1934–90 was as follows. During the period of sustained growth without structural crisis (1934–70), the total number of poor people increased, as can be seen in

Table 4.1. Within this period, the years from 1956 to 1970 saw a growth without inflation, a period labelled 'stabilizing development', that produced an increase in the number of 'extremely' poor and a quasi-stagnation in the number of 'non-extremely' poor. From 1970 to 1976, even though the government wanted support from corporate unions and to maintain the regulation of wages, there was an increase in the total number of the poor, though both the absolute and relative number of extremely poor went down (see Table 4.1). From 1977 to 1981, for the first time, poverty was reduced both in absolute and relative terms. This reduction is explained by the decline in the number of the extremely poor (by nearly three million), though there was a slight increase in the number of the non-extremely poor. Nonetheless, the 1982 crisis reversed not only the reduction of the total number of poor people during the oil boom years, but also the declining trend in relative poverty.

Table 4.1. shows, for 1990, a dramatic picture of the incidence of poverty, which has reached 77.9 per cent of the country's population according to the important research results obtained by Julio Boltvinik on the basis of the 1990 Census, utilizing the 'poverty lines' method. Boltvinik's (1994) findings make one doubt the figures for the 1980s, which probably underestimated the incidence of poverty.

Neo-liberal Anti-poverty Policy, Organizational Theory and the National Solidarity Program (Pronasol)

The influence of international institutions on policy and organization of social protection

In Latin America the neo-liberal policy implemented since the 1980s has not led to growth but rather to income concentration producing both extreme wealth and extreme poverty. Neo-liberal policy was implemented to take advantage of the foreign debt crisis, giving way to adjustment measures vigorously promoted by the IMF and the World Bank, that reduced public expenditure in order to obtain a budget surplus destined to service the debt. These measures created a still worse fiscal imbalance, hyper-inflation and an accelerating internal debt with massive income transfers to the rich as well as a loss of government legitimacy. This failure motivated international financial institutions to design and recommend new economic policies that would promote growth and stability, as well as the decline of a foreign debt serviced by means of country-by-country re-negotiation with creditors. These measures were accompanied by policies of financial and commercial liberalization, the cutting of subsidies to industry and the export sector, public-sector privatization, de-regulation and an adaptation of legislation to the new conditions in the fields of labour, fiscality and social development (Salama, 1995: 355). Along the same lines, there arose a policy of positive interest rates, to promote

TABLE 4.1 *Incidence of poverty and of extreme poverty, measured by the 'poverty lines' method, 1960–1990* (millions of persons and percentages)

Concept	1960		1963		1968		1977		1981		1984		1988		1990	
	No.	%	No.	%	No.	%	No.	%	No.	%	No.	%	No.	%	No.	%
Poor	27.5	76.4	29.8	77.5	32.8	72.6	36.7	58.0	34.6	48.5	44.6	58.5	46.1	59.0	63.3	77.9
Extreme	20.4	56.7	26.7	69.4	25.6	56.7	21.5	34.0	18.6	26.1	22.8	29.9	22.0	28.2	55.5	68.3
Non-extreme	7.1	19.7	3.1	8.1	7.2	15.9	15.2	24.0	16.0	22.4	21.7	28.6	24.1	30.8	7.8	9.6
Non-Poor	8.5	23.6	8.6	22.5	12.4	27.4	26.6	42.0	36.7	51.5	31.6	41.5	32.1	41.0	17.9	22.1
Total population	36.0	100	38.4	100	45.2	100	63.3	100	71.3	100	76.2	100	78.2	100	81.2	100

Sources: for 1960, Consejo Consultivo del Pronasol (1987: 2); 1963 to 1988, Enrique Hernández-Laos (1992: 108–9, Table 3.2); for 1990, Julio Boltvinik (1994: 87, Table 11.3); total 1990 Census population taken from Anuario Estadístico de los Estados Unidos Mexicanos, INEGI (1993, Table 2.1).

domestic savings and to deter the flight of capital out of the country. These policies achieved a limited, temporary success but their fragility ended in a collapse of most of the Latin American economies, as was the case for Mexico in December 1994.

This renovated liberal paradigm at the level of social and economic policy also has its replica at the organizational level, actively backed by the World Bank. The battle against bureaucratic structures and fixed procedures in organizations, as a banner of neo-liberalism, has also been reinforced by postmodern approaches. The World Bank and other international institutions have emphasized actions at the micro-economic and micro-social level as a basis for an increase in productivity and efficiency and as a way out of poverty. In this vein, strategies such as 'self-help' at individual and group levels, programme decentralization and flexibility are considered as fundamental to the raising of social well-being. Such strategies have shown their inability to reduce poverty, in the absence of re-distributive social policies and economic measures that promote employment and sustained growth.

In some anti-poverty approaches there is a glimpse of paradigmatic change, promoted by United Nations institutions such as the United Nations Development Programme and the Latin American Administration Center for Development. It is said that 'the bureaucratic-autocratic paradigm which postulated that a program could adequately function if mounted from the top down, is being put aside' (Kliksberg, 1993: 99). The emphasis is on 'flexibility' and decentralized structures, in which programme municipalization could play a role in reducing administrative costs (ibid.: 102–5).

Community members' participation has been an old worker and peasant demand since the 1950s. However today it is being presented by institutions, such as the World Bank, as an exigency, though it is a dependent participation limited by the rules of those institutions. The concept of participation acts in fact as a complement of neo-liberal economic adjustment policies. Thus it constitutes a 'socializing exercise for the excluded'. In other words, it is a 'participation on the assistential terrain and subordination on the economic' as Bascones (1995: 7) points out.[13]

In Latin America there exists a series of strategic problems in matters of social management, among which is a lack of coherence between economic and social policies, as well as in economic sector control, that leads to the minimization of social impact resulting from economic decisions. The counterpart to these problems is the 'institutional weakness' of the public social sector. Often the ministries of health and of education, which are the fundamental operators of the social sector, are found to be the most backward sectors in the management terrain (Kliksberg, 1993: 98).

United Nations institutions have put forth the notion of 'self-sustenance' for the anti-poverty programmes as a prerequisite for their survival and for them to have a durable impact upon social well-being. 'Articulation' strategies, to give coherence to the diverse social sector institutions, are also being highlighted to make such programmes more effective. This has led to the proposal of building inter-organizational networks to connect social institutions, non-governmental organizations (NGOs) and the communities themselves into a 'coherent whole', to strengthen anti-poverty programmes (Mandell, 1993: 193). To improve social institutions, a more sophisticated social management system is needed, one that can cope with the variability and non-predictability that comes out of social management practice. In other words, 'adaptive' managers, who are able to consider multiple scenarios and be 'in tune' with people, are required (Kliksberg, 1993: 106). This kind of manager must be relatively autonomous, possess a 'political awareness', and be 'proactive' in order to respond to the demands of the inter-organizational network (Mandell, 1993: 193–5).

What the organizational approaches to improving the management of the social sector, coming from the international organizations, have not incorporated is a complexity analysis of strategic planning (for a model of the complexity paradigm, see Ibarra, 1995: 51–70). Some awareness exists that social organizations in an underdeveloped country move inside a dialogical environment (the economic system's rationality that produces and goes on producing poverty goes side by side with the rationality of the social protection institutions which try to counteract poverty). Yet, the international organizations and the Mexican government do not dare to propose changes in the logic linked to the rationality that heightens poverty. They fear to acknowledge 'recursivity' within a divergent class system, that is, one where the production of riches also means the production of poverty, and vice versa. Therefore, it is necessary that some organizations exist to alleviate marginality to help the system to reproduce itself, though in doing so the conflict among social actors successively changes its form. In such systems the strategy of social welfare institutions is ineffective because it is beyond their reach to influence the systems, unless events emerge to cause an inflection in the system (e.g., workers' movements or popular movements). The system's unity is made up of divergent rationalities produced by disparate institutions and citizens, as well as by the recursivity coming from strange powers that regulate the system's reproduction in ever new forms.

In Mexico, as was described on pages 86–9, the dramatic increase in poverty between 1982 and 1988, caused by both crisis and economic adjustment policies, gave birth at the end of 1988 to the National Solidarity Program (Pronasol is the Spanish acronym). The formal, explicit objective of this was to reduce the extreme poverty of the Mexican population, though its real purposes were to build a hegemonic political consensus among the population and add lustre to the President of Mexico.

Pronasol's ties with the basic neo-liberal alignments stressed market primacy for resource allocation according to the economic orthodoxy of the IMF, limited intervention of the state in income redistribution, and the approach of 'trickle-down' theory in regard to the combat of poverty. Pronasol adopted some of the basic proposals of the World Bank: 'self-help', 'flexibility', 'participation', though the programme also partially followed other proposals such as decentralization and municipalization. Even though the Salinas administration tried to distinguish Pronasol from neo-liberalism by means of the artifice of 'social liberalism', its operation and results have shown a repeated failing of the dual liberal logic, deepened by the egomaniac attitude of its mastermind and agent, ex-President Salinas.

Pronasol's organizational structure

The so called 'reform' of the state in the sphere of social protection, during the administration of CSG, was justified in terms of the

> bureaucratic domination that ended in a hierarchical centralized social policy decision system; the increasing autonomy of the bureaucratic apparatus from the beneficiaries of social policy, as well as a trend to limitless growth of social expenditure . . . which was the source of legitimacy, reproduction and the power of bureaucracy. (Consejo Consultivo del Pronasol (CCP), 1994: 24)

The counterpart of the state bureaucratic outfit in charge of social protection, that is the benefiting population, suffered malfunctions in terms of intermediarism and a ballooning social demand negotiation supported by a 'popular petitionist and passive culture that feeds back state tutorship and clientelist practices towards society' (CCP, 1994: 25).

The former criticisms are severe and realistic; they lay bare the vices of Mexican bureaucracy in the domain of social protection. Nonetheless, as will be discussed later in this chapter, the new structure around 'social liberalism', developed by CSG's administration, added a new centralism, an increased bureaucracy and a renovated political clientelism that outdid the former vices of social protection institutions.

The top-level organizational structure of Pronasol

At the top of the structure is the President of Mexico, who presides over the Committee for the National Solidarity Program, established on 8 December 1988. It is made up of the Ministries of State, the Directors General of the Mexican Institute of Social Security, the National People's Food Program Company, the National Institute of Arid Zones and the National Forestry Co-operative. This Committee has the functions of policy definition and co-ordination, strategy and actions against poverty, as well as the securing of compliance with specific programmes. In addition, the Consulting Council of Pronasol (CCP) was established as an auxiliary organization for the Committee; the CCP is made up mostly of representatives of official trades unions and former government officers as well as a minority of intellectuals, business people and legislators.

During its first period, Pronasol was run by the Vice-Ministry of Regional Development, part of the Ministry of Programming and Budgeting, formerly directed by CSG, who later became presidential candidate, and then, President of Mexico. Additionally, an Evaluation Committee was created, presided over the Raúl Salinas de Gortari brother of the former president, to study the social and economic impact of Pronasol. The Solidarity Program took advantage of existing planning and development bodies at regional and state level. At the start of its fourth year, Pronasol entered into a second period, and the government tried to institutionalize it by means of the creation of a Ministry of Social Development (SEDESOL in the Spanish acronym). A Social Development Cabinet was also established for the co-ordination of the diverse institutions that intervene in social policy. In addition, the 'Unique Development Agreements' signed by the federal and state governments was transformed into the 'Social Development Agreements', but this time signed directly by the president and the state governors (CCP, 1994: 70).

Funds for Pronasol came from a variety of sources: the federation, state and municipal governments, the social and private sectors. The Federal Budget established a special heading (heading XXVI) for 'Solidarity and Regional Development', authorized annually by the Chamber of Deputies. Officially it was affirmed that the Pronasol budget was decentralized and was operated mainly by state and municipal governments and hardly at all by federal officers. In reality the regional and state allocation of funds was directly approved by the president in conjunction with top SEDESOL officers.

Pronasol's micro-social organizational core and its procedures

Pronasol's action was based on the establishment of a micro-social and micro-regional nucleus. The purpose of this was to institute a new relationship between the state and civil society, that 'would be linked to the decentralizing trends of the State, as well as the strengthening of regional development planning and the configuration of a new social policy' (CCP, 1994: 63). The procedures for the building of a micro-social and micro-regional core are as follows:

1 The Pronasol agents organize a public consultation, with representatives of the community, with the purpose of forming a 'Solidarity Committee' (SC) to obtain the participation and commitment of the members with regard to the public works to be carried out.
2 A general assembly is held with the possible beneficiaries of the project, who elect a board of directors (a president, secretary, treasurer and as many members as there are functions to be carried out). The assembly is validated by the Pronasol Delegate.
3 Through the co-ordination of the different SCs the social demand for the micro-region is added up and the projects are selected. By means of this process, social demand is rationalized.

4   An Agreement Act is drawn up with the Delegate of the SEDESOL, to list the commitments of the community.
5   A Technical File is established, with the assistance of the SEDESOL office or a municipal technician, which includes the works to be carried out, the resources needed, the costs and timetable, as well as the federal, state, municipal and community funds and resources. The community may participate with money, materials or actual hours of labour.
6   The community makes the follow-up, evaluation and control of completed actions during the whole process. The member in charge of Social Supervision keeps a log, informing the SC with regard to contractor selection, the quality and cost of materials, execution times, as well as the reporting of any irregularities.
7   If a contractor is in charge of works, the SC should formally accept the finished works and give the contractor a consent in writing only if the works fulfil the specified norms, otherwise the contractor cannot collect the corresponding amount of money.

A critical evaluation of Pronasol's operation

The evaluation of the Solidarity Program will be settled mainly according to an analysis of 'organizational imperatives', proposed by Clegg (1990: 184–207), to postmodern organizations. This chapter only mentions some of these facts in terms of available information. Lastly, the mode of rationality that lay behind Pronasol during the administration of CSG will be discussed, as to whether it contributed to the empowerment of the democracy of this social assistance organization and of the community to which it was related.

The articulation of mission, goals, strategies and main functions

The main goal declared by the programme was to combat poverty, specifically extreme poverty, even though this did not mean its eradication, due to the structural character of poverty.[14] It can be said that the aim of reducing total poverty proved to be a complete failure. Another aim that failed was the fight against extreme poverty, as INEGI affirms.[15] By reason of the programme's expense distribution, funds did not go to the very poorest communities.[16] Rather, the programme responded to political criteria for nullifying opposing political parties.

With an estimated budget of little more than 1 per cent of the Gross Domestic Product (GDP), it seems that Pronasol's objectives were over-ambitious. Moreover, macro-economic austerity policy and the encouragement of economic 'financiarization'[17] produced unemployment and a vicious concentration of income and wealth that dealt a blow to Pronasol's aims (see Table 4.2).

Two of Pronasol's non-declared but fundamental missions, judging by its own operation and results, were: (i) to establish a political hegemony based

TABLE 4.2 *Expenditure of the National Solidarity Program, 1988–93* (in millions of new pesos) (1988 = 100)[1]

Year	Expenditure	Annual rate	% of GDP
1988	1,226.4		0.31
1989	1,832.1	49.4	0.45
1990	2,946.4	60.8	0.72
1991	3,848.6	30.6	0.88
1992	4,972.5	29.2	1.08
1993[2]	3,004.6	−39.6	0.64

[1] Adjusted according to the Implicit GDP Deflator.
[2] Estimated expenditure at the end of the budget year.

Sources: for 1988 to 1992 Public Federal Financial Account; for 1993 SEDESOL, General Direction for Planning.

upon consensus rather than compulsion; and (ii) to legitimize and give lustre to the Republic's Presidency. The fight against poverty was set aside for two reasons: a quite small Pronasol budget and fund distribution decided on the basis of political criteria:

1   In view of the elections for Congress representatives in October 1991, and with the intention of achieving a majority that could guarantee the intense series of constitutional adjustments that would bring together a new regime of accumulation oriented towards foreign trade, Pronasol's expense had to suit this schedule.[18] All the construction was finished between January and September 1991, and some doubled their costs compared to the 1990s projects. For example, the total of renovated schools rose from 20,000 in 1990 to 80,000 in 1991 (Pineyro, 1992: 68).
2   The renewal of the IF of the Presidency. Under CSG's management, Solidaridad acquired a public image in Mexico and abroad like no other Mexican social development programme before. This could probably be a glimpse of postmodern management applied by the Salinas regime in order to seduce Mexican citizens, Washington politicians, and North American investors.[19]

The popularity gained by the president allowed him to associate the re-privatization of public banks and industries with the enhancement of welfare. For example, the sale of the Compañía Mexicana de Aviación would provide funds for electricity to be supplied to more than 500,000 residents of the poorest zones in Mexico. In other words, once again there was this false alternative on the decision of re-privatization as a pre-requisite to acquiring social justice for the poor population strata (Dresser, 1994: 275).

CSG's government strategy to establish a link, in the first place with social movements to reaffirm the government's legitimacy, and, once this was fulfilled, with community groups by means of the municipal governments, was carried out by direct negotiation. The goal was to 'establish direct discussion between the President, his staff and these groups, and to eliminate bureaucracy that restrains the negotiation task' (Dresser, 1994: 291). Every week the president made visits, inaugurated works set up by Pronasol, and established direct contact with poor people. Between December 1988 and January 1992, he had 254 meetings, 57 per cent of these with urban people's movements, 27 per cent with peasant communities, 5 per cent with Mexican Indian sectors, and 7 per cent with other sectors.

Pronasol's strategy was to establish three general programmes, each one divided into several sub-programmes and these into a 'project network'. Likewise, it was conceived as a national extended programme subdivided according to federal entities and municipalities, and furthermore, as a regional system. Moreover, the Presidency co-ordinated the Ministers' and local government's collaboration to establish sub-programmes and projects with Pronasol, therefore 'school renovation', 'children in solidarity', 'school breakfasts', 'CONASUPO solidarity stores', etc., gave Pronasol a greater dimension than its own budget could. Add to this the millionaire and intense publicity campaigns and presidential visits, so the programme's non-declared duties were also fulfilled.

Pronasol's strategy in terms of the market of social demand followed the World Bank and the World Health Organization (WHO) principle of 'focalization' as an effective way of going against extreme poverty. Pronasol's representatives said that the programme was focused especially on the fight against extreme poverty in indigenous communities, rural areas, and urban marginal areas. As Goicoechea's study (1994) shows, regions with medium poverty, but with the influence of opposition political parties, were favoured. Anyway, focalization suggests 'social assistance', which justifies the dualization of social protection and stratifies the types of citizenship, one 'first-class', and another 'second-class'.

In relation to the 'design of work', there was no influence coming from the programme to change its organization. The projects in which local communities participated, especially in public works such as disposal systems and drinking-water systems, were still developing old-fashioned artisan methods, using little machinery and equipment. The common type of labour used was the 'non-qualified', together with other craft skills that imply former training and practice. Some small or medium-sized subcontractors were hired, generally from local villages, and they continued to use contracted and non-qualified labour.

According to 'employment relationships' these were shaped by the international organizations' outlines, in terms of the communities' 'participation'. Pronasol established a procedure that gave birth to the so-called 'Solidarity Committees' (CS), and a proceedings agreement (concertation) was signed. It looks like some kind of 'subcontracting' between the government and the community. The government supplied funds and/or materials, and the community contributed labour as well as supervision and accomplishment of the entire project. The government gave the CS some 'empowerment' to perform these functions, but always limited by the budget and supervision of Pronasol's Delegate. Nevertheless, the highest production of poverty, driven on by the austere economic policy and the lack of any political reform that could bring society together, demonstrated Pronasol's illusion (mirage) to the country and to those observers abroad.

Arrangement of functional alignments

Pronasol, as an institution that tried to continue functioning by means of special forms of agency, focused on two levels. First, inside the government apparatus, in which a type of agency was created subject to the conditions of the power structure and inevitable co-ordination. This manner of agency can be considered successful because of a loyal, controlled bureaucracy that took advantage of the Mexican political class's habits of building 'groups' based upon personal loyalty to the group's leader. At this point the issue was that all the Salinas groups had positioned themselves in the highest and middle level offices of the federal government, and they did not stop until they controlled the majority. Secondly, the composition of agencies, including members from the poor population, was settled by a contract with a democratic community organization (a CS established in consultation with the community, and run by democratically elected members). However, functional relationships were not so democratic, given that they created new clientelist relationships.

First, the institutional framework built by the Salinas forces favoured an incorporation of the most radical people's movements, which allowed leaders of these movements to re-vindicate their struggle to achieve better material conditions. Secondly, it created a tighter, more dependent relationship. At the beginning of 1989, Pronasol's operation was more participatory and more democratic, due to direct agreement with established organizations, many supposedly 'social opposition',[20] in the assignation of community projects resources without the previous requirement of forming a CS. However, in 1990 there was an important turning point in the procedure. Resources were to be managed by means of municipal governments, which would create a CS with the community, putting aside the 1989 agreement with the social organizations (Méndez et al., 1992: 62).

Pronasol pushed on much further than traditional co-option strategies that merge governmental intervention with the internal decisions of community organizations. These organizations have had the liberty to install their own internal processes, limited only by the actions of the Pronasol Delegates and a central control in the form of the budget assignment. Anyhow, the result is linked to the state's distributive network. Organizations are much too vulnerable in the face of political loyalty to the official party and the government (Dresser, 1994: 281).

Pronasol's support procedure on work and services, that first of all regional social demand should be addressed and that the projects to be chosen should rationalize demand, was not respected. The regional social demand was centrally decided and projects chosen often had some political motivation behind them, that is, the overtaking of opposition political parties in some regions and communities.

Most of the projects did not contribute to the communities' social integration because of their temporary nature; once the project is completed, the CS disappears. However, those used for collective activities (e.g., theatre, school, sports areas), administered by the local community, or productive projects that have some community participation, have remained.

There is no quality control of the programme's services and works. Communities and Proposal Delegates demand that contractors finish work, but quality is often not taken into consideration. With regard to abilities and usefulness, the programme does not enhance these either. There are only a few productive projects, related to micro-industries, that have actually promoted better abilities and skills.

Control and co-ordination mechanisms

The Salinas administration wanted to establish, on several levels, a network of loyal public dedication to the economic project called 'social liberalism'. This network, it was hoped, might make CSR's administration survive beyond its term. The bet was, according to some high public officials, 'to continue for two administration periods after Salinas'. This generated some expectation on the part of middle-level staff groups on long-term projects, and it also encouraged people to work with loyalty and dedication; they were not going to be 'orphaned' at the end of the administration, as had happened in the past, as they would have a position in public service. This also happened with Proposal employees, mainly because of the creation of a new ministry designed around this programme, and later, because the Proposal Minister was chosen as a candidate for the Mexican Presidency. Nevertheless, the political system's disorder outdid itself in government. Private sector corruption and Salinas's Machiavellian-style machinations, which brought about conflict within the dominant elite, put an end to the dream of continuity.

Anyway, Pronasol was being closely monitored by the president, and fundamental decisions were still favourable to the federal government, in this specific case, the new Social Development Ministry (SEDESOL). The intention of de-centralizing the budget, and the fact that its execution was mainly in the hands of state and municipal governments, did not concur with the way the intention worked out in the end. The press and political analysts commented on Pronasol's discrimination in the allocation of expenditure to federal entities where governors were opposed to Salinas's push to modernity and the tight, centralized control of SEDESOL's technocratic elite.

Credibility and relationships between the roles of the different actors

It can be said that CSG's administration tried to establish a (de-differentiation) process to by-pass the traditional bureaucratic apparatus.

The administration's aim was to reduce the size of the state and to become an even more liberal state. In fact the 1982–87 crisis played a de-differentiating role in relation to state streamlining – nearly 400,000 government employees were made redundant. From 1988 the Salinas government emphasized direct control of processes that were linked to the regime's legitimization. In this field, Pronasol was the priority. In general, CSG's government tried to by-pass the bureaucratic web of the different ministries, creating a social assistance programme with fewer authority levels and with direct communication between the poor communities and the president. The creation of SEDESOL increased the number of authority levels, though it continued to have fluid contact with the community.

In terms of counter-balancing powers, Pronasol's technocracy did not meet any other entity that would obstruct its progress, because it operated as an autonomous programme directed by the president, even though it overlapped the functions of several ministries. From 1992, this situation started to change because members of the PRI began to become aware of the role that Pronasol had in the triumph of their party's candidates for Congress – the president supervised the naming of, or actually named, the candidates for the 1991 elections. Pronasol had become a political clientelist structure parallel to the PRI, but with real, effective power to promote the president's candidates. However, the PRI could do little to recover its position, as the president changed the party's general secretary at whim, thus making PRI autonomy impossible.

Incentives and performance

The incentives for the agents who belonged to Pronasol's techno-bureaucracy were material (good wages and work conditions), as well as symbolic in connection with the expectation of the survival of the Salinas project and programme beyond CSG's term. Furthermore, the fact of feeling 'the generation for change' itself and being able to say that the country was moving into modernity were also strong symbolic incentives.

Poor communities that had material improvement programmes, felt that this time they were being included, that they were 'participating' and it was worth it. The thousands of 'actions' that Pronasol had developed, accounted by SEDESOL and launched by Salinas propaganda, testified to the sense of participation. Nevertheless, general poverty continued behind the optimistic picture painted by the administration's propaganda.

Pronasol's modes of rationality

Pronasol became the dialogic hub of institutions such as the World Bank, the IMF, the Treasury Department of the USA and the international financial community, as they promoted a policy of economic austerity, regulation by the market, wage control, commercial and financial liberalization, privatization and deregulation, among other measures that led to a more generalized impoverishment rate. The foreign institutions also proposed a social assistance policy, focused on the poorest sectors of the population, in order to offset the effects of liberal doctrine. The dialogics of the CSG government also converged in this programme; on the one hand, the programme assumed higher efficiency of social programmes if traditional bureaucracy were put aside and authority levels eliminated, creating a more direct relationship with poor communities. On the other hand, it pursued political aims that lead to a centralized, authoritarian control of decisions that resulted in the limitation of distributive efficiency.[21]

Pronasol's rationale, in which several contradictory logics come together, could not consolidate a social policy built upon a false basis. The programme originated in a period where crisis and economic adjustment policy increased the incidence of poverty and reduced confidence in the government. This paved the way to using the Solidarity Program to try to legitimize the governmental regime and conserve the political monopoly that has existed for more than 60 years.

Pronasol cannot only be conceived as a material institution. It should be considered instead as an IF that had as its main objective the establishment of a political-clientelist hegemony and the giving of legitimacy and prestige to the Republic's presidency. The regulation of poverty was only a secondary objective. This IF has a transitory nature in view of its contradictory rationale.

This IF established new forms of agency that gave only temporary effectiveness to its main mission, connected to the power circuit that the Salinas regime built. The agents assumed a seduction mentality that tried to sell a programme that was not able to eradicate poverty. The community agents were impressed by a participatory spirit generated from this kind of programme, and tried to support government economic policies even where these policies had a noxious political effect, especially on poor people.

Final Commentaries and Summary

Although postmodernism has introduced a healthy criticism of determinism, functionalism, structuralism and other theories that promote the rational subject of self-regulation, equilibrium and stability, it does not escape from a certain ideological bias – for example, a pathological consumerism as the centre of sociality in advanced social formations, and a conceptual and methodological individualism. Therefore, it would be worth establishing a sort of counter-approach in line with Clegg's (see note 4) opinion that organizational analysis needs both modernism and postmodernism as well as modernity and postmodernity.

If the advanced world is currently living the sharpening of modernity and is being pricked by the charms and horrors that postmodernity seems to promise, the backward world is trying to leave behind the marks of archaism and pre-modernity to enter into the modern age. Mexico, too, is a mosaic of archaism, pre-modernity, semi-modernity, islands of modernity and some isolated postmodern foreign industrial plants. Such conditions, together with proximity to a country that is a paradigm of modernity and of entry into postmodernity, attracts and subordinates, both economically and politically, the Mexican nation. As a consequence of crisis and accommodation to the imperatives of its big neighbour, Mexico has lived almost 15 years of neo-liberal economic and social policy. One result has been Pronasol, a sadistic mixture of international pathology and the sickness of the previous two Mexican government administrations, together with the pathology of the present one. Pronasol has been an alchemy of arrogant actions of postmodernism brought to bear on a pre-semi-modern country.

Mexico was unable to cure endemic poverty in spite of substantial economic growth rates between 1934 and 1970, a period extended to 1981, though with evident symptoms of crisis. The explanation of impoverishment resides mostly in the rationale built into the regime of accumulation by import substitution, as well as in the bureaucratic-corporate mode of regulation in force up to the early 1980s. The irrationality coming out of the accumulation process contributed to curbing the strengthening of the capital and intermediate goods sectors, coupled with the animal spirits of business people who prevented income distribution more in line with the generation of effective demand. On the side of the mode of regulation, the rationality of corporate bureaucracy that led to the building and maintenance of political monopoly through the subordination of the labour movement impinged upon inequality and social stratification.

As regards the organizations of workers and capitalists, part of the explanation for the continuation of poverty in Mexico stems from the relative difficulty of the working class to build up effective organizations, and this seems to be a sickness of capitalism, as Clegg, Boreham and Dow (1986) have found in other countries. In Mexico the corporate-bureaucratic mode of regulation firmly incorporated trade unions into the aims of the governmental. Even though the state developed a corporate relationship with capitalists, big business and their representative organizations were able to influence the orientation of economic and social policy, and obtain substantial subsidies, protection against foreign competition and low taxes, in exchange for their abstention from direct politics. With the beginning of the political crisis in 1968 and the projected fiscal, educational and social protection reforms in the early 1970s, private enterprise began an increasingly intense struggle with government. It was this struggle, together with USA's interests in Mexico and the international configuration of affairs, that planted the seed that later gave birth to the neo-liberal era in the early 1980s.

The long crisis of the 1980s increased not only absolute but also relative poverty. Pronasol was a neo-liberal response to the enormous increase in poverty, but the programme was overshadowed by austerity economic policy. If in 1988 the incidence of poverty was estimated at about 59 per cent of the total population (most probably underestimated), the 1990 Census demonstrated that the incidence had risen to 77.9 per cent, measured by the lines of poverty method (see Table 4.2).

Pronasol was a bold anti-poverty programme built up by President Salinas both to legitimize his dubious triumph in the 1988 elections, as well as to consolidate the neo-liberal economic project. This was an accumulation regime whose engine was thought to be manufacturing exports. Salinas's government sought the building of an open, competitive economy regulated mainly by the marketplace, and the application of orthodox fiscal and monetary policies and a social policy focused on compensating people excluded from the market. On the political side, Pronasol tried to establish a new hegemonic relationship with the poor through the building of consensus rather than compulsion.

Pronasol was an institutional form of a transitory nature, in view of the contradictory modes of rationality that developed in terms of the explicit and hidden missions of the programme. The seduction campaign mounted by the presidency was not able, in the end, to persuade citizens that the programme's main mission was to combat poverty. Both the pathetically small budget (0.63 per cent of the GDP from 1989 to 1993) and its improper regional distribution, together with an economic policy that produced more poverty than that eradicated by Pronasol, finally revealed the fragility of this institutional form.

One interesting feature was the building of a micro-social and micro-regional core as the organizational cell for operating the anti-poverty programme. This core was designed to incorporate community traditions, and to operate in a democratic manner. However, once the programme had absorbed the opposition community leadership, bit by bit, the distribution of funds to states, regions and municipalities became centralized under the direct supervision of the president. Thus, the programme strayed from combating extreme poverty, and applied criteria designed to generate political loyalty and prestige for the president.

To ensure projects are effectively operated at the micro-social and micro-regional levels, a new type of community agency was built. The SC was the agency, formally constituted through a 'subcontract' type of relationship, that both formally and informally combined with cultural traditions and a community's modes of rationality with the aims of Pronasol. The SC was given some 'empowerment' to deal with the local project, and gave community members a sense of participation. The Pronasol Delegates were the other agency at the micro-social and regional level that applied some of the social management attributes mentioned by Klicksberg (1993) and Mandell (1993) that made them effective. Top and middle officers at the Pronasol were also an effective agency, loyal to and motivated by the symbolism of continuation of the Mexican neo-liberal project and of the bureaucrats in their posts.

It could be said that the programme reached a good level in the articulation of its real missions (the political ones), goals, strategies and main functions. The triumph of the president's candidates in the 1991 elections to Congress testify to the effectiveness of the articulation of the above-mentioned dimensions. The growing legitimacy and prestige of the president also show the functioning of the programme. However, the main declared mission, that is the combat of extreme poverty, was not accomplished. With the aggravation of political crisis in 1994, the real situation of the poor was unveiled, and the programme started losing its lustre.

Pronasol was the vehicle by which Salinas sought to de-differentiate the traditional bureaucratic apparatus by creating a new organization: a macro-core tied to neo-liberal alignments, a meso-technocracy well fitted to contact with a micro-core whose traditions and leaderships were incorporated. This organization had reduced the number of tiers of authority, and relied on agencies whose organizational arena was functionally designed. The presidency utilized a postmodern seduction machine to sell the programme. However, a political event – the Zapatista rebellion – introduced a point of inflection that catalysed the decomposition of the Mexican political system and demonstrated the overwhelming presence of poverty.

Notes

1. Stewart Clegg (1990: 10) remarks that the postmodernity emphasis on consumption diversification has as a counterpart the de-differentiation of production.

2. Bauman touches on the poverty problem coming as a residual of post-modernity: 'under modernism, power could be relatively violent, relatively brutal, relatively frank, relatively exposed, but the necessity for these forms of intervention on the world have now receded to the margins of everyday life, aimed now primarily at the dispossessed, the non-citizens, the non-subjects of postmodernity' (quoted by Clegg, 1990: 3).

3. The author's view is that 'on the one hand, we need the critical edge of the theorists of postmodernity, that is the ability, the facility, to be able to de-construct all grounding claims of the various forms of modernist theory produced. At the same time, I think we have to be alert to the way in which an increasing knowledge of global differences allows us to be able to point to the existence of what might well be discontinuous phenomena in terms of what we now recognize as the project focused on modern forms of organizing' (Clegg, 1990: 15).

4. 'Modes of rationality, as an analytical construct fabricated out of the available resources, fixed in and through circuits of power and institutional knowledge, which agencies find at hand, can be researched in many ways. It may be done through a well-constructed questionnaire, a documentary analysis, an organizational biography of elites and others in the picture, through the secondary analysis of the data of others, through discourse analysis of multiple accounts of organization realities and so on' (Clegg, 1990: 13).

5. The IF (or structural form) is defined as 'the social codification of one or several fundamental social relations which characterize the dominant production mode' (Boyer, 1986: 87). The concept of social codification admits both the

incorporation of a set of rules of social conduct and the assimilation of symbols that guide social behaviour. According to Luis Montano (1989), institutions have an integrating function for individuals and groups, even though such integration amply escapes to the sphere of conscience, remaining in an unconscious horizontal collective body. The institutional connection with reality is effected through symbolic mediations (according to Lacan), if the institution is to exist. Institutional forms follow an institutionalizational logic that emanates from social relations themselves, according to Théret (1988: 30), that is it is a logic internal to any social relation and not only is specific to the state, even though the latter is the one that gives cohesiveness to the set of IFs. In other words, capitalism has created its own economic and political institutions outside the state. For a detailed analysis of IFs, see Victor M. Soria (1989, 1991, 1994).

6. Clegg notes that 'agents are practical experimentalists confronted by a potentially far more uncertain, ambivalent, contradictory and ambiguous world than any natural scientist might anticipate finding in the laboratory. Upon this chaotic canvas they will seek to impose their own "circuits of power"' (1990: 8).

7. This mode of regulation started its incubation at the end of the 1910 Revolution and had its determinants in the structural and organizational transformations of social classes as well as in the surging of the authoritarian postrevolutionary state. The latter was sustained by a political elite at whose centre is found the president of the Republic. This elite hooked up workers by means of a political party with a monopolist scent mounted on corporate sectors, as well as the Mexican bourgeoisie represented by corporate-clientelist elites. The state applied all its political strength to the consolidation of the Mexican bourgeoisie by mean of a 'bureaucratic organization mode' that favoured capital accumulation. This mode is called 'bureaucratic' because of the authoritarian intervention of the state, exerted from above and with an incapability to recognize competitive forces coming from the world market.

8. Clegg, Boreham and Dow (1986: 260) remark, following Hyman and Fryer (1975), that trade unions are only capable of organizing workers in a 'secondary' form, given that they have been previously organized by capital or by the state in 'primary' organizations. Moreover, trade unions are confronted with the difficulty of the heterogeneity of interests on the part of their members, as a result of the double intersection of their position as non-proprietors of the means of production and being formed by civil society. The tension between democracy and bureaucracy is more profoundly immured in the organization of workers, due to the different practices of civil society that have differential effects on the diverse class positions, constituted by a different relation with the state (Clegg et al., 1986: 267).

9. In extreme cases of confrontation between unions and government, as in 1958 when the labour movement substantially increased the number of strikes, the government ordered both the police and the army to break up the main ones (those of railroad and telegraph workers), incarcerating their leaders. Also at that time, the army crushed the peasant movement and the government proceeded to jail its leaders.

10. The wage relation integrates an assembly of IFs which contributes to the cohesion of the different agencies related to the productive utilization of the labour force as well as the reproduction of the latter. The wage relation encompasses both the technical relations of production (the production process itself) as well as the labour relations regarding labour market conditions and the bargaining of working conditions and wages.

11. Currently the Zedillo administration has started auditing some of the enterprises acquired by Raúl Salinas de Gortari, the president's brother, as well as its bank deposits in Switzerland, and out of such investigations as well as from public denunciations, it seems that the privatization of commercial banks and public enterprises was full of corrupt practices. As an example, Teléfonos de

México, SA, the government's telephone monopoly, which was profitable with assets of more than 8,000 million dollars, was privatized in favour of Carlos Slim's group which got control of the company with a 400 million dollars investment. This company has doubled tariffs with the government's consent and still enjoys a monopoly position, although it is being challenged by foreign companies who are pushing to enter the Mexican communications market.

12. This was an heterodox type of pact that linked economic measures with political agreements on the part of the representatives of enterprises (who were committed to moderate their profits) and of workers (who compromised to accept wage increases according to expected inflation). Some of the main policies that accompanied the pact were to let the rate of exchange be overvalued and the rate of interest to be positive to put a brake to capital flight outside the country. For a detailed account of such a pact, see Victor M. Soria (1994).

13. Luis M. Bascones notes that 'since the beginning social policy is subordinated to an economic policy that consolidates and deepens inequality and exclusion for the majority. Social policy has a limited or even a nil redistributive purpose, but an ampler goal of "democratic" regulation of poverty that tries to build up consent and to motivate the active and even ardent adhesion on the part of the marginal' (1995: 23).

14. The battle against poverty has been based on three programmes: (i) solidarity for social welfare, focused on health, education, housing, basic services and land property legalization improvement; (ii) solidarity for regional development, centred on the construction of infrastructure and special development programmes in specific regions; and (iii) solidarity for the production on a project basis to create the conditions to develop capacities and productive resources for the communities.

15. INEGI points out that 'from 1984 to 1989 it was observed [that there was] an important increase of extreme poverty in Mexico, both at the national level and between rural and urban areas. However, between 1989 and 1992 the trend was reversed and it is observed [that there was] a decline of the population in this situation' (1993: 89).

16. Goicoechea (1994) has shown the lack of consistency in the distribution of Pronasol's expenditures according to the degree of marginality of regions. Thus, from 1989 to 1992 the per capita expenditure was about 500 pesos (1980=100) for middle poverty regions, nearly 520 for high poverty regions, 450 for very high poverty regions, 340 for low poverty regions, and 120 for very low poverty regions.

17. 'Financiarization' stands for a concept developed by French economists in order to identify a process of autonomization of the financial sphere which absorbs resources that should go to productive investment, by paying higher rates of interest than the rate of profits (Salama, 1989; Salama and Valier, 1992).

18. Due to the electoral objectives and the aim of Pronasol to acquire legitimacy during the Salinist administration, it has been qualified as an intent to install a new neo-corporate structure, and it includes the most miserable people from the countryside and from the city. The attempt was to have minimum and passive consensus so it could generate a hegemony to facilitate transition to capitalist modernization (Piñeyro, 1992: 70).

19. CSG put forth an intense and permanent publicity campaign that bombarded all mass media components day and night, the subject being the greatness of the Pronasol. CSG had several interviews with foreign journalists, interviews with politicians, international financial organization representatives and foreign business people. He also used public relation agencies that took care of his image abroad and his lobbying at Washington.

20. In the beginning Solidaridad co-opted a lot of opposition left ex-militants who, in the rising structural crisis of the Mexican social formation in the early 1970s, were making efforts to organize poor social sectors. It seems that within CSG's government some sectors connived at getting support from communitary

opposition (left) organizations and their leaders so new leaderships could substitute for traditional ones (Méndez et al., 1992: 65). Some analysts, such as Moguel (1992: 44), read this fact as a governmental way of fighting the social opposition (left) influence and autonomous leadership of urban popular sectors, using formulas and methods that these sectors use (i.e., democratic meetings and sectorial articulation by way of a National Co-ordinator, etc.).

21. The operation's 'planification' is not made from the bottom to the top as the programme postulates. Rather, it is made by the programme's techno-bureaucratic elite due to an already established budget and a regional assignation determined by the necessity to resist political opposition parties.

References

Banco Mundial (1990) *Informe sobre el desarrollo mundial, 1990: la pobreza.* Washington, DC: The World Bank.

Bascones, Luis, M. (1995) 'La exclusión participativa: el Banco Mundial y el combate a la pobreza rural', *mimeo*.

Bauman, Zygmunt (1982) *Memories of Class.* London: Routledge and Kegan Paul.

Boltvinik, Julio (1994) *Pobreza y estratificación social en México.* Mexico: UNAM–COLMEX–INEGI.

Boyer, Robert (1986) *La théorie de la régulation: une analyse critique.* Paris: La Decouverte.

Bromley, Simon (1991) 'The politics of postmodernism', *Capital & Class*, 45: 129–50.

Callinicos, Alex (1989) *Against Postmodernism. A Marxist Critique.* New York: St Martin's Press.

Cleaver, Harry (1992) 'La subversión del patrón de dinero en la crisis actual', *Taller sobre dinero global y Estado nacional.* Mexico: FLASCO, 15–17 July.

Clegg, Stewart R. (1990) *Modern Organizations. Organization Studies in the Postmodern World.* London: Sage.

Clegg, Stewart and Rouleau, Linda (1992) 'Postmodernism and postmodernity in organization analysis', *Journal of Organizational Change Management*, 5 (1): 8–25.

Clegg, Stewart R., Boreham, P. and Dow, G. (1986) *Class, Politics and the Economy.* London: Routledge and Kegan Paul.

Consejo Consultivo del Pronasol (1987) *El Combate a la Pobreza.* Mexico: El National.

Consejo Consultivo del Pronasol (1994) *El programa nacional de solidaridad. Una visión de la modernización de México.* Mexico: FCE.

Davis, M. (1985) 'Reaganomics magical mystery tour', *New Left Review*, 149.

Dresser, Denise (1994) 'Pronasol y política: combate a la pobreza como fórmula de gobernabilidad', in Felix Velez (ed.), *La pobreza en México. Causas y políticas combatirla. Lecturas 78 El Trimestre Económico.* Mexico: ITAM-FCE. pp. 262–99.

Goicoechea, Julio (1994) 'Desarrollo regional y pobreza en México', *mimeo*.

Harvey, David (1991) 'Flexibility: threat or opportunity?', *Socialist Review*, 21 (1) (January–March): 65–77.

Hernández-Laos Enrique (1992) *Crecimiento económico y pobreza en México*, Mexico: UNAM.

Hyman, R. and Fryer, R. (1975) 'Trade unions: sociology and political economy', in J.B. Mckinlay (ed.), *Processing People: Cases in Organizational Behaviour.* London: Holt, Rinehart and Winston. pp. 150–213.

Ibarra, Eduardo (1995) 'Strategic analysis of organizations: a model from the complexity paradigm', *Human Systems Management*, 14: 51–70.

INEGI (1993) *Magnitud y evolución de la pobreza en México 1984–1994. Informe Metodológico*. Mexico: ONU-CEPAL/INEGI.

Jensen, M.C. and Meckling, W.H. (1976) 'Theory of the firm: managerial behavior, agency and ownership structure', *Journal of Financial Economics*, 3 (4).

Kliksberg, Bernardo (1993) 'Gerencia social: dilemas gerenciales y experiencias innovativas', in B. Kliksberg (ed.), *Pobreza: un tema impostergable*. Mexico: CLAD-PNUD/FCE.

Laclau, E. and Mouffe, C. (1985) *Hegemony and Socialist Strategy*. London: Verso.

Lautier, Bruno (1993) 'Les malhereux sont les puissantes de la terre'. Paper presented at the conference L'Etat et le marché en Amérique Latine, Chantilly, France, 9–10 December.

Lyotard, Jean-François (1979) *La condition post-moderne*. Paris: Editiones Minuit.

Mandell, Myrna (1993) 'Gerencia intergubernamental: una perspectiva revisada', in Bernardo Kliksberg (ed.), *Pobreza: un tema impostergable*. Mexico: CLAD-PNUD/FCE.

Marques, Jaime and Prévôt, Marie-France (1994) 'Le programme national de solidarité, où la promotion d'une citoyenneté à géométrie variable au service d'un développement libéral au Mexique', *mimeo*.

Méndez, Luis., Romero, M.A. and Bolivar, A. (1992) 'Solidaridad se institucionaliza', *El Coridiano*, 49 (July–August): 60–72.

Moguel, J. (1992) 'Cinco criticas solidarias a un programma de gobierno', *El Cotidiano*, 8 (4): 41–8.

Montano, Luis (1989) 'Institución y estrategia. A propósito del trabajo de Victor M. Soria: Formas institucionales y estrategia empresarial', Department of Organizational Studies, *mimeo*, UAM-I, Mexico.

Montano, Luis (1992) 'Modernidad, cultura y organizaciones'. A commentary to the Seminar on Postmodern Organizations', presented by S. Clegg. UAM-I, Mexico.

Pineyro, José L. (1992) 'El Pronasol: ¿nueva hegemonía política?', *El Cotidiano*, 49 (July–August): 58–9 and 67–71.

Salama, Pierre (1989) *La dollarisation*. Paris: La Decouverte.

Salama, Pierre (1995) 'Pauvretés, les voies étroites d'une issue équitable en Amérique Latine', *Revue Tiers Monde*, XXXVI (142): 341–63.

Salama, Pierre and Valier, Jacques (1992) 'Politiques libérales et fin des processus hyperinflationistes en Amérique Latine', *Problèmes d'Amérique Latine*, 5.

Salama, Pierre and Valier, Jacques (1994) *Pauvretés et inégalités dans le tiers monde*. Paris: La Decouverte.

Secretaria de Programación y Presupuesto, Public Federal Financial Account, 1988 to 1992, Mexico.

SEDESOL (1993) The National Solidarity Programme, General Direction for Planning, Secretaría de Desarrollo Social, Mexico.

Soria, Victor M. (1989) 'La regulación, las relaciones sociales de producción y la empresas. Un análisis de la estrategia de relaciones industriales y los regímenes disciplinarios de fábrica', in *Estrategia, desarrollo y política económica*. Depto Economíam Mexico: UAM-I.

Soria, Victor M. (1991) 'La teoría de la regulación, las relaciones sociales y la organización', in E. Ibarra and L. Montano (eds), *El orden organizational. Poder, estrategia y contradicción*', Mexico: Ed. Hispánicas.

Soria, Victor M. (1992) 'Moneda, Estado y gasto social', *Taller sobre dinero y Estado nacional*. Mexico: FLASCO. 15–17 July.

Soria, Victor M. (1993) 'Desinflation, austerité et politique sociale au Mexique, 1982–1993'. Paper presented at the conference L'Etat et le marché en Amérique Latine, Chantilly, France, 9–10 December.

Soria, Victor M. (1994) 'Nouvelles politiques d'ajustement et the relégitimation de l'Etat Mexique, le rôle du Pronasol et de la privatisation des entreprises publiques', *Revue Tiers Monde*, XXXIV (135): 603–23.

Soria, Victor M. (1995) 'Regulation política, liberalización economica y la evolución de la pobreza en México'. Paper presented at the international conference Apertura económica y sociedades latinoaméricanas, National University of Colombia, 9–13 October.

Théret, Bruno (1988) 'La place de l'Etat dans les théories de la régulation'. Paper presented at the International Congress on Regulation Theory. Barcelona, 16–18 June.

Théret, Bruno (1992) *Régimes économiques de l'ordre politique*. Paris: PUF.

5   Post-Soviet Management: from State Dependency to Entrepreneurship?

Bruno Grancelli

The development of Schumpeterian entrepreneurship in Russia is by no means a smooth process. Indeed, in that country a process went on for 70 years which has been labelled *reverse entrepreneurship* (Buck et al., 1994: 1), by which is meant that inputs of high value on the international markets turned into products of lesser value. This process of value 'deduction' stemmed from the fact that the market was not controlled by the state, but was simply abolished. Thus, the reconstruction of economic institutions is not merely a matter of economic assistance or management training: this is necessary of course, but it is by no means sufficient if not accompanied by radical changes in the culture of economic agents at all levels. As has been pointed out, Soviet management training does not match up to the present needs, although post-Soviet managers are often able to revise and update their basic knowledge and techniques. This is because the need to cope somehow with the uncertainties of the command economy fostered in them an enterprising spirit which, along with a good level of education, enables the quite rapid absorption of management techniques that were unknown or under-utilized in the past (Warner, 1994).

The post-Soviet problem, though, is not that of learning new techniques: it is that of applying them in an environment in which two huge problems are closely interwoven: (i) largely corrupt institutional elites in an extremely turbulent environment; and (ii) widespread collusion among the managers and the work force to prevent privatization from being followed by radical restructuring.

It is clear that these problems are evidence of a basic difficulty: the lack of an institutional framework that is able to guarantee the efficient working of market processes (Boisot, 1994). The absence of a rational-legal model of bureaucracy is not a liability for Russia alone, although it is here that its consequences are more dramatic. Thus research on the current transformation of industrial governance in that country should try to clarify which liabilities stem from the institutional legacy of state socialism and which can be traced back to enduring cultural dispositions. This is not an easy task. Nevertheless, it can be attempted by conducting comparative analysis of specific aspects of management, involving a certain number of post-socialist countries in order to check the relative weight of the Soviet model and of cultural dispositions moulded in the pre-socialist history of labour and industrialization (Child and Markoczy, 1994).

This chapter is a preliminary step in that direction. The first two sections focus on the big firms which used to be 'high priority' for their strategic importance, the aim being to highlight some aspects of organizational change, entrepreneurial formation and creation of inter-organizational links. The last section discusses management training and practice in relation to the growing importance of business groups, the leading force in a transition process marked by the concomitant failure of market and hierarchy.

Russian Business Groups: Some Adjustment Processes

The process of privatization in post-Soviet Russia proceeded quite smoothly, contrary to many expectations. Thus the crucial issue is not privatization *per se*, but what lies ahead: is marketization coming about? In other words, is marketization emerging along with industrial restructuring? Will enterprise management be based on criteria of efficiency and productivity? Here I shall present some data on the problems and prospects of industrial restructuring in post-Soviet Russia, while also briefly discussing the role of top management therein.

Case studies carried out in various post-socialist countries of Eastern Europe point to the existence of three main groups of enterprises. The first includes firms bound to disappear unless massive help from the state is forthcoming. A typical example is an industrial conglomerate stemming from a largely spontaneous privatization process. In this case we have a holding which resembles an empty shell because it remains formally accountable for assets and liabilities while all its activities have been transferred to new-born firms. If the holding disappears, the possibility exists that at least some of the firms in the group will survive in the new economic environment. This kind of firm accounts for 15–20 of the total (Brada et al., 1994).

The largest group, however, is made up of 'shifting enterprises' (Brada et al., 1994: 96). These are technically bankrupt but are not about to disappear, at least not in the short run. This is due not so much to help by the state as to the fact that the overwhelming majority of post-socialist firms share the same conditions. Indeed, a wave of liquidations would bring about a social and economic earthquake, hence the management can adopt a wait-and-see attitude regarding a government policy which, almost certainly, will result in some kind of compromise between industrial clearance and decline. The structural change will be different in each country, but the common view is that at least one-third of the 'shifting' enterprises will be unable to survive in the long run. The fate of those that remain will depend both on the trends in their branch and on development processes at the regional level.

Structural changes also relate to the evolution of a third group of firms, that is those with a promising future which provides room for strategic planning. This group includes private enterprises possibly born out of subcontracting with firms belonging to the two previous groups or with a big monopolistic firm.

It is precisely on the 'shifting' enterprises, on their grouping and their strategies, that one should focus attention, since this is the typical context in which the organizational elites of the previous regime are going to become factory owners. The interesting question is to see how many of them are turning into entrepreneurs.

The bulk of 'shifting' enterprises is located in what used to be 'Sector A', that is the military-industrial complex (MIC) to which the majority of Soviet enterprises were linked in one way or another. The following considerations are based on data gathered by Russian scholars in 740 defence-sector enterprises, and in 25 companies with 3,000 to 10,000 employees in shipyards and electronics (Kuznetzov, 1994). The first finding of these investigations is that the firms must shift as they can, and they do so by grouping. Everywhere in post-Soviet Russia the perception that industry was on the verge of disintegration led industrial management to seek inter-organizational integration at the branch or regional level. This process is in progress to a greater or lesser extent in all Eastern European countries; the peculiarity of the Russian case, though, is that the MIC was, and still is, extremely important and will consequently influence the entire restructuring of the economy. But a caveat is in order here. Understanding the processes of industrial restructuring requires a reassesment of two widely held views. The first concerns the technological and organizational separation between MIC and the rest of the economy; the second concerns the alleged conservatism of managerial culture within these once privileged enterprises.

Indeed, if one bears in mind the results of informal innovation in the Soviet economy, one can find, for instance, that the organizational autarchy caused by uncertainty on the supply side led to the creation, by the big complexes of the MIC, of *internal* subcontracting systems which provided a wide range of goods and services to the *company towns* inhabited by their employees (Grancelli, 1988). Thus many enterprises formally included in the MIC were not technologically integrated into the MIC, but many others were, such as micro-electronics, a branch in which civilian production was completely subordinate to military production. But the main point is that, independent or otherwise from the MIC, each Soviet enterprise had to be able to shift quickly to military production should the necessity arise. Consequently, almost all enterprises in the civilian sector were conditioned to a greater or lesser degree (in their production, lay out, etc.) by the needs of the military (Kuznetzov, 1994: 474).

Nowadays, the main problem of economic transformation lies precisely in this idiosyncratic structure of the big industrial plants bequeathed by the Soviet company autarchy which was in turn an unintended result of a system in which horizontal relations were ruled out, at least officially because they were to be managed by industrial ministeries (Boisot and Child, 1988). Hence, the current difficulties encountered by conversion processes in the MIC can be traced back to three lines of segmentation of the command economy. The first relates to a pattern of labour management in an industrial system which, behind the official rhetoric on the worker's 'sense of being the boss', was quite similar to that in force half a century ago at the General Gypsum Company, as described by Alvin Gouldner in his *Pattern of Industrial Bureaucracy* (Beissinger, 1988; Boisot and Child, 1988; Grancelli, 1988). The consequence is a great deal of rigidity in the labour market which will be overcome very slowly as far as the majority of 'state dependent workers' are concerned (Zaslavsky, 1995; van Zon, 1996; Suesser, 1998).

The other two legacies of the ministerial structure of industry are the following. First, an informational asymmetry whereby firms once belonging to the same ministry can obtain better information on each other's competitiveness and comparative advantages. This in turn, implies differences in the research costs for new suppliers and entry costs in a new market. Secondly, given that self-sufficiency was being pursued by the ministries too by means of the creation of multi-functional products, today many firms experience high substitution and adaptation costs (Kuznetzov, 1994: 481; Brada, 1998; Gicquiau, 1998).

It is within these institutional rigidities that (starting in 1992) some adjustment mechanisms began to materialize. According to Kuznetzov they can be depicted as 'sustainable' (or real) or 'fragile'. This means that in the first case the adjustment can be based on some real structural and subjective advantages while, in the second case, the term 'fragile' implies that the adjustment depends almost only on the enterprising spirit of some top managers. Of course, the enterprising spirit may also find expression in rent-seeking activities as was common under the old regime. The differences between rent-seeking, and the two types of adjustment mentioned above are summarized in Table 5.1.

Among the strategies of 'real' adjustment, the one that warrants closest scrutiny is the pursuit of investment capital through the creation of close links with the only branch which continues to enjoy high export revenues: oil and gas. This strategy, although now not so widespread, is of special interest because it points up a couple of important trends. The first is the development of an informal financial market in which the grant of credit is linked not so much to objective budgetary controls as to the existence of an attitude of trust in managers able to get things done. The second trend is the building of long-term relations among vertically (and sometimes horizontally) integrated business groups (Kuznetzov, 1994: 482–4).

The research issue thus becomes that of verifying the subjective factors which may shift the process towards rent-seeking on the one hand or entrepreneurship on the other. That is, one has to investigate the likelihood that enterprise managers, who were 'virtual owners' and are now about to turn into 'actual' owners, will show a propensity for innovation and risk-taking.

TABLE 5.1   *Rent-seeking activities and adjustment processes in big post-Soviet firms*

Type of adjustment	Sustainable adjustment	Fragile adjustment	Entrepreneurial rent-seeking
General strategy	Diversification according to market demand, including export.	Diversification related to the possibility to keep production going without further investments and with scant attention to the market.	Pursuit of earnings mainly from the sale of firm properties and financial speculation.
Acquisition of capital	Sources in order of importance: 1 Government credits and subsidies. 2 More or less sophisticated forms of rent-seeking. 3 Foreign investments. 4 Credits granted on the basis of trust in the entrepreneurial qualities of managers. 5 Credits from commercial banks.	Sources in order of importance: 1 Government credits and subsidies. 2 More or less sophisticated forms of rent-seeking 3 Credits from commercial banks.	Predominance of credits from commercial banks which are being used almost only for salaries.
Export strategies	Gradual shift from occasional subcontracting agreements to long-term agreements. Subcontracting is not seen as just a source of revenue, but as a means to gain reputation on foreign markets and negotiating capabilities as a basis for exporting directly later on.	Subcontracting is seen only as a source of revenue. Exploitation of the very low value of the rouble.	Export inertia: the only contracts honoured are those signed before 1992.
R&D and new technologies	Start with low investment technologies, and subsequent investments in high-cost technologies to achieve a comparative advantage.	Static situations at low technological levels or even at high level, but less and less sustainable because the R&D function is inadequate.	Acquisition of all those technologies which can facilitate speculative activities.
Organizational development	Relatively rapid adjustment because of the presence of a great organizer and decision-maker (a 'charismatic manager').	Very slow adjustment also because of the tendency to disaggregate firms into independent units.	Quick learning of the best ways to take advantage of the persistent high rates of inflation.

Source: Kuznetzov (1994: 485–7).

If the starting point is 'reverse entrepreneurship', the implication is that attitudes, behaviours and transactions of economic agents used to be oriented by a logic of rent-seeking which expressed itself, for instance, in the semi-free supply of goods and services to the higher ranks of the *nomenklatura* on the part of enterprise directors as a sign of gratitude for their appointment. Rent-seeking also used to materialize in the guise of political-administrative protection to people involved in informal/illegal economic activities by 'cadre patrons' (Jowitt, 1983; Mars and Altman, 1983; Grancelli, 1988, 1992; Eberwein and Tholen, 1997). Thus, it is no coincidence that the cultural heritage of the command economy is labelled as 'entrepreneurial rent-seeking' (Kuznetzov, 1994: 474) – that is something which appears to be a well-tested ability to obtain credit and subsidies in order to keep more or less intact the previous enterprise welfare and, at the same time, substantially increase the salaries of top management. What is worth noting here is that a vicious circle will be created: in order to avoid conflicts, enterprise directors do not tackle the problems of redundancy, and sometimes favour worker mobilization to avoid cuts in subsidies, but this policy brings about an abandonment *en masse* of skilled workers and staff personnel in search of more rewarding jobs. The final result, at the macro-level, is a sort of alliance against restructuring between two state-dependent groups: low-skilled workers and ultra-paid managers who are often incompetent (Kuznetzov, 1994; Zaslavsky, 1995).

The investigations by Russian scholars, however, point to a reduction in the number of such cases. Kuznetzov (1994: 487) estimates that the quota of firms in the MIC engaged in these forms of survival strategies fell, between 1992 and 1994, from 35 per cent to 10 per cent. By contrast, the quota of firms trying to restructure rose, in the same period, from 25 per cent to 50 per cent. The reason was that government subsidies for the conversion of the MIC, which were 0.78 per cent of GNP in 1993, were less than half in 1994. Rent-seeking, then, is not going to disappear: it just will acquire more sophisticated forms.

A typical example of 'primitive' rent-seeking (along with the engineering of workers' protest) is the buying of goods at administered prices followed by the sale of the same goods at market prices. Nowadays, however, rent-seeking acquires more sophisticated features, such as the mobilization of personal networks to obtain credits from financial institutions to be converted later into high-interest loans to a third party, or finding a foreign party just to obtain high salaries for local managers or to safeguard a monopoly position. All this is evidence of a trend in which old *nomenklatura* privileges are being replaced by the monetary rent stemming from the control of one or more enterprises (Kuznetzov, 1994: 489).

Worth noting is that the sale of vouchers to employees has promoted rent-seeking in so far as the government saw it as the only rapid way to achieve a 'critical mass' of privatized firms. This set in motion a management and employees buyout as the only option in a context where the value of assets was usually low because of obsolescent machinery and 'social security passivity'. The dilemma was reaching the 'critical mass' while avoiding the eruption of social conflicts. Unfortunately, this kind of privatization is bound to recreate, in part at least, the precondition for a large amount of continuities in management practices.

That old wine is being poured into new bottles becomes clear when we see how widespread are strategies centred on short-term profitability and excessive productive diversification, or when we see how widespread organizational environments still are in which redundancy is not dealt with, and salaries bear no relation to productivity (Buck et al., 1994).

Another issue to bear in mind is the widespread propensity of employees to sell their shares, also in connection with the lifting of legal restrictions on this practice. This may actually represent a favourable precondition for significant changes in enterprise management through the formation of a group of core investors, as is already happening in a few cases (Buck et al., 1994; Kharkhordin, 1994; Brada et al., 1994).

The point, therefore, is that continuities and changes in post-Soviet management are to be addressed using an approach which focuses on both the vertical relations between management and labour and horizontal relations among firms within the new market structures and the largely old institutional practices. At the first level, an element of continuity is apparent in the strong pressure exerted by the *kollektiv* for the maintenance of company welfare and the purchasing power of salaries. By contrast, the setting up of new relationships among firms appears to be a significant aspect of change, although its full potential is far from having been realized up to now. The fact of the matter is that horizontal relations tend too often to be managed within a logic of reciprocity not dissimilar from its predecessor so that the informal/illegal deals are still widespread, although for different reasons. In other words, the informal/illegal dealings of today are no longer the by-product of uncertainty on the supply side brought about by central planning; they arise out of the need to avoid a chain of wind-ups.

As for the relations with the new market structures, such as stock exchanges or investment banks, the dominant attitude seems to be that of reducing them to a minimum. This is usually explained by the scant level of reliability of these structures which are also deemed as inadequate to the needs of these big companies.

To sum up, the situation which emerges from the available evidence is a tangle of market and hierarchy failures in which the incentives to restructuring are 'fragile' indeed. What makes the difference at the company level is the presence of a 'charismatic director' who identifies with the firm because such a person is confident that he or she is going to be the owner (Kuznetzov, 1994: 484). This possibility has appeared quite seldom so far, but it deserves further investigation. Here I shall make some preliminary remarks on this subject.

First of all, we should bear in mind an important fact: the institutional process of privatization took off in 1992, but a *crypto-privatization* process had already began to materialize in the early 1970s which brought about a second unofficial economy (Grossman, 1979; Jowitt, 1983; Mars and Altman, 1983; Rupp, 1983; Alessandrini and Dallago, 1987; Grancelli, 1988, 1992). The important conclusion drawn, then, is that privatization laws provided a socially acceptable framework for the legalization of transactions and of the results of previous spontaneous privatization (Kharkhordin, 1994: 417). In other words, the spontaneous process known as crypto-privatization used to be regulated, official norms notwithstanding, by the unwritten laws of an 'administrative market' of sorts in which transactions concerned not so much property rights as the assignment of management posts and opportunities to infringe official rules. What emerges here is that spontaneous privatization has granted directors *de facto* control of their enterprises. Well then, if this is how matters stand, one may ask why not legalize the possession and exchange of existing 'administrative rights' in order to facilitate the quick and peaceful privatization of the economy (Naishul, 1992).

The question, unfortunately, is not that simple, and precisely because one of the main legacies of the 'administrative economy' is that it is not enterprise directors alone who are turning into owners: state officials are also largely involved in the deal (Winiecki, 1990; Kuznetzov,1994; Grancelli, 1995b). This means that a variant of Weberian bureaucracy that is able to arbitrate and supervise the exchange of 'administrative rights' is not in place; and this brings us to the second issue. One of the troubles of post-Soviet Russia is the development of an *unlearning* process within state administration. If the best officials continue to flee away from government structures, and the inflow of new well-trained ones is limited, the capacity of the administration to operate in a market environment becomes more and more inadequate. Hence a vicious circle arises: a plethoric and segmented administration is completely unable to perform sophisticated forms of co-ordination and, in turn, this incapacity fosters the expansion of structures which are supposed to perform those functions but are incapable of doing so (Kuznetzov, 1994: 502–3). Furthermore, this inability to supervise and co-ordinate the economy is not just a matter of insufficient training of the administrative personnel: the trouble is that, more often than not, the state administration (as happens in developing countries) is a 'constellation of rent-seekers' (Grancelli, 1995b).

Finally, a third failure of post-soviet hierarchy is related to the fact that governmental authority in Russia finds itself in a sort of 'adolescent stage'. This implies that, at present, government administration is too subservient to pressure groups of various kinds. But the more dramatic fact is the bitter struggles going on within the administration which impede the imple-mentation of any political design whatsoever. In this institutional environ-ment, industrial policy (like any other policy) turns into an instrument for enhancing the power of various government agencies rather than an effective tool of economic regulation (Kuznetzov, 1994: 506).

The only way out today, as in previous stages of Russian history, is a radical improvement in the quality of the civil service (Bendix, 1973;

Kuznetzov, 1994; Kaminski and Kurczewska, 1995). This is a long-term solution, of course, but what should be tackled immediately at least, is, the problem of the recruitment and training of administrative personnel. In the meantime, in the no man's land between the end of the command economy and the beginning of the market economy, a process has developed in which the relations between polity and the economy are largely moulded by powerful business groups which were, under a different guise, already powerful in the past. Thus the research issue on the agenda should be the following:

- Will the organizational elites of these business groups demonstrate the capacity to turn into entrepreneurs able to show not just 'alertness' to whatever earning opportunity may appear?
- Will they be able to innovate and take risks, that is, bring about a 'creative destruction' in their economic environment?

A research hypothesis might take the *frailty* of incentives to restructuring as providing further confirmation that, as in developing economies or in the first stages of capitalist development, individuals matter more than economic institutions lacking in stability and authoritativeness. Within this framework one might expect management and entrepreneurial strategies to be influenced by personal experiences and learning abilities rather than by the basic laws of the market.

By now the basic legal premises of the market have been put in place to some extent. Accordingly, we should focus, in the first place, on the capacity of the ex-*Red Executives* to turn into Schumpeterian entrepreneurs. The research design should then be based on two main premises. The first is a shift in emphasis from the macro-level of polity to the *meso*-level of economic organizations, and within this level the focus should be on the values, attitudes and behaviour of managers and would-be entrepreneurs. The next section contains some preliminary remarks on this subject.

On the Study of Business Groups and Entrepreneurship in Post-Soviet Russia

The first issue is what kind of theoretical perspective should we adopt, given that the time has come to shift the emphasis from institutional to cultural preconditions of entrepreneurship? Should we use culturalist perspectives or should we place more emphasis on the legacy of Soviet industrial governance and its evolution?

In Russia, what seems to prevail is an interpretation of entrepreneurship in terms of cultural backwardness. The new entrepreneurs, according to Klimova and Dunaevsky (1993), are the bearers of a traditional-patriarchal culture in which the clan ethic plays an important role. Other scholars, such as Kuzminov (1992), emphasize the legacy of Soviet economic culture and the negative traits it came to acquire in the long period of co-existence between the official economy and the shadow economy (*tenevaya ekonomika*). These claims are criticized on the ground that Soviet culture cannot be labelled traditional in so far as in that system teleological rationality (the building of communism) co-existed with the instrumental rationality of technical and socio-economic development. It is true, however, that once the ideological tension faded away many features of a traditionalistic culture resurfaced because of the substantial continuity of the autocratic principle of government behind a new ideological façade. The conclusion is that the conditions of the Russian transition are not comparable to those of Western Europe in the early stages of capitalist development, nor to those of developing countries. The process of socio-economic transformation in this country is taking place in a kind of *limbo economy*, and this should be considered the main factor conditioning the study of attitudes and behaviour of Russian managers and entrepreneurs (Codagnone, 1995: 64–7).

If the problems of socio-economic transformation are conceptualized in terms of a limbo economy, perspectives are summarized by the statement: 'There isn't any market way to the building of a market society' (Codagnone, 1995: 77). Well, this reference to Polanyi's *The Great Transformation* (1974) is acceptable to a certain extent in so far as there is a general consensus that: (i) in Russia, at present, state and society interact in a context of general disarray, and (ii) the perspectives of economic modernization will be linked to the cultural heritage of the country as well as to the integration between the state and the economy. References to state intervention in the construction of a market society are to be found also in Russian literature on the management of privatized enterprises (Kharkhordin, 1994). But what is important to note here is that the emphasis is not only on the inability both of the state and the entrepreneurs to direct the transition process; also emphasized is the emergence of a strong actor at the *meso*-level the organizational elites in the industrial conglomerates. The mainstream of economic transformation lies precisely here. This is the environment that must be explored to see whether or not entrepreneurship will substitute for state-dependency in privatized enterprises.

What kind of concept can we use in the turbulent environment of the 'limbo economy', where forms of 'entrepreneurial rent-seeking' co-exist not only with 'alertness' to whatever profit opportunities but also with examples of 'creative destruction'? It seems to me that we may usefully start with the concept of the 'transformational leadership' of managers/ entrepreneurs in what used to be the high priority sector, that is, the leadership of a social group which is as powerful today as it was in the past (Kozminski, 1991). If we want to point to possible comparative references for this leadership, we may certainly indicate the fact that the legacy of Soviet socialism is not of a 'pre-industrial' or 'underdeveloped' kind. We should, however, bear in mind that the organizational reality of post-Soviet firms is, more often than not, quite similar to that of some firms in the industrial periphery of the USA just half a century ago.

A comparative investigation of the economic and social aspects of the transition process should not neglect the insights of the cultural-civilizational approach (Sztompka, 1998), anything else means that one risks mistaking aspects of the appearance of modern culture for such modernity in itself. An appearance in caricature does not form a perfect impression. It is important, then, to specify the possible ways in which elements of the culturalist perspective can be integrated with the industrial governance approach. This is the suggestion forthcoming from those studies of international management which include China, a country where the legacy of paternalism is very strong. The generalization arising from these studies is that 'system' and 'culture' are linked together, in the sense that the regime has been encouraging the reproduction of cultural predispositions which could reinforce it, such as respect for hierarchy or a particularistic conception of social relations. Conversely, values and traditions that are perceived as threatening (family or community ties, for instance) have been hampered. Something like this applies to the cultural legacy of the Soviet and pre-Soviet system (Grancelli, 1988). Thus, there seems to be sufficient grounds for the following generalization: the legacy of the Soviet system of industrial governance may provide the more direct and global explanation of current behaviour in privatized firms. This explanation should include, however, the influences stemming from the pre-Soviet processes of industrialization and modernization (Child and Markoczy, 1994; Grancelli, 1995b).

As for inter-organizational relations, the focus should be on business groups, a topic extensively addressed, especially in relation to the Japanese case. As has been pointed out in the literature on business groups, we may find answers to a series of *why* questions (Granovetter, 1994). For instance, business groups exist because of resource dependence (Pfeffer and Salancik, 1978) or because many firms try to extract 'rents' from the government or the economy through the formation of coalitions (Olson, 1982). According to Granovetter, it is becoming increasingly clear that one should also pose *how* questions, that is, questions on how the economic results may be improved or worsened by the links among firms belonging to the same conglomerate. These, indeed, are the kinds of question which allow us to go further than the mere understanding of what motivates economic actors in so far as they orient our interest towards issues such as the factors which favour the construction of conglomerates, the mobilization and use of resources through networks of relations, the structure of these networks and the scale of economic co-operation (Granovetter, 1994).

Business groups have been extensively studied, especially in the country where they have shown the highest degree of economic efficiency. The risk is that if we go no further than the why questions, a new variant of the convergence theory may be put forward, this time with Japan (instead of the USA) as the model (Granovetter, 1994: 456). However, I do not think that this applies to the Russian authors who have addressed this issue because they seem well aware that possible future outcomes are located along a continuum with the industrial monopolies of the ex-Yugoslavia at one extreme (Kharkhordin, 1994: 415). Some questions to address in the Russian case might then be the following. Will management style shift from paternalism (a *noblesse oblige* attitude towards employees) to a more individualistic stance? What is the impact of training programmes, sponsored or managed by Western institutions, or organizational behaviour? How do Russian managers react to these programmes? How fast do they learn? What do they prefer to learn? Is there turnover in managerial posts in big, privatized firms? How is it going? How widespread are the entries of core investors? What are the typical patterns? In conclusion, I shall briefly comment on the second of the issues listed above.

What Kind of Training for the Builders of 'Capitalism in One Country'?

Post-Soviet Russia has seen the mushrooming of management schools which, generally, are quite successful in the teaching of 'hard' aspects of management such as finance and marketing. The problems lie instead with 'transformational leadership', that is, with such cultural aspects of management as, for instance, negotiating and communicating skills (Kozminski, 1995).

This state of affairs points to the need for an 'artful adaptation' (Warner, 1994) of Western programmes of management training. The precondition for doing so is certainly clarification of the expectations by the actual and potential audience. Note that these are expectations of people who are right in the mainstream of economic transformation and work in an organizational environment made highly heterogeneous by the idiosyncratic structure of post-Soviet industry, a by-product of the previous ministerial organization of the production system. Thus, one may agree that the best way would be that of 'distancing as far as possible the enterprise from the residual institutions of real socialism' (Child and Markoczy, 1994: 145). This solution, however, would entail the massive creation of green-field factories along with an extensive programme of restructuring and conversion. But Western aid has been more limited than initially planned, and the consequence one can expect is that the resurfacing of a market economy will be linked mainly to the possibility of reorganizing the big firms of the former 'Sector A'.

A situation such as this calls for a comparison with the exigencies of re-industrialization and economic take-off that Russia had to face in the 1920s, when the slogan 'Socialism in one country' was coined. Indeed, one sometimes gains the impression that today a widespread feeling among the organizational elites of the industrial sector is pointing to the re-evaluation of national resources and traditions within a psychological framework which has been aptly labelled as 'Capitalism in one country' (Warner, 1994: 72).

Western management skills are, of course, still in high demand. The available evidence, though, suggests that they will be used within a markedly national form of capitalism. Indeed, a 'capitalism in one country' attitude seems to shine forth from statements like the following: 'We are interested in applying Western practice, not Western theory', or 'We are no longer so impressed by Western business as we used to be' (Warner, 1994: 73). Something not dissimilar happened in the early 1920s when 'scientific management' was to be adapted to the needs and priorities of the new Soviet regime. At that time, Russian scholars and managers would say they merely wanted to apply Tayloristic techniques after purging the logic of capitalist exploitation of labour from them (Beissinger, 1988).

The signs are that a peculiar Russian management style is going to emerge, maybe from a paradox: the greater than expected success of entrepreneurship in finance and commerce along with the failure of economic policy. These are the two processes within which to frame the incipient organizational transformation of industrial enterprises. Here the incentive to restructuring is surely 'fragile' because of the following dilemma: if credits to industry increase, the risk is hyper-inflation; if they decrease, the risk is a chain of firm insolvency. In other words, in the post-Soviet economic environment government policies may threaten firms' survival, and firms' behaviour may render the implementation of policies devoid of any effectiveness (Warner, 1994: 88). Hence, attention should be focused on the strategic behaviour of organizational elites, of those 'virtual owners' and would-be entrepreneurs.

Interestingly, this social group of ex-*nomenklatura* members is not made up of hardliners but of managers, not significantly different from their Western counterparts, who want generous credits from the governments while claiming a free hand in their 'free market' strategies (Warner, 1994: 70). The question, then, is what kind of training should be given to these managers/entrepreneurs? And also, what kind of learning is required of Western managers and consultants engaged in joint ventures and training activities?

If the psychological climate among Russian industrialists is as described above, what is apparently necessary is: (i) substantial but 'non-threatening' management training programmes, and (ii) a cultural 'sensibilization' of Western management and consultants (Child and Markoczy, 1994: 145). It seems to me that a 'non-threatening' training programme might include a comparative explanation of the relationships between institutions, financial/industrial conglomerates and economic efficiency. Such a programme should help the audience to think of issues such as the economic, institutional and cultural contingencies which make federations of firms more viable, and the nature and operating conditions of business groups in various countries with reference made to variables such as property rights, social solidarity structures, and authority relationships (Granovetter, 1994: 462–7).

As for the cultural sensibilization of foreign managers and consultants, the main issues to address are undoubtedly the knowledge both of Soviet training traditions and of the outcomes in terms of management style of socialist and pre-socialist industrialization drives. The first issue has been correctly addressed by those North American trainers who acknowledge the usefulness of Russian business games for understanding continuities and changes in industrial management as well as the difficulties encountered by many Russian managers in breaking psychologically with past priorities (Puffer, 1992; Warner, 1994). The second issue has been tackled by a French group which designed the establishment of two business schools (in Moscow and Alma-Ata) based on a study of Russian management culture. The method was similar to that elaborated by Bollinger and Hofstede (1987) for the comparison of the cultural values of middle and top managers in 72 countries. Russian culture was examined by referring to four main values: hierarchical distance, uncertainty control, individualism, and the masculine/feminine dichotomy. The results showed an autocratic culture of management in a still pre-capitalist country where wide hierarchical distance combines with a high level of communitarianism. Among the conclusions of this study, mention should be made of the alleged impossibility of resorting to management by objectives. What is lacking in Russia, according to this study, are such cultural prerequisites as a spirit of independence to sustain negotiations with superiors, the propensity to take risks, and the desire to reach an excellent level of performance (Bollinger, 1994: 46–7).

What is apparent in this investigation is the desire (not so common among foreign trainers) to understand Russian culture, along with the inadequacy of the culturalist approach to fulfil this desire. As a matter of fact, some kind of management by objectives was operating in Soviet factories, if nothing else because the main objective for all to fulfil, whatever the costs, was the production plan. The Soviet variant of management by objectives was called 'storming', and used to take place at the end of the month and the year (Grancelli, 1988). A spirit of initiative was necessary to cope somehow with uncertainties on the input side; risk was taken by directors, even if it was political and not economical; the individual desire to emerge from the masses was well developed among party activists and talented people; negotiations of various kinds used to be undertaken in the official and the shadow economy (Jowitt, 1993; Mars and Altman, 1983; Alessandrini and Dallago, 1987; Grancelli, 1988, 1995b).

To sum up, a culturalist approach may certainly be useful, but if it is being used as the sole tool of analysis, it cannot help to grasp the duality of social life in Soviet Russia, where a double level of consciousness and behaviour existed and has been documented (Zaslavsky, 1981; Shlapentokh, 1989; Grancelli, 1991). The culturalist hypothesis is, then, a quite fragile basis for the 'artful adaptation' of Western management training, and the same applies to the issue of the cultural sensibility of foreign trainers, managers and consultants. What is worth noting on this matter is that many of these persons tend to underscore the persisting heuristic value of many past theories and methods in relation to environments which are different from those of Western Europe and the USA. One example may suffice to illustrate this point.

In the recent history of organization studies, scientific management and its derivatives have been snowed under with criticism. During the 1970s numerous papers were written to demonstrate the necessity of 'escaping Taylorism', but none of their authors bothered to think for a moment of pre-Tayloristic forms of work organization, in comparison to which Taylorism was certainly a progression (Bonazzi, 1989). What, then, is the usefulness of such contributions to the understanding of (post)-Soviet organization which was, and still is, largely pre-Tayloristic, and has been framed within institutional assets which derive much more from patrimonialistic bureaucracy than from the legal-rational model? Thus, one may say that the culturalist approach in itself is not enough unless it is accompanied by knowledge of the institutional and sub-institutional aspects of Soviet industrial governance. But to acquire this knowledge, and to propose some interpretation of ongoing processes of organizational transformation, we must undertake a backward journey through the history of organization studies. This will be very useful for a comparative reassessment of two almost forgotten issues, that is to say, the industrial and the bureaucratic ones (Grancelli, 1995a, 1995b).

To conclude, if management training is to have an impact on organizational behaviour in post-Soviet firms, we should certainly possess updated knowledge. But it is advisable to rethink such classical works as Alvin Gouldner's *Patterns of Industrial Bureaucracy* (1970), Michel Crozier's *Le phenomene bureaucratique* (1969) and, above all, Reinhard Bendix's *Work and Authority in Industry* (1973). This 'back to basics' would contribute more than anything else to forming a more appropriate cultural sensibility in Western scholars and consultants. It might indeed provide some comparative understanding of organizational behaviour in a country which Marquis De Coustine and Sir Winston Churchill both labelled 'an enigma shrouded in a mystery'.

References

Alessandrini, S. and Dallago, B. (1987) *The Unofficial Economy*. Aldershot: Gower.

Beissinger, M. (1988) *Scientific Management, Socialist Discipline, and Soviet Power*. Cambridge, MA: Harvard University Press.

Bendix, R. (1973) *Lavoro e autorità nell'industria*. Milan: Etas Kompass.

Boisot, M.H. (ed.) (1994) *East–West Business Collaboration. The Challenge of Governance in Post-Socialist Enterprises*. London: Routledge.

Boisot, M.H. and Child, I. (1988) 'The iron law of fiefs: bureaucratic failure and the problem of governance in the Chinese economic reform', *Administrative Science Quarterly*, 33: 507–27.

Bollinger, D. (1994) 'Les fondements d'un nouveaux système de management en Russie', *Le courier des pays de l'Est*, 392 (September): 43–7.

Bollinger, D. and Hofstede, M. (1987) *Les differences culturelles dans le management*. Paris: Editions d'organization.

Bonazzi, G. (1989) *Storia del pensiero organizzativo*. Milan: F. Angeli.
Brada, J.C. (ed.) (1998) *Corporate Governance in Transition Economies*. New York: Sharpe.
Brada, J.C., Singh, I. and Török, A. (eds) (1994) *Firms Afloat and Firms Adrift: Hungarian Industry and the Economic Transition*. New York: Sharpe.
Buck, T., Filatotchev, I. and Wright, M. (1994) 'Employee buyouts and the transformation of Russian industry', *Comparative Economic Studies*, 36 (2): 1–15.
Child, J. and Markoczy, L. (1994) 'Host country managerial behaviour in Chinese and Hungarian joint ventures: assessment and competing explanations', in M.H. Boisot (ed.), *East–West Business Collaboration. The Challenge of Governance in Post-Socialist Enterprises*. London: Routledge.
Codagnone, C. (1995) 'New entrepreneurs: continuity or change in Russian economy and society?', in B. Grancelli (ed.), *Social Change and Modernization. Lessons from Eastern Europe*. Berlin: de Gruyter.
Crozier, M. (1969) *Il fenomeno burocratico*. Milan: Etas Kompass.
Eberwein, W. and Tholen, J. (1997) *Market or Mafia: Russian Managers on the Difficult Road towards an Open Society*. Aldershot: Ashgate.
Gicquiau, H. (1998) 'L'industrie russe d'aujourd'hui', *Le courrier des pays de L'Est*, 427: 3–16.
Grancelli, B. (1988) *Soviet Management and Labor Relations*. Boston, MA: Allen & Unwin.
Grancelli, B. (1991) 'Il meccanismo sociale della perestrojka: alcune riflessioni preliminari', in G. Delli Zotti (ed.), *Attori del mutamento nell'Est Europeo*. Milan: F. Angeli.
Grancelli, B. (1992) 'Organizational innovation and entrepreneurial formation: some comparative remarks', in B. Dallago, G. Ajani and B. Grancelli (eds), *Privatization and Entrepreneurship in Post-Socialist Countries. Economy, Law and Society*. London: Macmillan.
Grancelli, B. (1995a) 'Introduction: who should learn what?', in B. Grancelli (ed.), *Social Change and Modernization. Lessons from Eastern Europe*. Berlin: de Gruyter.
Grancelli, B. (1995b) 'Organization change: toward a new east–west comparison', *Organization Studies*, 16 (1): 1–25.
Granovetter, M. (1994) 'Business groups', in N.J. Smelser and R. Swedberg (eds), *The Handbook of Economic Sociology*. Princeton, NJ: Princeton University Press.
Grossman, G. (1979) *Notes on the Illegal Private Economy and Corruption in Soviet Economy in a Time of Change*. Washington, DC: US Government Printing Office.
Jowitt, K. (1983) 'Soviet neotraditionalism: the political corruption of a Leninist regime', *Soviet Studies*, 3: 275–97.
Kaminski, A. and Kurczewska, J. (1995) 'Strategies of post-communist transformation: elites as institution-builders', in B. Grancelli (ed.), *Social Change and Modernization. Lessons from Eastern Europe*. Berlin: de Gruyter.
Kharkhordin, O. (1994) 'The corporate ethic of *samostoyatelnost* and the spirit of capitalism: reflections on market-building in post-Soviet Russia', *International Sociology*, 4: 405–30.
Klimova, S. and Dunaevsky, L. (1993) 'Novye predprinimateli i staraia kultura' ('New entrepreneurs and old culture'), *Sotsiologiceskie Issledovanya*, 5: 64–8.
Kozminski, A. (1991) 'Framework for comparative studies of management in post-socialist economies', *Studies in Comparative Communism*, 4: 413–24.
Kozminski, A. (1995) 'From "nomenklatura" to transformational leadership: the role of management in the post-communist enterprises', in B. Grancelli (ed.), *Social Change and Modernization. Lessons from Eastern Europe*. Berlin: de Gruyter.

Kuzminov, I. (1992) 'Sovetskaya ekonomicheskaya kultura: nasledie i puti modernizatsii' ('Soviet economic culture: legacies and paths of modernization'), *Voprosy Ekonomiki*, 3: 44–57.

Kuznetzov, E. (1994) 'Adjustment of Russian defence-related enterprises in 1992–94: macroeconomic implications', *Communist Economies and Economic Transformation*, 4: 473–513.

Mars, G. and Altman, Y. (1983) 'The cultural basis of Soviet Georgia second economy', *Soviet Studies*, 3: 546–60.

Naishul, V. (1992) 'Liberalism, customary rights and economic reform', *Communist Economies and Economic Transformation*, 1: 29–44.

Olson, M. (1982) *The Rise and Decline of Nations: Economic Growth, Stagflation, and Social Rigidities*. New Haven, CT: Yale University Press.

Pfeffer, G. and Salancik, G. (1978) *The External Control of Organizations: a Resource-dependence Perspective*. New York: Harper & Row.

Puffer, S. (1992) *The Russian Management Revolution*. New York: Sharpe.

Rupp, K. (1983) *Entrepreneurs in Red*. Albany, NY: SUNY Press.

Shlapentokh, V. (1989) *Public and Private Life of Soviet People*. Oxford: Oxford University Press.

Suesser, J.R. (1998) 'L'emploi industriel en Russie dans les premières années de la transition (1991–1996)', *Le courrier des pays de L'Est*, 427: 17–26.

Sztompka, P. (1998) 'The lessons of 1989 for sociological theory', in P. Sztompka (ed.), *Building Open Society and Perspectives of Sociology in East-Central Europe*. London: Sage.

van Zon, H. (1996) *The Future of Industry in Central Eastern Europe*. Aldershot: Avebury.

Warner, M. (1994) 'How Russian managers learn', *Journal of General Management*, 4: 69–88.

Winiecki, J. (1990) 'Obstacle to economic reform of socialism: a property right approach', *A.A.A. P.S.S.*, 507 (January): 65–71.

Zaslavsky, V. (1981) *Il consenso organizzato. La società sovietica negli anni di Breznev*. Bologna: Il Mulino.

Zaslavsky, V. (1995) 'Contemporary Russian society and its Soviet legacy: the problem of state-dependent workers', in B. Grancelli (ed.), *Social Change and Modernization. Lessons from Eastern Europe*. Berlin: de Gruyter.

6 Alternative Socio-technical Systems in the Asia-Pacific Region: an International Survey of Team-based Cellular Manufacturing

Paul Couchman and Richard Badham

In cell manufacturing, workers are divided into teams – usually of between two and 50 employees – grouped around the manufacturing equipment that each needs. A single cell makes, checks and even packages an entire product or component. Each worker performs several tasks, and every cell is responsible for the quality of its products. As such, cell manufacturing is the ultimate factory-floor refinement of other team-management techniques that western companies have embraced in recent years. (*The Economist*, 17 December 1994: 61)

This chapter aims to contribute to contemporary academic debates on the so-called 'new production paradigms'. Such debates most recently focus on the diffusion of Japanese management systems and practices in the West (or 'Japanization' as the phenomenon has been referred to; Wilkinson et al., 1992) and on the advantages and disadvantages that these 'new' approaches offer to employers and employees. Of particular interest has been the 'Toyota Production System' (Monden, 1994), a distinctive approach to manufacturing that has been dubbed 'lean production' by the MIT Commission on Industrial Productivity (Womack et al., 1990). Key questions addressed in many of the more critical studies have been: is the Japanese approach a further development of traditional labour rationalization strategies, or does it offer the potential for genuine worker empowerment through the creation of self-regulating, multi-skilled team work? Do Japanese management approaches represent 'ultra-Taylorism' (Dohse et al., 1985) or a new form of 'democratic Taylorism' (Adler and Cole, 1993)? Do the Japanese management practices offer 'positive tension' (Domingo, 1985) or 'management by stress' (Parker and Slaughter, 1988) in the workplace? It is increasingly acknowledged that such Japanese management practices offer a particular model of techno-organizational development, contrasted with alternative 'European' or 'socio-technical' approaches by a number of authors (e.g., Benders et al., 1995; Dankbaar, 1997; and Mathews, 1995). Some of the crucial issues facing research on new forms of work organization are the costs and benefits of these different models, and the form and degree in which they are being diffused world-wide.

In this chapter we hope to be able to shed light on some of these issues. The chapter will focus on cellular manufacturing (CM), a socio-technical system with elements common to both the 'European' and 'Japanese' models, and investigate the different forms of work organization being taken up by companies introducing this system in the Asia-Pacific region. The chapter will present preliminary findings from a recently-completed exploratory survey of the implementation of CM among manufacturing firms in the Asia-Pacific region. The Asia-Pacific survey, which complemented an earlier survey of Australian manufacturers (Syed et al., 1995), was an initial attempt to explore the human resource issues associated with the introduction of CM in the region, and the extent to which the solutions adopted were closer to the 'Japanese' or 'European' model. It must be emphasized that the findings are at present preliminary and are in the process of being analysed. An important goal of this ongoing research programme is to expand the empirical base informing debates about new production paradigms.

Competing Models of Cellular Manufacturing

> Cellular manufacturing is an application of group technology where a portion of a firm's manufacturing system has been converted to cells. A manufacturing cell is a cluster of dissimilar machines or processes located in close proximity and dedicated to the manufacture of a family of parts (a cell family). The parts are similar in their processing requirements (required operations, tolerances, machine tool capacities, etc.). (Wemmerlöv and Hyer, 1989: 1511)

The concept of CM is not new but is based on the earlier engineering concept of 'group technology' (GT) which aims to exploit product and process similarities in order to achieve smoother production flows in job-shops producing batches of parts or products. The origins of GT have been variously identified: Brödner (1988), for example, traces it to the concept of 'group production' ('*Gruppenfabrikation*') which was introduced during the early 1920s in Germany. This was an attempt to address the disintegration effects of Taylorist work rationalization, and sought re-integration through the production of whole families of parts or products by teams of workers conducting complete work sequences. By contrast, Alford (1994), among others, identifies the roots of GT in the USSR of the 1940s with the development of the 'group machining method' by Mitrafanov (Mitrafanov, 1966; Ivanov, 1968). Gallagher and Knight (1973), on the other hand, trace the origins of GT back to a set of principles adopted in the manufacture of machine tools in the USA in the 1920s. It is significant to note that the latter two origins (the two most frequently identified with GT) were concerned with improving the flows of batches of work-in-progress through multi-sequence operations, such as the machining of component parts, and were not so concerned with work organization issues.

But while there is considerable agreement about the nature of GT, the use of the term 'manufacturing cell' is more flexible and can refer to a range of organizing methods. Furthermore, the concept of CM is now, as Alford (1994) points out, commonly applied to a whole manufacturing systems approach, and is no longer used solely in relation to batch-producing machine and job-shops. This broader usage is illustrated, for example, in Peter Drucker's (1990) 'new theory of manufacturing' wherein one of the four basic concepts underlying the 'post-modern factory of 1999' is modular or cellular organization of the production process (the future factory as a 'flotilla' of modules in contrast to today's 'battleship').

A new form of divergence exists, however, between two very different approaches to CM deriving from two competing models of production efficiency. The first of these, originating in Germany and informed by Scandinavian studies of work-group autonomy, was the 'autonomous production island' (*Autonome Fertigungsinseln*). During the 1980s the idea of GT, combined with semi-autonomous work-groups and shop-floor computer support, re-emerged as a craft skill-based solution that addressed problems of changing world markets with increasing demands for custom-ized high-quality products (Badham and Schallock, 1991). The concept of 'production island' was first formally defined by Ahlmann (1980), and the new autonomous organizational structure was developed in response to three main factors (Hartmann, 1989):

1 Changes in the markets for capital goods and high end consumer products (both important market sectors for German manufacturing industry).
2 Increasing demands among the work force for improvements to the quality of working life.
3 Recognized problems with conventional Fordist/Taylorist production methods, such as high logistics and quality costs.

A more developed definition of 'autonomous islands of manufacture' was proposed by the Ausschuss für wirtschaftliche Fertigung in 1984 (AWF, 1984) and had four key features:

1 *The production of wholes* – the production island manufactured com-ponent parts or a whole product from raw material as completely as possible.
2 *The grouping of facilities* – all the necessary production facilities (tools, fixtures, machines, etc.) are located within the production island and are operated by the personnel therein.
3 *Semi-autonomous work-groups* – the work team within the production island is self-regulating and is responsible for the co-ordination, planning, production decision-making and control of work within re-defined boundaries.

4 *Multi-skilled and multi-functioned personnel* – there is no fixed division of labour among the team members.

This approach to CM contrasts markedly with the application of the concept in Japan. There the approach to production system design is exemplified by the 'Toyota Production System' (glorified in the West as 'lean production', and heralded by many commentators as *the* future for competitive manufacturing) with its philosophy of constantly reducing production costs through the progressive elimination of waste (*muda*). This waste is seen everywhere in the manufacturing operation, and includes excessive production resources (e.g., of people, facilities and inventories) and excessive work or 'over-production' (which creates the excessive inventories). There are four key principles underlying this approach. First, 'just-in-time' (JIT), rather than 'just-in-case' production – JIT is a simple principle, succinctly described by one of the earlier Western acolytes of Japanese production methods, Schonberger, as 'produce and deliver finished goods just-in-time to be sold, sub-assemblies just-in-time to be assembled into finished goods . . . and purchased materials just-in-time to be transformed into finished parts' (1982: 16).

Secondly, 'Autonomation' (*jikoda*), a necessary quality control adjunct to JIT which seeks to ensure that defective units are not shipped from one process to another, thereby disrupting the downstream process. Thirdly, a flexible (both in terms of numbers and skills) work force (*shojinka*), and finally the capacity to capture 'creative thinking or inventive ideas' from the work force (*shikufu*). The layout of machines and other production facilities to create 'U-shaped cells' is an important means used to realize this approach. In this configuration, work-stations are arranged in sequence in a U-shape. Work enters at the top of one arm, moves linearly from station to station, then exists from the other arm. The U-shaped cell is used to achieve three goals. The first of these is *shojinka*, flexibility in the number of workers in the cell so that demand changes can readily be adapted to. Working inside the 'U', operators are required to operate more than one work-station simultaneously and must learn to perform all operations through job rotation. The second goal is the progressive reduction, through the continuous improvement of work processes and machines, of the number of operators required in a work cell (an activity that is aptly termed 'process razing' by Sekine [1992]). The third is the introduction of 'one-piece flow' of work-in-progress units by replacing 'planned-centred production' with JIT demand–pull, eliminating large-batch production (based on economic order quantities) and drastically reducing machine set-up times. Through the achievement of these goals the manufacturing 'cell' becomes an important weapon in the war against waste, and it can often be a 'half-way house to automation'.

Clearly, the two competing models of CM are closely linked to the industrial culture and human resource development characteristics of Japan and Germany. Within Japan, the 'lean production' cell model is closely linked to a focus on internal labour markets and training, company-based trade unions, so-called 'life-long employment' for core groups of employees, and a tightly disciplined industrial culture. The Japanese approach has also been supported by specific institutional structures. The four most famous of these have been wages connected to individual workers (not labour grades) which increase with years of service, enterprise-based rather than craft or occupational unions, the life-time employment system which uses overtime as a buffer against demand fluctuations, and high levels of on-the-job training. Within Germany, the 'production island' model of CM is directly tied to a strategy of 'diversified quality production' (Hyman and Streeck, 1988) which entails production for higher quality and more customized product markets requiring highly qualified labour, apprenticeship training, craft or industry-based trade unions, and a 'high trust' industrial culture. The model of 'semi-autonomous group work' involved, however, is not necessarily restricted to this specific national culture, as suggested by the diffusion of self-managing team work within the USA.

In our survey, we were interested in finding out the extent to which these different approaches had informed the implementation of CM in firms within countries that had very different human resource development profiles and industrial cultures. In order to address this issue we employed a very general definition of CM as a guideline to respondents:

> Cellular manufacturing is the grouping of machines, processes and people into cells dedicated to the manufacture or assembly of a family of similar parts or *products*.

We then explored the different ways in which CM systems were introduced and how these were associated with different human resource strategies (such as changes to job design, the nature of any team work and training). We also sought details of the types of benefit that were obtained. The remainder of this chapter presents preliminary findings from the study.

Cellular Manufacturing and Work Organization

Group technology and cellular manufacturing do not necessarily require team work, but, as has been noted, they are conducive to this form of work organization and are often associated with it. However, there are many different forms of team work. Notably, the Japanese 'team concept' differs markedly from the autonomous work-group approaches that have been advocated in Europe.

> The Japanese concept of team work is . . . in danger of being misunderstood. Japanese workers typically perform jobs that have been designed according to traditional scientific management principles. Japanese workers thus employed form teams to examine how their otherwise traditionally run manufacturing

facility can be continuously improved. This is quite different from the Anglo-Scandinavian concept of autonomous group working. (Buchanan, 1994: 221)

In the critique by Dohse, Jurgens and Malsch (1985) of 'Toyotism' it is argued that the Japanese approach to work organization extends the logic of mass production by providing new ways of rationalizing and intensifying the labour process. Delbridge, Turnbull and Wilkinson (1992) are similarly critical. They contend that the Japanese practices increase the surveillance and monitoring of shop-floor employees, intensify work processes and reduce individual discretion with respect to working methods. To them, the result is 'a highly regulated and regimented labour process with many of the characteristics of bureaucratic control' (Delbridge et al., 1992: 102).

A key issue here is the degree of autonomy that is given to cell teams. But despite the fact that the first systematic studies of semi-autonomous work teams were conducted by the Tavistock Institute in the 1950s, and that further studies were initiated in Ireland, the Netherlands and Norway in the mid-1960s (with Sweden following in the late 1960s), the notion of work-group autonomy remains poorly conceptualized (Buchanan, 1994). An early attempt to systematize the concept was that of Gulowsen (1972), who specified ten criteria of autonomy and formulated a one-dimensional scale of autonomy based on these, but this appears not to have been developed further.

A later attempt at a more rigorous definition of autonomy was that of Sandberg (1982), who argued:

> An autonomous group is a way of organizing work whereby the work group has responsibility for the whole activity cycle and the right to decide on questions in connection therewith. The autonomy of the work group is a function of three interdependent factors. First, the degree to which the activity cycle is an independent whole. Second, the degree to which the work group can influence the boundary conditions of the activity cycle. Third, the degree of influence of the work group on the internal conditions of the activity cycle. A work group cannot be said to be autonomous or not autonomous, it is autonomous in certain respects and to a certain extent. (Sandberg, 1982: 5)

Using this approach, Sandberg contrasted autonomous work with Taylorist/Fordist forms of work organization and 'human relations' attempts at job redesign (i.e., job rotation, job enlargement and job enrichment) both of which are 'based on connecting individual workers and individual activities in a predetermined manner out of the workers' control' (Sandberg, 1982: 53). On the other hand, autonomous group work 'is possible when job design and job distribution are characterized by a moderate horizontal and vertical specialization which is not too rigid', and group decision-making is 'possible when job design and job distribution are not settled once and for all externally but the group can influence the necessary decisions' (ibid.: 53).

The interest in autonomous work groups seems to have diminished in the late 1970s and early 1980s, but there appears to have been a revival of interest, especially in the management literature, since the mid-1980s (e.g., Lawler, 1986; Peters, 1987; and Parnaby, 1988). The later advocates have failed to clarify the definition of team autonomy, and may even have weakened its content by restricting its meaning, for example, to degrees of freedom of choice, over work pace and methods.

Whatever interpretation of group autonomy is adopted, it is clear that the Japanese team concept embodies a somewhat different approach from that of the European models. As Professor Haruo Shimada has noted, in Japan

> the team concept is not intended to increase workers' autonomy but to help them find out the problems in the production line so that no defective goods will be produced. In the US, workers tend to take participation as having a voice in all kinds of things that in Japan are determined by management and engineers. (Cited in Hoerr, 1989: 61)

In Japanese management practice, the team concept is mainly associated with *kaizen* or continuous improvement, the constant drive to remove waste from the production process. Central to this are suggestion schemes which capture the *so-ikufu*, creative thinking or inventive ideas, from workers, either as individuals or through the team-based activities of quality circles. The use of cross-functional teams to improve operations and increase productivity is not new. In the USA, as long ago as the 1930s Mogenson's 'work simplification' process (Mogenson, 1932) utilized problem-solving teams (some members of which were drawn from the shop-floor), and the so-called 'Scanlon Plan' involved the establishment of 'productivity committees' to explore ways of improving productivity (Lesieur, 1958). The Japanese adopted this team method of production process improvement in the 1950s and have developed it to a fine art. But under the Japanese management regime, workplace discipline – imposed by the demands of JIT, *jikoda*, *shojinka*, *shoninka* and *kaizen* – is tight, and so team autonomy becomes problematic. As Janice Klein (1991) has pointed out, the process controls associated with Japanese management practices impose constraining limits on the ability of teams to exercise control over their work activities. For example, short task-cycle and highly standardized jobs leave little or no discretion for the operator to decide how work activities are to be carried out, and the tight coupling of adjacent production process via JIT demand–pull, in conjunction with an absence of buffers (which are seen as waste in the Japanese approach), leaves no room for workers to decide when to produce, or the pace at which to work.

The contrast between the two different approaches to team work, the European autonomous group work versus the Japanese team concept, can be illustrated using Adler and Cole's comparison of the Japanese car

TABLE 6.1 *Contrasting models of team work – team work organization in a Japanese–US joint venture auto company (NUMMI) versus that in a Swedish auto company (Volvo Uddevalla)*

Feature	NUMMI (USA) Toyota–GM	UDDEVALLA (Sweden) Volvo
Assembly layout	Fordist assembly line.	Parallel 'dock' assembly.
Job design	Highly standardized, but team can re-define standards subject to management approval ('democratic Taylorism').	Much less standardized, focus on balance of tasks within assembly cycle.
Work-cycle time	1 minute.	2 hours.
Process coupling	Tight: internally via machine-paced line, externally via JIT delivery.	Much looser: no paced line and buffer stocks.
Team size	4–5	10
Team leader	Selected by union representatives and management.	Teams select their own leaders and may rotate role.
Team responsibilities	Assembly, quality control, preventative maintenance, team job rotation schedules, improvement of work process.	Assembly, balance work tasks, quality control, preventative maintenance, job rotation schedules, set overtime schedules, select own members.
Training	High emphasis.	High emphasis.
Pay for skills	No.	Yes.

Source: Adler and Cole (1993).

manufacturing transplant in the USA with Volvo's Uddevalla plant in Sweden (Adler and Cole, 1993), as in the Table 6.1.

While certain common features are shared (e.g., job rotation, multi-skilling, team responsibility for quality control and a high emphasis on training) the Japanese team concept involves a much lower degree of autonomy, both in terms of internal responsibilities and external constraints on worker discretion. The key issue for us focused on whether any of these concepts had been applied along with CM in the Asia-Pacific region.

The Survey: Methods and Sample

There has been growing interest in CM since the mid-1980s, and this builds on an earlier interest in GT. Surveys of companies using GT have been conducted in the USA (e.g., Ham and Reed, 1977), the UK (e.g., Burbidge, 1979) and Japan (e.g., Honda, 1980), and there have been more recent surveys on CM in the USA (e.g., Wemmerlöv and Hyer, 1989), the UK

(Ingersoll Engineers, 1990) and Australia (Syed et al., 1995). Complementing these surveys, there have been a number of detailed case studies (e.g., Buchanan and Preston, 1992; Sewell and Wilkinson, 1992; Dawson, 1994; Procter et al., 1995). Although there has been at least one cross-national survey of CM (Magjuka and Schmenner, 1992), which covered firms in the USA, Western Europe, the Far East and other countries, until our pilot survey there had been no comparative study of the implementation of CM within the Asia-Pacific region. In setting up our survey we discovered that CM had diffused among manufacturing firms in the region, but there was an extremely broad interpretation among the firms of what constituted a manufacturing 'cell' – this clearly affects the level of standardization and, consequently, the significance of comparative results.

The survey was conducted through a network of collaborating researchers in eight APEC (Asia-Pacific Economic Cooperation) countries (i.e., Australia, Canada, Malaysia, New Zealand, the Philippines, Singapore, South Korea, and Thailand). A questionnaire was developed and this was administered by a researcher to an appropriate company manager (usually a manufacturing manager) via telephone or in a face-to-face interview. In each country, three to six firms that had introduced cells in the last five years were selected to comprise the sample. (Initially the sample selection criteria were more stringent (in an attempt to control for the effects of any confounding variables), but not all research collaborators could identify firms to meet these criteria, so we relaxed these where this was necessary. The result was a sample that was more diverse than desired, but still sufficiently focused to provide useful comparative data.) Given the nature of the sample we would emphasize that the study is an exploratory one and that its findings cannot be seen as definitive or conclusive.

The sample obtained was made up of 30 firms in eight APEC countries. In sum, the firms in the sample:

- ranged in size from 38 to 43,000 employees (median size was 653);
- exported between 0 per cent and 100 per cent of their production (median = 40 per cent);
- came from a range of industries (one-half produced cars or auto products);
- had mostly increased their annual turnover in the past five years;
- had mostly first introduced cells one or more years ago;
- were mainly moderate to high-level exporters.

The Introduction of Cellular Manufacturing

Introducing cells in the firm

The introduction of CM can involve a major transformation in the organization and management of production processes. A common method of introduction (invariably recommended by the advocates of this approach to manufacturing; e.g., Burbidge, 1979) is to establish a cross-functional team to design, plan and implement the new system. This was confirmed in the survey, where all but two firms (both in New Zealand) had established a team to design and implement the cells. Of particular interest was that in just over a half of the firms (16 out of the 30) one or more shop-floor employees were part of the design team, but in only four cases was a trade union representative a team member. There was a distinct cross-national pattern in these findings. Shop-floor representatives were more likely to be involved in Australia (3/3) and Canada (5/6), but were less likely to be involved in the Philippines (1/3), Korea (1/4) and Thailand (1/3). Trade union representatives were only members of the CM design teams in Australia (1/3), Canada (1/6), Malaysia (1/6) and New Zealand (1/1). It is very likely that this variability is a result of differences in the industrial cultures (and most notably of differences in the specific institutional frameworks of employment relations) among the countries surveyed.

Procter, Hassard and Rowlinson observed that '(t)he means by which an attempt to introduce cellular manufacturing is made . . . become as important as the ends to which it aspires' (1995: 50). In doing so, they follow Geary (1994), and draw on Fox's attempts to delineate the principles underlying relationships of trust in the workplace in the context of the discretionary content of work roles (Fox, 1974). They contend that more attention needs to be paid to the process through which new work roles are created. That is, if 'task participation' is to be successfully executed with the introduction of CM, then all affected personnel should be actively involved from the outset. Our survey data showed that there was clearly a significant variation in the degree of shop-floor participation in design teams, particularly by trade union representatives.

The perceived benefits of CM

Why should firms replace more conventional production systems with CM? CM has been widely advocated as a relatively low-cost 'best practice' solution to the problems confronting manufacturing in an increasingly competitive globalized environment. As Alford has put it, 'CM is an idea that has come of age' (1994: 3), an optimistic view supported by our survey respondents, as in other surveys. In most of the firms, the investment in resources and facilities required to set up CM was relatively modest. Interestingly, and again reflecting cross-national variations in the institutional frameworks of employment relations, investment in people-resources for CM varied across the countries, with firms in Australia, New Zealand and Thailand more likely to invest in people, compared to their counterparts in Canada, the Philippines and Korea.

Despite the modest investment in implementation, the introduction of CM significantly improved manufacturing operations (notably through reduced lead times, improved product quality, increased flexibility of labour, increased on-time delivery, lower work-in-progress inventories, and increased labour productivity). The great majority of firms (25 out of the 30) reported an increase in job satisfaction. These improvements translated into business benefits for the firm, with nearly all reporting a significant or moderate impact on competitiveness, human resource development and financial performance.

Employment and Work Organization in the Cells

While CM is widely perceived by managers as making a significant contribution to the success of the business, the implications for employees are somewhat more ambiguous and are contingent on the form of CM introduced. The two main findings we will discuss here relate to changes in employment levels and work organization in the manufacturing cells.

The effect of CM on employment levels

Does the introduction of CM have any effect on the number of different types of employees in the firm? Our survey findings clearly showed that it did. In the majority of the 30 firms surveyed, both direct and indirect production labour was reduced as a result of CM: the number of direct labour employees had been reduced in 20 of the firms, and in 16 there had been reductions in the number of indirects. One half of the firms had also reduced the number of supervisors on the shop-floor, and 13 firms had reduced the number of staff involved in production planning and control. Such reductions are due to the improved productivity of cells and to the associated reorganization of work. It is the latter that lowers the need both for indirect labour outside the cells (such as separate materials handling or progress workers) and for supervisors (functions normally performed by these staff become the responsibility of the cell members). Of all employee categories, production engineers were the most prominent exception, with only six firms indicating a reduction and nine saying there had even been an increase in the number of these employees. This clearly has implications, as discussed later, for any discussion of the extent to which production engineering tasks have really been devolved on to cell teams. None of these changes in employee numbers varied significantly by country, by industry, by firm size or by export level.

Work Organization in the Cells

In nearly all of the cases, the introduction of CM was associated with changes in work organization and job design. In 25 of the firms, operators

performed a wider range of work tasks than they did before the introduction of CM. In only four cases did the range of work tasks stay the
same and in one the range became narrower. The jobs of operators were
generally expanded horizontally to encompass more tasks (job enlargement) and vertically to take on more responsibilities (job enrichment). The
functions performed by cell operators reflected this broader task range: in a
majority of the firms the operators carried out quality inspection (26/30),
machine set-ups (20/30) and the transfer of materials to and from the cell
(16/30) in addition to their direct production duties. Furthermore, three
functions usually associated with supervisors and other indirect labour
were brought into the cells and performed by a cell leader in many of the
firms; that is production reporting (21/30), work scheduling (19/30) and the
establishment of output goals (15/30).

But did this work reorganization mean that the operators gained more
discretion over the performance of their work tasks? Our survey data
suggests, as indicated by Klein (1991), that a reduction in autonomy of
task execution may be occurring, while there is some increase in collaborative input into task design. In total, 28 of the 30 firms said that their cell
operators were required to follow detailed written task instructions (often
referred to as Operation Sheets or Standard Operating Procedures). In only
two cases were cell operators not required to do so. This is a typical feature
of the Taylorist and Japanese approaches to job design. But Taylor also
encouraged workers to suggest improvements ('the first step is for each
man to learn to obey the laws as they exist, and next, if the laws are wrong,
to have them reformed in the proper way' (Taylor, 1972: 133)), an
approach that has been adopted and further developed under Japanese
management practice. In most cases, operators had some responsibility for
improving the way that they performed their jobs (in just ten firms were
they required to 'only follow instructions'), and 17 of the firms had quality
circles where operators met regularly to discuss improvements and submit
suggestions for change. In five firms, operators were even allowed to make
their own changes to Standard Operating Procedures.

Another constraint on cell operator discretion is the existence of JIT
demand–pull scheduling of work. Under JIT, cells are often more tightly
coupled to downstream operations and only produce to meet demand
(rather than to stock 'just in case'). Just over half of the firms (17) in the
sample operated under JIT, a finding which revealed that CM is not
necessarily associated with demand-driven production, as in the Japanese
model. The adoption of JIT along with cells varied across the different
countries; that is firms in Australia (1/3), Canada (3/6), the Philippines (1/3)
and Singapore (0/2) were less likely to have adopted this form of production. It is not clear, given the nature of our sample, whether this variation
is due to national differences which limit the diffusion of Japanese
management practices or due to differences in the firms sampled. For
example, could our findings be interpreted to confirm the beliefs expressed
in the following statement?

Many senior Japanese executives appear to think that it is more challenging to transfer lean management styles to Australia than to most other countries in the Pacific region, whose cultural predispositions may be closer to those in Japan. By contrast with their neighbours in South East Asia, Australians are seen as more individualistic yet also more solidaristic with potentially militant unions. (Bamber and Shadur, 1995)

A further indicator of tightness of coupling, whether using JIT or other scheduling methods, is how long the cell operators can stop work during production time without stopping any downstream production operations (on a moving assembly line, for example, this time for any work station would be zero). This varied greatly between the firms, although 12 (not all of them operating under a JIT system) reported that their cells could not stop work: these were the most tightly coupled. The majority (18/30) could stop work, for times ranging from ten minutes to several days. The longer this length of time, the less coupled the cell is and the greater the autonomy it has in managing its activities.

CM *and teamwork*

Manufacturing cells, as noted above, do not necessarily require team work; in conventional Fordist production, cells can be run by one or more individual operators who do not work together as a team, for instance. However, in every one of the firms in the sample, the people within the cells were organized into teams. In every case these cell team members were multi-skilled in that they shared tasks and rotated their jobs. In nearly all cases (26/30) the cell team had a team leader, and the great majority of these were selected by management rather than elected by the team members. In 24 of the firms, the cell teams met regularly to discuss a wide range of work-related issues. The most frequently cited of the issues discussed were: quality (11 firms), cell performance (10), production problems (8), human resource issues (8), process improvement (8), occupational health and safety (5), and the working environment (4).

On the basis of the responses to the job and team-work questions, we were able to group the cell teams into three main groups, as shown in the Table 6.2. As discussed earlier, there are different forms of team work, and the two models we were interested in were the Japanese model (which is closer to conventional mass production work organization) and the European model of semi-autonomous work-groups. These models differ in the degree of autonomy that is given to the team. Type A cell teams (13 firms) were closer to the semi-autonomous work-group model. A sub-group of five of these were the most autonomous in that they were able to change their standard operating procedures (SOPs) themselves. Type B cell teams (12 firms) were an intermediate category with a lesser degree of autonomy, due either to tighter coupling or to a lack of regular team meetings. By contrast, Type C cell teams (five firms, the smallest group)

TABLE 6.2 *Characteristics of different types of cell teams in respondent firms*

TYPE A	TYPE B	TYPE C
Broader task range.	Broader task range.	Same or narrower task range.
Able to stop work.	Either able to stop work or meet regularly.	Less likely to be able to stop work.
Meet regularly.	—	May meet regularly.
Suggest changes to standard operating procedures or even make changes themselves.	May suggest changes.	May suggest changes.

were closest to the Japanese model: while most of these teams did meet regularly (*kaizen*), they had the same or a narrower range of work tasks and were more likely to be coupled to downstream production (JIT). None of the cell teams came very close to the autonomous work-groups model advanced in Europe. Overall, these cell teams had more in common with the Japanese team concept although some did have higher levels of autonomy.

The cell team types did seem to be related to particular industrial cultures. Type A (more autonomous) were more likely to be found in Australia, New Zealand, the Philippines and Singapore, while Type C teams were more likely to be found in Malaysia. The team types were significantly related to firm size, with Type A teams more likely to be found in smaller firms and less likely to be found in larger ones. The more autonomous teams were associated with a greater degree of labour flexibility and a higher level of job satisfaction. This latter finding appears to support the claim that the greater the autonomy of the team (i.e., the more control it has over its work environment), the more job satisfaction its members will obtain. In those firms where there were type A cell teams, CM was more likely to be seen as having a significant impact on human resource development. However, there was no significant relationship between the other business performance indicators and the team types. That is, the level of team autonomy did not seem to be related to the reported effects of CM on financial performance or competitiveness, a finding which clearly requires further investigation.

Conclusions: CM as a Tool of Control or Empowerment?

We began this chapter by identifying a key question arising from current debates over the diffusion of new forms of team-based production organization: are they approximating towards a Japanese model, developing many traditional labour rationalization strategies, or do they offer the potential for more developed forms of group autonomy and genuine worker empowerment? Our survey sought to shed some light on this hotly-debated issue by examining the implementation of CM in firms throughout the Asia-Pacific region. As a background to the survey, we contrasted different forms of CM (i.e., German 'autonomous production islands' versus Japanese 'U-shaped cells') and identified the different models of team work (European autonomous work-groups versus the Japanese team concept) associated with these forms. The two central issues arising from these contrasts relate to performance and work-group autonomy. While the European approach to CM seeks to contribute to more effective and efficient performance through autonomous work-groups, the Japanese approach achieves high levels of performance through tighter discipline and lower levels of team autonomy. More critical studies of Japanese management practices contend that they represent an extension of the logic of mass production by providing new ways of rationalizing and intensi-fying the labour process.

However, there are also many critics of semi-autonomous group work, even from among its traditional supporters. Buchanan argues, for example, that

> [t]he key questions for the future, therefore, concern how the thinly sustained credibility of the autonomous group approach and its socio-technical systems underpinning can survive the continuing lack of conceptual clarity, the demon-strable lack of rigorous and strong supporting empirical evidence, and the invidious comparisons with Japanese manufacturing methods. These questions imply an interesting research agenda which will require organizational as well as academic commitment if they are to be addressed effectively. (Buchanan, 1994: 222)

Our survey findings certainly confirmed the operational and business benefits obtained from CM – within the very varied forms in which it was introduced and with greatly different types of team work. The process advantages offered create productivity and organizational gains which our survey showed lead to reductions in labour, particularly direct and indirect shop-floor labour and supervisors. There is, however, little support for the claim that the introduction of CM has succeeded in realizing its 'radical potential' for 'the development of self-regulating, multi-skilled teamwork, for a transformation in the role of first line supervision from policeman to coach, and for a movement towards a high (employee) involvement management style' (Buchanan and Preston, 1992: 71).

In many cases, the form of team work identified in the firms in our sample appeared to be closer to the Japanese than the European model (i.e., closer to NUMMI than Uddevalla). Under this, the jobs of team members in most cases were enlarged and enriched and the cell teams were given responsibility for continuous improvement in their work activities. The job discretion of cell team members was higher, therefore, than under conventional Fordist mass production. However, this increasing discretion often appears far from the developed model of empowered and auto-nomous group work. In general, the survey results confirm the note of caution made in many previous case studies of CM introduction (e.g., Dawson and Webb, 1989; Dawson, 1991; Buchanan and Preston, 1992; Magjuka and Schmenner, 1992; Sewell and Wilkinson, 1992). Although data analysis is presently preliminary, there are suggestions that, as Sewell and Wilkinson found, it often seems to be the case that management is using '*empowerment and trust as rhetoric and the centralisation of power and control as the reality*' (Sewell and Wilkinson, 1992: 102). As indicated by our survey, however, there is more complexity in the types of team work being developed than fits easily into a 'bi-polar' model of different types of team work. Moreover, the nature of team work and its effectiveness both varies and shares similarities across firm sizes and industrial cultures in a complex pattern. A more distinctive analysis of such conditions must wait upon further analysis.

References

Adler, P.S. and Cole, R.E. (1993) 'Designed for learning: a tale of two auto plants', *Sloan Management Review*, Spring: 85–94.

Ahlmann, H.J. (1980) 'Fertigungsinseln – eine alternative producktionsstruktur', *Werkstatt und Betrieb*, 10: 641–8.

Alford, H. (1994) 'Cellular manufacturing: the development of the idea and its application', *New Technology, Work and Employment*, 9: 3–18.

Anon. (1994) 'The celling out of America', *The Economist*, 17 December: 61–2.

AWF (ed.) (1984) *Flexible Fertigungsorganisation am Beispiel Fertigungsinseln*. Eschborn: Ausschuss für wissenschaftliche Fertigung e. V.

Badham, R. and Schallock, B. (1991) 'Human factors in CIM development: a human-centred view from Europe', *International Journal on Human Factors in Manufacturing*, 1 (2): 121–41.

Bamber, G.J. and Shadur, M.A. (1995) 'Lean production: the transferability of Japanese management strategies to Australia'. Paper presented at the First Asia/Pacific Conference on Rapid Product Development, 11–13 December.

Benders, J., de Hann, J. and Bennett, D. (eds) (1995) *The Symbiosis of Work and Technology*. London: Taylor & Francis.

Brödner, P. (1988) *The Shape of Future Technology: the Anthropocentric alternative*. Berlin: Springer-Verlag.

Buchanan, D. (1994) 'Cellular manufacturing and the role of teams', in J. Storey (ed.), *New Wave Manufacturing Strategies: Organizational and Human Resource Management Dimensions*. London: Chapman.

Buchanan, D. and Preston, D. (1992) 'Life in the cell: supervision and teamwork in a "manufacturing systems engineering" environment', *Human Resource Management Journal*, 2 (4): 55–76.

Burbidge, J.L. (1979) *Group Technology in the Engineering Industry*. London: Mechanical Engineering Publications.

Dankbaar, B. (1997) 'Lean production: denial, confirmation or extension of sociotechnical systems design?', *Human Relations*, 50 (5): 567–83.

Dawson, P. (1991) 'From machine-centred to human-centred manufacture', *International Journal of Human Factors in Manufacturing*, 1 (4): 327–38.

Dawson, P. (1994) *Organizational Change: a Processual Approach*. London: Chapman.

Dawson, P. and Webb, J. (1989) 'New production arrangements: the totally flexible cage?', *Work, Employment and Society*, 3 (2): 221–38.

Delbridge, R., Turnbull, P. and Wilkinson, B. (1992) 'Pushing back the frontiers: management control under JIT/TQM factory regimes', *New Technology, Work and Employment*, 7 (2): 97–106.

Dohse, K., Jurgens, U. and Malsch, T. (1985) 'From "Fordism to Toyotism"? The social organization of the labour process in the Japanese automobile industry', *Politics and Society*, 4 (3): 22–4.

Domingo, R. (1985) 'Kanban: crisis management Japanese style', *Euro-Asia Business Review*, 4 (3): 22–4.

Drucker, P.F. (1990) 'The emerging theory of manufacturing', *Harvard Business Review*, 68 (3) (May–June): 94–102.

Fox, A. (1974) *Beyond Contract Work, Power and Trust Relations*. London: Faber & Faber.

Gallagher, C. and Knight, W. (1973) *Group Technology*. London: Butterworth.

Geary, J. (1994) 'Task participation: employees' participation enabled or constrained?', in K. Sisson (ed.), *Personnel Management: a Comprehensive Guide to Theory and Practice in Britain*. Oxford: Blackwell.

Gulowsen, J. (1972) 'A measure of work group autonomy', in L.E. Davis and J.C. Taylor (eds), *Design of Jobs*. Harmondsworth: Penguin.

Ham, I. and Reed, W. (1977) 'First group technology survey', *Machine and Tool Blue Book*, 72: 100–8.

Hartmann, M. (1989) 'A West German lesson for increased flexibility and innovation in manufacturing: autonome fertigungsinseln'. Paper presented for the Program in Science Technology, 12 May, MIT, Cambridge, MA.

Hoerr, J. (1989) 'The payoff from teamwork', *Business Week*, 10 July: 56–62.

Honda, F. (1980) *Group Technology*. Tokyo: Japan Society for the Promotion of Machine Industry.

Hyman, R. and Streeck, W. (1988) *New Technology and Industrial Relations*. London: Routledge.

Ingersoll Engineers (1990) *Competitive Manufacturing: the Quiet Revolution*. Rugby: Ingersoll Engineers.

Ivanov, (1968) *Group Production, Organization and Technology*. London: Business Publications.

Klein, J. (1991) 'A reexamination of autonomy in light of new manufacturing practices', *Human Relations*, 44 (1): 21–38.

Lawler, E.E. (1986) *High Involvement Management: Particular Strategies for Improving Organizational Performance*. San Francisco: Jossey-Bass.

Lesieur, F.G. (ed.) (1958) *The Scanlon Plan*. Cambridge, MA: MIT Press.

Magjuka, R.J. and Schmenner, R.W. (1992) 'Cellular manufacturing and plant administration: some initial evidence. *Labor Studies Journal*, 19 (2): 43–62.

Mathews, J. (1995) *Catching the Wave*. Sydney: Oxford University Press.

Mitrafanov, S.P. (1966) *Scientific Principles of Group Technology*. Boston Spa: National Lending Library for Science and Technology.

Mogenson, A.H. (1932) *Common Sense Applied to Motion and Time Study*. New York: McGraw-Hill.

Monden, Y. (1994) *The Toyota Management System: Linking the Seven Key Functional Areas*. Cambridge, MA: Productivity Press.

Parker, M. and Slaughter, J. (1988) *Choosing Sides: Unions and the Team Concept*. Detroit: Labour Notes.

Parnaby, J. (1988) 'A systems approach to the implementation of JIT methodologies in Lucas Industries', *International Journal of Production Research*, 26 (3): 483–92.

Peters, T. (1987) *Thriving on Chaos: Handbook for a Management Revolution.* London: Macmillan.

Procter, S., Hassard, J. and Rowlinson, M. (1995) 'Introducing cellular manufacturing: operations, human resources, and high trust dynamics', *Human Resource Management Journal*, 5 (2): 46–64.

Sandberg, T. (1982) *Work Organisation and Autonomous Groups.* Lund: LiberForlag.

Schonberger, R. (1982) *Japanese Manufacturing Techniques.* New York: The Free Press.

Sekine, K. (1992) *One Piece Flow – Cell Design for Transforming the Production Process.* Cambridge, MA: Productivity Press.

Sewell, G. and Wilkinson, B. (1992) 'Empowerment or emasculation? Shopfloor surveillance in a total quality organization', in P. Blyton and P. Turnbull (eds), *Reassessing Human Resource Management.* London: Sage.

Syed, M., Ashman, C., Kaebernick, H., Couchman, P.K. and Badham, R. (1995) *Survey of Cellular Manufacturing: Cellular Manufacturing's Impact on Australian Industry.* Sydney: IE Management Consultants.

Taylor, F.W. (1972) *Scientific Management: Comprising Shop Management, the Principles of Scientific Management [and] Testimony before the Special House Committee.* Westport, CT: Greenwood Press.

Wemmerlöv, U. and Hyer, N.L. (1989) 'Cellular manufacturing in US industry: a survey of users', *International Journal of Production Research*, 27: 1511–30.

Wilkinson, B., Jonathan, M. and Oliver, N. (1992) 'Japanizing the world: the case of Toyota', in J. Marceau (ed.), *Reworking the World.* New York: de Gruyter.

Womack, J.P., Jones, D.T. and Roos, D. (1990) *The Machine that Changed the World.* New York: Rawson Associates.

7 Japan in Britain, Japan in Mexico: Production Supervisory Practice in the Electronics Industry

Jonathan Morris, James Lowe and Barry Wilkinson

The critical role of supervisors and front-line managers in manufacturing organizations is once again a subject of scrutiny (Storey, 1992; Lowe, 1993). Three major factors appear to be at work. First, there is a purported shift from personnel management to human resource management (HRM). Thus, it is argued that line managers and supervisors assume far greater importance for the management of human resources as such responsibility is devolved to them. Secondly, as part of a diffusion of Japanese management systems to Western countries, it is suggested that supervisors have an enhanced, or intensified role for 'technical' responsibilities as part of total quality management (TQM) systems. Line managers thus take on a greater role for monitoring and implementing quality improvements and ensuring the maintenance of their processes. Thirdly, these developments occur as part of a wider debate where the low skills, authority and ambiguous role of supervisors has been characterized as a 'supervisory problem', at least in the UK. In recognizing these developments and debates, this chapter reports on a comparative empirical study of supervisory roles in one Japanese-owned consumer electronics company with plants based in the UK and Mexico.[1]

Some Theoretical and Conceptual Issues

Our theoretical starting point is that there are (at least) two somewhat overlapping models of managing human resources: first, the Human Resource Management (HRM) model, and secondly, a 'Japanese' model. Both models have significant implications for front-line managers and supervisors. The HRM model, emanating from the USA in the 1980s, has several tenets: that the management of human resources should be tied to business strategy; that employees should be viewed as a 'strategic resource' for achieving competitive advantage; that HRM policies should be flexible; that the goal of quality should be paramount; and, most vitally from this chapter's perspective, that HRM is integrated and not marginal, because responsibility for HRM is devolved to line management from Personnel (see Legge, 1995).

Human Resource Management has sparked a debate about the role of the supervisor because one of the key ways in which the strategic integration of HRM is to be achieved is through line management (Guest, 1987). For Sissons 'the locus of responsibility is now assumed by senior line management' (1990: 5), while Poole emphasizes that HRM 'involves all managerial personnel (and especially general managers)' (1990: 3). Under this new agenda, line management is no longer restricted to monitoring and organizing, but is concerned with commitment, quality and flexibility. Storey (1992) regards line management as the 'crucial delivery mechanism' through which practices such as employee involvement, team working and 'counselling' are realized. In addition, it is evident that the introduction of HRM practices, such as more sophisticated selection, appraisal and payment systems, and forms of labour deployment, imply changes to line management responsibilities (Armstrong, 1989; Townley, 1989).

The 'Japanese' model also emphasizes quality and is embraced by the just-in-time/total quality control (JIT/TQC) ethos. Quality products at the lowest possible cost forms the core of this philosophy, supported by industrial relations and personnel policies. The model embraces a number of notions: quality comes first; customer focus; continuous improvement or *kaizen*; employee involvement, and suppliers as partners (Morris et al., 1995). The JIT/TQC system has some similarities with HRM in that quality is the responsibility of everyone, and, as part of this ethos, responsibility is devolved to the 'line', including production workers, who must ensure that they strive to produce products 'right-first-time'. While there are also considerable differences between HRM and the 'Japanese' model, notably the team ethos of the latter and the individualistic orientation of the former, both imply a heightened role for supervisors in securing the objectives of management.

Similarly, in the case of 'Japanese' manufacturing and management systems, a number of writers have emphasized the specific technical role of front-line management in bringing about continuous improvement and perfecting quality (Schonberger, 1982; Wickens, 1987; Mallory and Molander, 1989; Lowe, 1992, 1993). On a functional level these writers share the analysis of the HRM model with regard to the supervisor's role in involving and managing subordinates. However, what marks these writers out is their suggestion that specific technical or organizational changes at the shop-floor level imply a restructuring of the supervisor's role. For example, the use of cellular organization implies that supervisors become virtual mini-managers and absorb many activities traditionally performed by specialists. Moreover, devolution of quality management to the shop-floor means that supervisors become key actors in ensuring that product quality is met.

Front-line Management in Context

Any analysis of the role of front-line management and its interface with the shop-floor must be set within specific historical and institutional contexts. In the UK and USA, the roots of the modern industrial supervisor can be traced back to the systems of internal contracting at the end of the nineteenth century (Gospel, 1983), with work organization and control left to a subcontractor, typically a skilled craftsman. By the turn of the century, management were adopting a supervisory system that exerted more direct control over labour costs and the labour process (Littler, 1982). Initially, craftsmen were employed as supervisors and maintained high status and pay, but gradually their role, power and authority were diminished as organizations grew and 'Taylorist' functional specialization emerged (Williams, 1915; Pollard, 1968). Moreover, as Edwards (1979) notes, employers sought to gain more direct control through the use of assembly-line technology. Finally, the emergence of a shop steward movement undermined the supervisor's position (Phelps-Brown, 1959) and proto-personnel functions took over matters of selection, grievance and discipline management, etc. (Edwards, 1979; Littler, 1982; Tyson, 1987).

Gradually, supervisors became caught in a promotion trap due to the growing professionalization of management and technology (e.g., accountants and engineers). A demarcation between qualified managers and uneducated supervisors opened up with the result that they became increasingly marginalized (Roethlisberger, 1943; Child and Partridge, 1982; Child et al., 1983).

The current state of supervisory practice is somewhat difficult to ascertain due to a relative lacunae of recent empirical research. The *Workplace Industrial Relations Survey* (Daniels and Millward, 1986) and Edwards's (1987) studies indicate a far greater involvement by works managers in personnel matters. Macro-survey data also points to supervisors moving from 'overseer' to 'manager' (IDS, 1987, 1988, 1991; IRS, 1990). Storey's (1992) case analysis of 15 companies found a much (and radically) expanded role for supervisors involving selection, training and induction, as part of a new approach in employee relations and emphasizing communications, devolved management accountability, greater appraisal and more individualized pay.

In a wider context, both practitioner and academic studies have attempted to link the status of the supervisor with organizational performance. A NEDO (1992) report in the UK, for example, highlighted differences in supervisory systems between the UK, Germany and Japan. Academic studies, however, have established that the 'supervisory problem' is a peculiarly Anglo-Saxon phenomenon, arguing that it may be linked to the relatively low status of the production function in the UK and USA (Lockyer, 1979; Weiner, 1981). By contrast, in Germany and Japan, the production function is held in far greater esteem so that the supervisory 'class' occupy positions of high status in industry and society. In Germany, for example, the *Meister* and *Vizemeister* will have served a formal apprenticeship and are usually skilled workers with several years' experience (Jürgens and Strömel, 1985; Partridge, 1989). As such, they are expected to have a detailed knowledge of the section, liaise with other departments and have more direct input into training, all aspects which would typically fall under the remit of specialist departments in the UK or USA. This is reflected in greater staff specialization in UK firms and a greater preference for bureaucratic forms of control (Maurice et al., 1980; Child et al., 1983).

Similarly, in Japan, most supervisors have at least ten years' experience and benefit from greater access and promotion to higher levels of the management hierarchy. Indeed, Jürgens and Strömel's (1985) study of the German and Japanese automobile industries argues that 'supervisory density' is far greater in Japan than in Germany. They further argue that 'the foreman (the supervisory equivalent) in Japan is clearly the most important person in day-to-day production and manpower deployment' (Jürgens and Strömel, 1985: 4). Further, 'he (or she) is involved in manpower allocation, selection or transfer, line balance, and dissemination of information to the shopfloor and the foreman [sic] still has the classical management tools and powers unrivalled by staff, or professionals, etc.' (Jürgens and Strömel, 1985: 15).

Ogasawara (1992) adds a further dimension in a comparative study of a Japanese electronics plant and a sister plant in the UK. He notes the role that both team leaders and supervisors play in the system of *jinji koka seido* (performance appraisal) and in potential promotion arising out of this system.

The dynamics of the supervisor's role in other national contexts has been partly highlighted by such comparative studies. However, perhaps more important has been the 'comparison factor' in the management practices of foreign direct investors, predominantly from Japan, who have tended to adopt organizational structures and systems which locate supervisors clearly in managerial positions and in very different roles from that described in the UK (see above) (Kenney and Florida, 1993; Morris et al., 1993; Lowe, 1995). These issues raise a number of questions. What is the nature of front-line management roles in Japan? To what extent are these roles being transferred? What are the social, institutional and cultural barriers to transfer? The answers to some of these questions are provided by the research outlined in the next section.

The Research Results

Introduction

The research data reported herein extends evidence on supervisory practices in an international context. It offers an assessment of two plants, one in the Mexican *Macquilladores* and one in the UK (in order to keep the plants anonymous, we will refer to the Mexican plant as DM and the UK plant as DUK). Both are under the same Japanese parent, both produce (for North America and Europe respectively) CTVs, and they use similar technologies. Yet there are clear differences in supervisory practice between home country and transplant practice, and between the two plants themselves.

The research methodology combined extensive interviews with detailed observations. The interviews were carried out at two levels: with relevant managerial staff (general, personnel, production, engineering), and with supervisors themselves. The observation element involved the researchers 'tracking' a number of supervisors in a line setting for half a shift each, although this was used more extensively at DUK where access and language problems were less of a constraint.

After we had gathered the data, and in the light of our theoretical interests, it seemed that five issues stood out for consideration: supervisors' attitudes; supervisors' status; supervisors' roles; supervisors' authority; and supervisors' training and development. Each of these themes will be addressed for these two plants before making some conclusions.

A number of terminological problems exist in comparing supervisory roles across different organizations. In particular, formal job titles vary and often do not take account of those performing quasi-supervisory functions, for example chargehands, team leaders and so on (Thurley and Wirdenuis, 1973). For this reason writers in the area have advanced that the concept of a 'supervisory system of control' be adopted. This supervisory system refers to a network of interrelated roles that both formally and informally relate to those personnel performing supervisory functions (Dawson and McLoughlin, 1986). At the research sites, therefore, different terms were used to denote roles of similar status and function. First-line management were referred to as 'foremen' and 'forewomen' at DUK while at DM they were called 'supervisors' and would have responsibility for managing between four and five production lines. These personnel were supported by semi-or quasi-supervisory roles (one per production line) termed 'utilities' and 'group leaders' at DM while at DUK a highly stratified grading system resulted in eight different job titles, rising from 'float' to 'senior chargehand' at the top of the scale. While these different titles carried theoretical differences in status and minor increments in pay, our observations, and comments by the management, confirmed that these personnel were fulfilling the same functions and had primary responsibility to cope with the so called 'disturbance handling' elements of production work, such as chasing material supplies, covering toilet breaks, and calling for maintenance in the event of a major breakdown. Indeed, those at the lower end of the scale at DUK were also critical of this system as they recognized that they were doing a job equivalent to, and sometimes more demanding (in the case of dealing with more subordinates or complex processes) than colleagues who were of a higher grade. (In outlining these distinctions we use the broad terms 'supervision/supervisors' throughout the chapter to refer to those identified formally at the front-line of supervision and those performing semi- or quasi-supervisory functions and highlight specific job positions and titles at the various sites with the use quotation marks.)

Supervisors' attitudes

In both the UK and Mexican plants it was evident that there was a high level of commitment by supervisors to their work, evident not only in comments made during interviews, but also in their behaviour on the job. This was not unexpected, particularly in DUK where most of the super-vision had been recruited from the shop-floor, and a key criterion for promotion to supervisory positions was performance and commitment, rather than formal qualifications. Typically, the supervision at DUK would 'pull out all the stops' to meet the needs of the 'customer', including in situations where they had attributed a problem to an upstream area or a specialist group. It was not unusual for the supervision to arrive at work early (often one hour or more before the official start time) or to continue for several hours at the end of a shift, often at very short notice (i.e., during a shift) and with considerable disruption to family and out-of-work commitments. A similar level of supervisory commitment was evident at DM.

The high supervisory commitment to target achievement and customer requirements was, unsurprisingly, extremely stressful. The tracking exercise confirmed an extremely high-stress working environment, particularly in the UK case. Supervisors recognized that stress was inherent in the job, and indeed this appeared to some extent to be seen as positive. However, certain stressors were seen as negative and undesirable: in the UK case negative comments were made about perceived excessive bureaucracy ('doing paperwork in triplicate'), short notice overtime, and, most com-monly, uncertainties and disruptions to smooth operations caused by other sections of the plant or specialist groups.

A further observation is pertinent here and arises from the more chaotic JIT system in operation at DUK when compared to DM. This resulted in supervisors having to become engaged in fire-fighting activities stemming from problems such as material shortages, internal defects, and unplanned change-overs following difficulties experienced up or downstream. At DM, however, the plant benefited from smoother production schedules and operated closer to established plans. 'Supervisors' (foreperson equivalent) were observed to be somewhat removed from the minute-to-minute problems of the line, partly as a result of more stable production but also because a clearer division of responsibility appeared to exist between them-selves and their subordinates (the 'utilities'). 'Utilities' at DM thus appeared more willing and able to deal with many of the unanticipated problems that occurred on the line when compared to their counterparts at DUK.

Despite the differences highlighted above, the supervisors at DUK were mostly positive about the attitudes and capabilities of their 'teams' of employees, and there was evidence that employees were genuinely treated as part of the team – for example, supervisors would sometimes sit with their members during tea breaks. An expressed emphasis on the central importance of team work was pervasive. At DUK supervisors did, however, use language which distinguished them from operators. In conversations between supervisors, for example, there was widespread use of the term 'bodies' to refer to operators, and poor performers were known as 'woofers'.

At DUK the supervision perceived that they had to be strict on efficiency and quality targets with their employees, though potential conflict with subordinates over the strictness of supervision appeared to be deflected by blaming this on 'the system' at DUK or on 'the Japanese way'. Each supervisor could typically identify a small number ('one or two') who had to be 'kept a close watch on' because of quality problems or absences. The information and disciplinary systems in place forced supervisors to take appropriate action against the 'one or two', but again action taken was sometimes justified by reference to higher authorities – in the case of absences, 'Personnel won't like this', etc. Whatever the approach used, supervisors stressed the need to show a high degree of sensitivity to individual subordinate problems and needs. At DM, similar strictures applied, but roles seemed more clearly defined.

In both plants, the supervisors were always willing to do whatever was necessary to maintain production but there were frequently complaints that other sections were the cause of their problems (see above). It is difficult to assess whether this is reflective of a 'blame culture', but clearly the operation of a JIT environment that emphasizes 'right first time' could contribute to this.

At DUK there appeared to be relatively little awareness of pressures and the root causes of problems which were affecting other sections. In the process of tracking supervisors across sections they could be observed dealing with problems on a parochial and narrow basis and had difficulty in seeing the wider implications of their actions. Managers were also critical of the 'business awareness' of their supervision, particularly for not being able to understand the financial impact of decisions. For example, the managing director of DUK said that supervisors were often keen to undertake work in overtime without recognizing that it impacted on the profitability of the company.

At DUK supervisors appeared to have problematic relations with specialist groups, particularly engineering and maintenance. In one respect they recognized the skills and competencies of these groups, their dependence on them and the importance of maintaining good relations with them. Yet there were occasional comments about the relatively privileged positions of the specialists, with most referring to their status and conditions ('easy life'; 'it's another world up there'; 'if we upset them they can make life very awkward for us', and so on). Although in principle specialists were answerable to the line, this was not apparent in the displays of deference and demeanour in day-to-day interactions, and our impression was that there were considerably greater stresses on line supervisors than on specialists. At DM, the relationship between specialists and supervisors was less tense. Two factors seemed to account for this. First, laxer health and safety legislation meant that more line maintenance could be done by supervisors and operators.[2] Secondly, because supervisors were more technically qualified at DM than at DUK there was a greater level of understanding between the two groups (to the extent that 'group leaders' could also perform minor maintenance tasks).

At DUK, as one might expect, the supervision typically felt ambiguous towards managers. Managers were respected for their own long hours and hard work, and individual supervisors generally made positive comments about their own individual 'boss'. On the other hand, 'management' as a group were seen as the source of some of their problems, particularly stress at work. Recently, a small number of managers at DUK had been promoted from the shop-floor and, in the view of the supervision, this had help to lessen the feeling of 'them [management] and us [supervision]'.

At DUK a significant change of climate over the preceding few months was reported to us by several supervisors. Meetings between managers and supervisors, which had been occurring since autumn 1994, were felt to have resulted in beneficial outcomes in terms of relieving supervisors of some of the pressures they faced (in particular it was commented that more realistic manning levels had been established) and in terms of making supervisors feel they had a greater say ('let's be fair to them, they did listen and they did respond' was a typical comment). Our impression was that managers at DUK had gained (or restored) a semblance of credibility over the previous few months. Supervisors were also supportive of management's attempts to extend NVQ (training) and to attract IIP (Investors in People – a UK-wide HRM standard) accreditation, and genuine disappointment was expressed at the failure to gain the latter. These initiatives also appeared to have lent credibility to the 'management'.

Supervisors' status

One of the striking differences between DUK and DM was the question of status. At DM, as we have already stated, 'supervisors' were typically graduates of technical college. At DUK supervisors typically had few formal educational qualifications and had generally been promoted from the shop-floor. Indeed, a number of managers at DUK had come through this route. At DM, meanwhile, the typical route to becoming a 'supervisor' was not via progression from the shop-floor but via recruitment from the outside labour market. Thus, 'utilities' infrequently became managers at DM.

Unsurprisingly, therefore, the status of supervisors at the two plants was markedly different. At DUK, for example, while supervisors typically felt themselves to be crucial to plant performance, they certainly did not have an inflated perception of their status. When asked which other occupational groups they would compare themselves with, they never chose professional groups and they voluntarily pointed out their lack of qualifications. Moreover, they saw their remuneration as appropriate to their position.

Where there was a clear distinction (in status terms at least) in DUK's supervisory system it was in the role of the 'foreperson', who took on broader responsibilities and reported directly to managers. The behaviour of the lower levels of the supervisor system suggested that this distinction was clearly recognized by them: 'forepersons' carried a much higher status and a greater degree of authority. For instance, in the course of tracking one 'senior float', an operator refused to transfer lines despite being needed and said 'I'm not moving unless [the foreman] tells me to'. In response to this the 'senior float' went to the foreman and requested that he ask this operator to transfer which he then did without any further hesitation.

Supervisors' roles

Supervisors at both DUK and DM were invariably clear of their priorities: to satisfy their customers' needs by meeting output and quality targets. A wide range of technical, operational and human skills were used to strive towards these.

A good deal of time was spent collating output, quality, labour efficiency and attendance information and reporting it appropriately in line with system requirements, for instance via production boards, computer input, or to personnel. 'Forepersons' at DUK would examine this information and make decisions about labour allocation, batch change-overs, etc. Generally, these personnel were observed to have a detailed knowledge of the operations under their control and were methodical in establishing priorities and organizing others.

At DUK, the largest amount of time spent by 'floats/chargehands' during the tracking phase was in taking actions necessary to cope with unanticipated events which affected output against targets. For instance, dealing with unexpected changes to schedules, coping with parts shortages and upstream problems, and handling problems with quality, re-work, missing stock and machine malfunctions. Often these problems were associated with the introduction of new product lines. Below 'foreperson' level, supervisory activities were typically directed to ensuring that their own line met targets; 'forepersons' themselves were typically concerned to co-ordinate activities across a group of lines. But regardless of status, such fire-fighting activities took up most of their time. While this was evident at DM, it was much less prevalent. This was a function of several inter-related factors. First, 'supervisors' and 'group leaders' were more highly educated than their 'foreperson equivalents'. Indeed, most had some form of technical qualification. Secondly, management seemed to have a greater expectation that 'supervisors' would 'manage' their lines, that is it was emphasized to us that they should ensure that they are able to pursue more 'off-line' strategic priorities by training and preparing their 'utilities' so that they would be able to cope with all but the most unanticipated problems.

At both plants, and to these ends, supervision played a key role in gathering, processing and passing on information between themselves and others. 'Others' were mostly maintenance, engineering, quality and purchasing specialists, and up- and downstream supervisors. At DUK however, those below 'foreperson' level expressed some frustration about the lack of information supplied to them or how slow information was in arriving, for example impending parts shortages or schedule changes. They felt that the provision of more accurate and timely information could help them plan better to release labour for NVQ training, schedule overtime, prepare for batch change-overs, etc. Yet again at DM, the day-to-day interface with specialist groups such as maintenance tended to be delegated from managers to 'supervisors'.

At both plants the supervision typically attempted to address uncertainty by being proactive in seeking detailed information not provided by formal systems – visiting downstream sections, purchasing or engineering staff, for instance – in order to assess the exact progress of activities in their sections. Good interpersonal skills were at a premium in gathering such information and where necessary persuading others to facilitate the supervisors' objectives.

In addition, our data demonstrate that the supervision at both plants performed a critical role as a communication link between management and system requirements on the one hand and the demands of operators on the other. On a day-to-day or hour-to-hour basis this entailed the supervisor informally discussing with operators their individual work allocations and quality and efficiency performances, and where necessary re-allocating tasks and re-balancing lines.

In the case of DUK the plant management had attempted to improve the communication structures by instituting monthly meetings with the supervision and by devolving more responsibility to them via the introduction of daily and monthly team briefing sessions. After some initial disappointment following its introduction, this had been modified so that supervisors deliver a monthly core brief to make it less dry and more accessible. The accompanying local brief has apparently been accepted with enthusiasm by supervisors, and operators. One supervisor described it as 'the best thing they've ever done' and we were told that workers 'really participate' in the monthly brief. This may have contributed to the perceived change in climate referred to above. However, our limited observations of the pre-shift brief suggests that they are conducted hurriedly and are largely a one-way process.

In general, 'supervisors' at DM appeared to perform a broader role. For example, day-to-day maintenance tasks were delegated at DM to 'supervisors' while at DUK these were performed by specialists. In general, this was reflective of the higher status of supervisors and production managers at DM *vis-à-vis* other specialists.

AT DUK we saw little evidence of supervisory involvement in improvement activities. Much of their time was taken up by fire-fighting activities and this appeared to squeeze any 'thinking time'. Such pressures were probably exacerbated by current pressures at the plant, given that it had gone through a period of rapid growth and was operating above its capacity. Thus, at DM 'supervisors' were more involved in implementing process improvements; 'everything is done by the supervisor' was a typical comment, which referred to having a major say in equipment investment (although they did not hold budgets).

At DUK supervision had some role in the disciplinary process – formally in the early stages only. Counselling operators was seen as an unpleasant, though necessary, activity. Such activities were infrequent, and not directly observed. Our impression was that supervision frequently used informal comments and suggestions ('a word in the ear'). A further interesting responsibility of 'utilities' at DM was to become involved in designing rhetoric appeals for better quality and productivity from operators. This manifested itself in the 'utilities' literally plastering the assembly-line with pictures of Disney characters exhorting their subordinates to improve and get things 'right first time'. We are unclear as to how seriously these were taken by the operators and whether these brought about significant changes in their behaviour. Nevertheless, this finding at DM does imply a greater willingness of those at this level of the organization to 'mouth the words' of management than was the case at DUK. At DM, furthermore, supervision is involved to a greater degree in discipline, although the lack of a union or even a company advisory body and a grievance procedure helps explain this. 'We just tell them [the workers]' said one manager.

Interestingly, both plants operated with a different structure in their respective auto-insert/surface mount technology (SMT) sections. Here, operators were generally more highly skilled and more experienced. In addition, operators themselves took some responsibility for 'switching', machine setting, parts feeding, problem diagnosis, etc. Operators worked in teams, most were capable of running different machines and would frequently help each other in switching. Many operator responsibilities were those which, in other sections of the plant, would be taken by 'utilities'.

'Cell leaders' at DUK (different titles applied to this section too) in the SMT/auto-insert appeared to spend less time 'directing' and exerting detailed control over their operators. Rather, they had more space for planning and co-ordination activities, and for analysing problems. 'Cell leaders' at DUK appeared to be more genuinely 'managerial' than in other areas (note also that in SMT the cell leader is an engineer). Thus, our data confirm the importance of the dual contingencies of process technology and worker skill in influencing the supervisory role and style employed (Woodward, 1965; Walton, 1985).

Supervisors' authority

At both plants, supervision had authority over detailed line balancing and work allocation within their lines yet they had more limited discretion over personnel issues. What authority they enjoyed was highly circumscribed by bureaucratic rules (for instance on absence and discipline) and by efficiency and quality targets set by managers. There was little evidence of supervisory influence over these matters although at DUK the supervisor–management meetings referred to earlier appeared to have given supervisors the feeling, at least, that they were being informed of planning decisions that affected them.

Supervisory authority and influence with regard to specialist groups (purchasing, production control, engineering, etc.) was also limited. Clearly, supervision is highly dependent on those groups in attempting to achieve objectives. It was often unclear who was answerable to whom, if anyone, and the skills of persuasion, cajoling and exchanging favours appeared to take on great importance. At DUK, the idea that 'customer needs' were paramount was invariably expressed, though it was not always clear that the needs of upstream (customer) supervisors took priority over their downstream (supplier) supervisors. This problem could have been exacerbated by the elaborate supervisory hierarchy at DUK. Sometimes a customer supervisor could be making demands on a relatively senior supplier supervisor. For example, one junior supervisor complained of issuing paper work to upstream sections which did not appear to initiate corrective actions.

At DUK, supervisory authority over personnel issues was limited. Supervisors were clearly the key to the motivation of operators, but basic personnel decisions were either taken directly by the Personnel department, or the supervision would be expected to follow a set of established rules and procedures. At DM, 'supervisors' were not formally involved in operator selection but they had a high degree of involvement in the choice of their 'group leaders' and 'utilities' and their pay and appraisal.

At DUK, supervisors generally perceived themselves to have very limited authority. A telling comment frequently made was that 'we have budgets, but don't know how much they are'. Even junior managers commented on their limited authority over budgets. In contrast, 'supervisors' at DM had little control over budgets but they perceived themselves to have some influence over and to be informed about it. One caveat to this is the 'hidden hand' of the Japanese 'shadows' that operated at both plants. Both supervisors and managers at DM commented on the pervasive authority of the Japanese personnel and some used this to their advantage. For instance, one Mexican production manager told us (commenting on a recent problem he had experienced with his counterpart in maintenance), that if he wanted something changed he would not bother asking his Mexican colleague. Instead, he suggested that he would go directly to his compatriot's Japanese 'shadow', partly because this would in turn allow the other affected 'shadows' to discuss the issues and collectively sanction any changes.

Supervisors' training and development

Supervision at DUK received six days off-the-job training in a variety of skills when taking up their positions. Furthermore, there are training opportunities in the event of certain training needs being identified, such as team briefing. From our wider sample (see note 1) six days is a relatively short period of formal training. Nissan's 'supervisors' (foreperson equivalent) receive 35 days off-the-job training; at Ford 15 weeks off-the-job is typical.

One 'foreperson' at DUK suggested that the training of supervisors was inadequate and did not sufficiently prepare them for the demands of the job. A lot of the supervisors' development, he said, depended on picking things up from more senior colleagues. His point was that the quality of the supervisors' development was a reflection, in part, of how good their immediate superior was.

At DM, no formal training was required but less quantifiable amounts of on-the-job training formed a large part of the development provision for the supervision. Nevertheless, this did not appear to impede their ability to perform the job. Primarily, this was due to more selective selection techniques and a labour market which was able to provide 'group leaders' with technical backgrounds. In management's view, performing a 'group leader's' role was a sufficient preparation for progression to a 'supervisor's' job (primarily because the differences between the two were seen as minor). The presence of better incoming labour at these levels meant that DM was able to ensure its 'group leaders' and 'supervisors' had a much broader role than was the case with their equivalents at DUK.

Supervisors at DM, Supervisors at DUK

Although the two plants, DM and DUK, were in many ways very similar in terms of products, product technology and production systems, the characteristics of the labour force were very different. At shop-floor level, the work force at DUK was much more stable than at DM. At DM the labour turnover figures were 5 per cent per month, rising to 11 per cent in bad months. Labour was very transient, typically immigrants from Southern Mexico, who frequently moved to other jobs in the immediate locale or, often illegally, to the USA.

Meanwhile, at the 'supervisor' level, and indeed management level, employees were far more technically qualified having spent three or four years at technical college. Nearly all managers were engineering graduates. This appeared to bring great differences between supervisory roles, skills and attitudes at the plants. At DM, for example, 'supervisors' were clearly more 'managerial' than their equivalents (the 'forepersons') at DUK (or even production managers in certain cases at DUK). This included an observed dedication to achieving production objectives and, very much in contrast to the *mañana* stereotypes that exist about Mexican work habits, the factory manager was critical of Western approaches:

> If the bell rings, then you [Westerners] go and everyone leaves. Here, if there's a problem then we solve it that day. So what we have here is a Japanese company in Mexico, run by Mexicans [see above comments regarding shadows] but showing the same type of dedication and professionalism as the Japanese.

From the authors' observation, such rhetoric was close to reality with managers, supervision and workers often at the plant 12 hours a day for at least six days a week.

These issues highlight the impact of varying hierarchies at the plants. At DM the supervisory structure was much less elaborate than at DUK. At the same time it was in some ways much more rigid. Operators could become utility workers, but utility workers did not usually get promoted to 'group leader'. 'Group leaders' were drawn from the ranks of technicians and could in turn be promoted to 'supervisor' and ultimately progress to management. At DUK this kind of 'glass ceiling' effectively occurred much higher, between 'forepersons' and management, a finding confirmed in other studies of supervisory systems in the UK (Child and Partridge, 1982).

A last comment might be made on gender composition. Both plants are overwhelmingly female at operator level and utility and sub-foreperson level. But up the hierarchy, males dominate. This is much more the case at DM which is, in part, perhaps a reflection of societal differences, but is also indicative of the differing promotion routes in the two plants.

Conclusions

This chapter has undertaken a comparative analysis of supervisory practice across two countries. Clearly, however, international variations are only one variable, other obvious ones being industry-specific and ownership-specific factors. This plant comparison has attempted to control these variables by keeping the product variable (CTV production) and ownership variable (DM and DUK) constant. In doing so, some salient differences emerge.

Technology differences appear to have an important influence on the supervisory structures within the two plants with the SMT areas requiring greater skills from both workers and supervisors when compared to manual insertion and assembly areas. Some major differences at the supervisory level do appear, however, such as differences in the vocational education and training systems in the two countries. Slightly alarmingly, from a British perspective, the higher levels of the supervisory cadre in

Mexico appear to be much better educated. This has major implications for their status, authority, roles and their relationships with other groups of workers at the organizational level. It suggests that 'supervisors' at DM are much closer to the HRM and Japanese models outlined earlier. At DM, group leaders at the top end of the supervisory system thus have the skills, attitudes and authority to fulfil these more broader roles when compared to their counterparts in DUK. The DUK plant seems to 'suffer' from the classic 'supervisory problem' in that the context in which it operates and some of its own historical practices creates ambiguous supervisory roles. The supervisory system was also constrained by the relatively low status and skills of those performing supervisory jobs. This was undoubtedly exacerbated by the stresses and strains of trying to co-ordinate and supervise processes that were more unstable and problematic than was the case at DM. Lastly, the 'group leaders' at DM clearly acted and thought of themselves as part of management and appeared to be accepted as such by their superiors, whereas at DUK forepeople were uncertain of their status and authority, unaware of strategic business priorities and unconvinced of their superiors' rhetoric that they should act, think and behave as part of the wider 'management team'.

Notes

1. This chapter reports on one case study of a wider project comparing supervisory practice in Japan, North America and the UK in two sectors – consumer electronics and automotive. This project is funded by the Economic and Social Research Council (R000221410). Originally, the substantive empirical focus was to be an analysis of supervisory practice at two Japanese-owned sister transplants in the UK and USA. However, our choice of industry (consumer electronics and colour television (CTV) manufacture) and the nature of the emergent international division of labour and production precluded this. In short, CTVs are, by and large, no longer produced in the USA. Rather, production capacity has shifted to the Tijuana and Chihuahua regions of Mexico such that the country as a whole is now the world's largest producer of CTVs, with an output of approximately eight million units per annum.

2. A 'solder bath' is used to solder components on to printed circuit boards. This involves heating solder up to around 55°C. In DUK the solder bath was encased in a protective casing. At DM there was a barrier, equivalent to a fire guard, that could be easily removed (or knocked) out of the way. The latter offered easy access for maintenance purposes but was potentially dangerous for employees.

References

Armstrong, Peter (1989) 'Limits and possibilities for HRM in an age of management accountancy', in J. Storey (ed.), *New Perspectives on Human Resource Management*. London: Routledge.

Child, John, Fores, Michael, Glover, Ian and Lawrence, Peter (1983) 'A price to pay? Professionalism and work organization in Britain and West Germany', *Sociology*, 6 (3): 363–93.

Child, John and Partridge, Bruce (1982) *Lost Managers: Supervisors in Industry and Society*. Cambridge: Cambridge University Press.

Daniels, M. and Millward, N. (1986) *British Workplace Industrial Relations Survey 1980–84*. Aldershot: Gower.

Dawson, P. and McLoughlin, I. (1986) 'Computer technology and the redefinition of supervision: a study of the effects of computerization on railway freight supervisors', *Journal of Management Studies*, 23 (1): 116–32.

Edwards, Paul K. (1987) *Managing the Factory: a Survey of General Managers*. Oxford: Blackwell.

Edwards, Richard (1979) *Contested Terrain*. London: Heinemann.

Gospel, Howard (1983) 'The development of management organization: a historical perspective', in K. Thurley and S. Wood (eds), *Industrial Relations and Management Strategy*. Cambridge: Cambridge University Press.

Guest, David (1987) 'Human resource management and industrial relations', *Journal of Management Studies*, 24: 503–21.

IDS (Incomes Data Services) (1987) *Supervisors of Manual Workers*. IDS Study 386, May.

IDS (Incomes Data Services) (1988) *Teamworking*. IDS Study 419, October.

IDS (Incomes Data Services) (1991) *Supervisors*. IDS Study 479, May.

IRS (Industrial Relations Services) Focus (1990) *From Overseer to First Line Manager: the Changing Role of the Supervisor*. IRS Employment Trends 476, November.

Jürgens, Ulrich and Strömel, Hans-Peter (1985) *The Communications Structure between Management and Shopfloor – a Comparison of a Japanese and German Plant*. International Institute for Comparative Research and Labour Policy, Wissenschaftszentrum, Berlin.

Kenney, Martin and Florida, Richard (1993) *Beyond Mass Production: the Japanese System and its Transfer to the United States*. Oxford: Oxford University Press.

Legge, Karen (1995) *Human Resource Management: Rhetorics and Realities*. London: Macmillan.

Littler, Craig (1982) *The Development of the Labour Process in Capitalist Society*. London: Heinemann.

Lockyer, Keith (1979) 'The British production Cinderella: two effects', *Management Today*, June: 70–1.

Lowe, James (1992) 'Locating the line: the front line supervisor and human resource management', in P. Blyton and P. Turnbull (eds), *Reassessing Human Resource Management*. London: Sage.

Lowe, James (1993) 'Manufacturing reform and the changing role of the production supervisor', *Journal of Management Studies*, 30: 739–58.

Lowe, James (1995) *The Role of the Supervisor in the Automobile Industry*. Unpublished PhD thesis, University of Wales, Cardiff.

Mallory, G. and Mollander, C. (1989) 'Managing the front line: the changing role of supervisors', *Journal of General Management*, 14 (3): 35–46.

Maurice, M., Sorge, Arndt and Warner, Malcolm (1980) 'Societal differences in organizing manufacturing units: a comparison of France, West Germany and Great Britain', *Organization Studies*, 1: 59–86.

Morris, Jon, Munday, Max and Wilkinson, Barry (1993) *Working for the Japanese*. London: Athlone Press.

Morris, Jon, Wilkinson, Barry and Munday, Max (1995) 'Farewell to HRM? Personnel management in the UK's Japanese-owned plants'. Paper submitted to *Journal of Management Studies*. Available from Jon Morris.

NEDO (National Economic Development Office) (1992) *What Makes a Supervisor World Class?* London: NEDO.

Ogasawara, Koichi (1992) 'Japanese personnel appraisal: individualized race for power and imposed involvement'. Paper presented to a Workshop on Japanese Management Systems: An International Comparative Perspective, University of Wales, Cardiff Business School, September.

Partridge, Bruce (1989) 'The problem of supervision', in K. Sissons (ed.), *Personnel Management in Britain*. Oxford: Basil Blackwell.

Phelps-Brown, E. (1959) *The Growth of British Industrial Relations*. London: Macmillan.

Pollard, Sidney (1968) *The Genesis of Modern Management*. Harmondsworth: Penguin.

Poole, Michael (1990) 'Editor's Introduction', *International Journal of Human Resource Management*, 1 (1): 1–15.

Roethlisberger, Fritz (1943) 'The foreman: master and victor of double talk', *Harvard Business Review*, 23: 283–98.

Schonberger, Richard (1982) *Japanese Manufacturing Techniques*. New York: The Free Press.

Sissons, K. (1990) 'Introducing the human resource management journal', *Human Resource Management Journal*, 1 (1): 1–11.

Storey, John (1992) 'Developments in the management of human resources', Warwick Papers in Industrial Relations, 17, Industrial Relations Research Unit, University of Warwick.

Thurley, Keith and Wirdenuis, Hans (1973) *Supervisors: a Reappraisal*. London: Heinemann.

Townley, Barbara (1989) 'Selection and appraisal: reconstituting social relations', in J. Storey (ed.), *New Perspectives on Human Resource Management*. London: Routledge.

Tyson, Shaun (1987) 'Management of the personnel function', *Journal of Management Studies*, 24: 523–32.

Walton, Richard E. (1985) 'From control to commitment', *Harvard Business Review*, 64 (3): 76–84.

Weiner, M. (1981) *English Culture and the Decline of the Industrial Spirit, 1850–1980*. Cambridge: Cambridge University Press.

Wickens, Peter (1987) *The Road to Nissan*. London: Macmillan.

Williams, A. (1915) *Life in a Railway Factory*. London: Duckworth.

Woodward, Joan (1965) *Industrial Organization: Theory and Practice*. London: Oxford University Press.

PART 3

CRITIQUING THE GLOBAL WORLD OF MANAGEMENT THEORIES

8 **Total Quality Management in the UK Service Sector: A Social Constructivist Study**

Mihaela Kelemen

A great deal has been written on total quality management (TQM) in the last few decades. A recent search on ABI Inform shows that between January 1994 and February 1996 there were 1,078 articles published on this subject, which accounts to more than two articles per working day. Yet, despite this immense effort, TQM remains essentially an ambiguous concept. As Spencer (1994) notes, there is a wide range of definitions and approaches to TQM but little agreement as to what TQM is all about. This may not be surprising given the modernist nature of most TQM writings. Modernism presupposes that the more science one applies to a social phenomenon, the closer one gets to the truth about it.

In this chapter, I argue that one may need to question the modernist grounding of existing research and adopt a stance that feels more comfortable with the partial nature of knowledge, for example, social constructivism. Social constructivism acknowledges the multi-faceted but partial nature of knowledge. In so doing, it challenges the taken-for-granted meanings of social phenomena and throws up other potential meanings, particularly those which may be suppressed.

This chapter focuses on the most powerful TQM constructions, namely those which manage to win out temporarily at the expense of the others. This is not to say that I am a supporter of these constructions. Such potential support would contradict my earlier concerns about modernist research. This focus is informed by the attempt to explore the very process by which certain constructions get elevated and others are downplayed. The chapter discusses this political process in the context of four UK service organizations embarked on allegedly successful TQM programmes.

Theoretical Controversies in the Total Quality Management Field

The origins of total quality management (TQM) are usually ascribed to Japan's search for quality improvements in the 1950s and its success in moulding ideas on quality into a coherent operating philosophy. Much of Japan's transformation was associated with the introduction of statistical quality control in Japan by the US Army over the period 1946–50 and the visits by three key American quality gurus in the early 1950s. These were W.E. Deming (1982), J.M. Juran (1989), and A.V. Feigenbaum (1962). The Japanese adopted, developed and adapted the methodologies that the Americans brought in and, by the late 1950s, had begun to develop clearly distinctive approaches deemed suitable for their own culture (i.e., quality circles and team work, Pareto and fish-bone diagrams, quality built in the design of the product, etc.). The Japanese gurus, K. Ishikawa (1985) and G. Taguchi (1986) emphasized mass education, the use of simple tools and team work.

Much of the increased awareness of the importance of quality in the West in recent years has been associated with a new wave of gurus, for example, T. Peters (1980) and P. Crosby (1979). Crosby's name is perhaps best known in relation with the concepts of 'doing it right first time' and 'zero defects', whereas Peters is best known for his customer orientation and for identifying leadership as being central to the quality improvement process.

A succinct review of the some of the extant TQM literature shows that different quality experts emphasize different aspects of it. For example, TQM is described as a new way of thinking about the management of organizations (Chorn, 1991), a comprehensive way to improve total organizational performance and quality (Hunt, 1993), a systematic approach to the practice of management (Olian and Rynes, 1991), an alternative to 'management by control' (Price, 1989), a paradigm shift (Broedling, in Spencer, 1994), a business discipline and philosophy of management aimed at satisfying the customers in the market place (Hill, 1991) and as a totalizing narrative which silences any other voice but the most powerful one (Steingard and Fitzgibbons, 1993). Furthermore, in the TQM field, the evidence of contradictory advice abounds:

> Consider the following prescriptions of four of the leading gurus . . .: Juran advocates setting quality objectives and managing the quality plan according to these objectives. On the other hand, Deming is strongly opposed to management by objectives as well as the use of merit ratings and slogans to achieve objectives. Peters favours rallies, slogans and reward to promote excellence. Crosby is

against material rewards but recommends recognising contributions towards the quality effort. He also recommends zero defects as a quality objective, whereas Juran and Deming are against this because the inherent variability in all processes renders such an objective unrealistic. (Chatterjee and Yilman, 1993: 16)

The elusiveness of TQM has given rise to an increased sophistication of theories as well as a tendency to anchor them in contingency thinking. However, both universal and contingency-driven TQM theories attempt to impose structure, clarity and intelligibility upon a phenomenon that slips through the net of modernist thought. For what follows, I argue that TQM is socially constructed and this is why there can be no rational, objective and 'ultimate' explanations of such a phenomenon.

Social Constructivist TQM

Constructivism is a term fraught with difficulty. As Schwandt (1994) notes, constructivism is a term widely used in sociological analysis, yet its particular meaning is shaped by the intent of its users. For example, radical constructivism (von Glasersfeld, 1991) signals a particular relationship between mind and world where knowledge is thought to be valid if it works to achieve a goal. Social constructivism (Gergen, 1985), on the other hand, focuses on the collective generation of meaning as shaped by conventions of language and other social processes, while feminist constructivism (Riger, 1992) is concerned with portraying the lived reality of women's experiences. This chapter draws on Gergen's version of social constructivism which suggests that power is paramount in the social construction of reality. In so doing, the chapter explores some of the mechanisms by which certain constructions become more 'powerful' than the rest to the extent that they replace the multi-faceted reality of TQM.

There have been relatively few empirical attempts to research TQM from a social constructivist perspective (Munro, 1995; McArdle et al., 1995). These studies document processes of 'interest translation' (Latour, 1987) in manufacturing organizations embarked on TQM. 'Interest translation' is defined by Latour as a process in which the explicit interests of the 'enrolled' (i.e., the employees) can be translated so that in the end they appear to become synonymous with the interests of 'the enrollers' (i.e., top management). One way to ensure that people accept TQM is to tailor its message in such a way that it caters to employees' explicit needs. Another type of translation takes place when employees embrace TQM because their usual way of doing things is cut off.

In this chapter, I argue that TQM serves not only interest translation purposes, but also 'examination' purposes. Examination is a technique aimed at structuring a particular arena in such a way that it can be observed and monitored, or in Foucault's words:

it provides a way to know where and how to locate individuals . . . to be able at each moment to supervise the conduct of each individual, to assess it, to judge it, to calculate his [*sic*] qualities or merits. It is a procedure, therefore, aimed at knowing, mastering, and using. (Foucault, 1977: 143)

A social constructivist approach allows one to problematize the taken-for-granted meanings hidden behind TQM's seductively instrumental façade. As Wilkinson and Willmott (1995) argue, one should move beyond the benign vision of quality gurus by questioning the way total quality management is identified and pursued, as well as by uncovering some of the unchallenged assumptions and implicit power relations hidden within this ostensibly neutral concept. Indeed, TQM may not just be a benign methodology for increasing quality and pleasing the customer, but also a powerful determinant of every-day reality for many organizational members.

Approach to Study

For this study, I targeted a bank, a mail carrier, an insurer and a logistics company. The choice of these companies was determined by several criteria, among which were their service orientation, their leading role in the sector, as well as their allegedly 'successful' TQM approach to providing services. The fieldwork was carried out in the light of the idea that there are many legitimate ways in which the researcher can go about researching TQM, none of them, however, being able to collect and recuperate all the existing meanings. This chapter relies on three sources of data: field notes, interview transcripts and company documents. The research was confined to a relatively short period of time – five weeks in each organization on average, effectively providing a snapshot with single-shot interviews. This may well raise methodological problems for the implementation of a TQM programme is a long-term process (Redman and Wilkinson, 1995), and, therefore, such snapshots provide limited information. Such processes do not proceed smoothly and one cannot assume that the snapshot was appropriately timed. As a result, I had to assemble views on TQM in a shorter time than would be expected from an ethnographic study which typically involves digging, exploring and questioning over time.

The Official TQM Accounts

As I mentioned earlier, the focus of the chapter is represented by those TQM accounts which, at least temporarily, are more persuasive and powerful than the rest, in this case, the so-called official accounts. More specifically, the chapter explores the mechanisms by which these accounts are elevated at the expense of the others.

Official accounts in the companies studied define TQM as:

- 'A philosophy that allows the bank to predict and satisfy the needs of the customers, through increased employee involvement and continuous improvement' (In-house magazine No. 24, the bank).
- 'The way of working which will enable the business to achieve customer satisfaction in a manner consistent with our values' (TQM Booklet, the mail carrier).
- 'Our commitment to meeting client and employee needs' (Annual Report, 1993, the insurance company).
- 'The means by which the company will build a better future for all stakeholders (i.e., shareholders, customers, employees) and achieve world-class standards of quality and productivity' (Annual Report, 1993, the logistics company).

The empirical data suggests that there are contentious individual interpretations of TQM which differ by hierarchical level and across departments. This may not be surprising, given top management's alleged expectations that employees will translate the TQM official definition in ways that are meaningful to them. As the general director of the mail carrier put it: 'the company's definition of TQM sends across a certain philosophy which must be understood correctly by people. I don't really care what words they use when they talk about it'. However, individual translations are welcome only to the extent that they support the general framework set out by the official account. The evidence suggests that those individual accounts which resist the official version of TQM are constantly downplayed and discriminated against.

Let us now illustrate these claims. The data suggest that the closer to the task employees are, the less likely they define TQM according to the official account. Indeed, top management define TQM in line with the official account, whereas subordinates tend to define TQM in a close relation to the task they perform. For example, one of the top managers interviewed said 'it is difficult to define TQM in my own terms because I know what the official definition says' (the logistics company's marketing director). On the other hand, a processing worker in the mail carrier defined TQM as 'making sure that the mail goes properly from start to finish and treating all mis-sort correctly', while a depot worker in the logistics company said 'TQM is about good management of the machinery to minimize problems'.

Similarly, the closer employees are to the customers, the more likely they define TQM in accordance with the official account. Indeed, front-office people appear to embrace the rhetoric of the official account to a greater extent than the back-office people who tend to be more technical and task-driven in defining TQM. For example, a delivery worker in the mail carrier defined TQM as 'keeping our customers happy', and a salesperson in the bank said that 'TQM is a chain in which everybody is everybody else's customer'. In the back-office, TQM was defined as 'having standards in place to account for our quality' (the bank's operations director) and as 'best practices which allow us to meet the required standards' (middle manager in the insurance company).

While the plurality of TQM meanings is encouraged by the top management, all those individual accounts which do not fit the official pattern are constantly downplayed. The evidence suggests that top management enforce the official TQM account via quality initiatives. These initiatives have the alleged aim to promote a more unified total quality management understanding within the organization. This is not to say that there are no disagreements within top management teams concerning the mechanisms by which TQM should be enforced. As the chairman of the insurance company said: 'We don't agree all the time on how to make quality a workable item, but most of us believe that the initiatives we have in place send the right message to the people.'

The evidence suggests, however, that these initiatives actually restrict the active role of the individuals in the social construction of TQM. They are perceived by 88 per cent of the employees interviewed to be aimed at quantifying, controlling and predicting human behaviour. As one of the mail carrier's employees said: 'Nothing has changed as a result of TQM; there are more meetings to attend, more papers to fill in, more controls in place and less freedom to do your job.' As Thompson (1980) notes, by providing strict determinants of behaviour rather than loose conduct guides, quality initiatives can easily become devices for translating all situations in measurable and controllable terms, making the organization a more visible and, therefore, a more controllable place.

Quality Initiatives

There seem to be numerous quality initiatives in the organizations studied. These initiatives are grouped for the purpose of this chapter in four distinct categories: standards-related initiatives, consulting-related initiatives, incremental initiatives and training-related initiatives. In what follows, I argue that quality initiatives serve purposes of 'interest translation' (Latour, 1987) and 'examination' (Foucault, 1977).

Standard-related initiatives of 'silencing other views'

The bank and the insurance company are embarked on various standards campaigns such as British Standards BS 5750 (the bank), ISO 9000 and PAM (professional account management) standards (the insurance company).

The BS 5750 initiative was originated by senior managers in what may be described as the bank's back-office. This linking of TQM and BS 5750 may be explained by their technical orientation and inclination to quantify most aspects of their business. While the motivation behind adopting BS

5750 is heralded by a back-office senior manager to be 'a genuine concern for the customer, for the society as a whole', other views, coming from the front-office claim that 'we went for BS 5750 because somebody else (our main competitor) had already gone for it'.

The insurance company is also embarked on two similar initiatives. The first initiative, the PAM standards, which was originated and enforced by the company's quality professionals, has the alleged objective of 'creating a consistent quality of service throughout the company's international network' (Annual Report, 1993: 10). Again, others see this differently. For example, the sales and marketing director expresses a feeling that 'PAM emphasizes the administrative side of the business and not the potential benefits for the clients or the employees'. One of the middle managers who was involved in the PAM launch said: 'We did not launch PAM. We threw it at people. Launching is about winning people's minds and hearts and making sure they understand what PAM is all about, not about copying what other people already did.' At the time the study took place, the insurance company was also involved in ISO 9000 accreditation across a number of European offices. The already-achieved UK accreditation was considered to be 'evidence that our success in this field is recognised externally as well as internally' (Annual Report, 1993: 11).

The institutional pressure from various constituencies (customers organizations, competitors, the general public, the European Foundation for Quality Management) appears to be the favourite leitmotiv of top managers in promoting and supporting quality standards. The insurance company's chairman, for example, said that 'ISO is just a marketing tool but does not put too much internal discipline into the company. It is just a gloss, something that the market requires.' Another board member held a similar opinion: 'ISO is much more to do with marketing, it is a means by which you can explain to the world how clever you are.'

Institutional pressure may be the preferred explanation for the concern with standards but there is another equally powerful explanation to account for. Top management may also support the BS 5750, PAM standards and ISO initiatives because standards help to measure reality as well as to enact it in a particular way. As the insurance company's chairman has written: 'Standards are very tangible and allow measurable objectives and deadlines to be put in place' (chairman's letter to staff, 1994). The insurer's sales and marketing director also noted that 'what gets measured gets done; we can get our people to work towards the company's objectives'. However, Czarniawska-Joerges (1993) notes that standards are monologues because they reflect a simplified view of the world as decided by those who rule.

One may conclude that top management's concern with quality standards has serious political implications. Quality standards appear to be devices by which complexity is reduced to relatively simple patterns, as decided by top management, a process which may eventually transform the organization into a more pellucid and controllable place. In their attempt to order reality according to their preferred rationality, top management use quality standards as lenses through which individuals are viewed, judged, measured and compared against the others (i.e., *examined*). Those individuals who do not conform to the prescriptions laid down by these standards are 'given help' (via training programmes) to adjust themselves, or are simply discriminated against. As the mail carrier's facilities director said: 'There are a few people here from the old guard, the dinosaurs, as we call them, who do not want to accept that TQM is the only way forward for the business. Hopefully, we will be able to get rid of most of them soon.'

Consulting-related initiatives of 'fixing the way forward'

These initiatives are a consequence of top management's persistent use of consultants and other external bodies. This is not to suggest that managers actually believe consultants to be a panacea to the problems the organizations may face in implementing total quality management. Rather, the evidence suggests that most organizations use consultants as vehicles of change, by encouraging the belief that consultants are neutral entities who can provide objective information on various aspects of total quality management. The bank's board of directors, for example, hired a number of external consultancies, one of which was used to provide evidence on the achievements of their TQM programme. This evidence was then used by the board for internal and external communication purposes.

The mail carrier's board of directors also supports a quality initiative which relies on external remedies, namely the Business Excellence Review (BER). Company documents define BER as an 'objective, systematic assessment carried out across all parts and addressing all aspects (i.e., culture, process, results) of a business unit with the objective of identifying strengths and improvement opportunities' (internal document, March 1993). The quality director said that BER will 'help the organization to be more successful in achieving its quality goals by comparing it against a credible, external, world-class model of business excellence – the European Foundation Quality Management model'. A majority of board members appears to support this view because, in their opinion, it helps to measure the company's progress in an objective way.

A similar stance is taken by the insurance company's board of directors. They state that EFQM membership is an important milestone on the road towards TQM. As the quality director said: 'In order to create the culture of quality in our company, we became a member of EFQM.' The wide support for the EFQM model at the top of the organization may be related to the attractiveness and simplicity of the EFQM model which assumes a causal relationship between organizational variables and an 'objective way' of measuring quality.

While the alleged reason for relying on external consultants is their objectivity and neutral nature, I would argue that the accounts provided by these consultancies are meant to enhance the legitimacy of top management's actions, actions which are typically directed at ordering the organization according to their preferred interests. The recourse to external agencies may also be interpreted as a knee-jerk response to the overt expression of tensions concerning the power relations between top management and their subordinates (Conrad, 1983). As Bloomfield and Vurdubakis (1994) noted, consultancy reports have traditionally constituted a powerful set of devices for organizational self-reflection.

In Bloomfield and Vurdubakis's view, the power of these reports resides in a double translation movement. On the one hand, there is the move from 'external reality' (i.e., the way total quality is managed) to its representation in a text. This allows the construction of a textual order in terms of which TQM problems and opportunities can be diagnosed in a way that fits top management's interests. On the other hand, there is a move in the opposite direction, from the text to the world 'outside' the text, embodying a regulatory dimension whose aim is to re-order the organization (i.e., to improve total quality management in this case) through the stipulation of recommendations of best practices by top management.

One may also conclude that consultancy reports are a significant means by which examination of employees takes place in the organization studied, for, on the one hand, they collect data about employees and, on the other hand, they provide prescriptions as to how employees' lives should be ordered in the future. Where the 'external accounts' do not support the preferred 'rationality', the board disregards them. In the logistics company, for example, an external consultancy conducted a study aimed at quantifying and evaluating the state of health of the company's organizational culture. The results were never made public for the board did not like them: 'We did not think the consultants measured what they were supposed to. Their stuff was very questionable in terms of statistical validity and overall coherence. Such results could not be made public because they did not mean anything' (the operations director).

Incremental initiatives of 'getting people in line'

These initiatives support the most essential principle of TQM, namely the need for continuous improvement. The mail carrier's and the logistics company's boards of directors originated a number of initiatives aimed at continuous improvement. While their alleged purpose is in line with employee participation, enhanced motivation and commitment, they appear to facilitate the achievement of increased efficiency and control (Grenier et al., 1991).

In the mail carrier, quality improvement projects (QIPs) were set up in order 'to identify and prioritise improvement opportunities, to plan and implement solutions and to continuously improve everything we do in the company' (Support Pack for QIPs, p. 3). One might want to start looking critically at the statistics regarding the implementation of these quality initiatives, given that numerous middle managers and subordinates expressed their concerns about how the statistics were constructed. The facilities manager, for example, said: 'We have five teams of engineers who are doing exactly the same QIP and so, the fact that we achieved 38.7% quality improvement as opposed to 20%, our target, is a lot of rubbish.' A quality manager supported this idea by saying that 'there is a tendency to be number driven and, for example, in processing, where the percentage is low, the functional director sends a memo around just before the statistic is due, ordering his managers to increase participation'. Another personnel manager also appeared to be critical by stating that 'we talk about involvement in quality but what we do is we force people to participate in QIPs to get our figures up'. A processing worker mentioned a particular QIP in which they were asked to 'come up with recommendations which were never implemented', and another one said that 'what's annoying about QIPs is that they imply that there are only certain ways to do things around here, top management's way'.

The logistics company's top management enforce a similar initiative called 'our contribution counts circles' (OCC circles). Company documents describe this initiative as a way for the employees 'to get together in a structured way to identify, evaluate, recommend and implement improvements in quality, customer service and the way things are done in general' (OCC circles document). One of the quality managers considered OCC circles as 'mechanisms that destroy the spontaneity of people and alienate them'. Similarly, a finance manager said that 'the philosophy is right but they are too bureaucratic and people are deterred from participating because of their formality'. It may be that this initiative is supported by the top management because it allows quantification and, therefore, control. One of the back-office employees argued that 'the director wants everyone to sit on a circle to get the numbers up', while another one said that 'the company is playing a numbers' game'.

One may well argue that both QIPs and OCC circles are means by which top management order the organization in ways that make it more visible and therefore, more controllable. Indeed, having QIPs and OCCs in place allows top management to observe and monitor (i.e., examine) the employees and to categorize them in terms of people who behave à la TQM and people who choose not to behave à la TQM. Consequently, the former will be encouraged while the latter will be discriminated against to the extent that TQM becomes the only acceptable way of behaving. This form of interest translation cuts off any other alternative way of doing things around the place, forcing the employees to comport themselves according to the prevailing philosophy.

Training-related initiatives of 'fixing those who fall off'

In the organizations studied, training on TQM techniques appears to play a significant role in ordering the organization. The traditional view of training assumes that the individual is a given which the organization recruits and trains on a number of topics, among which is TQM. Furthermore, if training endorses the company's mission and values, the chances to improve self-fulfilment and motivation are higher. A social constructivist approach rejects this view by arguing that the individual is not a given, but is actively constructed through various TQM discourses and practices (Townley, 1994). Training on TQM in the organizations studied is specifically designed to equip the employees with new visions of work, à la TQM, in the belief that there is no conflict between the pursuits of productivity, efficiency and competitiveness, on the one hand, and the humanization of work, on the other (Rose, 1990).

The logistics company's case seems to be the most relevant example in terms of how training is used to shape people's attitudes towards fundamental issues, including themselves. This organization has its own 'university' and training issues are surrounded by an academic language. For example, the university has a principal, a rector, a number of deans as well as numerous committees and advisory boards. The organization has established ten faculties, which include The Warehousing and Distribution Faculty, The Commercial Faculty and The Core Faculty. The physical surroundings, comprising spacious class-rooms, computing facilities and video monitors, give the feeling that it is a 'real' university. The university publishes its prospectus as well as a number of leaflets on course availability. Its stated mission is to 'develop, train and inspire people to achieve world class performance and to build the world's best lean enterprise' (University Prospectus, 1994: 3).

On each corridor there are monitors presenting snapshots with the mission of the university. The chairman appears to play a pivotal role in these snapshots; he either speaks to people about total quality and 'world class', or presents awards to those who are considered to be role models for the rest of the organization. One can also see numerous photographs in which the chairman congratulates other organizational members for their achievements. The chairman's words are everywhere: on the corridors, in the class-rooms, on people's uniforms. The symbolic facet of the chairman's activity supports Brown's (1994) argument that symbolic actions and artefacts are important means by which individuals and groups seek to legitimate their privileged power relations.

In the logistics company, training and power are intertwined to a greater extent than in the other organizations under study. The financial manager, who is also a trainer, recalled a story in which two individuals, one from the vehicle office and the other from the post office, went on an accounting course because it was the shortest (only 3 hours), not because it was relevant to their jobs. When asked who sent them on that course they said that they had volunteered themselves in order to meet the training norms. This example illustrates that people feel internally pressurized to go on courses and, on certain occasions, they volunteer themselves. This instance supports Steingard and Fitzgibbons's (1993) idea that individuals eventually internalize the network of TQM power relationships and comport themselves into an ideal type of TQM employee. Employees know that if they do not attend 15 days of training a year, they will lose their privileges. In addition to the internal pressure, there seems to be a great deal of external pressure which comes from managers. On many occasions managers have to force their people to go on courses in order to get the numbers up. This is because managers are measured, *inter alia*, by the number of people sent on training.

One may well argue that training in this organization is related to education for self-enhancement but only to the extent that it optimizes the profit and overall performance of the business. In other words, training is aimed at institutionalizing a new way of thinking subordinated to the TQM official accounts. In all companies, employees have to endorse the training related initiatives because any other ways of doing things are cut off (Latour, 1987). Employees are thus implicitly forced into the TQM way of operating because there are no other ways of carrying out their work. As one of the processing workers in the mail carrier commented: 'If you don't attend the required amount of training you won't get any increase in your salary and your boss will look down on you.'

Conclusions

This chapter casts doubt on benign views which claim that TQM is a neutral technique which enables organizations to please their external customers via employee involvement. By adopting a social constructivist stance, I was hoping to add to the TQM debate by providing a critical view on what counts as TQM in four UK service organizations which claim to be embarked on successful TQM programmes. The insights gained during this exercise are, therefore, contextual and may not be generalized outside the organizations studied.

While the focus of the analysis is represented by those accounts which win out at the expense of the rest (i.e., the official TQM accounts), the chapter does not take a pro-management stance. Rather, it explores the political process by which official accounts are temporarily elevated and get to replace the multi-faceted reality. In the organizations studied, there are contentious individual meanings of TQM and some of them are suppressed as a direct manifestation of the power/knowledge deployed by 'significant' organizational actors (i.e., top management).

The evidence suggests that top management actively create and order organizational reality through quality initiatives. Quality initiatives are aimed at reinforcing the TQM official account on a constant basis. Employees are thus inscribed in the temporary order prescribed by these initiatives which makes their participation in the process of reality construction easier to manage and control. Indeed, quality initiatives allow top management to examine the employees (Foucault, 1977) and translate their interest (Latour, 1987) in accordance with the prevailing rationality.

One may conclude that, in the organizations studied, TQM is a set of practices and discourses in the hands of top management aimed at making the organization more transparent for control purposes. Through TQM, the organizations studied are self-legitimized in their pursuit of profit, rationality and workers' submission.

Acknowledgements

I would like to thank Valerie Fournier and Rolland Munro for their insightful comments, as well as Keith Grint for commenting on an earlier version of this chapter.

References

Bloomfield, B.P. and Vurdubakis, T. (1994) 'Re-presenting technology: IT consultancy reports as textual reality constructions', *Sociology*, 28 (2): 455–77.

Brown, A.D. (1994) 'Politics, symbolic action and myth making in pursuit of legitimacy', *Organisation Studies*, 15 (6): 861–78.

Chatterjee, S. and Yilman, M. (1993) 'Quality confusion: too many gurus, not enough disciples', *Business Horizons*, 36 (3): 15–18.

Chorn, N.H. (1991) 'Total quality management: panacea or pitfall?', *International Journal of Physical Distribution and Logistics Management*, 21 (8): 31–5.

Conrad, C. (1983) 'Organisational power, faces and symbolic forms', in L.L. Putnam and M.S. Pacanowsky (eds), *Communication in Organisations: an Interpretive Approach*. Beverly Hills, CA: Sage. pp. 173–94.

Crosby, P.B. (1979) *Quality is Free: the Art of Making Quality Certain*. New York: Mentor Books.

Czarniawska-Joerges, B. (1993) *The Three-Dimensional Organisation: a Constructivist View*. Sweden: Studentlitteratur.

Deming, W.E. (1982) *Quality, Productivity and Competitive Position*. Cambridge, MA: Massachusetts Institute of Technology.

Feigenbaum, A.V. (1962) *Total Quality Control*. New York: McGraw-Hill.

Foucault, M. (1977) *Madness and Civilisation*. London: Tavistock.

Gergen, K.J. (1985) 'The social constructionist movement in modern psychology', *American Psychologist*, 40: 266–75.

Grenier, G., Holger, R.L., Tausky, C. and Chelte, A.F. (1991) 'Labour law and managerial ideology: employee participation as a social control system; employee involvement: a comment on Grenier and Holger', *Work and Occupation*, 18 (3): 313–42.

Hill, S. (1991) 'Why quality circles failed but total quality management might succeed', *British Journal of Industrial Relations*, 29 (4): 541–68.

Hunt, V.D. (1993) *Managing Quality: Integrating Quality and Business Strategy*. Homewood, IL: Irwin.

Ishikawa, K. (1985) *What is Total Quality Control? The Japanese Way*. Englewood Cliffs, NJ: Prentice-Hall.

Juran, J.M. (1989) *Juran on Leadership for Quality: an Executive Handbook*. New York: The Free Press.

Latour, B. (1987) *Science in Action: How to Follow Scientists and Engineers through Society*. Milton Keynes: Open University Press.

McArdle, L., Rowlinson, M., Procter, S., Hassard, J. and Forrester, P. (1995) 'Total quality management and participation: employee empowerment or the enhancement of exploitation', in A. Wilkinson and H. Willmott (eds), *Making Quality Critical: New Perspectives on Organisational Change*. London: Routledge. pp. 156–73.

Munro, R. (1995) 'Governing the new province of quality', in A. Wilkinson and H. Willmott (eds), *Making Quality Critical: New Perspectives on Organisational Change*. London: Routledge. pp. 127–55.

Olian, J.D. and Rynes, S.L. (1991) 'Making total quality work: aligning organisations, performance measures, and stakeholders', *Human Resource Management*, 30: 303–33.

Peters, T.J. (1980) 'Management systems: the language of organisational character and competence', *Organisational Dynamics*, 9 (1): 3–26.

Price, F. (1989) 'Out of Bedlam: management by quality leadership', *Management Decision*, 27: 15–21.

Redman, T. and Wilkinson, A. (1995) 'Is quality management working in the UK?, *Journal of General Management*, 20 (3): 45–59.

Riger, S. (1992) 'Epistemological debates, feminist voices: science, social values and the study of women', *American Psychologist*, 47: 730–40.

Rose, N. (1990) *Governing the Soul: the Shaping of the Private Self*. London: Routledge.

Schwandt, T.A. (1994) 'Constructivist, interpretivist approaches to human inquiry', in N.K. Denzin and Y.S. Lincoln (eds), *Handbook of Qualitative Research*. London: Sage. pp. 118–38.

Spencer, B.A. (1994) 'Models of organisation and total quality management: a comparison and critical evaluation', *The Academy of Management Review*, 19 (3): 446–71.

Steingard, D.S. and Fitzgibbons, D.S. (1993) 'A postmodern deconstruction of total quality management (TQM)', *Journal of Organisational Change*, 6 (5): 27–42.

Taguchi, G. (1986) *Introduction to Quality Engineering: Designing Quality into Produce and Process*. Tokyo: Asian Productivity Organisation.

Thompson, K. (1980) 'Organisations as constructors of reality', in G. Salaman and K. Thompson (eds), *Control and Ideology in Organisations*. Milton Keynes: The Open University.

Townley, B. (1994) *Reframing HRM: Power, Ethics and the Subject at Work*. London: Sage.

von Glasersfeld, E. (1991) 'Knowing without metaphysics: aspects of the radical constructivist position', in F. Steiner (ed.), *Research and Reflexivity*. Newbury Park, CA: Sage. pp. 12–29.

Wilkinson, A. and Willmott, H. (1995) *Making Quality Critical: New Perspectives on Organisational Change*. London: Routledge.

9   Intelligent Organizations?

Stewart Clegg and Thomas Clarke

Towards the Future . . .

What characterizes 'intelligent organizations'? Until quite recently if we wanted to answer this question we would have looked for it in manufacturing concerns in the automobile industry, such as Toyota. Until very recently the 'lean production' associated with Toyota would have been seen as the very model of ultra-modern and intelligent management. Today, as the automobile age is overtaken by the software age, we might look instead at a firm like Microsoft.

What would the management literature of 'best practice' prepare us to see? We would expect to see organizations that were:

1 Customer driven for service. Customers, both internal and external, will be sovereign.
2 Destructured through distributed and networked technology.
3 Focused on quality as the crucial leadership factor.
4 Premised on full participation to drive quality as the accountable basis for everyone's work.
5 Linking rewards to quality to ensure its continual support.
6 Characterized by reduced cycle time. 'Do it better, do it faster' is the maxim.
7 Focused on prevention not detection: try to make it right first time.
8 Practising management by analysis. 'If you can analyse it, you can manage it', pushes management to imaginative analytic techniques.
9 Long-term in outlook. How will they do what they will do, better, in the foreseeable future?
10 Practising partnership development. The quality of the business will reside in the quality of its long-term partnering networks with other firms and customers.
11 Exemplars of civic responsibility. The organization will be a corporate citizen and will abide by good citizenship rules.

Underlying this list is the 'learning organization', as we shall see. Now, the sceptical reader might say that none of this seems exceptionable. Why, then, is it regarded as something new? It is not as if in the past managers consciously designed 'stupid organizations'. On the contrary: what are now seen as outmoded were, once upon a time, the very model of modern management.

In the Past: the Model of Modern Management

At the beginning of modern management theory was Weber's account of bureaucracy. In its day it was enormously influential in shaping the thinking of management researchers (see Clegg, 1990). Bureaucracies were the inevitable design for rational organization, pronounced Weber. Such organizations would be:

1 Differentiated into discrete areas subject to unified functional control.
2 Governed internally and linked as a unity through a hierarchy of offices, with clear responsibilities and duties attached to them.
3 Managed on the basis of a detailed knowledge of 'the files'. Each functional area would have a staff whose job was constantly to update these records.
4 Comprised of roles where individual duties and actions would be defined 'without regard for persons': hence, everyone was to be treated in accordance with the rules rather than in accordance with their social identity or status.
5 Staffed by competent individuals, formally and certifiably trained to do the tasks of the bureaucracy, with opportunities to make their career in the service of the bureaucracy, slowly moving up through its ranks.

In many ways Weber foresaw one element of the modern paradigm of organizations: bureaucracy. In addition to bureaucracy, the paradigm of modern organizations comprised two other key elements, contributed by F.W. Taylor and Henry Ford.

1 Highly differentiated and consciously designed jobs, de-skilled along Taylorist lines.
2 A system of semi-automatic assembly-line production, referred to as 'Fordism', based on intensive, divided labour linked together mechanistically.

Taylorism is well known: it was the adoption of systematic measurement and redesign of tasks to make their execution as simple, efficient and controllable as possible. The origins were in the military emphasis on drilling troops in the appropriate techniques of assembling, loading, firing, and re-loading muskets in such a way that they formed a disciplined and coherent body of men.

The Fordist element of 'modern organizations' derived from the Chicago meatworks. By the end of the nineteenth century, with cattle being freighted into the railhead from all over the west, the Chicago meatworks had become a fully automated process based on a moving line of livestock being slaughtered and butchered in a predetermined sequence. The carcasses were hung from chains that moved, automatically, along a complex line of overhead gantries. It was the origin of the conveyer belt, a technology that spread from the meatworks to the production of mass consumer goods produced in large production runs. The system of conveyors and handling devices ensured the movement of materials to the appropriate work-station. A semi-automatic assembly-line organized work into a linear flow of sequential transformations applied to evolving raw materials. Workers became adjuncts to the moving line, repetitively repeating a few elementary movements, in a predetermined work-flow designed by engineers.

There was a pyramid of control, designed in a classically bureaucratic fashion. Authority resided in individuals by virtue of their incumbency in office and/or their expertise. Employment was based on specialized training and formal certification of competence, acquired prior to gaining the job. Individuals in the managerial chain of command held an office – both figuratively and literally. These offices were organized hierarchically, instruction was expressed in terms of universal fixed rules that legitimated imperative command – 'managerial imperative' – or 'giving orders'. Direct surveillance and supervision, as well as standardized rules and sanctions, were the norm for ensuring work was done according to plan.

Fordism was a system of mass production. Work occurred in large, spatially concentrated organizations. Real wage and productivity growth were linked in this system, and the higher real wages encouraged demand for standardized consumer goods because mass workers were also mass consumers with families and homes in the new suburbs. Ford had a 'sociological department' whose task it was to see that only family-men of moral probity, with no vices, such as alcohol, drugs, promiscuity or socialism, were employed.

For managers under Fordism, management constituted a career in which either seniority or achievement might be the basis for advancement. Impersonality, where relations would be role based, segmented and instrumental, was the ideal, as Weber recommended. Incentives, arranged in a career ladder with differential rewards related to place in the hierarchy, were the primary sources of motivation. Motivation of employees was principally through the wages system, the manipulation of bonus rates, and the extensive number of job classifications used. Prestige, privilege and power would be consistent with one another in the hierarchy.

Division of labour was extreme. Intellectual work of design, conception and communication distinguished its practitioners, the managers, from those who did manual work. The latter were so many interchangeable 'hands' executing and making possible superordinate designs, in a high specialization of jobs and functions and an extensive differentiation of roles. Production was planned against inventories of stock and raw materials. In those countries, such as the USA and the UK, that had vestiges of occupational craft unionism, these classifications became the basis of union organization and the defence of 'relativities' and 'occupational monopoly', leading to frequent demarcation disputes – about which trade is allowed to do what.

Parts and components were transported into huge warehouses in the plant, from subcontractors who had bid the lowest price for the contract, usually secured for one year at a time. The market supplied and the company stockpiled. Customer service was secondary to shipping product.

By the 1970s the model began to falter. A slowdown in productivity growth, fierce international competition, and upward pressures on wages squeezed profits. Productivity slowed down and there began a process of 'internationalization' and associated 'de-industrialization' of areas and enterprises that were previously strongholds of Fordism. Companies decentralized standardized production to new, dispersed localities, initially within the industrialized nations, later to newly industrializing countries, but kept managerial and financial functions within head offices in existing large metropolitan areas (Albertsen, 1988: 347).

Customers deserted the goods manufactured by this system. Widespread dissatisfaction began to be expressed by consumers with quality problems. Workers were dissatisfied as well, expressed in sabotage (sometimes the source of quality problems), frustrated outbreaks of truculence at work, sometimes tipping into industrial militancy, and increasing turnover and diminishing productivity. Consumers began to choose new imported products from Japan, a story that played out across diverse fields such as consumer electronics and automobiles.

Something was afoot. Not only were these Japanese products cheaper and more reliable – but management writers began to urge that they were so because their manufacturers followed a different paradigm in their production. By 1990 this had become known as 'lean production', based on developments at Toyota.

Lean Production: More Intelligent Organization?

Just as one element of 'modern organizations' began in the auto industry, so too some elements of the most popular model succeeding it were nurtured by Toyota in Japan. The Toyota system developed from a visit by Sakichi Toyoda to the Ford plant in Detroit in the early 1950s during the post-war reconstruction of Japanese industry, under American tutelage. While there he saw much to admire, but realized that much could, and would have to, be done differently in Japan (Cusamano, 1985). What were some of the differences?

- The Japanese market was not characterized by a similar demand to the USA for a small range of relatively large cars produced in vast quantities.

- The domestic market in Japan demanded many different types of car.
- Not only was there a greater variety of models, but they were produced in smaller batches than was typical in the USA.

Toyota responded to these market differences with innovations such as new techniques of die changing that speeded up work processes. Rather than fiercely competitive tendering between many suppliers, the firm established long-term relationships on the basis of mutual benefit. Suppliers became involved in design decisions with the firm. Toyota implemented their management systems in suppliers but did not vertically integrate to minimize transaction costs. Instead, they used 'just-in-time' (JIT) systems.

Just-in-time systems establish complex market relations with component subcontractors to ensure that supplies arrive where they are needed at the appropriate time. Large inventory stocks are dispensed with, and the circulation of capital in 'dead' buffer stock is minimized. Large JIT production complexes spatially organize so that subsidiary companies, suppliers and subcontractors exist in close relationships with each other. A number of distinct advantages flow from the JIT system: wage costs relocate from the more expensive core work force to the cheaper peripheral work force; stable long-term relations develop with suppliers, opening up multi-directional flows of information between the partners in the subcontracting network; personnel as well as ideas are freely exchanged; and innovations accelerate through the system.

Closely linked to the JIT system is *jikoda*, the principle of designing a machine with automatic defect detection, signalled by an immediate shutdown when a fault is detected. Inspection is built into the machine. When this is combined with JIT systems, it ensures defect-free production. Additionally, it eliminates the need for machine watching: the machine runs as long as everything is satisfactory. It stops if not. Hence, one worker can mind several machines simultaneously, not just watch one. As a team member, even greater flexibility attaches to them. Employee teams acquire multi-functional skills, making them able to work on different machines and processes.

At the same time that Toyota made technological innovations they introduced management innovations. In the post-war recovery, management yielded to union pressure and introduced lifetime employment for core employees and pay based on seniority, tied to company profitability. The effects were apparent: employees had a considerable stake in the success of the enterprise and considerable incentive to stay within the enterprise. On the basis of these conditions Toyota developed the skills of their core members over their career. The firm provided the context for the entire career; the firm rewarded career-workers through the seniority wages system. Consequently, production workers learnt a range of skills denied in the Fordist system. These skills were partly intellectual in character (Koike, 1987), involving tasks such as problem-diagnosis and responsibility for taking remedial action to fix problems. And, after time in the system, the core employees (invariably men) were well-remunerated.

The Toyota system, while it was a more intelligent organization than its Fordist counterparts, at its core was still based on many of the same principles. Retained were the precepts of the Taylor system, stressing both a horizontal and a vertical division of labour, together with hierarchical control structures. The differences were important. The skill basis was greatly enhanced. The development of multi-functional skills tied in with the definition of work tasks in terms of standardized competencies. Precise analysis of competencies available in teams, and graphic display of these on the shop-floor, meant better management of many areas of relative scarcity. The lead production system increased both the quantitative range of skills and their sharing, even if skill-ranges did not increase in all dimensions. Less strict specialization meant that first-line supervisors, 'foremen', were replaced with working team leaders. It was the teams that became responsible for the quality of their work, rather than a separate, and essentially, reactive-to-failure, inspectorate, nurturing a more proactive attitude to quality.

Both employees and customers trust manufacturers more in this system. Dealers develop 'relationship marketing' with buyers. They guarantee that the cars that they supply will pass the comprehensive and strict three-year compulsory tests in Japan. For employees, the line was not subject to arbitrary 'speed-ups' that exhausted workers at times of increased demand, nor 'slow-downs' at times of diminished demand. Continuous improvement rather than speed-up was the creed. When new methods improved productivity, workers were not made redundant but moved to other areas: the remaining pool of workers were expected to maintain the same level of intensity and productivity of work. Japanese work organization uses self-managing teams rather than workers striving against each other under an individualistic and competitive bonus payment and production system. Within self-managing teams work roles overlapped with continuous, rather than discontinuous, task structure, in which workers allocated tasks internally. Work skill content is not simplified inexorably as in the classical modernist organization under Fordism.

Work teams change the pace of production by adding or removing workers. Management and team members experiment with different configurations. Workers often moved with the production line and work-groups perform routine quality control. Management focused on non-routine aspects of quality control, such as advanced statistical measurement or work redesign. Work-groups detected and corrected mistakes quickly, saving considerable rework and scrappage. Quality control and shop-floor problem-solving were integrated (Kenney and Florida, 1988: 132). Workers were expected to make improvements in work processes to make it faster or smarter. This is where quality circles come in. Quality circles include both operatives and staff specialists such as engineers in the same circle, oriented not only towards reducing the wastage rate, but also to improving technological and process improvements. Much of the routine preventative maintenance is done by the operatives who use the machines. It is easy to see why, compared with Fordism, this way of working might be thought a more 'intelligent organization'.

- It does not treat employees as stupidly as Fordism: workers are more skilled and they develop abilities to work together, and learn together, in teams, through 'quality circles'.
- The model does not assume that customers take whatever they are offered.
- It involves suppliers and components manufacturers in the production cycle.
- It diminishes the amount of dead capital tied up in stock and warehousing.

MIT discovered Toyota's use of 'lean production' as a new paradigm in the course of a research project known as the 'International Motor Vehicle Program' conducted at the Toyota plant in Toyota City, Japan (Womack et al., 1990). Once discovered in Japan, it was not long before reports of the first sightings of the lean production paradigm in the USA and the UK came in, albeit that the export model underwent modifications that took account of different social structures, according to Oliver and Wilkinson (1988) and Morris and Wilkinson (1995). Management that followed the lean production model of just-in-time (JIT), flexible manufacturing, quality circles and *kaizen* (or continuous improvement) could share in the economic success of Japan. The paradigm provided a model for translation, irrespective of context. It boiled down to some simple precepts: 'Lean production is lean because it uses less of everything compared with mass production American style' as the Swedish management writer, Bengt Sandkull (1996: 71) puts it.

The circumstances in which 'lean production' triumphed have to be considered. At the outset Japanese cars sold well in overseas market dominated by high-cost models produced locally. For the 1970s and well into the 1980s, Japanese manufacturers, whatever other advantages they had from 'lean production', certainly expended less of one vital ingredient – wages – and got more of another – labour time (Williams et al., 1994). Japanese wages were about half of those in the USA and they worked several hundred hours a year more. By the mid-1990s the wage disadvantages had disappeared and the increasing value of the Yen placed great pressure on costs.

Japanese auto firms today are much like their competitors in Europe. They have a high break-even point and a high need for cost reduction, usually through opening plants overseas, in lower labour-cost economies with a high propensity to import components and ready-mades for assembly in the inwardly-invested sites. This describes Japanese investment in Asia as well as it does in the USA or the UK (Haslam et al., 1996: 36) and raises some questions about claims of a special advantage attaching to the 'lean production' problematic, its methods of just-in-time, *jikoda*, flexible manufacturing, and quality circles. Additionally, while once the talk may have been of the 'Japanese challenge', newer, cheaper cost-production centres have come on-stream, in countries such as South Korea, premised on similar cost-reduction strategies as once characterized Japan.

Flexible specialization

Lean production is usually identified in technological terms with flexible manufacturing systems, where small batches can be rapidly set-up, produced, and equipment rapidly reconfigured to start-up manufacturing another set of small batches. Flexible specialization based on information technology (IT) is the hallmark.

The 'flexible' aspect refers to the restructuring of the labour market and the labour process, while the 'specialization' aspect refers to the ascendancy of niche or specialist markets and marketing, as opposed to mass markets. It is the 'push' of the latter which is seen to require the response of the former. Changes to more differentiated consumption cause production changes away from organizations based on tight managerial control through surveillance, de-skilling and mechanization (Smith, 1989: 204).

Sabel (1982: 220) initially proposed that these changes would result in a 'high technology cottage industry' where craft forms of production would be enveloped by new forms of technology. In the Italian cases that he studied these were fostered by local state initiatives. The Benetton-type models of Emilia-Romagna provide the paradigm case. Later, in collaboration with Michael Piore, he extended the focus to include not only high-technology cottage industry, but also the restructuring of mass-production industry, adopting new technologies and new practices (Piore and Sabel, 1984). Thus, Piore and Sabel's focus on small and medium-sized enterprises in Northern Italy shifted to the restructuring of large US corporations, such as Boeing, General Electric, General Motors and Ford, which sought to learn from Japan and restructure. Flexible specialization enabled market-responsive manufacturing to be based on generalist skills and technologies rather than on ones which were highly differentiated.

Engineering and production changes alone were insufficient, however. Katz and Sabel (1985) and Piore (1986) identified major blockages to the realization of a restructured system in existing labour institution: these had to change to accommodate the new production systems (also see Smith, 1989: 210–11). In order that organizations have the flexibility to respond to changing market conditions they have had to develop a core of committed and flexible employees. Employers invest heavily in training costs, and, as a corollary, core workers develop company-specific skills. Employers protect these as an investment through offering core workers security, frequent retraining, and every opportunity to integrate into the organization culture. Peripheralized workers, by contrast, remain less-skilled with none of the benefits of those in the primary sector.

Critics have responded that what is occurring is less a new kind of 'lean production' and more a further twist on Fordism: they call this neo-Fordism. Neo-Fordism is seen to solve contradictions which the previous Fordist regime could not. The major contradiction was that the Fordist regime had reached the limits of its ability to increase productivity. Fordism ran up against the obstacle of its own design. This became apparent as labour productivity began to slow down. It was in those countries which developed enhanced commitment by the workers, notably Japan, that productivity increases were gained. The re-integration of the active consent and knowledge of the workers back into the production process proved the centre-piece of lean production. Of course, this poses some old problems in a new guise: if more 'intelligent organization' empowers workers and their team-based enterprise, how do we determine that their newly encouraged 'intelligence' gets exercised in line with managerial objectives?

Benchmarking the Intelligent Organization

Benchmarking studies are used extensively by the promoters of lean production. Womack, Jones and Roos (1990) speculated that lean production, as it was emulated by firms seeking to acquire 'world's best practice', would create 'plants . . . populated almost entirely by highly skilled problem solvers whose task will be to think continually of ways to make the system run more smoothly and productively' (Womack et al., 1990: 102). Evidence is emerging that where lean production benchmarks 'world-class' performance levels in firms, the stress on the lean way as the best way is one that neglects the interests of one important group of stakeholders: employees.

> Workers are employed in jobs which offer them little real control over working conditions and at tasks that can be learned in a very short period of time. Most workers lack any real control over how they work, how fast they work, or when they work. Workloads are high and increasing, health risks are high and increasing, work is stressful and becoming more stressful. (Lewchuck and Robertson, 1996: 79)

None of this is inconsistent with the results attributed to 'lean production': more may be produced, better, more rapidly, but if the surveys that register this do not at the same time register the human consequences of lean production, the real costs will never be accounted:

If a particular company, for example, had the highest throughput in the industry but also had the fastest line speed, the highest incidence of RSIs (repetitive strain injuries), the highest accident claims, and the most problems with the placement of injured workers, then its status as best-in-class around throughput would have to be offset against these other measures. (Lewchuck and Robertson, 1996: 61)

Wise management would insist on as broad-based an audit as possible: there is little point building intelligent organizations on fundamental stupidity.

Knowledge-workers

Adler (1993) and Adler and Cole (1993) provide detailed research of continuous improvement based on knowledge-workers at NUMMI, in the USA, an aspirational benchmark for many firms. Adler and his associates clearly share the 'lean production' paradigm fascination for detailed pre-scription of the task as the best basis for learning, constituted principally in terms of production efficiency where knowledge-based workers learn as they work and thus enhance the organization.

At NUMMI, a joint Japanese–American venture in automobile manu-facturing, teams of four or five workers perform tasks of relatively short duration, that are highly specialized, have detailed work procedures and a modest degree of job rotation. The system lends itself to rapid learning. Workers at NUMMI learn from making an explicit model of what they already know, applied to relatively short, focused tasks. Explicitness about rules and routines facilitates learning, they suggest. Adler and his col-leagues identify knowledge-workers as those who work in rule-enabling organizations rather than rule-constraining ones. The NUMMI case is thus an example of 'enabling' rather than 'coercive' rule-setting. In rule-enabling settings continuous improvement develops through the structuring of desire, understanding and trust:

- Workers learn to share with managers a 'desire' to achieve excellence and to work towards a job well done.
- Workers come to 'understand' that their jobs depend on the com-petitive success of the organization and the best way to protect their jobs is constantly to improve the way that they do them, and thus continuously improve the competitive position of their employers.
- Managers and workers develop 'trust' in each other and this trust is amplified through the commitment that the workers show.

Weick and Westley (1996) refer to the findings of Adler and his associ-ates as demonstrations of knowledge-workers practising 'exploitative' learning which they contrast with 'exploratory' learning, terms derived from the work of James March (1991 especially, also see 1995; and Levinthal and March, 1993).

- Exploitative learning is typical of the learning that occurs in more bureaucratic organizations, where learning develops from existing routines. It is associated with defining, measuring and improving performance. It advances through redefining work in terms of systematic reasoning, improvements to existing capabilities and technologies, and cost-reductions. It refines existing capabilities, forcing through standardization and routinization. Generally, exploitative learning is risk-averse. Its benefits are relatively immediate and fairly predictable. Exploitative learning tends to continue existing trends, perhaps accelerating them slightly.

- Exploratory learning allows for different type of learning than learning simply from routines. It is associated with complex search, basic research, innovation, variation, risk-taking and more relaxed controls. The stress is on flexibility, investments in learning and the creation of new capabilities. It may be thought of in terms of coaching and cajolery, and their articulation as training, advice and recommendations: think of a sports team and the role of the coach in continuously improving both individual and team performance. Exploratory learning characterizes more intelligent organization, where innovation, rather than refining what already exists, produces creative discontinuities. Exploratory learning offers distant time horizons and uncertain benefits as its vision. It offers the chance of increasing performance levels significantly beyond or below trendlines (if risky ventures fail).

Typically, exploratory learning comprises fleeing, flexible moments within the overall orderly flow. Take humour: its role in relieving tension in organizational settings, or of surfacing criticism in a way that is socially acceptable, is well known. Humour disrupts the routines of everyday seriousness: it expresses criticism, contradiction, ambiguity and contrary worldview. Humour is a classically improvisational form: unscripted, contextualized, creative and potentially code-breaking. If attended to, improvisations pose unique opportunities for insight and innovation among routines as they break on through to the other side of structure. Action-oriented organizations in the heat of action, like fire-fighters (Weick, 1996) or combat units (Janowitz, 1959), provide an organization model of improvisation over, above, beyond, around, sometimes in harmony, sometimes in counterpoint. with the script that steers normalcy. All organizations have moments of improvisation; not all organizations seem capable of capturing these and making them work for their future. In many, structure strives to overwhelm novelty rather than feel the shock of the new.

The premises that Adler and his associates begin from, as well as the specifics of the NUMMI case, privilege the 'lean production' model of clear and detailed standardization. Weick and Westley (1996: 450) suggest that Volvo's Uddevalla plant offers a contrast. Here the teams comprised about ten workers, working collectively on tasks that took about two hours, in ways that were much less-well documented than at NUMMI. The conditions are more craft-like. Adler and Cole (1993) suggest that in such craft circumstances, lacking in clear structure, it is more difficult to learn. Here, individuals learn more than the organization does because the lack of structure of the latter means little of what is innovated is incorporated: it does not shift from the individual's skill-set to that of the organization. Within a two-hour work cycle it is hard to spot the improvements that produce a positive effect.

> The Volvo model is a concept characterizing the willingness of Volvo, when new production facilities are about to be planned (either completely new or renewed) to allow people in project groups to develop new production systems not necessarily located in the body of mainstream ideas. The result is that people's unique creativity has been left free, and recurrent innovations have been made when new plants are built. The Volvo-model concept thus implies a company's trust in the project groups' abilities. This implies flexibility and an orientation towards trying out new solutions to production-related problems. (Ellegård, 1996: 118)

By contrast to the stress on routines in exploitative learning that Adler and his associates promote, Weick and Westley (1996: 450) suggest attention be oriented to the unexpected, the idiosyncratic, and the serendipitous that flies in the face of tight control: these are the harbingers of exploratory learning.

> If moments of balance between exploration and exploitation are transient, then researchers need to look at uncommon, often inconspicuous events to spot learning. And practitioners need to be less enamored with large-scale training programs and campaigns of transformation and more alert to places and moments where canons and dogma become suspect. (Weick and Westley, 1996: 450)

A new plant in a new site is an organizational opportunity to achieve the type of learning that Weick and Westley propose. The Volvo plants of Kalmar and Uddevalla, were such occasions.

> In such new factories there are no immediate signs of inertia where human manners, habits and values are taken for granted. Newly recruited people are open-minded regarding their opinions of work content and organization, at least if they have not been employed in the same company before. They are creating the culture of the new plant, a culture which will be the basis for the new traditions. These newly shaped traditions will obviously differ from the traditions of the older plants. (Ellegård, 1996: 120)

However, the learning that occurred did not get generalized around the Volvo system. Not only that. In the early 1990s the two innovative plants were closed down and Volvo's learning concentrated around the more exploitative learning conditions that prevailed in the parent plant at Torslanda. Volvo lacked a strategy for diffusing its learning through the company: it depended on the commitment of individuals to ideas, and the politics that surrounded any influence they might have. The moral is clear: there has to be a strategy for linking exploratory learning to exploitative learning. Levinthal and March (1993: 105) propose that the survival of any organization depends upon being sufficiently exploitative as to ensure current viability and sufficiently exploratory as to ensure its future viability. Too much exploitation risks organizational survival by creating a 'competency trap' where increasingly obsolescent capabilities continue to be elaborated. Too much exploration insufficiently linked to exploitation leads to 'too many undeveloped ideas and too little distinctive competence'.

Strategies for Organization Learning

Strategies for achieving the linkage between exploratory and exploitative learning characterize the latest developments in the lean production system. Rawlinson and Wells (1996: 203) provide an example. Work teams under lean production solve problems. But the learning from the problem solved does not stay within the team. Manufacturing engineers, as in Taylorism, take suggestions for making work smarter or faster and recode them into standard job sheets or operating procedures. This becomes the benchmark for work within the plant. But the process does not stop there.

The benchmark, once achieved within one team and one plant, can be virtually circulated throughout the entire organization, world-wide. The interlinkage of plants by Electronic Data Interchange (EDI) allows for the learning to be distributed globally, immediately, virtually. Imagine an improved process being exploratively innovated in a plant in the UK. How could management make it virtual, distribute it freely and widely? This is a technical problem with two dimensions: portability and embeddedness.

The first dimension, that of portability, includes three aspects that must be met, if it is to be achieved. First, the exploratory learning must be standardized and made more exploitative. This means that the moment of insight, disorder, in the orderly routine, must be codified into standardized terms that all can understand. Secondly, standardized information must be commodified. The dependence of the exploratory insight on the individuals who produced it must be eliminated by commodifying tacit knowledge. It must be rendered as something that any person could do, not something that one person might have done. If management can reduce their dependency on individuals as the bearers of knowledge and skills by rendering it into computer-based artifacts, it is possible to manipulate and combine it with other factors of production in ways that are impossible if it remains a human possession. This means a shift from the knowledge-worker to knowledge as a pure factor of production. Thirdly, abstract proprieties need to be developed for the phenomena that have been standardized and commodified. Examples include the registration of a house or land title: the title allows for the property to be alienated, to be exchanged across time and space in a recognizable commodity form. Abstract property rights simplify the preservation of assets over time and their movement through space.

The second dimension, that of embeddedness, flows directly from the properties of the digitalized corporation and technologies such as EDI. Exploratory learning embedded in innovation becomes tangible when embedded in a computer program. It is easy to transmit this throughout the world. But a program may not capture the tacit knowledge that is involved in making the exploratory innovation work. It is here that EDI can assist. The work process can be videoed, scanned on to computer, and downloaded instantly by the globally networked corporation. The tacit knowledge that created an exploratory breakthrough in one plant becomes a part of the strategy of competitive advantage of the global, digitalized, intelligent corporation. As Rawlinson and Wells conclude, 'the pace of work is no longer controlled and defined on a plant basis but on a global basis' (1996: 203).

The implications of portable embeddedness are massive in the age of the smart machine. Innovation premised on the tacit learning and embedded skills of the work forces of the cleverest countries can rapidly be standardized, commodified and abstracted into organizational processes in the least clever of countries. Here, workers with lower standards of schooling and education can be organizationally tooled-up to match the competencies of more creative employees in the cleverest of countries.

The implications of these developments are substantial for those organizations that can achieve these gains. They are even more substantial for the national systems of governance within whose administrative frameworks such break-throughs may occur. Being a clever country is no longer a sufficient basis for ensuring national competitive edge: it is not so much nations, but firms, that are competing globally, and they are able to ensure that better learning is no longer the preserve of nationally superior systems. Instead, it can be globalized through digitalization virtually anywhere.

Virtual Organizations

'Virtual' is a term with considerable currency in the natural sciences. Since the mid-nineteenth century in physics the term indicated 'structure and objects whose ontological status lies in the fuzzy realm between facts and apparition', such as a 'virtual image' referring 'to an image from which light *seems* to emanate but does not in truth do so' (Nohria and Berkely, 1994: 113). Most readers will probably be familiar with the computer concept of 'virtual memory', even if they remain unclear what it is exactly. Users of the Internet know that when they 'surf the net' they exist in cyberspace, a virtual space. Virtual organizations share many features with these other uses of 'virtual': members of networked organizations interact with others whom they may not know face-to-face, and rarely, if ever, see face-to-face, and their transactions take place in a virtual space. Computers make virtuality possible.

Intelligent organizations would be impossible without computers and information technology. Only a decade ago the nature of the relation was still a matter for speculation: *Fortune* magazine in 1988 ventured that, in the future, organizations would not just be aided by computers, but that 'companies will live by them, shaping strategy and structure to fit new information technology'. Some of the early oft-cited prodigy of the relationship are airline reservations where strategic advantage attaches to the booking system rather than the flying system; automated teller machines, the number of outlets of which now exceed conventional bank sites with staff, in developed economies like Australia; and computer-aided design/manufacturing (CAD/CAM) which has developed within, if not always been integrated by, many organization systems (Copeland and Mckenney, 1988; Ohara, 1988). However, the most significant impact of information technology is not in specific products or services but in the way that it dematerializes modern organization. Electronic information can be everywhere simultaneously, worked at by everyone simultaneously, from anywhere in the world with electronic access. Organization, as a container or an envelope of activity, ceases to be important.

In the past considerable resources were committed to organization design, including IT. For many years its adoption mirrored the organizations that produced it (IBM) and used it: they were bureaucracies in which IT enhanced centralization, formalization, standardization and control. More recent developments make virtuality possible, and flatter. Leaner organizations began to emerge that no longer needed armies of supervisors: supervision became both more immediate through technologies and employees became less subject to an external supervisory gaze and more subject either to team or self-supervision, in an environment measured and monitored electronically. Organization structure loses its historic role of managing power relations at a distance: for one thing, distance disappears electronically; for another, power relations flatten as teams proliferate, work becomes a series of projects, and the supervisory gaze is both internalized and becomes part of peer pressure.

Davidow and Malone identified *The Virtual Corporation* (1992) as a distinctive model premised on these changes. A simple thesis characterized their book. New technologies make old assumptions irrelevant. Organization design needs to catch up with the technological capacities of personal computers, remote access, networked data-bases, and e-mail. Yet, as should be apparent from the discussion thus far, digitalization is just one part of the tendencies towards 'virtuality'. It is the enabling mechanism that allows time and space to be collapsed, and the informational controls inscribed in bureaucracy, which sought to manage across them, superseded.

TABLE 9.1   *Contrasts between modern and virtual organizations*

Modern organization	Virtual organization
• Functionality in design structure.	• De-functionalized project-based design held together by network capabilities.
• Hierarchy governing formal communication flows and managerial imperative – the major form and basis of formal communication.	• Instantaneous, remote computer communication for primary interaction; increase in face-to-face informal interaction; decrease in imperative actions and increased governance through accountability in terms of parameters rather than instructions or rules.
• The files.	• Flexible electronic immediacy through IT.
• Impersonal roles.	• Networking of people from different organizations such that their sense of formal organizational roles blurs.
• Specialized technical training for specific careers.	• Global, cross-organizational computer-mediated projects.

> In the virtual organization . . . the file cabinets of bureaucratic ritual disappear, replaced by devices that shatter the traditional physical instantiation of information and knowledge. . . . When employees in contemporary organizations use electronic mail or build reports from network databases, there is no original physical reality to what this information refers, unless such reference be to a tangle of code and wiring that, to most workers, remains opaque or even mystical. (Nohria and Berkely, 1994: 119)

The virtual organization is almost the exact opposite of the modern organizations that Weber first identified in the ways that it organizes its basis for authoritative action. Recall the Weberian model that we introduced at the outset of the chapter: Table 9.1 contrasts it with its 'virtual' counterpoint.

Microsoft is an interesting case in point. While it is not a virtual organization itself, its products help make virtuality possible, and it uses some virtual ideas to facilitate more effective and faster communication among its staff at its principal location.

Microsoft

Microsoft hires smart people whom it makes sure know the software business really well – otherwise they don't get hired. Many heed the call but few achieve selection: only 2 or 3 per cent of those who apply to be software developers are invited to join Microsoft. But Microsoft is not so successful just because it makes good selection decisions. Of course, this is important, but it is not sufficient. Microsoft also nurtures creative people and technical skills through its organization design. (See Cusamano and Selby, 1996: 9. What follows is taken from this account.) Multi-functional teams are the norm, comprising distinctive functional skills and responsibilities that overlap at the boundaries. As new competencies are required they are hired in, as people who learn on the job, rather than from formal rules, regulations or training programmes. Effort is made to ensure that technical skills have career paths associated with them. Of course, if there are to be careers there have to be products and services shifting rapidly in the marketplace. Microsoft's strategy has always been to make its own products the market standard and then to make them obsolescent before their competitors do so: hence, the market grows dynamically.

Managing dynamic, technologically discontinuous markets premised on complex innovation can be the reef of unmanageable creativity on which enterprise founders. Not at Microsoft. Development is project based, and project teams must maintain market, not just technical, focus. Market focus is maintained through orientation not to the technically feasible but the commercially marketable in innovation, innovation performed under pressure of managerial limits on time, people and other resources. At any time there will be many project teams working in parallel, but also infrequent communication with each other, and under central co-ordination. The co-ordination encourages project teams to synchronize design and iron out conflicts in parallel process development with other teams. Strict time guidelines achieve this: teams have to report progress by a pre-specified time and date so that any problems of design incompatibility that require debugging are spotted immediately. Similarly, any bugs that designers build-in to the program inadvertently must be fixed by them – rather like the rule on the Toyota 'lean production' line that operatives fix faults that they spot or create, as Cusamano and Selby (1996: 12) note.

Microsoft is an entirely innovative and marketing-focused company. Frequent incremental innovation is aided by staff sharing open-plan offices, being in a single-site location, using common tools, and receiving frequent customer trials (and feedback – there are over 2,000 people receiving customer calls in the USA alone). Also, regular use is made of a small range of specific measures to monitor progress (such as individual daily reports on project development; monthly status reports on project team progress that are brief and formatted in terms of sets of headings and sub-headings, both of which are e-mailed to supervisors; and three monthly program reviews for each project chaired by Bill Gates and other senior executives, at which one or two key people from each project team are represented). The use of quantitative metrics and benchmarks at Microsoft became a well-established practice over the years. Whatever is at issue, any case that relies on politics or emotion more than data is unlikely to be received favourably by senior management. Use of such data typically addresses issues of quality, product and process.

Microsoft is based on teams whose members learn from each other, from other teams, from customers and from past mistakes. Teams seek to:

share knowledge is project management and quality control, as well as to build components that more than one project can utilize. Sharing and standardization save engineering and testing costs, make products more coherent to customers, and reduce the need for large customer support staffs. (Cusamano and Selby, 1996: 12–13)

All of this takes place in a context where teams are continually pushed by senior management to imagine tomorrow today, forcing continuous innovation and improvement in a process that Cusamano and Selby (1996: 13–19) term 'synch-and-stabilize' in an iterative, incremental and concurrent process that:

continually synchronize[s] what people are doing as individuals and as members of different teams, and periodically stabilize[s] the product in increments – in other words, as the project proceeds, rather than once at the end. (Cusamano and Selby, 1996: 14)

The cultural, structural and personnel context in which this occurs, while it may be 'fervently anti-bureaucratic' (Cusamano and Selby, 1996: 15), is also simultaneously structured. The structure is less one of rules for, and formalization of, operating procedures, but is based more on formal reporting of loosely structured project work. The basis for this is to make manageable chunks of process development constructed by small teams and tightly to couple these to customer feedback from the marketplace. Loosely but firmly structured reporting mechanisms on daily progress are where the structure bites in, as well as in sophisticated personnel management practices that are required to compensate for the overwhelming technical, rather than managerial, skill biases of most of the managers. The staff are the brightest and the best technically available from the elite universities in the USA, thus 'it is not surprising that the company culture emphasizes technical competence and shipping products rather than adhering to rules and regulation, respecting formal titles, or cultivating skills in political infighting' (Cusamano and Selby, 1996: 70–1). The down-side of this culture is that solutions are continually being re-invented because they have not been abstracted and systematized into the operating practices of the firm. As Microsoft develops its metrics, what it is attempting to do is to transform the tacit knowledge of its employees into generalizable abstractions standardization, commodification, and abstractification.

None of the systems that Microsoft use were the result of a conscious design decision; rather, they were emergent from the process of Microsoft's historical development, the problems that it faced, and the disasters and solutions that it stumbled into, or shipped in, with the buying-in of key management expertise that brought solutions pioneered elsewhere. One of these solutions was the realization that as Microsoft's product-range grew, it resembled a series of distinct business lines that were best managed as organic entities rather than as projects staffed by interchangeable people, without 'ownership' of the projects. Organic entities grew into distinct small business units where functional specialists worked in small team with overlapping responsibilities. While Microsoft employees are expected to be flexible, they are not expected to be so at the expense of career path and career ladders within the company. As stakeholders in the company, not just employees, they receive generous stock-options as part of their compensation package.

Microsoft developed as a company that wanted to make 'paradigm shifts' that flow from technological discontinuities in the digital world. Talk of 'paradigm shifts' is not regarded as academic at Microsoft but is the core business, overlooked by a 'Brains Trust' of a dozen senior people who 'run the key product areas and new initiatives as well as constitute an informal oversight group to critique what everybody else is doing' (Cusamano and Selby, 1996: 56). Many of its members were previously senior executives or professors elsewhere before joining Microsoft.

Microsoft has learnt not only from professional expertise hired in from elsewhere; it also learns from its customers. Customer support is regarded as a part of the product and as data for improvement. Such a strategy allows Microsoft to make a strength out of a weakness, the weakness being their propensity to ship products that are not totally de-bugged, despite all the in-house work. Over time they have evolved a complex cycle of customer input as a part of the product cycle.

The cycle of customer input begins by integrating internal data analysis with that derived from customers through phone-in services. These are of two types: 'Wish Lines' and 'Off-line Plus'. 'Wish lines' are where customers recount what they wish to see developed; 'Off-line Plus' analyses data from the thousands of customer calls that come in on a monthly basis. Information derived from these sources is fed into the internal product development that occurs around the testing of prototypes in Microsoft's usability labs. While these prototypes are widely tested within Microsoft, they are also released to elected customers for testing as well. Microsoft's product support services division also tests its 'supportability services' through the usability labs to find out to what extent the new features are supportable, as well as experimenting with new ways of diagnosing problems. At product-release time product developers and testers staff the product support services telephone lines so that they can hear, respond to, and learn from customer complaints directly. Product support services also run extensive market research post-launch on customer satisfaction, not only with the new products but with the levels of customer support and the company as a whole. Finally, the product support services division also run focus groups with marketing agencies to discover how customers actually use the products as well as releasing versions of the product that have been manufactured to track every mouse move and keyboard entry that the customer uses when working with the product (see Figure 6.1 in Cusamano and Selby, 1996: 361). Customers are key stakeholders in Microsoft. (Cynics say that they have to be, given the problems that are shipped out to them.)

Intelligent Organizations, Technologies and Power

Microsoft is a classic case of a company founded on the initial intelligence of a few people who have systematized that intelligence into an organization that learns through continuous self-critique, feedback and sharing of information. While Microsoft make extensive use of the virtual technologies that they design, they are also a spatially quite concentrated company, headquartered in Redmond, Washington State, in the USA. Consequently, as well as the 'virtual' systems of feedback and communication, there are many opportunities for face-to-face communication, often of a quite informal kind. Retreats are widely used. 'Postmortem reports' are also used for most post-project launches. These are almost like Maoist self-criticism, where one reflects rigorously and self-critically on the project process. The postmortem report may take between three and six months to produce. They address not just what went well, but also what could have gone better or failed, looking at a detailed inventory covering the people involved, the product, its quality, the schedule, and the process of production. (Cusamano and Selby (1996) detail with remarkable frankness the many glitches involved in the development of major Microsoft products such as the various versions of Word and the slowness, and costs, with which the emergence of a learning organization took place in Microsoft.)

Intelligent organizations constantly monitor the environment that they enact (Weick, 1990). Specific enactments constitute distinctive management problems. Enactment creates events subject to distinctive treatments, which Weick (1990) identifies as distinctive phenomena constituted by stochastic, continuous, or abstract forms of reckoning.

Stochastic events are probabilistic, not deterministic, because they have no clear cause-and-effect relations between 'what is to be done, how it is done, and when it is to be done' (Roberts and Grabowski, 1996: 411). Most recent management fashions founder on the reef of stochastic events. For instance, if an organization trained its members rigorously and prescriptively in one-best-way processes, it would never learn. This is because organizations require more skills than they know. The repertoire of skills that must be maintained if that organization is to learn, if it is to be intelligent, must be larger than the skill-set in use at any time. This is particularly the case where a new procedure or technology is introduced, and especially where diagnosis is required to make the start-up work smoothly. In these circumstances learning occurs through error and its rectification: if an organization knew already, there would be no error, and no learning. A further corollary of this is that diagnosis and monitoring, as much as operation, become crucial skill-sets. Stochastic events form the essence of an organization's exploratory learning about *reliability*, the hallmark of the industrial era (Roberts and Grabowski, 1996: 412). Employees should be able to offer more skills than, vocationally, they need right now, and much of Microsoft's unorthodox selection procedures (such as asking candidates impossible questions and studying the processes that they go through in trying to answer them) seek to identify people who do.

In the post-industrial era, where continuous events tie together disparate geographical spaces, *efficiency* has become the hallmark of quality. Here, exploratory learning arises not so much from learning how to avoid unanticipated or random events, but in learning from the way that irruptions of disorder impact upon the order of due process and its management. The emphasis is on rapid responses to emergencies, the ability to keep cool while managing tense environments, on early detection of malfunctions in continuous systems. Much of the 'bug-testing' that occurs in Microsoft is of this order: processes are in simultaneous development, and, as existing bugs may be resolved in one application, they may simultaneously introduce errors in another. As Cusamano and Selby (1996) detail, in Microsoft this has led to several disastrous or late product launches. In such environments, 'supervisors often pay more attention to processes and products than to people' (Roberts and Grabowski, 1996: 412). Microsoft is typical: while the technical management skills are excellent, the people management skills have not been so well developed. Over attention to process and under attention to people produces problems. Process does not encourage causal analysis: when events flow seamlessly it is much more difficult to work out what is responsible for what, or who is responsible for what. One consequence is that as supervisors pay more attention to process, people working closely with the processes pay less attention to their conception of the causal linkages at work in sound and unsound operation, thus compounding the stochastic probabilities. The cognitive interactive capacities of people working close to continuous processes in intelligent organizations routinely produce dumber learning capacities, unless closely monitored, as Microsoft learnt slowly. Intelligent organizations, paradoxically, can produce dumber people who rely on process rather than intuitive judgement. And if that intuitive judgement cannot be standardized, commodified and abstracted, then the learning that smarter people achieve will not be generalized.

Increasingly, technology in the postmodern era is a source of abstract events, for which the hallmark is neither their reliability nor their efficiency, both of which are assumed, but their *representation*. New technologies have an essentially dual character: one aspect is the essentially invisible material processes that unfold in applications, while the other is the equally unavailable mental maps of the imagined processes with which operators work. In this, we all try to construct socially a sense of the world in which we live and work: as it becomes ever more remote and inaccessible technologically, the less able we are to learn what to attend to. Operating a lathe through feel, rhythm, visual cues, is a very different operation from reading from a computer graphic applied to an automatic process from which the usual sense data are absent. 'The result is inadequate sampling of displayed information, inattention to information on the periphery, and distractions when building problem representations' (Roberts and

Grabowski, 1996: 412). Abstract events require a kind of learning without environmental stimuli in the form of cues: hence, organizations that make use of technologies premised on the abstraction of events require learning capacities that are equally abstract, that 'can intervene at any time, pick up the process and assemble a recovery' (Roberts and Grabowski, 1996: 412, after Weick, 1990). Learning is often sufficiently abstract as to be tacit, ineffable, not capable of being caught in a programme. A further corollary of this is that diagnosis and monitoring, as much as operation, become crucial skill-sets (Weick, 1990: 4). Intelligent organizations are not smart enough to know all of what they need to know: that's why they need people to work in them who are smart enough to know that they need to know more than they do (the definition that determined Socrates to be the wisest man in Ancient Athens). Learning is often sufficiently abstract as to be tacit, ineffable, not capable of being caught in the programme, but if one puts the activity on video, given sufficient experience, one translates the ineffable into the do-able, learning from the captured image, as Microsoft developers have done in trying to transmit tacit learning.

Technology Entails Power/Knowledge

Technology is much more than just 'hardware' or 'software', not merely material artifacts, but also encompasses complex relations of knowledge embodied in practices, procedures, and their codification, and is always fused with power. Hence we should think of these as power/knowledge relations (Foucault, 1976; Clegg and Wilson, 1992) where the materiality of power is always implicit and tacit in the immateriality of knowledge (and visa versa).

Organizations and networks, concrete or virtual, are systems built from the flows of power/knowledge that people use to enact them, where their structure is the medium and the outcome of their use in these flows. And their use fuses around technologies that carry both past design and future applications. The trick is to create learning in the intelligent organization that is not so locked into past design that it cannot reach for future, unknown applications.

The widespread use of the software that Microsoft produces within the company, while it is still in process, leads to a network-based organization. Networks may be characterized in terms of the strength or intensity of their linkages, symmetricality, reciprocity and multiplexity of their flows. The strength of a network linkage depends on the extent to which it is an 'obligatory passage point' in the network: can information flow elsewhere or must it route that way? The greater the amount of information, affect or resources flowing through the passage point, then the more powerful will be those whose knowledge decodes it (Clegg, 1989; Roberts and Grabowski, 1996: 416). The relations of different knowledges, embodied in different peoples, around these obligatory passage points may be more or less symmetrical: that is some will be more or less dependent or independent within the flow of relations. Reciprocity refers to the degree of mutual or non-reciprocal obligation that occurs in the relationship. Multiplexity refers to the degree to which those who relate to one another do so more or less exclusively or also are involved in other networks. Finally, the content of the linkages is important, in terms of its degree of 'classification' and 'framing': how strongly or loosely framed or bounded it is, and how tightly or loosely coded is its classification?

Under these circumstances it should be clear that while intelligent organizations may not have the same kind of vicious, zero-sum power that characterized the hierarchical and industrial relations power plays of modern organizations, they are certainly not bereft of power. Power need not be negative, though: it depends on the type of learning, whether virtuous or vicious. Learning implies both outcomes and processes. The notion of virtuous learning circles suggests comparative improvement in efficiency, however one chooses to measure it, in whatever stakeholder terms: profits; quality of working; supply of jobs; consumer satisfaction; environmental impact or macro-economic outcomes. Vicious learning, by contrast, implies diminished efficiency.

Vicious power and learning characterizes situations in which the tacit knowledge of the operator is greater than that of the designer and where this tacit knowledge is something to hang on to for personal gain: perhaps to win respite from hard labour through short-cuts, or sabotage; perhaps to achieve a greater output bonus without the supervisor knowing how or why. Vicious power relations depend on work situations where transparency is not evident.

There are those who argue that the shift to intelligent organizations is based on such an increasing transparency of power/knowledge that the creativity of all employees is effortlessly incorporated without resistance for use by the organization (for instance, Rule and Brantley, 1992). Hence, virtuous learning (seen from the point of view of the organization's management) will characterize the future. Employees will be subject to such surveillance, either through technology or through the gaze of their work-team as a normative device, picking up on *kanban* cues displayed prominently in the workplace, so that the transparency of their actions allows space only for virtuosity and virtuousness. In such conditions some commentators see a good thing, allowing for the exercise of enhanced individual discretion (Zuboff, 1992), while others see it as a bad thing indeed, reflecting a totalitarian nightmare of total control through total surveillance (Robins and Webster, 1993). Neither view is likely to be correct. While employee desire, understanding and trust may become aligned with employer governance strategies, they are highly unlikely to do so seamlessly. Intelligent organizations will still operate in stupid ways, on stupid things, using stupid systems; intelligent people will still strive for selective advantage; intelligent systems of surveillance will still break down, fail and be subverted. But the rhetoric of intelligent organizations does open opportunities for employees to try to make them live up to their slogans.

Wouldn't most of us prefer to work in more, rather than less, intelligent organizations? Future organizations and networks, concrete or virtual, will be systems built from the flows of power and knowledge that people use to create them, fused around technologies that carry both past design and future applications. The trick will be to create learning in the intelligent organization that is not so locked into past design that it cannot reach for future, unknown applications.

References

Adler, P.S. (1993) 'The learning bureaucracy: New United Motor Manufacturing, Inc.', *Research in Organization Behaviour*, 11: 111–94.

Adler, P.S. and Cole, R.E. (1993) 'Designed for learning: a tale of two plants', *Sloan Management Review*, 34 (3): 85–94.

Albertsen, N. (1988) 'Postmodernism, post-Fordism, and critical social theory', *Environment and Planning D: Social and Space*, 6 (3): 339–66.

Clegg, S.R. (1989) *Frameworks of Power*. London: Sage.

Clegg, S.R. (1990) *Modern Organizations: Organization Studies in the Postmodern World*. London: Sage.

Clegg, S.R. and Wilson, F. (1992) 'Power, technology and flexibility in organizations', in J. Law (ed.), *A Sociology of Monsters: Essays on Power, Technology and Domination. Sociological Review Monograph, No. 38*. London: Routledge.

Copeland, D.G. and Mckenney, J.J. (1988) 'Airline reservation systems: lessons from history', *MIS Quarterly*, 12 (3): 353–69.

Cusamano, M. (1985) *The Japanese Automobile Industry: Technology and Management at Nissan and Toyota*. Cambridge, MA: Harvard University Press.

Cusamano, M.A. and Selby, R.W. (1996) *Microsoft Secrets – How the World's Most Powerful Software Company Creates Technology, Shapes Markets, and Manages People*. New York: HarperCollins.

Davidow, W. and Malone, M. (1992) *The Virtual Corporation*. New York: HarperCollins

Ellegård, K. (1996) 'Volvo – a force for Fordist retrenchment of innovation in the automobile industry?', *Asia Pacific Business Review*, 2 (4): 117–35.

Foucault, M. (1976) *Discipline and Punish*. Harmondsworth: Penguin.

Haslam, C. and William, K. with Johal, S. and Williams, J. (1996) 'A fallen idol? Japanese management in the 1990s', *Asia Pacific Business Review*, 2 (4): 21–43.

Janowitz, M. (1959) 'Changing patterns of organizational authority: the military establishment', *Administrative Science Quarterly*, 3 (4): 473–93.

Katz, H.C. and Sabel, C.F. (1985) 'Industrial relations and industrial adjustments in the car industry', *Industrial Relations*, 24 (2): 295–315.

Kenney, M. and Florida, R. (1988) 'Beyond mass production: production and the labor process in Japan', *Politics and Society*, 16 (1): 121–58.

Koike, K. (1987) 'Human resource development and labor management relations', in K. Yamamura and Y. Yasuba (eds), *The Political Economy of Japan (Vol. 1): the Domestic Transformation*. Stanford, CA: Stanford University Press. pp. 289–330.

Levinthal, D.A. and March, J.G. (1993) 'The myopia of learning', *Strategic Management Journal*, 14: 95–112.

Lewchuck, W. and Robertson, D. (1996) 'Working conditions under lean production: a worker-based benchmarking study?', *Asia Pacific Business Review*, 2 (4): 60–81.

March, J.G. (1991) 'Exploration and exploration in organizational learning', *Organization Science*, 2 (1): 71–87.

March, J.G. (1995) 'The future, disposable organizations, and the rigidities of imagination', *Organization*, 2 (3/4): 427–40.

Morris, J. and Wilkinson, B. (1995) 'The transfer of Japanese management to alien institutional environments', *Journal of Management Studies*, 32 (6): 719–30.

Nohria, N. and Berkely, J.D. (1994) 'The virtual organization: bureaucracy, technology, and the implosion of control', in C. Heckscher and A. Donnellon (eds), *The Post-Bureaucratic Organization: New Perspectives on Organizational Change*. Thousand Oaks, CA: Sage. pp. 108–28.

Ohara, M. (1988) 'CAD/CAM' at Toyota Motor Company', in T. Kitawaga (ed.), *Computer Science and Technologies*. New York: North Holland.

Oliver, N. and Wilkinson, B. (1988) *The Japanisation of British Industry*. Oxford: Blackwell.

Piore, M.J. (1986) 'Perspectives on labor market flexibility', *Industrial Relations*, 25 (2): 156–66.

Piore, M.J. and Sabel, C.F. (1984) *The Second Industrial Divide: Possibilities for Prosperity*. New York: Basic Books.

Rawlinson, M. and Wells, P. (1996) 'Taylorism, Lean Production and the Automotive Industry', *Asia Pacific Business Review*, 2 (4): 189–204.

Roberts, K.H. and Grabowski, M. (1996) 'Organizations, technology and structuring', in S.R. Clegg, C. Hardy and W. Nord (eds), *Handbook of Organization Studies*. London: Sage.

Robins, K. and Webster, F. (1993) '"Revolution of the fixed wheel": information, technology and social Taylorism', in P. Drummond and R. Paterson (eds), *Television in Transition: Papers from the First International Television Studies Conference*. London: BFI Publications.

Rule, J. and Brantley, P. (1992) 'Computerized surveillance in the workplace: forms and distribution', *Sociological Forum*, 7: 405–23.

Sabel, C.F. (1982) *Work and Politics*. Cambridge: Cambridge University Press.

Sandkull, B. (1996) 'Lean production: the myth which changes the world?', in S.R. Clegg and G. Palmer (eds), *The Politics of Management Knowledge*. London: Sage. pp. 69–79.

Smith, C. (1989) 'Flexible specialization, automation and mass production', *Work, Employment and Society*, 3 (2): 203–20.

Weick, K.E. (1990) 'Technology as equivoque: sense-making in new technologies', in P.S. Goodman and L. Sproull (eds), *Technology and Organizations*. San Francisco: Jossey-Bass.

Weick, K.E. (1996) 'Drop your tools: an allegory for organization studies', *Administrative Science Quarterly*, 41 (2): 301–13.

Weick, K.E. and Westley, F. (1996) 'Organizational learning: affirming an oxymoron', in S.R. Clegg, C. Hard and W.R. Nord (eds), *Handbook of Organization Studies*. London: Sage.

Williams, K., Haslam, C., Johal, S. and Williams, J. (1994) *Cars: Analysis, History, Cases*. Oxford: Berghahn Books.

Womack, J.P., Jones, D.T. and Roos, D. (1990) *The Machine that Changed the World*. New York: Rawson.

Zuboff, S. (1992) *In the Age of the Smart Machine*. New York: Basic Books.

10 Metaphors and Organizational Action: Postmodernity, Language and Self-regulating Systems – a Mexican Case Study

Luis Montano

And all the world's a stage,
and all the men and women merely players:
They have their exits and their entrances;
and one man in his time plays many parts . . .
W. Shakespeare, As You Like It

The question of considering organizations as self-regulating systems has recently attracted the attention of many scholars. The contemporary developments of the systems approach, such as the proposal on *autopoietic* systems (Maturana and Varela, 1972) or on complex systems (Morin, 1981), have triggered an intense debate about the possibilities of transferring these new methodological elaborations into the social sciences (Luhmann, 1991) and Organization Studies (Desmarèz, 1983; Montano, 1987; Kickert, 1991; Ibarra, 1995). The main purpose of this chapter is to participate in this debate, studying the metaphorical nature of informal relations and their self-regulating role in organizations.

The import of the Human Relations School has generally been reduced to the recognition of spontaneous behaviour in small work-groups. The criticisms that many scholars have addressed against this analytical frame have not yet taken into consideration the social constitution of this 'spontaneous' behaviour (Montano, 1996). On the other hand, the cybernetic nature of the organization as a system has remained as an abstract thought which has hardly helped to understand members' behaviour in organizations. Thus, it becomes necessary to overcome these limitations and give an explanation both of the nature of informal relations and of their relevance in a self-regulating system.

The debate on organizations as self-regulating systems has been with us since the early 1930s. It started when the concepts of *milieu interieur*, autonomy, and equilibrium were first employed in order to study organizations within a systemic context. These debates are not only part of an historical outlook on ideas, but aid understanding of organizations as a blend of social, and symbolic, spaces, at the base of self-regulating operations. These debates will be revisited here, not merely out of a sense of history, but also out of a sense of their continuing relevance.

The chapter is divided into three sections. The first develops a short description and criticism of the theoretical conclusions advanced by Roethlisberger and Dickson (1976). The second introduces the notion of a metaphorical figure in order to explain the self-regulating process in organizations. Finally, the third section provides an empirical example that arises from exploratory research conducted in Mexico.

The Human Relations School and the Relevance of Informal Organization

The Human Relations School contributed to building a systemic approach, very close to the present cybernetic conception of self-regulation. Among the most important authors were L.J. Henderson,[1] who had a great influence over many scholars, such as N. Wiener,[2] T. Parsons, R.K. Merton, E. Mayo, F. Roethlisberger and W. Dickson, M.P. Follett and C. Barnard. For Henderson, every social phenomenon could be analysed through a systems approach. In this perspective a system is a methodological tool, not a reality, one that is composed of a rigid structure, a set of elements and flexible relations that allows the relation between the elements themselves and the structure. The emphasis was placed on the present concept of *homeostasis*, which represents the ability of a system to resist the process of corruption and degeneration. This is interpreted as a 'negative entropy' and is a measure of the degree of system organization (Wiener, 1969: 11). Organization and self-regulation have remained related to each other since then.[3]

For Roethlisberger and Dickson, the organization as a system is a set of dual organizations.[4] 'Technical' organization is totally different from 'human' organization, which in turn is divided into 'individual' and 'social'. The social is then subdivided into the 'formal' and 'informal' organizations. The first division accepts the distinction between the material and the human fields. The second attempts to differentiate the strictly personal from the social one; finally, the third stresses the lack of connection between the planned organization and the one which emerges from unexpected behaviour. A very close link between each pair of organizations is needed in order to preserve the notion of a system.

From this point of view, we can say, according to the authors, that the equilibrium of an organization is obtained when both structures of the same level have similar change rates (technical and human; formal and informal). However, it is known that one of them changes more rapidly than the other: technical and formal organizations change faster than human and informal ones, thus provoking a temporal imbalance. One major difficulty in obtaining equilibrium comes from the fact that one system is more controllable than the other, that is technical, social and formal organizations are more controllable than human, individual and informal ones. So, for example, the change in the formal organization can be very rapid and meet few obstacles, while the informal organization requires much longer periods of adjustment, during which time workers' resistance to change plays a dominant role. Individual organization represents a special case because it does not really change faster than social organization. It is a more complex structure because personality starts its development from an early age, under the family's influence.[5]

The systems approach basically developed as an attempt to achieve articulation between the two types of organization: the formal and the informal. The compulsion to re-establish the equilibrium of the system thus reduces the conception of the organization to a very simple one: that of either formal or informal relations. Moreover, informal organization is just that which is not formal.[6] In other words, spontaneous or unexpected behaviour is not planned behaviour. Thus, organization is always defined around formal aspects (Montano, 1994a).

The essential aspect of any organization is the way time and space are conceived. Without discussing the conception of time, we will focus on one of the most important representations of space in organization. We are referring to the act of establishing physical limits, that is the establishment of an inside and an outside. This is framed within a very crisp logic. Membership is then defined in a binary manner – yes or no. If someone is outside, then he or she is not considered as a member; but, on the contrary, someone who is inside is seen as if he or she was just, and only, a member. The fact of not considering the individual structure does not allow us to consider members as human or social beings. It is true, of course, that Roethlisberger and Dickson had introduced feelings in the informal structure, but they did so framed within a formal context.[7]

When we mention that the project turned around the formal organization, it is because the economic objectives of the enterprise were incorporated within this formality,[8] a very important statement that allows one to understand better the project of Roethlisberger and Dickson (1976). It seems, at first glance, that the authors were not concerned about technical organization, but were just interested in human aspects. However, because they introduced the notions of *cost and efficiency logics* into the formal organization in order to establish a systemic position, they accepted the leading position of economic relations over social ones. Theirs was not a humanistic or social project but an economical one. It is the economic function that leads the interpretation of space and thus the context of informal organization. The informal organization is despoiled, far from any rational behaviour, and one is forced to interpret it within the physical limits of the organization. The recognition of the role played by informal organization was made within this economic context: it could propitiate a larger collaboration or, on the contrary, restrain it.[9]

We propose a reinterpretation of Roethlisberger and Dickson's proposal. first we will explicitly establish some relationships between technical,

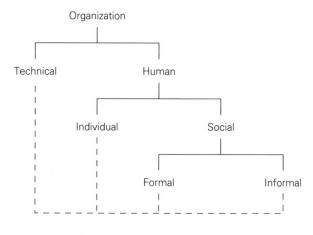

FIGURE 10.1   *Organization as a system*

individual, formal and informal organizations that were not considered in the original model (see Figure 10.1). Secondly, we will reformulate the concept of individual organization and develop a metaphorical approach in order to explain some features of the organization as a self-regulating system. We will stress in this exposé some arguments that question the idea of accurate organization frontiers.

1   The relationship between technical and formal structures can be grasped as a series of 'drifts', considered as (i) technological, (ii) institutional and (iii) metaphorical. The drift is obviously located in a spatial conception, even if it remains usually unconscious:

(i)   *Technological drift.* In a very strict sense, we are referring to a special technological transfer. Results obtained in a particular industry or institution attract the attention of others. The diffusion of these advances plays a very important role in this trend. This is the case, for example, of the quality control chart proposed by Shewhart in the Western Electric Company. This technological transfer becomes possible because theoretical proposals assume the form of administrative objects that sustain formal organization (Bayart, 1995).[10]

(ii)   *Institutional drift.* It refers to the fact that every organization which emerges into the social spectrum does so by taking some main features of other organizations (Castoriadis, 1975), justifying and giving direction, during a certain period of time, to the organization's future conduct. For example, we can remember the statement proposed by H. Fayol (1961) who argued that industrial organization became possible because it had been based upon military structure.

(iii) *Metaphorical drift.* This is a very special process in which some other social discourses are introduced into organizations to give them a new sense of their values and practices in order to face environmental disturbances. This is the case of strategic thought – Knights and Morgan (1991), Knights (1992) – and excellence discourse – Aubert and Gaulejac (1991).

2 The relationship between technical and informal structures also implies a spatial ingredient as an administrative tool. At first, it was reduced to the physical space in which a small work-group laboured. As the technical aim leads the formal organization, interpersonal relations are limited to this space. However, this relationship has been recently studied by W. Heydebrand (1989), who argues that the development of informatics usually broaden informal spaces by the incorporation of bureaucratic rules into the software repertory.

3 The relationship between individual and formal structures has been generally approached through the relationship between educational background and formal control. Some scholars, such as K. Thompson (1984), underline that visible aspects of formal control tend to vanish when educational background of organization members increases. This statement has been confirmed by H. Mintzberg (1991) who mentions that socialization in educational institutions is important not just for acquiring a technical knowledge, but also for obtaining a common way of thinking and behaving. This is relevant in the case of some organizational configurations, such as in the *professional bureaucracy.*

4 The relationship between individual and informal organizations is, in our opinion, fundamental in order to have a better understanding of organizations. We do not agree with Roethlisberger and Dickson's behaviourist approach because it implies the possibility of total conscious manipulation of organizations over individuals and because it overstresses economic objectives over symbolic life. It is by reformulating the concept of the social individual that we will propose a metaphorical approach that considers the importance of informal organization in self-regulating systems.

Towards a Metaphorical Approach

The study of metaphors has been recently incorporated into Organization Studies more as a methodological tool than as a recognition of a social complex phenomenon. This approach does not question explicitly the idea of organization limits, but it establishes that an organization can be seen as if it were another social space, such as a game (Crozier and Freidberg, 1977), a culture (Alvesson, 1993), a political arena, a brain, a psychological prison (Morgan, 1990), and so on. Nevertheless, we can develop a more comprehensive scope about the nature of metaphors if we ask whether the metaphor is a way of seeing the world, or if it is a result of the manner in which we see the world, or if it is a brand new world, or if it is the world itself. There are answers for each question. For example, for a sociologist such as Morgan, it is a methodological instrument; for someone interested in second-order phenomena, such as von Foerster, it is a consequence of the manner in which we face reality; for a poet such as Paz,[11] it is always the creation of a new reality; and for a radical postmodern philosopher such as Derrida (1989; Cooper, 1989), language is always metaphorical.

A further question asks if these approaches are different. The answer could be rather negative. To give a clearer answer, we will take von Foerster's approach to the second-order view. A second-order operation is usually defined as the operation upon the same operation, for example to learn how to learn, to see how we see. In a recent article, von Foerster argues that it is because of the blind point[12] that we do not see that we do not see: we are not aware of our partial blindness. The author establishes a distinction between invention and discovery. The metaphor appears always in the ambit of invention, in a connotative context, while discovery belongs to the sphere of denotative context. The function of language is quite different: invention implies that language creates the world; discovery, on the contrary, establishes that language is reduced to a mere image of the world (von Foerster, 1994: 102).[13] Based on these elements, we can say that the only way we have of understanding second-order operations is by contextualizing them. Then, this strategy implies a movement through space. To combat the blind point we need to move in order to register images in the right zone of the eye.[14] To fight against our ignorance of our mental blind point, we must consider other social spaces in which individuals transit.

A metaphor is not just an image because it is not a denotative operation; it is a connotative one because of its symbolic content (Montano, 1993). We cannot choose a specific metaphor to explain or give directions to organizations. Furthermore, as Alvesson has recently suggested, there also exists a second-order metaphor that, as we will further review, means that metaphors are always related to other metaphors. Organizing is an invention which implies a dynamic contextualization process, and studying it is just a discovery. Discovery, then, is a recognition of invention. However, to discover how we discover means that we must know how we invent. Thus, the second-order discovery must be very close to, or even be, an invention.

Organizing the organization also represents a second-order process that we usually call self-organizing. This operation implies the concept of autonomy which precedes the concept of adaptation.[15] Autonomy does not mean freedom or closeness,[16] but dependence and openness (Morin, 1994). Thus, self-organizing cannot recognize any bounded system. Physical limits are just an artificial device that has raised a mistaken discovery strategy. We need, then, not just to broaden the concept of limits in a formal approach[17] – for instance, considering some current organizational practices such as the subcontracting programme or the just-in-time process – but to incorporate the concept of organizational drift already mentioned above. Furthermore, we need to reinterpret the concept of informal behaviour in order to overwhelm the simple idea of spontaneous behaviour and relate it to the concepts of autonomy, dependence and self-organization.

The relative autonomy required by the concept of organization under scrutiny was achieved by means of the psychological process of internalization of external spaces. Thus, schematically speaking, we can say that informal organization does not abstractly represent spontaneous behaviour. Informal relations mostly represent, from our point of view, institutional spaces which the individual has internalized over the years of his or her everyday life, such as religion, school and family (Montano, 1996). These spaces do not need to be 'real' in the sense of a personal experience, but they are also imaginary personal accounts – which are as real as the real ones (Atlan, 1991) – such as prison, the army, psychiatric institutions, and so on. But they are not just institutional spaces. Our proposal also contemplates some other social activities, such as playing or dreaming, and some objects, such as machinery or organism. To advance in our project we need to make explicit our conception of metaphor.

Metaphors were first considered as a rhetorical device and were used to decorate or give relevance to a discourse. It was established later that metaphors were an 'epistemological obstacle'[18] because, instead of studying a specific object, the attention was concentrated on another one. From a linguistic point of view, the construction of a metaphor always requires a double process. First, a metonymy, which consists of withdrawal, removing one segment of a discourse, and secondly, a process that requires fulfilment of that empty space. It is true that we can face a metonymic process alone, but a metaphorical one always requires the double process. It is true that the metaphorical process could be a 'willing' process, such as in the case of poems, but it is also an unconscious process, where social actors are not aware of its construction. Metaphors are not just the union of two realities, but the invention of a new one.[19] That is why the activity of discovering reality becomes so complex and so enriching.

Alvesson (1993) proposes an interesting approach to metaphors. He introduces the concept of second-order metaphors and argues that the metaphorical process is not neutral. He approaches organizational metaphors from a methodological point of view in order to criticize simple images. He argues that behind each metaphor we can find another one that gives direction to the former. For instance, behind the metaphorical approach of organizations as a game (Crozier and Friedberg, 1977), mention that we can find another one, such as the jungle, that remains hidden but gives a new signification to the game and then to organizations. Alvesson mentions that the number of metaphors involved in an organizational analysis could be very high and their deconstruction would become a very complex operation. Nevertheless, he does not pay any attention to the metonymic process which is not represented in his diagram. This process is, as we will see further, central in explaining the

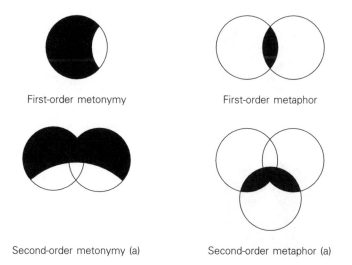

First-order metonymy   First-order metaphor

Second-order metonymy (a)   Second-order metaphor (a)

FIGURE 10.2   *First- and second-order metaphors*

contradictory sense of discourses. Moreover, this second-order metaphor implies a second-order metonymy.

In Alvesson's proposal we see a union between two sets, the object and the modifier. For illustrating the first-order metonymic zones, we have not illuminated the withdrawn zone. Let us suppose we have two sets (A = the object and B = the modifier): we can thus define the metaphor as follows: $A \cap B = A \cup B - (A' + B')$. The union of two sets gives the impression of totality, but notice that two important spaces are eliminated; A', which could represent important – mostly negative – aspects of the object, and B', which has the same effect on the modifier and could also represent some aspects that cannot be introduced into A.[20] For the second-order metonymy we have two possibilities: first, to consider the second-order metaphor as affecting both the object and the first modifier, and secondly, according to Alvesson, to consider only that affecting the first modifier. In Figure 10.2, we show the first and second processes, considering the first option. Figure 10.3 shows the second option of this second-order process and the possibility of a third-order one, always taking into account the second option. For example, let us consider that an organization is seen as a game which at the same time is considered as a jungle. The metaphor of the jungle does not directly affect the way we observe the organization but it does so indirectly through that of the game. That is why Alvesson considers that this second-order metaphor is hidden.

How can we interpret the relationship between the individual and the informal organization? In a first attempt we had illustrated Roethlisberger and Dickson's proposal on formal/informal organizations as it is shown in Figure 10.4 (Montano, 1994b). In this figure we had considered the informal organization mainly as the internalization of a set of exterior

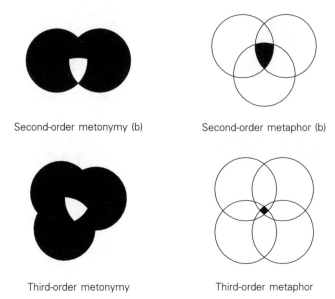

Second-order metonymy (b)   Second-order metaphor (b)

Third-order metonymy   Third-order metaphor

FIGURE 10.3 *Second- and third-order metaphors*

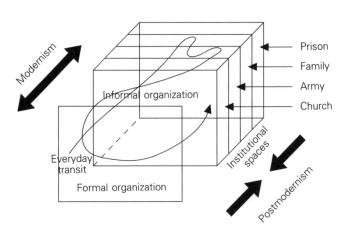

FIGURE 10.4 *Formal and informal organizations*

institutional spaces. Autonomy was then achieved not by refusing the exterior but by internalizing it. Thus the company becomes also a school, an army, a church, a prison, and so on. From this point of view, self-regulation consists, among others, in a process of anticipating conflicts. A problem raised in the formal organization could be transferred to one of these other institutional spaces. For instance, when an employee complains that her or his salary is too low, directors can argue that work should be seen as an opportunity of learning, as if she or he were at school, emphasizing that the present is not as important as the future. This new contextualization of the company implies a metonymic process which consists of rejecting the economic space and then evoking an ambit in which certain solidarity and long-term aims play a major role. However, metaphors also go in the contrary direction, meaning they can also reinforce the negative organizational aspects, such as the impression of being a prisoner. Then we have a frequent transit between these two poles: an open conflict and a falling in love (Pagés et al, 1979).

The process of anticipating conflicts implies the internalization of the exterior. It remains dependent on other institutional spaces and functions through an intermediate zone that generally does not reach these extremes of open conflict and falling in love. This is a very important component of the self-regulating process. The daily imaginary transit that members make in organizations implies the non-recognition of its physical limits. Thus, a self-regulating system is really bounded by meaning. The self-reference operation becomes crucial to assure a partial equilibrium. This is not, however, achieved just inside formal organizations, as suggested by Luhmann (1991: 199), but, as we are observing, it takes place basically in the informal organization.

This metaphorical process is contradictory and recursive and has important consequences over individuals. The relationship between individual and informal organizations is bi-directional, giving rise to a kind of a loop which reinforces the relation. The individual can be inside the organization in many institutional spaces in the same journey of time. Each institutional space has its own patterns of behaviour – even if they share many other aspects. For instance, some institutional spaces are driven mostly be freedom and solidarity values and others by discipline and obedience. Each institutional space presents at the same time positive and negative aspects. Typically these dual characteristics are managed in order to take advantage of positive aspects, meaning that they are considered in a partial manner. We can now return to the idea of second-order metaphor in order to be aware of the elimination of negative aspects and thus the reinforcement of specific discursive strategies.

We still face two major problems. The first one is the metonymic process which always implies the presence of an absence.[21] In other words, there is always the possibility of rejecting the metaphor – we mean the first modifier – and of returning to the object; or, to say it better, the metonymic space is always present and gives a contradictory direction to the discourse. The second problem is the possibility of a double-bind process which leads to the metaphorical loop. Double-bind theory was *invented* by G. Bateson[22] when he studied schizophrenic behaviour. A double-bind appears when an individual is captured between two simultaneous contradictory orders – for instance an act demanding love and an energetic rejection. This process is compelled by the second-order metonymy mentioned above and provokes in the individual a schizophrenic reaction which leads to an evasion of reality. Individuals are not able to manage the situation. They are not aware of their condition and cannot explain it

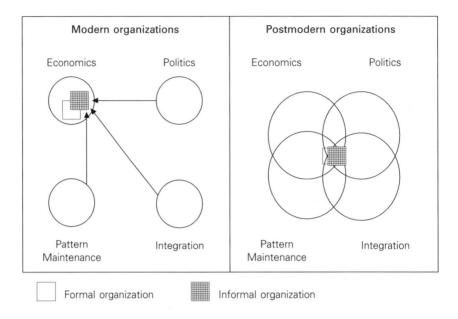

FIGURE 10.5 *Modern and postmodern organizations*

except through a metaphorical language (Bateson et al., 1956).[23] The metaphorical process then becomes the cause and the effect of human behaviour. Adopting Bateson's double-bind means that it would no longer be possible to sustain the Parsonian idea of a society divided into main social functions in which different organizations are accurately inscribed, legitimizing their objectives. As Touraine (1969) proposed, these functional social spaces overlap in the so-called post-industrial society as formal and informal organizations are overlapped (see Figure 10.5).

According to Parsons (1970), in a modern society, the functional spaces are supposed to be clearly separated. Because they serve functions every society needs to fulfil, different kinds of organizations are supposed to contribute to the satisfaction of these social needs. However, what we can appreciate is that, through the bias of the metaphorical process, every other social function is incorporated into the informal organization. On the other hand, in a post-industrial (sometimes also called postmodern) society, we notice that these functional spaces overlap somewhat, giving rise to a new relation between formal and informal organizations (Montano, 1994b). As Burns and Stalker (1961) recognized, one of the main characteristics of (their) contemporary organizations was that the net distinction between formal and informal tends to disappear. Additionally, Heydebrand (1989) mentions that in post-bureaucratic organizations – which are inscribed in a post-industrial capitalism – formal and informal organizations are strongly overlapped. The modernization process of organizations suggests the idea of a complex organization as a small society, not just because of all the

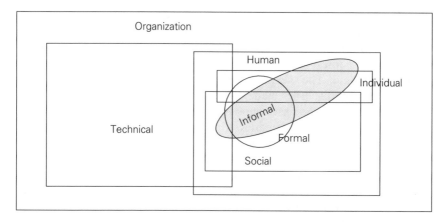

FIGURE 10.6 *An overlapped version of Roethlisberger and Dickson's proposal*

facilities they have – dormitories, restaurants, medical services, recreative, sports and cultural activities, magazines, etc. – but because of the metaphorical construction of reality that attends and constitutes their dominance. With the growing importance of economic organizations, we assist the birth of a new metaphor: society as a large organization (Ouchi, 1984). In this post-industrial trend, economic organizations occupy the central overlapping zone, giving direction to the other social functional spaces.

At the organizational level, we propose that there is also a trend to overlap all kinds of sub-organizations. Thus, the formal and informal organizations represent a kind of synthesis of an organization (see Figure 10.6). Such a proposal leads to a more complex approach to organizations and requires a more careful study of the overlapped zones.[24]

The Mexican Case: an Exploratory Approach

Theoretical discussion of the metaphorical process for studying organizations is quite difficult to translate into an empirical approach. In this chapter our objective is related to an exploratory study that recognizes some important trends in organizational behaviour in a small company in Mexico. The study was made in the frame of a general crisis in Mexico, which can be characterized mainly in three functional spaces: economic, social and political.

The economic crisis was triggered in December 1994 with the Mexican currency devaluation. The recognition of the economic crisis was a crucial point of meaning for neo-liberal discourse, based on an economic globalization, which intended, from an official perspective, to incorporate Mexico into the sphere of industrialized and modern countries. On the other hand, the guerrilla movement in Chiapas, which started in January 1994, signalled the recognition of an important social conflict which underlined the contradictory results of the national modernization process. Chiapas is the poorest state in Mexico, and the Zapatist Army is formed by indigenous people. The weapons used by the Zapatist guerrillas are very archaic; they even use rifles made of wood. However, they have been using what is called a postmodern communication strategy, based on new technological advances in informatics. Finally, political instability increased with the assassination of the candidate to the presidency of the official party (Partido Revolucionario Institucional or PRI). The assassination took place in a context where, to achieve modernity, political parties underlined the necessity of a real process of democracy, the existence of which had previously been widely questioned.

We can observe that modernity is located in several functional social spaces, that new technologies have been introduced in some arenas and that they share some pre-modern social aspects, giving rise to the creation of modernity niches. In the economic field we can notice the rise of such modern niches in some large enterprises.[25] Notwithstanding the lack of infrastructural technology, most enterprises have adopted the search for excellence, flexibility and quality in their formal discourses. The cultural aspects present in the informal organization aided most of these organizations in achieving a better performance. However, latterly, in order to face the terrible consequences of the globalization process, medium and large enterprises have adopted what is now called a *re-engineering* approach (see Hammer and Champy, 1994) which dramatically reduces the employment rate.[26] In addition, the bankruptcy of micro and small enterprises has worsened the unemployment situation.

Even if some of the most important enterprises in Mexico have incorporated these new programmes, affecting the formal organization – such as the introduction of quality or excellence groups – the informal organization remained anchored in other social values, such as friendship, religion and family. By contrast, micro-enterprises generally 'suffer' from a lack of formality, where business is not considered as a way of accumulating money but remains, in most cases, just a familiar activity. The lack of formality does not represent automatically the rise of informality. Informal organization always remains an unconscious and an important component of the self-regulating process.

We have studied a small company in which informal organization is apparently not well developed because of the lack of formal actions tending to create an internal environment. However, we will propose that informal organization is a self-regulating mechanism which is always present because of the internalization of other social spaces.

The company was founded in 1952 and has two small plants in Mexico City. It has 36 workers, who were interviewed through a questionnaire which was designed to reveal the significance of some of the most important metaphors mentioned in the specialized literature. The company has three family stockholders and is administered by the eldest, who is about 65 years old. Its main product is a label used on some important consumer goods. The production technology is simple and the company has not introduced any significant changes for a long time. Salaries are really low, working conditions are hard and insecure, and the internal environment is rather tense. The average time workers have remained in the company is 8.91 years but at 9.39 the standard deviation is very high, signalling a high turnover.

From the questionnaire we have chosen some items referring to seniority, formal relations among workers, working time, importance of salary, internal environment and quality, and whether work had become more competitive or co-operative. These variables were correlated with the rep-resentations of the organization as a family, a church, an army, a group of friends, a game, a machine, a prison, an organism, a theatre, a place of domination, a political arena, a jungle, a culture and a system. The main results are shown in Table 10.1. We can observe that the metaphor most mentioned was the theatre, which is highly and positively correlated[27] with formal relations among workers[28] and the importance of salary,[29] but negatively correlated with the importance that workers assign to quality. We can observe, then, that the theatre was not conceived as a neutral metaphor. To have a better understanding of the sense workers give to metaphors we correlated them with other variables, such as those mentioned above. This is an indirect way of studying second-order metaphors proposed by Alvesson. In a second moment, we estimated correlation indexes for metaphors themselves in order to have a more direct second-order approach. These are shown in Table 10.2.

On the basis of the second correlation we can now complement our first observation about the theatre. We found that it is positively correlated with the prison and jungle metaphors. The theatre was interpreted not as a cultural activity but as a space in which actors are placed just in order to play a role. Moreover, behind the theatre we also find, in a second-order approach, those metaphors of system, machine and political arena. These two ways of finding the interpenetration of metaphors are illustrated in Figure 10.7. The figure shows no clear borders among, but the overlapped nature of, representation of social spaces.

We can observe in Figure 10.7 a shadowed zone composed of the meta-phors of family, group of friends, and church, which have some positive correlations among them as well as with the variable of co-operation. This zone is clearly separated from other metaphors by a negative correlation, through the intermediation of other variables such as the importance of quality and the jungle/theatre; and co-operation and political arena/system. We want also to underline that very important variables for improving organizational performance are inside this zone: the importance of quality and co-operation.

We can observe that it is not enough to study metaphors and their relations, but that we need to introduce other variables in order to explain

TABLE 10.1 Coefficients of correlation between metaphors and some chosen variables

	SEN	FOR	TIM	SAL	QUA	COO	MEAN	STD
				Average and Standard Deviations of metaphors' scores				
FAM	-0.1342	-0.1086	-0.2031	-0.0377	-0.0448	0.3259	4.4400	2.9100
CHU	0.1954	-0.1613	0.1430	0.2850	-0.0921	0.2164	2.8300	2.6600
ARM	0.2343	-0.3417	-0.0321	-0.1337	-0.1449	0.1520	3.0000	1.7700
FRI	0.0506	-0.1593	-0.0481	-0.1095	0.2341	**0.4439**	4.8100	2.5200
GAM	0.1713	0.2206	-0.0145	-0.2595	-0.0608	-0.0928	4.1700	2.6100
MCH	0.3500	0.1051	0.3587	-0.2054	0.0099	-0.0977	5.3900	3.2800
PRI	0.2792	0.0695	0.3872	-0.1617	-0.0133	0.1298	3.8900	3.0700
ORG	0.3845	0.1904	**0.4332**	-0.0144	-0.1732	-0.2537	5.6000	2.7800
THE	0.1972	**0.4751**	0.3011	-0.3475	**0.4692**	0.0210	7.0800	2.5700
DOM	0.3583	0.0039	0.0937	-0.1884	-0.0274	-0.0681	2.5600	1.9300
POL	0.3131	0.3916	0.3790	0.0467	0.1368	-0.3805	3.6900	2.9400
JUN	0.1649	0.3164	0.2306	**0.4650**	**0.5219**	-0.2293	3.8100	2.8900
CUL	-0.0306	0.0944	0.0430	-0.0636	0.1197	-0.2043	6.5600	2.6200
SYS	0.3164	0.0443	**0.4346**	-0.0417	-0.1165	-0.3913	4.8100	2.8200

TABLE 10.2 *Coefficients of correlation between metaphors*

	FAM	CHU	ARM	FRI	GAM	MCH	PRI	ORG	THE	DOM	POL	JUN	CUL	SYS
FAM	1.000													
CHU	-0.0714	1.0000												
ARM	-0.0221	0.0243	1.0000											
FRI	**0.26298**	**0.3412**	-0.1345	1.0000										
GAM	-0.2578	0.0494	**0.34538**	0.1050	1.0000									
MCH	0.0861	-0.0809	-0.0540	-0.0183	0.1456	1.0000								
PRI	0.0696	-0.1110	0.1366	0.2376	0.0665	**0.4671**	1.0000							
ORG	0.1709	0.0163	-0.1206	0.1406	0.0895	0.2710	0.0905	1.0000						
THE	-0.0853	-0.1152	-0.1381	-0.0328	-0.2704	0.1385	**0.39648**	-0.1295	1.0000					
DOM	-0.0349	-0.2150	**0.3917**	0.0052	-0.0471	0.1271	**0.367**	0.0076	0.1745	1.0000				
POL	-0.0772	-0.0067	-0.1867	0.0613	-0.0714	0.1284	0.0786	0.1289	0.2309	0.2774	1.0000			
JUN	-0.0268	-0.2763	-0.0837	-0.0329	-0.0713	0.2013	0.2652	-0.0218	**0.4725**	0.2502	**0.5289**	1.0000		
CUL	0.0154	-0.0355	-0.1106	0.0991	0.0403	-0.0092	-0.1270	0.3215	0.0141	0.1289	0.2156	-0.0080	1.0000	
SYS	-0.0588	0.1254	0.1602	0.0711	0.0589	0.1167	**0.32802**	0.2490	0.1129	0.2407	0.2794	0.1147	0.1929	1.0000

Key

FAM	Family	SEN	Seniority
CHU	Church	FOR	Formal Workers Relations
ARM	Army	TIM	Working Time
FRI	Group of friends	SAL	Importance of Salary
GAM	Game	QUA	Importance of Quality
MCH	Machine	COO	Cooperation
PRI	Prison		
ORG	Organism	MEAN	Average
THE	Theatre	STD	Standard Deviation
DOM	Domination place		
POL	Political Arena	**p<0.05**	
JUN	Jungle	**p<9.01**	
CUL	Culture		
SYS	System		

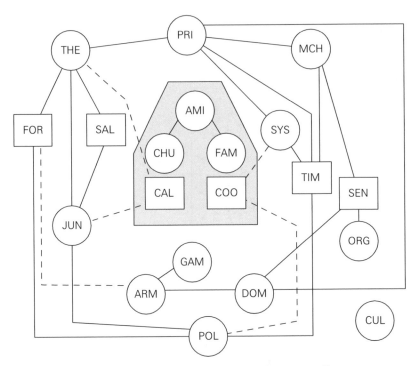

FIGURE 10.7 *Relationship among metaphors in a Mexican small company*

workers' perceptions. Thus, for example, working time and the importance of salary are nowadays two fundamental aspects in the frame of the general crisis in Mexico. Because of the lack of technology, one way to improve productivity is extending labour hours – which are positively correlated with the machine – giving us an accurate picture of Taylorist strategy. Working time is also correlated with metaphors of the prison, system and political arena. We must underline that it is also indirectly related with co-operation through the perception of the organization as a system and a political arena. On the other hand, the importance of salary has also become a central workers' claim and it is positively correlated with the metaphors of theatre and jungle, and establishes a negative second-order relation with the importance of quality.

We also want to mention that formal relations among workers affect not just the perception of the organization as a theatre and as a political arena, but that formality among workers affects the whole organization through 'n'-order relations. We could even find some important circuits in order to explain diverse partial aspects of the organization. For instance, we could analyse the path from considering the organization as a group of friends to a theatre. We also have to notice that, in this case, the metaphor of culture is apparently not related to any other element. We propose two non-exclusive interpretations. First, we probably did not study other metaphors

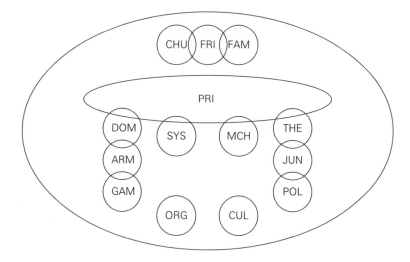

FIGURE 10.8 *Organization as an 'n' order metaphor*

or variables that might be related to it. Secondly, this is a special case that is not really well integrated into the system. The cultural discourse is generally introduced and administrated by directors in a formal manner. We know that it has been normally adopted in large organizations, using a highly developed informatic technology. Thus, metaphors with low correlation indexes represent a more fragmentary perception of reality.

As we have noticed, not only the metaphor of theatre, but also those of machine and system, are not neutral. They are related mainly to that of prison, which is one of the best concrete examples of the informal institution of internal and external spaces. We are not saying that metaphors always have the same sign – positive or negative. We know that most of the time they are considered in that way, but, for example, the army could sometimes represent an acceptable or good place. This is the interpretation we propose for the negative correlation between this metaphor and the formal relations. Game, for instance, could represent a recreational activity, a space strictly regulated by rules, or it could even be a very free action. In Figure 10.8 we have drawn the company as an organization of 'n'-order metaphors. Even if we are aware of the risk of adopting an endless deconstruction approach (Alvesson, 1993), to go further than the second-order metaphor avoids giving just a positive or negative sign to each metaphor.

Concluding Remarks

Organization Studies are not a social science because they study organizations which are in society, but because society is, metaphorically speaking, inside organizations. Organizations, in their everyday transit through a wide range of social spaces, and their ambiguous perception, signal to us that we face a complex and dynamic phenomenon that, through the bias of internalization, represents a kind of 'synthesis' of society. As Morin (1981) mentions, the part is inside the whole as the whole is contained in every part. The new paradigms which have been developed in order to explain new organizational forms are useful not only for the study of postmodern organizations, but also to understand 'pre-modern' ones. Symbolic life is to a great extent just a metaphorization of the world, a social perception of time and space, a connotative strategy, that constantly recreates the world. During the organization period of modernization – from the early years of the present century to the 1960s – Organization Studies considered rationalization as a substitute for symbolic life, characterizing organization pre-modernism as being anchored in a symbolic ground. Symbolic life has now emerged as a main feature of postmodern organizations but we have to recognize that it has never really disappeared, and that the metaphorization of social relations has been a constant component of organizations, one that has played a very important role in the self-regulating process.

We would like to allude to an idea developed by Foucault in his most methodological book, *L'archéologie du savoir* (1970). We refer to the emergent surfaces – *surfaces d'émergence* – that represent social spaces in which new practices can appear, be designated and be analysed. Diverse social spaces, such as in the case of madness: family, close social groups, working environment and religious community, work together to preclude new objects and new practices. That is why in the construction of every new object we can find a social *intertextuality*, until this new object reaches the status of a discourse and gives direction to other discourses, when it is internalized, sometimes through the door of informal structure, to other organizations. The metaphorical process resides therefore in the very social construction of reality and is not just a methodological tool for studying or directing action (see Figure 10.9).

Notes

Agustin Montano supported me in the statistical analysis and Ma. Teresa Flores helped me to make this chapter more readable. My colleagues Antonio Barba, Eduardo Ibarra and Marcela Rendón made valuable comments which enriched this chapter. A first version of this chapter was presented at the 12th EGOS Colloquium at Istanbul in July 1995 and received important suggestions to improve it, mainly from Rita Smeds from Helsinki University of Technology, and Ulrich Heisig and Wolfang Littek from Bremen University. I had the opportunity to work on it with Denis Bayart and Jacques Girin, at the Ecole Polytechnique in Paris. Finally, my students of the Doctoral Programme in Organization Studies at Universidad Autónoma Metropolitana discussed it and made helpful observations. To all of them I would like to express my gratitude. However, the author assumes, as always, all the responsibility.

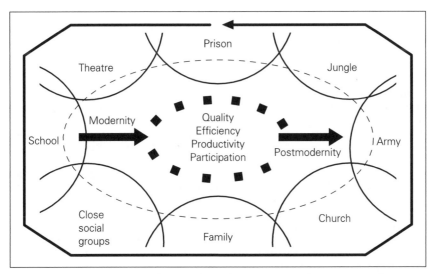

FIGURE 10.9   *Emergence surfaces and social construction of organizational reality*

1. 'This physiologist (L.J. Henderson), a professor of the Philosophy of Science at Harvard University, was as strongly influenced by the work of the French doctor Claude Bernard as by that of the Italian writer Vilfredo Pareto, from whom he acquired the concepts of "internal environment" and "equilibrium". The former is taken from Bernard and has to do with the discovery of the constancy and conservation of the composition of blood, and was evidence for an internal environment – *milieu intérieur* – which constitutes the "condition of a free and independent life" (Henderson, 1970: 153). The latter is taken from Pareto, originally developed in a thesis on the subject of solid objects and later transferred to economics and finally to sociology' (Montano, 1996).

2. Norbert Wiener, one of Henderson's most prominent students, commented: 'There was also Professor Lawrence J. Henderson, the physiologist, who combined some really brilliant ideas about the fitness of the environment with what seemed to me to be a distressing inability to place them in any philosophical structure . . .' (Wiener, 1966: 166).

3. As Morin explains: 'Cybernetics is the first science which, after Western science's advances of the seventeenth century has established its method, has brought about its operational success, and has achieved the recognition of other sciences through its treatment of a physical system, the machine, not in the operation of its constitutive elements, but in the operation of its organizational features' (Morin, 1981: 285).

4. 'By "system" is meant something which must be considered as a whole because each part bears a relation of interdependence to every other part' (Roethlisberger and Dickson, 1976: 551).

5. An important nuance has to be introduced. Roethlisberger and Dickson assumed the behaviourist perspective and then the possibility of totally modelling human personality. They did not pay any attention to the symbolic life of early age.

6. 'The term "informal organization" will refer to the actual personal interrelations existing among the members of the organization which are not represented by, or are inadequately represented by, the formal organization' (Roethlisberger and Dickson, 1976: 566).

7. The logic of sentiments 'represents the values residing in the interhuman relations of the different groups within the organization. Examples of what is meant here are the arguments employees give which center around the "right to work", "seniority", "fairness", the "living wage". This logic, as its name implies, is deeply rooted in sentiments and feelings' (Roethlisberger and Dickson, 1976: 564).

8. 'The formal organization of an industrial plant has two purposes. It addresses itself to the economic purpose of the total enterprise; it concerns itself also with the securing of co-operative effort. The formal organization includes all the explicitly stated systems of control introduced by the company in order to achieve the economic purposes of the total enterprise and the effective contribution of the members of the organization to those economic ends' (Roethlisberger and Dickson, 1976: 558).

9. 'It is well to recognize that informal organizations are not "bad", as they are sometimes assumed to be. Informal social organization exists in every plant, and can be said to be a necessary prerequisite for effective collaboration. Much collaboration exists at an informal level, and it sometimes facilitates the functioning of the formal organization. On the other hand, sometimes the informal organization develops in opposition to the formal organization. The important consideration is, therefore, the relation that exists between formal and informal organizations' (Roethlisberger and Dickson, 1976: 559).

10. 'Dans la routine d'un atelier, une fois le contrôl statistique "implanté", ce n'est plus la théorie qui sert, mais l'objet carte de contrôle et la procédure organisationnelle associéee. La procédure, appliquée de façon automatique, ne nécessite aucune réference à la théorie statistique. L'activité de l'ouvrier peut s'analyser comme une succession d'opérations congitives élémentaires' (Bayart, 1995: 14). The lack of a complete theoretical context allows the administrative object to be transferred to other organizations. This is the case, described by Bayart, of the control chart which was transferred from an industrial context to a control medical practice. This is an approach that complements the Foucaultian's perspective of the *Panoptics*, which was transformed from an object into a disciplinary principle – *Panoptism* (Deleuze, 1987; Foucault, 1980).

11. 'El erotismo es sexualidad transfigurada: metáfora. . . . ¿Qué dice esta metáfora? Como todas las metáforas, designa algo que está más allá de la realidad que la origina, algo nuevo y distinto de los términos que la componen. Si Góngora dice *púrpura nevade*, inventa o descubre una realidad que, aunque hecha de ambas, no es ni sangre ni nieve' (Paz, 1993: 10). Notice that Paz does not make any distinction between invention and discovery, which is crucial to von Foerster.

12. The blind point is a small part of the eye, near the optical nerve, in which there are no visual receptors. Thus no image can be captured.

13. This is a very important distinction historians usually make when the mention that America was not discovered but invented. We can say, in this same direction, that organizations are invented before being created.

14. Fernando Leal, a colleague from Universidad de Guadalajara, in Mexico, told me about a certain intelligent machines project in which researchers had established that intelligence is closely related to spatial displacements. Thus, machines were constantly moved in order to improve their learning ability.

15. The concept of autonomy was substituted by that of adaptation and dominated the study of organizations for a long period. Some writers, such as N. Luhmann, have proposed that of self-reference in order to overcome the limitations of the adaptation process. The concept of self-reference, according to the author, is quite close to those of self-organization and the autopoietic system (Luhmann, 1991).

16. As C. Castoriadis remarked, paranoia is an extreme case of autonomy that tends to eliminate any kind of dependence (Castoriadis, 1994).

17. We can mention, as an example, that Berquist argues that the postmodern

organization emphasizes its mission and makes their formal boundaries less visible (see also Clegg, 1992; and Thompson, 1993).

18. Let us remember that for G. Bachelard, an epistemological obstacle was a discursive strategy that avoided to study the real object: 'A science that accepts images is, more than any other one, a victim of metaphors. That is why, the scientific spirit must fight incessantly against images, analogies and metaphors' (Bachelard, 1981: 45).

19. I always enjoy the definition of a female flamenco dancer, by Garcia Lorca: she is a woman half bronze, half dream (quoted by C. Fuentes, 1992). In this case, the blend of two substances, whose natures are totally different, invents a new reality.

20. There is another way of interpreting metaphors. Instead of dealing with an object and a modifier, we could say that it is a double synecdoche process (Kittay, 1989). A synecdoche is a figure of speech in which a part is used for the whole (as *hand* for *worker*) or the whole for a part (as *the law* for *police officer*). It has the same effect in our figure by withdrawing A' and B' but it allow us to stress two other acts: the fractionary and accumulative way in which man has been perceived by scholars (worker is a hand plus feelings plus memory) and the organization's self-regulating capability, due to the physical or logical identity – the metonymy zone plus/or minus A' – that the parts preserve from the whole, as in the case of loosely coupled systems: 'Loose coupling lowers the probability that the organization will have to – or be able to –respond to each little change in the environment that occurs' (Weick, 1976: 6).

21. The absence can be an attempt to evade censure, but it never disappears. The presence or absence is at least as strong as the same presence. See, for example, Cardoza y Aragón, a Guatemalan poet (1986).

22. For G. Bateson, a theory is always invented; it cannot be found in the natural world (Bateson, 1993).

23. See also Benoit, 1985.

24. Our research project also includes the possibility of using fuzzy logic in order to overcome some of the limitations inherent to the crisp logic. This will allow us to have a more flexible concept of organizational limits (Salazar, 1995).

25. Industrial establishments in Mexico are classified as micro (up to 15 workers), small (up to 100 workers), medium (up to 250 workers), and large (more than 250 workers). Most of them are micro (77%) and small (17%), the rest are medium (3%) and large (2%). Micro and small companies employ about 33 per cent of the total workers (Montano, 1992).

26. For some other important consequences, see Heisig and Littek, 1995.

27. We have considered only those variables in which $p < 0.005$.

28. Formal relations were perceived by workers as the opposite of friendly relations.

29. The importance of salary, internal environment and quality were measured in a descendent scale. Thus, correlation indexes with a negative sign are really positive indexes, and vice versa.

References

Alvesson, M. (1993) 'The play of metaphors', in M. Parker and J. Hassard (eds), *Postmodernism and Organizations*. London: Sage. pp. 114–31.

Atlan, H. (1991) *Con razón y sin ella. Intercritica de la Ciencia y del Mito*. Barcelona: Tusquets.

Aubert, N. and de Gaulejac, V. (1991) *Le coût de l'excellence*. Paris: Seuil.

Bachelard, G. (1981) *La formación del espiritu cientifico. Contribución a un psicoanálisis del conocimiento objetivo*. Mexico: Siglo XXI.
Bateson, G. (1993) *Una unidad sagrada. Pasos ulteriores hacia una ecología de la mente*, edited by R.E. Donaldson. Barcelona: Gedisa.
Bateson, G., Jackson, D., Haley, J. and Weakland, J. (1956) 'Toward a theory of schizophrenia', *Behavioral Science*, 1 (4): 251–64.
Bayart, D. (1995) 'Des objects qui solidifient une théorie: l'histoire du contrôle statistique de fabrication', *Ecole polytechnique*, Paris (mimeo).
Benoit, J.C. (1985) *El doble vínculo*. Mexico: Fondo de Cultura Económica.
Burns, T. and Stalker, G.M. (1961) *The Management of Innovation*. London: Tavistock Publications.
Cardoza y Aragón, L. (1986) *El rio. Novelas de caballeria*. Mexico: Fondo de Cultura Económica.
Castoriadis, C. (1975) *L'institution imaginaire de la Sociéte*. Paris: Seuil.
Castoriadis, C. (1994) *Los dominios del hombre: las encrucijadas del laberinto*. Barcelona: Gedisa.
Clegg, S.R. (1992) 'De las culturas antiguas a la fatuidad posmoderna?', *Gestión y Política Pública*, 1 (1): 103–53.
Cooper, R. (1989) 'Modernism, post-modernism and organizational analysis 3: the contribution of Jacques Derrida', *Organization Studies*, 10 (4): 479–502.
Crozier, M. and Friedberg, E. (1977) *L'acteur et le système. Les contraintes de l'action collective*. Paris: Seuil.
Deleuze, G. (1987) *Foucault*. Mexico: Paidós.
Derrida, J. (1989) *La deconstrucción en las fronteras de la filosofia*. Barcelona: Paidós.
Desmarèz, P. (1983) 'La sociologie industrielle. Fille de la thérmodynamique d'équilibre?', *Sociologie du Travail*, 3: 261–74.
Fayol, H. (1961) *Administración industrial y general*. Mexico: Herrero Hermanos.
Foerster, H. von (1994) 'Visión y conocimiento: disfunctiones de segundo orden', in F. Schnitman (ed.), *Nuevos paradigmas, cultura y subjetividad*. Buenos Aires: Paidós.
Foucault, M. (1970) *La arqueología del saber*. Mexico: Siglo XXI.
Foucault, M. (1980) *Vigiliar y castigar: nacimiento de la prisión*. Mexico: Siglo XXI.
Fuentes, C. (1992) *El espejo enterrado*, Mexico: Fondo de cultura económica.
Hammer, Michael and Champy, James (1994) *Reingeniería*, Bogota: Norma.
Heisig, Ulrich and Littek, Wolfang (1995) 'Reorganisations of trust-based self-organisation. Changes of trust relations in the work process'. Paper presented at the 12th EGOS Colloquium, Istanbul.
Henderson, L.J. (1970) *On the Social System*. Chicago: University of Chicago Press.
Heydebrand, W.V. (1989) 'New organizational forms', *Work and Occupations*, 16 (3): 323–57.
Ibarra, E. (1995) 'Strategic analysis of organizations. A model from the complexity paradigm', *Human Systems Management*, 14 (1): 51–70.
Kickert, W. (1991) 'Autopoiesis and the science of (public) administration: essence, sense and nonesense', *Organization Studies*, 14 (2): 261–78.
Kittay, Eva Feder (1989) *Metaphor. Its Cognitive Force and Linguistic Structure*. Oxford: Clarendon Press.
Knights, D. (1992) 'Changing spaces: the disruptive impact of new epistemological location for the study of management', *Academy of Management Review*, 13 (3): 514–36.
Knights, D. and Morgan, G. (1991) 'Strategic discourse and subjectivity: towards a critical analysis of corporate strategy in organizations', *Organization Studies*, 12 (2): 251–74.
Luhmann, N. (1991) *Sistemas sociales. Lineamientos para una teoría general*. Mexico: Universidad Iberoamericana/Alianza. Editorial.

Maturana, H. and Varela, F. (1972) *Autopoiesis*. Facultad de Ciencias, Universidad de Chile, Santiago.

Mintzberg, H. (1991) *La estructuración de las organizaciones*. Barcelona: Ariel.

Montano, L. (1985) 'La escuela de las relaciones humanas: premisas para un debate', in E. Ibarra and L Montano (eds), *Historia del pensamiento administrativo*, Vol I. Mexico: Universidad Autónoma Metropolitana-Iztapalapa. pp. 351–6.

Montano, L. (1987) 'El orden sistémico: algunos avatares del paradigma organizacional', in E. Ibarra and L. Montano (eds), *El orden organizacional: poder, estrategia y contradicción*. Mexico: Universidad Autónoma Metropolitana-Iztapalapa. pp. 1–58.

Montano, L. (1992) 'Micro enterprises in Mexico. A metaphorical approach'. Paper presented at the Eastern Economic Association Conference, New York.

Montano, L. (1993) 'De la metáfora al poder. Algunas reflexiones acerca de las aproximaciones organizacionales a la educación superior', in E. Ibarra (ed.), *La universidad ante el espejo de la excelencia. Enjuegos organizacionales*. Mexico: Universidad Autónoma Metropolitana-Iztapalapa. pp. 1–17.

Montano, L. (1994a) 'Modernidad, postmodernismo y organización. Una reflexión acerca de la noción de estructura postburocrática', in Luis Montano (ed.), *Argumentos para un debate sobre la modernidad*. Mexico: Universidad Autónoma Metropolitana-Iztapalapa. pp. 67–92.

Montano, L. (1994b) 'At the edge of modernity: boundaries, mediations and overlappings. The lessons of the Japanese organization', *Osaka City University Business Journal*, 35–57.

Montano, L. (1996) 'Intelligent machines and organisational spaces. A metaphorical approach to ethics', in K.S. Gil (ed.), *Information Society: New Media, Ethics and Postmodernism*. London: Springer. pp. 90–103.

Morgan, G. (1990) *Imagenes de la organización*. Madrid: Ra-ma.

Morin, E. (1981) *El método: la naturaleza de la naturaleza*. Madrid: Cátedra.

Morin, E. (1991) *Introduction à la pensée complexe*. Paris: ESF Editeur.

Morin, E. (1994) 'La noción de sujeto', in F. Schnitman (ed.), *Nuevos paradigmas, cultura y subjetividad*. Buenos Aires: Paidós.

Ouchi, W. (1984) *The M-Form Society: How American Teamwork can Recapture the Competitive Edge*. Reading, MA: Addison-Wesley.

Pagès, M., Bonetti, M., de Gaulejac, V. and Descendre, D. (1979) *L'emprise de l'organisation*. Paris: Presses Universitaries de France.

Parsons, T. (1970) 'Social systems', in O. Grusky and Miller, G.A. (eds), *The Sociology of Organizations: Basic Studies*. New York: The Free Press. pp. 75–82.

Paz, O. (1993) *La llama doble. Amor y erotismo*. Mexico: Seix Barral.

Roethlisberger, F. and Dickson, W. (1976) *Management and the Worker*. Cambridge, MA: Harvard University Press.

Salazar, J. (1995) 'Notas sobre "fuzzies o fusos"', *Doctoral Programme on Economics*, Universidad Autónoma Metropolitana-Iztapalapa.

Thomspon, K. (1984) 'La sociedad organizacional', in G. Salaman and K. Thompson (eds), *Control e ideología en las organizaciones*. Mexico: Fondo de Cultura Económica.

Thompson, P. (1993) 'Postmodernism: fatal distraction', in M. Parker and J. Hassard (eds), *Postmodernism and Organizations*, London: Sage. pp. 183–203.

Touraine, A. (1969) *La société post-industrielle. Naissance d'une société*. Paris: Denoël.

Weick, Karl E. (1976) 'Educational organizations as loosely coupled systems', *Administrative Science Quarterly*, 21 (1): 1–19.

Wiener, N. (1966) *Ex-prodigy. My Childhood and Youth*. Cambridge, MA: MIT.

Wiener, N. (1969) *Cybernetics: or Control and Communication in the Animal and the Machine*. Cambridge, MA: MIT.

PART 4

RETHINKING VALUES, COLLABORATION AND GLOBAL MANAGEMENT AS POLITICAL PRACTICES

11 Antagonistic Values or Complementary Value Systems? The Chances and Limitations of Dialogue in Organizations

Fernando Leal

The Problem

In a recent book dealing with the intervention of social scientists in organizations, the authors eloquently express the situation which is the starting point of the present chapter:

> In many ways Western industrial society has not come to terms with being an industrial society at all. It continues to struggle with conflicting value systems, all of which are important, but which are difficult to reconcile and integrate, and which have internal contradictions. In particular there is one value system concerned with economic growth, development and expansion: there is a second one concerned with the intrinsic value, autonomy and personal growth of human beings; and there is a third concerned with research, the development of knowledge and the exercise of skills for their own sake. (Klein and Eason, 1991: xiii)

Although these conflicts can be readily appreciated in the relations between organizations dedicated to serve those antagonistic values (as Klein and Eason immediately point out), they can at least as often be felt and suffered within any one single organization. Thus a researcher has to fight, and negotiate with, the administrators in funding institutions about values and priorities (say, about the usefulness of her research project or about its costs) as well as those working *within* her university or even within her own department. In her turn, the administrator in a funding institution must not only deal with researchers in universities, but also with politicians or business people who have a say *internally*, that is in the management or public image of the very same institution she works for. And again, a politician does not have an easy life in trying to reconcile *her* values and priorities *vis-à-vis* a businessperson and vice versa, nor does any of them against all sorts of social agents and groups both in the community at large they belong to and *inside* the particular organization or organizations they lead or manage. In general, we can extend the reasoning in the passage quoted above to the internal life and strife of organizations. Indeed, one way to spell our what organizational complexity means is to say that different and conflicting values are all the time in operation.

It must be noted from the start that value conflicts can, and often do, lead in the real world to conflicts of *interest*, without being identical with them. According to some authors this only happens because interests gave birth to values, say in the form of ideology, false consciousness, rationalization, projection, sublimation, and whatnot. Be that as it may, we must distinguish between the two things. A good example is Kant's famous anecdote concerning the King of France. When fighting the King of Spain for the possession of some Italian city the French king is supposed to have commented that there was no point of contention between him and the Spanish king, and that theirs was not at all a case of disagreement; on the contrary, he said, they really wanted exactly the same thing, namely Naples (or whatever the city was). This was a conflict of interests, and obviously not a conflict of values. They both held political domination in high esteem, and the problem arose just because their ambitions happened to focus on the same object. This kind of thing may of course happen in organizations, and it may even be the case that some, or even all, value conflicts are a surface phenomenon hiding a deeper, and uglier, conflict of interests. This idea is very popular with Foucaltians, for example, who tend to assume that everyone wants power. Thus researchers and administrators may really be fighting over control of financial resources, although the former do it under the cover of scientific freedom and the latter would rather appeal to efficiency. The question is a very old philosophical one.[1] Given its complexity, I want to propose here that we put the question in brackets for the time being and just assume there is a distinction between values and interests, if only in the way the actual conflicts are actually conducted. I shall return to it at the end of the chapter.

The present chapter is above all a *theoretical* exercise, in other words it is an attempt at finding a better way of looking at value conflicts which, by enhancing our understanding of what is going on when they occur, may hopefully help us in finding better ways to deal with them *practically*. Now there are, as far as I can see, only two known practical methods to handle conflicts in organizations, namely *by force* (imposing a solution from above and breaking any opposition to that solution) or else *by dialogue* (which takes many forms, but all of them have at least this in common, that they aim at a peaceful negotiation, that is an at least temporary solution of the conflict which will more or less satisfy the parties involved in the conflict). Quite apart from the fact that force is a rather lousy method of conflict resolution in that value struggles will most certainly re-emerge somewhere else and very possibly with a vengeance (resentment is a bad counsellor after all), I can safely assume that no reader of this book will favour force (persons who do tend to despise books). That leaves us with dialogue as a method, so that what I will say about value conflicts, if it has to have practical value, must have some consequences for our understanding of the possibilities of dialogue as a method of conflict resolution.

The Origin of the Problem (a Hint from Classical Political Philosophy)

How do value conflicts arise? When one is involved in one of these conflicts, it is often hard to avoid thinking that the other party is being stubborn, stupid or downright perverse – how is it possible that he (or she) thinks that way? How is it possible that he (or she) doesn't see reason?[2] At least in those cases it is difficult to see a way out of the conflict and this seems to be pretty bad news for dialogue as a method of conflict resolution. However, this is as should be expected. If people could easily agree on values, then we might not be tempted to talk of value conflicts at all, only perhaps of minor disagreements to be solved pragmatically. I want to say that value conflicts arise because no value exists in a vacuum, unsupported by anything else.[3] On the contrary, values tend to cluster into what (for want of a better word) we may call value systems.[4]

This is borne out by the quotation we started with: people who put money first also tend to put economic expansion first and not, say, knowledge or job satisfaction, and people who put knowledge first, also tend to put research first and not money (except, in both cases, when the opposite value can be safely harnessed as a means to produce the real good). Thus a researcher would like to have free exchange of ideas, because this usually fosters knowledge even though it may hamper economic success; alternatively, the money people might prefer secrecy. (All this, of course, has to be taken with a pinch of salt. Not even researchers may want the business to go bankrupt lest they lose their jobs). Values thus always hang together and exist in more or less coherent clusters; and this is what gives values their peculiar resilience and causes the visible effect of stubbornness we find in actual value conflicts. And all negotiations are trade-offs in which we accept some loss of things we cherish in order to preserve other things we also cherish within the same system of values. Single values clash only because whole value systems clash. (By the way, I shall go on simply talking of values for simplicity's sake, but I will always mean whole value systems.)

All this may be a bunch of truisms, but there is a catch to it. For it sometimes happens that value systems appear to be incompatible. Historically, this was first observed and minutely commented upon by Macchiavelli. The story is complex, but suffice it to say that he found out that the medieval project of conceiving a Christian ruler (as evinced in closely reasoned tracts by the Church Fathers and the Schoolmen) was doomed to failure, in that politics could only be conducted within the framework of Pagan values. Thus treachery and the ruthless elimination of rivals (but also magnificent showing off and spending) were essential to successful government, whereas humility and charity were a recipe for political losers. There was just no way, Macchiavelli argued, that Christian values may be adopted, adapted or integrated into good government (where good meant effective and successful). This was an intellectual scandal of no mean proportions in Early Modern Europe, as is witnessed by the numerous attempts at refutation by philosophers, theologians and politicians (the most famous or infamous of which was penned by no less a figure than Frederick the Great, who probably knew better but had a stake in hiding the truth).[5]

But not even Macchiavelli, living as he did in Florence and this means outside the Italian cities where modern capitalism was being born (Genoa and Venice), foresaw that Pagan values were also to be opposed by the growth of commerce. And he couldn't have foreseen that because the process took several centuries to be deployed in full force. The point is here that the values of commerce, that is things like keeping contracts or being thrifty, are also incompatible with the Pagan values.[6] The big clash between those gigantic value systems have reverberated ever since the Renaissance and keep reverberating to this very day. The so-called industrial-military complex is necessarily a fragile arrangement, because the values associated with war-mongering are uneasily married with those of commerce. Of course, the people involved have interests in common, but this commonality of interest is always at risk. Somehow, the two great wars of the twentieth century and its technological attendants have taught us that, even if (as the cynics among us say) war is the best business ever, it may also destroy everything.[7]

Anyway, none of these value systems (and others as well) has been actually superseded by each other. They co-exist, come into conflict with each other and negotiate for power. And this mixture of co-existence, conflict and negotiation does not only occur at the macro-level which I have been discussing for the sake of dramatic effect. It occurs at all levels, from international and domestic politics and policy-making, through all sorts of communities, institutions and organizations, down to small groups, nuclear families and maybe even the single self.[8] To take just one example, the corporative values associated with the old extended family have completely given way in modern industrial societies (and are giving way in developing countries) to the more individualistic values of the nuclear family; and the latter have also started to give way to all sorts of new arrangements and experiments (communes, single-parent families, childless couples, homosexual marriages, and whatnot). What philosophers like Heidegger have called the planetarization of human life and some publicists refer to as the global village has produced, and keeps producing, larger and more complex clashes between value systems than ever before in the history of humankind. Those clashes are not going away because sometimes we wish them to (sometimes we enjoy the variety, of course). They are here to stay. We have to live with them and try to understand them.

Relativism and Common Aims (a Further Hint from Classical Political Philosophy)

When values are in conflict, the modern recipe is relativism. Nobody wants to be dogmatic, least of all in matters of value, which we know to be beyond exact knowledge and assessment. This at least seems to be what every civilized denizen of the modern world would say. Relativism was first envisioned by the old sophists in Ancient Greece about 2,500 years ago, probably as a consequence of the great Greek migrations at the social level and of much travelling at the personal one: nothing like coming into contact with strange customs to give a healthy mind some relativistic twist! But relativism didn't take root in the Ancient world. The second relativistic wave came with the great sea voyages, especially since the sixteenth century and particularly with the so-called discovery of America. Those were strange people with strange customs indeed. But the power of dogmatism and intolerance (both civil and religious) was too great to yield easily. Only after about 500 years of increasing globalization did relativism and tolerance manage to get some hold in general culture. Of course, there still are big chunks of the opposite attitudes everywhere, or else why should there be such a resurgence of fundamentalisms, nationalisms and racisms? But this does not concern us civilized people, who are thoroughly tolerant, relativistic and generally nice to other people's notions and values, are we not? When a value conflict arises, we would immediately (or if not soon enough, when the first heat has passed) agree to disagree, would we not? Only primitive, simple-minded people would fight over what are, after all, only matters of opinion, wouldn't they?[9]

It is easy to see that relativism, tolerance and other nice attitudes are easy to adopt in practice *as long as* we are only talking about other people being in conflict with each other, or as a philosopher says, as long as we are talking *in the third person* (Tugendhat, 1993). But the moment the conflict touches us, and we start talking *in the first person*, the moment the values in conflict are *our* values and thus essentially connected with the matter at hand, the nice attitudes seem to 'melt, thaw and resolve themselves into a dew'. We care and that's the difference. Relativism doesn't then seem to be the answer after all. Well, as a matter of fact it is, or at least it is up to a point. But in order to see how, or how far, the argument has to become a little more complex. And first of all, we have to get rid of a notorious red herring. Let us suppose someone would say: 'Yes of course, relativism is a more precious conquest of the Enlightenment and we should cherish and respect it. And it is probably the best policy in intercultural relations, but not really when a conflict appears *inside an organization*, because here there is a job to be done. No relativism can help when there is a joint project and decisions have to be taken. So let's keep relativism out, nice though it may be. The very essence of organizations makes it wholly irrelevant.' If this is true, it would mean that one very widespread attitude, which I suppose to be a part (an essential part and a hard-earned part) of modern civilized life has no role to play in organizations. Could the gap between general culture and organizational needs be that big?

In order to answer that question I propose to take a hint from classical political philosophy. According to Collingwood and Oakeshott (two contemporary philosophers, both British, both professors at Oxford), there are at least two ways to understand an association of people as first conceived in Ancient Roman law. The distinction was then appropriated by late medieval political philosophers (from the fifteenth century on) in order to come to terms with the new political realities then emerging, when the various arrangements popularly called the Feudal Order started to give slow and painful birth to what would come to be called the Modern European National State, which is of course the arrangement which has imposed itself on all peoples on this planet and which is so familiar to us as to make it very difficult to conceive any alternatives.[10] The Roman legal terms were *societas* and *universitas* and the difference between them was spelt out by Oakeshott as follows:

> The idea *societas* is that of agents, who, by choice of circumstance, are related to one another so as to compose an identifiable association of a certain sort. The tie which joins them, and in respect of which each recognizes himself to be *socius*, is not that of an engagement in an enterprise to pursue a common substantive purpose or to promote a common interest, but that of loyalty to one another. . . . Juristically, *societas* was understood to be the product of a pact or an agreement, not to act in concert but to acknowledge the authority of certain conditions in acting. . . . It was a formal relationship in terms of rules, not a substantive relationship in terms of common action. . . . Analogically, *universitas* is not difficult to understand. It is persons associated in a manner such as to constitute them a natural person. . . . [W]hen the jurists of the later Middle Ages came to explore this notion of corporate association in connection with collegiate churches, boroughs, universities, etc., it gradually received a more elaborate specification. A corporation aggregate was recognized as persons associated in respect of some identified common purpose, in the pursuit of some acknowledged substantive end, or in the promotion of some specified enduring interest. . . . And

since association was in terms of a common substantive purpose, membership entailed a choice to be associated in pursuit of this purpose, an undertaking (perhaps a vow) to promote this purpose and acceptance by those already associated. (Oakeshott, 1975: 201–4)

According to both Collingwood and Oakeshott (although only the latter explains the Roman distinction), a good part of the intellectual confusion in the debate about nations and the practical difficulties that nations have within themselves and with each other stem from the tension produced by the fact that these two concepts are so mixed up in our institutions, practices and ideas. What I want to submit is, very simply, that this tension also exists in the case of our modern organizations. We also find here both aspects, although perhaps some organizations are rather more similar to a *universitas* than to a *societas* or the other way round. In an important sense, it is a matter of degree whether in a given organization people attach more weight to the sharing of a common purpose and the pursuit of common aims, or else whether the convivial and 'fair play' ruling of what is a common predicament rather than a common purpose is emphasized.

Now, because this is a matter of degree, the objection voiced before is, as I said, a bit of a red herring. Incidentally, it may be of interest to observe that, as far as a given organization behaves like a *universitas*, a conflict of value seems almost ruled out from the start. The common aim may be considered the highest value in such an organization, so where could the conflict of values come from? Take again the case of a university. The common aim is higher education and scholarly research. They all agree to *that*. However, there are many ways in which we can try to attain that aim, and there are many criteria by which we may judge whether we are attaining it or not. The familiar examples of value conflicts between the staff and the administration readily come to mind. So, a common aim does not by itself guarantee that values will be the same for all. Since we have assumed that such conflicts should not be solved by imposition and brute force, we may want to take recourse to the *societas* aspect of organizations. The solution must somehow refer to certain rules agreed beforehand.[11] And the following of such rules open the space for nice attitudes like relativism and tolerance.

This would be the place where dialogue enters the picture; and the temptation is difficult to resist to go immediately into it. I have two reasons for delaying discussion of dialogue. One is that, although dialogue is certainly *en vogue*, most philosophical discussions of it (e.g., in Habermas, 1983) seem to me to be of little use when trying to figure out how things might work in real life and real organizations. The second one is that, although there are some proposals concerning how dialogue might be (and has actually been) conducted which strike me as quite realistic, their lessons can only be really understood if we effect a change in perspective on what value conflicts are for.

From Conflict to Complementarity: a New Way of Thinking about Values

Philosophers have always viewed conflict or opposition in one of two ways: the *dogmatic* way, according to which only one side may be right (or correct or true or valid) and the other will have to give, and the *dialectic* way, according to which the opposites must be reconciled, either by finding a hidden unity or harmony between the opposites or else by a higher synthesis. The former has become a huge question mark ever since Gödel proved that adequate knowledge implies contradictions and consistent knowledge cannot be adequate (Gödel's proof concerned elementary and easily formulated theories, so that we can assume it is *a fortiori* valid for any theory).[12] Yet dogmatism is today as alive as it ever was. In fact, it is vastly more popular than dialectics, which has usually been deemed a bit esoteric if not mystical. Be that as it may, when applied to conflicts of values the traditional methods of dealing with it closely follows these two models. People think either dogmatically or dialectically, that is they think that either at most one of the conflicting values is correct (whatever that means) or else that they are merely surface phenomena of a deeper consensus.[13] There seems to be no third way.

This was indeed the position until Niels Bohr came along and showed how we could accept conflict and opposition without either having to decide for one party or having to find a higher synthesis.[14] This move was made possible by the introduction of the concept of *complementarity*. The experimental facts were as simple as they were baffling: light behaved sometimes like a wave and sometimes like a particle. The experiments could not be dismissed; so the dogmatic resolution was discarded. However, the dialectic idea of a deeper unity between these two undeniable manifestations of light could not be sustained (talk of 'wavicles' among physicists was always intended as a joke). Moreover, the duality thus found to apply to light was soon generalized to matter. It seemed that at the most elementary level, all nature should behave in this curious dual manner. The whole thing seemed to be as impossible as it was undeniable and unavoidable. After much thinking about this very deep puzzle, Bohr proposed we think of duality as complementarity (for a semi-technical account of Bohr's intellectual struggle, see Murdoch, 1987). It bears emphasizing that complementarity has not the usual sense, that is the sense in which we say of two pictures of an elephant taken from different angles that they are complementary (the image stems from John Bell, see d'Espagnat and Klein, 1993). Rather, it is as though one of the pictures of the elephant would show an eagle and the other picture would show a snake! If this should happen every time we photograph the elephant, then both pictures would then be complementary in Bohr's sense, that is they would be both necessary and mutually exclusive pictures.[15]

It is here impossible to enter into the details of Bohr's theory; its interpretation is a matter of controversy and I am far from being an expert.

Nevertheless, I find the idea of complementarity fascinating, especially since it was introduced into linguistic theory, a subject I really know from the inside. Very briefly put, it is a usual procedure to think of some words and expressions as having the function of *pointing to objects* and of other words or expressions as having the very different functions of *signifying an idea*. For instance, in the sentence 'That cat is black', you would say that the words 'that cat' point to the animal and the words 'is black' say of it that it is black (applies the idea of blackness to the cat, as it were). This is of course a very simple example; but something like it has been the stock-in-trade of every analysis of language proposed by logicians, grammarians, philosophers, and something like it was naturally part and parcel of linguistic theory. Both properties, pointing and signifying (or indicativity and predicativity, as the technical terms go), are both necessary for language but mutually exclusive. A given word or expression is necessarily one or the other, but it cannot be both. Now what some linguists started to propose in the late 1970s and early 1980s was that every word and expression in every language actually had both properties, even if it sounded monstrously implausible on the face of it. The key concept was again complementarity; and, as in physics, you could not analyse the pointing function together with the signifying function of a given word, but the tools for seeing how the word functions this way or the other way, were completely different.[16]

Now what I want to propose is that organizations also evince complementarity, at least when it comes to values. The idea came to me when reading the most recent book of Jane Jacobs, a maverick political philosopher and economist (1993). According to her, social and political life is torn between two conflicting, indeed incompatible, value systems incarnated by two different and opposed groups of people. These two systems she calls moral syndromes. In medicine a syndrome, the reader may remember, is a bunch of symptoms. So the symptoms which together make up the syndromes can be summarized and opposed to each other as shown in Table 11.1 (Jacobs, 1993: 23–4).

It is rather easy to picture military people as prototypical representatives of Moral Syndrome B and tradespeople as prototypical representatives of Moral Syndrome A; as such they constitute quite different 'systems of survival'.[17] Jacob's book is a rich and agile commentary upon these conflicting kinds of people, their historical origins and their metamorphoses across time and space.[18] To give an example, scientific research (and its concomitant values) could only flourish under Moral Syndrome A and the gang and mafia culture is only possible within Moral Syndrome B. I cannot go into the rich detail of these value systems here. And it must be said at once that Jacobs is mainly interested in showing how the application of one value system to problems pertaining to an unappropriate realm (say, the application of the value 'respect of hierarchy' to the realm of scientific research) can only have disastrous results; showing that is why she wrote the book in the first place – it is intended as an analytic

TABLE 11.1

Moral Syndrome A	Moral Syndrome B
Shun force	Shun trading
Come to voluntary agreements	Exert prowess
Be honest	Be obedient and disciplined
Collaborate easily with strangers and aliens	Adhere to tradition
Compete	Respect hierarchy
Respect contracts	Be loyal
Use initiative and enterprise	Take vengeance
Be open to inventiveness and novelty	Deceive for the sake of the task
Be efficient	Make rich use of leisure
Promote comfort and convenience	Be ostentatious
Dissent for the sake of the task	Dispense largesse
Invest for productive purposes	Be exclusive
Be industrious	Show fortitude
Be thrifty	Be fatalistic
Be optimistic	Treasure honour

Source: Jacobs, 1993: 23–4.

instrument to clear up the malaises of our civilization. Nevertheless, I think that her book can be read in such a way that we understand the above 'syndromes' to be jointly necessary for our survival. Now I want to suggest we should again leave the macro-level of political analysis and try to apply that insight to organization theory, that is try to see organizations as surviving only because of the co-existence of opposing value systems within them, systems which (and people who) fight each other and cannot be reconciled. In other words, organizations would need complementarity of value systems, even though such complementarity shows up as conflict. It is not at all difficult to see that, say, a university needs both scientists and administrators; and it is clear that the values of both groups (and not just their interests) are often opposed to each other. This is the kind of complementarity I want the reader to concentrate upon.

Now, there is a different approach which gives a dynamic twist to the idea of complementarity: the brief and tantalizing insights offered in a recent book on the differences in organizational culture within what appears to be one style of economy, namely capitalism.[19] According to Hampden-Turner and Trompenaars (1993), one of the aspects of capitalism which differ across cultures can be expressed as the tension between individualism and communitarianism. Phrased as a question:

> Is it more important to focus upon the enhancement of each individual, his or her rights, motivations, rewards, capacities, attitudes, or should more attention be paid to the advancement of the corporation as a community, which all its members are pledged to serve? (Hampden-Turner and Trompenaars, 1993: 11)

The opposition between these two attitudes is clear, but it is far from being absolute once we take the right perspective. According to the authors, Anglo-Saxons follow Adam Smith in taking for granted that focus on individuals has beneficial consequences for the community by some 'invisible hand' mechanism, and they have trouble understanding why other people (like Continental Europeans and Asians) cannot see the force of this logic. This would be the correct and obvious solution to a false value conflict. Only it does not work that way. Our authors think that

> the French, Germans and Japanese . . . stand [Adam] Smith on his head. They would say that if the needs of the group are considered first, then the invisible hand will . . . reach down and automatically take care of the desires of the individual. (Hampden-Turner and Trompenaars, 1993: 14)

If this analysis is correct, what separates two value systems is not so much the causal chain as such (which is circular in both cases), but the starting point of the reasoning. Yet this apparently small difference cannot be easily resolved:

> In a dilemma in which individual and group needs seem to diverge irreconcilably, managers from different countries will begin to repair the split in precisely opposite ways. Because of this, a multicultural group working on a minor crisis can be overwhelmed with bafflement and suspicion as managers from different cultures each wonder what the foreigners are up to. (Hampden-Turner and Trompenaars, 1993: 15)

This also seems to be a kind of complementarity, and it is certainly one which the authors exploit in order to better understand other cases of value conflict. But somehow, it doesn't quite look like the kind I illustrated before as resulting from Jacobs's book. Nevertheless, it may be instructive to think whether Jacobs's 'moral syndromes' or 'systems of survival' might be related to each other by a circular causal chain. I am sure this has to be the case if those 'systems' are really complementary. This is pretty clear for Jacobs's macro-political examples. Suppose there is a society or group where everyone is military and no one is productive. Such people can only survive because they prey upon the productive life of some other society or group (think of the bandits in Kurosawa's *Seven Samurai*). And in the long run the military life will be harnessed by the productive life as an organic part of a mixed society (as with modern armies which are obedient to a civil government). On the other hand, the productive life of a people is only possible if it has some protection from outside aggression, and that protection is given by the military people (like the samurai in the above-mentioned film). This is a simple but effective argument. And what I want to suggest is that this is what probably happens within any given organization. The weird thing is that conflict happens, even though the people involved could become wise and see through the situation. At this point, we should be prepared to examine the question of what are the chances and limitations of dialogue when a conflict of values (reflecting a deeper phenomenon of complementarity of values) arises in an organization.

Dialogue as a Solution to Value Conflict

The first problem here is that dialogue, as commonly understood, is conceived as a form of negotiation. A good example is the German institution of the *Betriebsrat*, the Corporate Council formed by representatives of the administration and the working force. Whenever there is a problem, say the perpetual issue of rising wages, the members of the *Betriebsrat* sit down to talk and negotiate a trade-off. Now the notion of negotiation, and the actual practice of it as usually conceived, has more to do with interests than with values. Management wants to keep production costs low and workers want a rise. These two interests are clearly in conflict, but what about the values? Are they different? The question cannot be answered yet. But in order to prepare the terrain for a considered answer, let's choose an example where we can more readily locate different values in conflict.

Suppose a team of social scientists who know about organizations are approached by a company interested in developing an information system to help the chief engineers do a complex job. The system should be developed in tight collaboration with the company's system designers. We have here three groups, the academics, the engineers and the designers, each one of which has not only interests to defend but values to uphold. Thus, the engineers (the end users) want the system to be of real use without it robbing them of the interesting parts of the job. Similarly, the designers (organized in a development team) look forward to building an interesting, original, complex, challenging system. And the social scientists (as advisers to both users and designers) are anxious to show how their favourite ideas and theories about the way organizations work and how a badly designed system can wreak social and organizational havoc in a particular working environment. This is a case where value conflicts could very easily arise; and one whose consequences would be a wonderful technological toy which cost an enormous amount of money and energy but which nobody actually uses (for an example, see Ord, 1995). According to the report given by the social scientists on the real-life story which underlies my example (Eason et al., 1995), the conflict was avoided by a methodology of so-called 'user-centred systems design' which entails five steps (I have changed the wording somewhat):

1 Potential users identify an application area for information technology.
2 Working teams are organized so as to ensure user participation throughout the process.

3 The teams work out progressively more detailed user and task analysis and develop a progressively more detailed system prototype; here the main point is to avoid specification before the users can have a say.
4 The system prototype is actually used in realistic trials so that users are enabled to evaluate it and propose their actual requirements.
5 The system is implemented in pilot studies all the while observing what consequences it has on the job and on the organizational life; here the main point is to avoid rushing into full implementation before the people involved have been given the chance to see whether unforeseen but undesirable effects happen.

This list gives an outline of how dialogue can take place in an organization in an orderly fashion, so as to ensure that the people involved (the bearers of the potentially conflicting value systems) step on each other's toes.[20] One of the most interesting parts of this methodology is that it was invented by academics who thereby are quite effectively hindered in taking decisions which would run counter to the wishes and values of the users; in fact, the designers (the computer people) are also restrained, in that users are put at the centre of things. So a certain hierarchy of values is pre-ordained, according to which the users' values are given priority without destroying or eliminating the values of the designers or the intervening academics. In fact, these are as necessary as ever (certainly as necessary as the users' own values) to the functioning of the designing enterprise. Moreover, this hierarchy is only a momentary affair, so to speak a snapshot of the whole process. When the authors analyse the role of the academic partners in the project, the actual description shows a complexity which belies the simple label 'user-centred':

> What was the rôle of the academic partners? The overall process of development was proposed by the academics. . . . [They] provided specific help at a number of stages. . . . [Their] experience . . . was that, in the act of taking over and using this advice, the development team [i.e., the designers] followed the principles *but varied the practice. They did not perform these activities as systematically as the academics would have felt necessary or appropriate. . . .* The development team feel that they would be able to plan and undertake a user-centred approach without support in the future (and indeed have set out to do so). *In following this course, the development team recognise that with their technical background, there will remain a tendency to concentrate upon completing technical development and they have to remind themselves to make the effort to go to users with incomplete systems. . . .* There is one further conclusion to draw about the takeover of user-centred approaches. This study shows it can be achieved as a series of methods to replace . . . the current methods of systems development. Technical development staff and users can utilise these methods. *The difficulty is that when it comes to generating alternative organisational visions or of understanding how people and technology might interact, for example, in different allocations of function, the development staff and the users may not know of relevant theories and findings. This was the one rôle in the present study the academics could not hand over.*
> (Eason et al., 1995 my emphasis)

The italics show where the priorities change; sometimes it is technical factors that become more important, as when the designers 'vary the practices', but they are aware that they will tend to 'concentrate' upon the technical bits and forget about the users, so priorities change again; and a final change of gears appears when the authors insist upon the necessity of intervention by social scientists so that users and designers come to understand 'alternative organisational visions', that is they are enabled to avoid undesirable social consequences within their organizations, a possibility non-academics ignore as long as they focus only on technology or on the actual use of the system. In fact, I would say that the label 'user-centred' is only appropriate because it tries to avoid adapting people to the system to be developed, but it is really not at all exclusively centred on users; but then sometimes it is. Sometimes it becomes centred on technology, and sometimes it becomes centred on organizational life. Each one of these terms refers to profoundly different and eventually conflicting value systems incarnated by the three groups of people we mentioned, namely the engineers (who are going to use the system), the designers (who are going to develop it), and the academics (who have to worry about both the users and the organization).

It is clear from this example that conflicts of value such as these cannot be resolved by compromise. There is no bargaining and negotiation going on here. I said in the last section that 'organizations need complementarity of value systems, even though such complementarity shows up as conflict'. Well, this is not correct. Quite the contrary in fact: it is *because* complementarity shows up as conflict that organizations need it at all: without conflict (and the deeply felt convictions behind it) complementarity couldn't really work. Only because engineers, designers and social scientists in the above example are each *committed* to the values they represent (I would even say the values them embody), can potential conflict be resolved in a dialogue in which complementarity becomes clear.[21] This would then be the main difference between interests and values: you can compromise when it comes to interests (that's the whole point of bargaining), but you cannot compromise when it comes to values. That is why values, far from being some sort of cognitive garbage, are absolutely essential to organizations. But we can only understand it when we see ever-threatening conflict of values as a manifestation of complementarity.

Concluding Thoughts

Dialogue can be seen in the first place as a way to become more sensitive to the perspective of the other members of an organization without surrendering the unique commitments that make each member necessary. In the above examples, the engineers did not renounce their engineering values, nor did the designers or the social scientists renounce theirs; they only attuned those values to each other's in order to better reach the common goals.[22] Thus can the double aspect of *societas* and *universitas* be best redeemed: an organization which cultivates the over-arching values of dialogue acts like a *societas* but, again, by using dialogue to achieve common goals through the civilized interaction of opposing values and commitments, acts like a *universitas*.[23]

However, dialogue can only work when there are deeply felt values which are at least in potential conflict. And the aim of dialogue is not *theoretical* (the one abstract truth that Habermas (1983) is so concerned with and even obsessed about) but *practical* (action undertaken in co-operation with other people). It is because of this active, practical character in the middle of conflict that values have a role to play over and above goals, aims and interests, as I hope to have shown. As such, values are, so to speak, bearers of truth, but not pale theoretical truth expressible in some abstract statement, but full-blown and lively practical truth as embodied in real agents dealing with a real complex world – a world where conflict should not be seen as *unavoidable* but as *indispensable*, that is not as a necessary evil to be tolerated but as a necessary good to be fostered.[24] For if ever one value system should obliterate the other one (as the dogmatics would have it), the whole organization, and its purpose, would also be obliterated.

Notes

This is an amended version of a text I submitted to the participants in the APROS '95 conference (Cuernavaca, Mexico, 11–14 December, 1995). I would like to thank Luis Montano and Eduardo Ibarra, who took the risk of inviting a philosopher and linguist to such a conference; I only hope they do not regret it. My appreciation also to all the people who attended the session on 'Ethics and Commitment' and particularly to my rapporteur, John Hassard of Keele University; their questions, comments and complaints were extremely helpful. Finally, a grant from the Society for the Furtherance of the Critical Philosophy (London) made both the work on the chapter and my participation in the conference possible.

1. Its first manifestation is probably the Ancient Greek idea, voiced by Aristotle, when he reasoned that 'if everyone is looking for some good, then there is a good that everyone is looking for' (*Nicomachean Ethics*, book I, chapter 1). He referred to this good by the traditional name of *eudaimonia* or happiness; and some contemporary philosophers have argued that the argument contains a logical fallacy (see e.g., Geach, 1972). I cannot explore the issue here for lack of space.

2. Simon's penetrating discussion of rational processes and the opposed phenomena of limited, that is 'serial' attention (faddishness and one-issue politics) readily comes to mind in this context, but I don't want to complicate the description here (see Simon, 1983, part 3).

3. This problem is *deep*, but I must rest content with a couple of hints here in order not to break the chain of argument. The Ancients used to say that nature hates a vacuum (i.e., matter fills everything) and this attitude persisted until good theories were proposed that showed how a vacuum was possible (i.e., how there could be places in nature where nothing was). Many philosophers had the opposite idea concerning value: they thought there could be things which people might be

able to avoid attaching a value to. This is what the ideal of cool reason amounted to. But other philosophers refused to believe so and recent scientific research has obliged them at long last by showing not only that we are as a matter of biological fact inveterate *valuers*, but also, and much more interestingly, that not even reason could function without concomitant processes of valuing (see Damasio, 1994).

4. The issue has been studied extensively in recent philosophy, although with no particular emphasis on values as such. For instance, somebody says during a conversation that contemporary organizations are increasingly postmodern. Now, barring insincerity, bad faith, conceptual confusion or just the understandable wish to pull our leg, he who says that believes it. But in order to believe it, he must believe a lot of other things (relating, e.g., to how organizations used to work in the past, to how organizational changes come about, and so on). As a matter of fact, we who hear him must also believe a lot of things if we are to understand what he is saying. Statements do not exist in a vacuum; they are sustained by all sorts of other (explicit or implicit) statements. In philosophical shop-talk we say statements (and the beliefs associated to them) are *inferentially* connected, which just means that what anybody believes or says follows from some other thing he or she also believes or may say (if pressed) and that all sorts of other things follow from it (see Davidson, 1984). In philosophical parlance we would say that statements (or beliefs) are *holistic*. So I would say that values are as holistic as statements (or beliefs).

5. The best reference for this historical development is Isaiah Berlin's priceless essay on Machiavelli (Berlin, 1979: ch. II).

6. For the development of capitalism, see Braudel, 1985. For the clash between the Pagan value system and the modern commercial value system, see Hirschman, 1977.

7. It has recently been claimed that war-mongering on the grand scale is dead (see Kennedy, 1988). The sheer uncontrollable resurgence of religious and ethnic wars should sober us up a little in that respect.

8. This is at last what is suggested in Gergen, 1991. See also Elster, 1986.

9. I shall later argue that viewing values as 'just matters of opinion' is a wrong-headed attitude. As such it is the worst possible reason for adopting relativism or tolerance. Values are not *cognitive garbage* but rather represent deep, if somewhat obscure, insights without which human action would lose ground, become difficult and unfocused and finally break down (see 'Dialogue as a Solution to Values Conflict' on p. 237).

10. Collingwood, 1942: part II; Oakeshott, 1975; part III. A quotation might give the flavour of the argument: '[The] effort to understand [the new political situation] lit upon several well-worn analogies, some of which we may neglect . . . because they soon revealed themselves to be inadequate and implausible: the notion, for example, that a state is like a "family" and that the relations between its members were like family relations; or the suggestion that a state is like an "organism" and that the relationship between its members was like that of the components of an organic process. But there are two ideas, each promising enlightenment and each proving itself to be capable of absorbing a whole direction of thought, round which European reflection on this matter has continuously circled since the fifteenth century: a state understood in the terms of *societas* and a state understood in the terms of *universitas*. They derived from Roman private law, where the words stood for two different modes of human association; and from the twelfth century they had become familiar whenever argument had to do with the legal specification of associations. . . . In the late Middle Ages the words *societas* and *universitas* were already in use to denote and to distinguish some actual associations and communities. . . . [But] their English equivalents ("partnership" and "corporation") came to be used indifferently . . .' (Oakeshott, 1975: 198–200). For the use of the organic and family metaphors in modern organizations, see Montano, 1995.

11. On the other hand, it is not clear that we know beforehand what the rules are. In fact, it would seem that we do not know that and perhaps never will. Witness the endless invention of new rules as new kinds of (unforeseen) problems and conflicts in society keep popping up (think, e.g., of the endless changes in legislation). Besides, it has often been observed that the rules of society are partially contradictory – one of the many issues judges have to decide concerns which of two incompatible laws apply to a given case. Ethnomethodologists have suggested that this is the general situation in any regulated interaction (see Garfinkel, 1967: ch. 2). All this is closely related to what I am going to say in the next section about traditional methods of conflict resolution, and particularly about the dogmatic method.

12. Readers familiar with Gödel's theorem may find my reference to it a trifle baroque, if not straightforwardly wrong. I would like to defend myself against the charge. The dogmatic perspective assumes that only one of two conflicting positions can be right. If instead of 'positions' we say 'propositions' and instead of 'conflict' we say 'contradiction' (which in the cases we are discussing is just a matter of making things more precise), then the dogmatic is saying that of two contradictory propositions only one is true. This prima facie implies acceptance of the old Aristotelian laws of contradiction and excluded middle, either in the direct syntactic version given by Whitehead and Russell (1910: *2.11 and *3.24) or in the sophisticated semantic version given by Tarski (1935: sec. 2, props. 1 and 2). Yet things are a bit more complicated than that in that we are presupposing that the method of conflict resolution is dialogue, that is dialogue would be a decision procedure to establish which of the two contradictory propositions is true. It is here that Gödel enters the picture. He proved that for a relatively elementary formal system there are true propositions which it is not possible to prove (the system, if consistent, is not complete). What I was trying to say above is that if this is true for simple formalized systems, it is all the more so for sets of propositions which are neither formalized nor easily formalizable – apart from being far from simple and inaccessible to comparable decision procedures as are available in mathematics. In other words, dialogue is a great method, but no one which could decide (*pace* Habermas) who is right in a value conflict.

13. I am not talking rhetorics here. Of course, it does not escape me that a manager or a PR man can argue dogmatically or dialectically (saying, for instance, that workers and managers have *au fond* the same values, in spite of appearances). The dialectical strategy, which is rather subtler, might even succeed with some people; but I want to focus on what people really think about the conflict.

14. I am not suggesting here that quantum physics can be directly applied to other fields of inquiry, as has become fashionable in recent times: all I am saying is that Bohr has taught us to think in new ways – but how to do so remains the responsibility of the practitioners of any given discipline (a task which demands respect to their own concepts, methods and problems). On the other hand, Bohr's historical priority, as all other priority claims, is of course subject to changes in scholarship: an older author who anticipated complementarity may anytime be found (thus d'Espagnat and Klein, 1993, hesitatingly refer to Kierkegaard, another Dane). I just want to say that Hegel is most certainly not a candidate. For his version of dialectics (which is probably the most famous one) presents itself rather as a kind of combination of the dogmatic and the dialectic, suggesting that reconciliation by synthesis is never achieved or definitive but has always a temporary character. Bohr's vision is not like that at all.

15. Murdoch, 1987: 60: 'Two or more concepts or statements may be said to be complementary in Bohr's sense if and only if: (a) they are different in meaning, or predicate different properties, (b) together, or jointly, they constitute a complete description or representation of a thing, (c) they are mutually exclusive or incompatible either in a logical sense or in an empirical sense.'

16. See the magisterial exposition of Seiler (1986). By the way, I suspect complementarity may be a much more pervasive feature of language than the original example shows (see Leal, 1992). Anyway, only time will tell whether this similarity between physics and linguistics is only superficial. The latter discipline is anyway still too underdeveloped as a science for a protracted comparison to be of much use.

17. See the historical reference to the clashes between Pagan (highly military) and modern (highly commercial) values in section 2.

18. Although Jacobs's ideas are particularly useful to support my case for complementarity, she has some interesting forerunners, both in historically informed political philosophy (Hirschman, 1977; Berlin, 1979; Oakeshott, 1993) and in general moral philosophy (Nagel, 1979: ch. 14; Nagel, 1986; Hampshire, 1989).

19. In another chapter (Ibarra and Leal, 1995) a comparison of the ideas of Hampden-Turner and Trompenaars (1993) with those of Albert (1991) is proposed.

20. For a case where something like the above methodology failed to be implemented, see Klein and Eason, 1991: 106–14. The by far common case of ordinary dialogue being just a useless expedient is illustrated by Ord (1995).

21. I would like to remind the reader again of Simon's discussion of the limited attention problem (people appear to be inherently incapable of concentrating on more than problem at a time) (see note 2). If he is right, then complementarity looks like an example of what Hegel termed 'the cunning of reason' installed right at the heart of human organizations.

22. A *similar* idea seems to underlie the application of Socratic method to organizations by Joseph Kessels in the Netherlands. This method, which is also the first historical model of dialogue, was invented by Socrates in the middle of a far-ranging value crisis as a unique means of analysing what our values amount to. It was further developed and refined by German philosopher Leonard Nelson (1929) in the beginning of this century and, through the work of his disciples, has been continuously cultivated up to this day (see Heckmann, 1981; Krohn et al., 1989). Kessels is original in trying to use it to help participants 'develop an analysis of a controversial policy matter, a fundamental decision or a practical dilemma' (taken from the prospectus of Dialogue Consultants, located in Amsterdam; see also Kessels, 1996). The main *difference* from the methodology of 'user-centred systems design' is that Kessels's version of the Socratic dialogue takes place away from the nitty-gritty details of the workplace, whereas dialogue (in the example of the section on pages 237–9 above) is actually *embodied* in the actual work and has a separate existence only in so far as meetings of the involved teams are needed at different stages of the process.

23. The over-arching values are emphatically not superordinate values of the organization, but rather general presuppositions of dialogue and more generally of civilized life.

24. I do not apologize here for talking of truth. Postmodernists don't like it, I know (and I remember being forcefully reminded when giving the chapter at the colloquium from which this book emanates). Unfortunately, a proper defence of this unfashionable position would need a different chapter. In the meantime, the interested reader may want to compare the discussion of knowledge in Leal (1993).

References

Albert, Michel (1991) *Capitalisme contre capitalisme*. Paris: Seuil.

Berlin, Isaiah (1979) *Against the Current: Essays in the History of Ideas*. London: The Hogarth Press.

Braudel, Fernand (1985) *La dynamique du capitalisme*. Paris: Arthaud.

Collingwood, Robin George (1942) *The New Leviathan*. Oxford: Clarendon Press.
Damasio, Antonio R. (1994) *Descartes' Error: Emotion, Reason, and the Human Brain*. New York: Putnam.
Davidson, Donald (1984) *Inquiries into Truth and Interpretation*. Oxford: Clarendon Press.
d'Espagnat, Bernard and Klein, Étienne (1993) *Regards sur la matière: des quanta et des choses*. Paris: Fayard.
Eason, K.D., Harker, S.P.D., Raven, P.F., Brailsford, J.R. and Cross, A.D. (1995) 'Expert or assistant? Supporting power engineers in the management of electricity distribution', in P. Shipley and F. Leal (eds), *Ethics and New Technology*. Special issue of *AI & Society*, 9 (1).
Elster, Jon (ed.) (1986) *The Multiple Self*. Cambridge: Cambridge University Press.
Garfinkel, Harold (1967) *Studies in Ethnomethodology*. Englewood Cliffs, NJ: Prentice-Hall.
Geach, Peter Thomas (1972) 'The history of a fallacy', in *Logic Matters*. Oxford: Blackwell. pp. 1–13.
Gergen, Kenneth (1991) *The Saturated Self: Dilemmas of Identity in Contemporary Life*. New York: Basic Books.
Habermas, Jürgen, (1983) *Moralbewusststsein und kommunikatives Handeln*. Frankfurt am Main: Suhrkamp.
Hampden-Turner, Charles and Trompenaars, Fons (1993) *The Seven Cultures of Capitalism: Value Systems for Creating Wealth in the United States, Britain, Japan, Germany, France, Sweden, and the Netherlands*. New York: Doubleday.
Hampshire, Stuart (1989) *Innocence and Experience*. Cambridge, MA: Harvard University Press.
Heckmann, Gustav (1981) *Das sokratische Gespräch: Erfahrungen in Hochschulseminaren*. Hannover: Hermann Schroedel.
Hirschman, Albert O. (1977) *The Passions and the Interests: Political Arguments for Capitalism before its Triumph*. Princeton, NJ: Princeton University Press.
Ibarra, Araceli and Leal, Fernando (1995) 'Capitalismos realmente existentes', *Espiral: Estudios sobre Estado y Sociedad*, 1 (3): 29–60.
Jacobs, Jane (1993) *Systems of Survival: a Dialogue on the Moral Foundations of Commerce and Politics*. London: Hodder and Stoughton.
Kennedy, Paul (1988) *The Rise and Fall of the Great Powers: Economic Change and Military Conflict from 1500 to 2000*. London: Unwin Hyman.
Kessels, Jos (1996) 'The Socratic dialogue as a method of organizational learning', *Dialogue and Universalism*, 6 (5–6): 53–67.
Klein, Lisl and Eason, Ken (1991) *Putting Social Science to Work: the Ground between Theory and Use Explored through Case Studies in Organisations*. Cambridge: Cambridge University Press.
Krohn, Dieter, Horster, Detlef and Heinen-Tenrich, Jürgen (eds) (1989) *Das sokratische Gespräch: ein Symposion*. Hamburg: Junius Verlag.
Leal, Fernando (1992) 'Der zweite Grundsatz der operationalen Linguistik', *Zeitschrift für Phonetik, Sprachwissenschaft und Kommunikationsforschung*, 45: 164–77.
Leal, Fernando (1993) 'Hacia una nueva filosofía del trabajo', *Debate feminista*, 7: 129–67.
Montano, Luis (1995) 'Organisational spaces and intelligent machines: a metaphorical approach to ethics', in P. Shipley and F. Leal (eds), *Ethics and the New Technology*. Special issue of *AI & Society*. 9 (1): 43–56.
Murdoch, Dugald (1987) *Niels Bohr's Philosophy of Physics*. Cambridge: Cambridge University Press.
Nagel, Thomas (1979) *Mortal Questions*. New York: Cambridge University Press.
Nagel, Thomas (1986) *The View from Nowhere*. New York: Cambridge University Press.

Nelson, Leonard (1929) 'Die sokratische Methode', *Abhandlungen der neuen Fries 'schen Schule*, vol. 5. Translated into English as 'The Socratic method', in *Socratic Method and Critical Philosophy: Selected Essays by Leonard Nelson.* New York: Dover, 1949. pp. 1–43.

Oakeshott, Michael (1975) *On Human Conduct.* Oxford: Clarendon Press.

Oakeshott, Michael (1993) *Morality and Politics in Modern Europe: the Harvard Lectures*, edited by S.R. Letwin. New Haven, CT: Yale University Press.

Ord, Jackie (1995) 'The ethics of NHS computing: a terminal case', in P. Shipley and F. Leal (eds), *Ethics and New Technology.* Special issue of *AI & Society*, 9 (1): 80–90.

Seiler, Hansjakob (1986) *Apprehension: Language, Object, and Order.* Tübingen: Gunter Narr.

Simon, Herbert A. (1983) *Reason in Human Affairs.* Stanford, CA: Stanford University Press.

Tarski, Alfred (1935) 'Der Wahrheitsbegriff in den formalisierten Sprachen', *Studia Philosophica: Commentarii Societatis Philosophicae Polonorum.* I: 261–405.

Tugendhat, Ernst (1993) *Vorlesungen über Ethik.* Frankfurt am Main: Suhrkamp.

Whitehead, Alfred N. and Russell, Bertrand (1910) *Principia Mathematica* (vol. I). Cambridge: Cambridge University Press.

12   Towards a Relational Theory of Organizational Collaboration

Thomas B. Lawrence, Nelson Phillips and Cynthia Hardy

Organizational collaboration has been an important managerial issue since the development of large-scale business enterprises in the early 1800s (Blackford and Kerr, 1994: 203). As we near the end of the twentieth century, collaboration remains an important organizational activity and an increasingly important topic in management research (see Alter, 1990; Huxham, 1995; Smith et al., 1995). Yet, despite the growing number of articles, books, and conferences on the subject, the notion of organizational collaboration remains diffuse. Arrangements such as strategic alliances, trade associations, joint-marketing agreements, and roundtables on the environment are all discussed as forms of collaboration, despite the obvious differences in these co-operative relationships. Similarly, the theoretical approaches adopted in examining collaboration have varied widely. Researchers have employed a range of approaches, including exchange theory, power and conflict theories, modelling theories, institutional economics, negotiated order, stakeholder theory and social structure theories (Wood and Gray, 1991; Smith et al., 1995). While each of these approaches has value, the underlying nature of collaboration – the social dynamic that makes collaboration a distinctive organizational phenomenon – remains unclear. The theoretical framework that we develop here is intended to provide a means of understanding the social processes that underlie collaboration and that link collaboration to the wider context in which it occurs.

Our argument is structured in three parts. We begin by defining collaboration and outlining the general questions about collaboration that form the foundation of our discussion. We also examine several existing alternative theories of collaboration and introduce a discursive perspective that we find helpful in understanding the process of negotiation that underlies the social accomplishment of collaboration. In the second section, we present the theoretical framework that we find most useful in understanding collaboration as an ongoing and emergent process. Finally, we conclude with a discussion of the implications of our perspective for the study and practice of collaboration.

The Analysis of Collaboration

By collaboration we mean a co-operative, inter-organizational relationship that relies on neither market nor hierarchical mechanisms of control (Ouchi, 1980). This definition is inclusive, yet provides a set of critical characteristics that distinguish collaboration from other forms of organizational activity. The first and most straightforward aspect of our definition is that collaboration occurs between organizations rather than at the individual or organizational level. The study of collaboration therefore requires an aggregate focus and is part of the increasing move to studying populations, sectors, domains, and fields rather than the single organization and its environment (e.g., Meyer and Scott, 1983). Secondly, collaborative activity is not mediated by market mechanisms. In other words, collaborative activity is carried on 'outside' market structures and co-operation depends on some alternative to the price mechanism. Finally, unlike hierarchy, collaboration does not involve the use of control through legitimate authority (Ouchi, 1980). Whereas hierarchies are associated with a willingness on behalf of members to submit to both direction and monitoring by their superiors, collaboration involves the negotiation of roles and responsibilities in a context where no legitimate authority sufficient to manage the situation is recognized.

Current Approaches to the Study of Collaboration

Collaboration between organizations has been considered from a number of different perspectives. One approach stems from the notion of 'collective' strategy where businesses co-operate rather than compete (e.g., Astley, 1984; Bresser and Harl, 1986; Carney, 1987; Bresser, 1988). Such collaboration takes a variety of forms: joint ventures (Harrigan, 1985); strategic partners (Lorenzoni and Baden-Fuller, 1995); alliances (Kanter, 1990); networks (Thorelli, 1986; Powell, 1990; Alter and Hage, 1993); network alliances (Gomes-Casseres, 1994); modular corporations (Tully, 1993); outsourcing (Winkleman, 1993); virtual corporations (Byrne, 1993). This work examines how these forms of inter-organizational collaboration can improve strategic performance by, for example, helping to spread risk; share resources; enhance flexibility; increase access to technological know-how and information; enter new markets; and secure assets (e.g., Amara, 1990; Barley et al., 1993; Nohria and Eccles, 1993; Powell and Brantley, 1993).

Similar to this approach is the work of organizational economists (see Barney and Hesterley, 1996). In this work, the previous focus on, and negative connotations of, collusion have more recently been replaced with an interest in strategic alliances and joint alliances (e.g., Kogut, 1988, 1991). Hennart (1988) distinguishes between contractual alliances such as long-term supply relationships, licensing arrangements, and distribution arrangements and joint ventures where two or more firms co-operate through the creation of a separate firm; other writers offer diverse definitions of the various forms of co-operation. Organizational economists have used Transaction Cost Economics (Williamson, 1975, 1985) to explain the emergence of joint ventures and alliances as alliterative forms of governance structure to the more traditional markets and hierarchies (Buckley and Casson, 1988; Koenig and Thiétart, 1988; Hill, 1990; Hennart, 1991; Williamson, 1991).

Another approach to collaboration has been developed by writers on inter-organizational domains (e.g., Gray, 1989) which, in turn, draws on negotiated order theory (e.g., Strauss et al., 1963). This work draws from the work of Emery and Trist (1965) who introduced the notion of turbulent environments, where problems characterized by uncertainty, complexity and unclear boundaries are beyond the ability of a single organization to solve. They call for inclusive (Warren, 1967; Warren et al., 1974 or collaborative (Gray, 1989) decision-making where organizations pool their expertise and resources (Trist, 1983)). Domains form as individuals perceive that mutual problems can be resolved collectively. It is not an objective, predetermined process but one of social construction (Altheide, 1988; McGuire, 1988) where social order is negotiated (Strauss et al., 1963; Gray, 1989; Nathan and Mitroff, 1991).

> Domains are cognitive as well as organizational structures . . . one can only too easily fall into the trap of thinking of them as objectively given, quasi-permanent fixtures in the social fabric rather than ways we have chosen to construe various facets of it. (Trist, 1983: 273)

As individuals come to share a vision of the problem and see themselves, collectively, as part of the solution, they become stakeholders. This shared appreciation of the problem helps acquire an identity for the domain which may produce mutually agreed upon directions and boundaries, which may then become manifested in a more permanent structure (Trist, 1983).

There is, then, a variety of different approaches to collaboration, with different terminology, definitions, agendas, assumptions, and methodologies. It seems that the differences between strategic, economic, government/ business and inter-organizational domain approaches to understanding collaboration overshadow the fundamental similarities – the aspects of collaboration that make it a distinct organizational phenomenon. And, although each of these approaches has contributed significantly to our understanding of collaboration, their proliferation has produced a set of theoretical and empirical understandings of collaboration that are largely non-cumulative. We believe there is merit in returning to a simple set of research questions that are concerned with investigating the basic nature of collaboration.

Questions about Collaboration

In two recent special journal issues on organizational collaboration (Smith et al., 1995; Wood and Gray, 1991)[1] the editors summarize the issues surrounding collaboration with three major questions: (i) what are the antecedents of collaboration?; (ii) what are the dynamics of collaboration?; and (iii) what are the outcomes of collaboration? The first of these questions is concerned with the conditions and resources that facilitate collaborative organizational behaviour. Trust, for example, has been argued to be a fundamental condition for development of collaboration (Hardy and Phillips, 1995; McAllister, 1995; Smith et al., 1995). Smith, Carroll and Ashford (1995) suggest that despite significant amounts of research on the antecedents of collaboration, the focus has largely been on formal collaboration. Consequently, 'additional research is needed on the conditions that give rise to naturally occurring cooperation' (Smith et al., 1995: 15).

The second question concerns the nature of collaboration as a process, including such issues as the stages of collaboration (e.g., Gray, 1989; Zajac and Olsen, 1993), the politics of collaboration (e.g., Gray and Hay, 1986; Hardy, 1994) and the emotional aspects of collaboration (McAllister, 1995). Approaching this question can lead to an emphasis on conscious, rational decision-making processes as in Browning, Beyer and Shetler's (1995) examination of SEMATECH. It can also lead to a focus on processes of social construction and negotiated order, as in Nathan and Mitroff's (1991) study of collaborative strategies in the management of a product-tampering crisis. While the study of collaboration has examined many aspects of its dynamics, these results remain somewhat diffuse. Divergent theoretical perspectives seem to examine similarly divergent empirical phenomena, such that the results are largely non-cumulative.

The third question asks about the results of collaboration. According to Smith et al., 'most of the previous research that has linked cooperation to outcomes has focused on performance variables and individual satisfaction variables' (1995: 17). We concur with their call for the examination of a broader range of outcomes, including non-economic impacts such as social ties, political power and technological innovation (Smith et al., 1995). Collaboration can also be associated with other, less attractive consequences. Outcomes such as concentration of power (Pfeffer and Salancik, 1978), homogenization of ideas (Janis, 1972), exclusion of marginal members (Gray and Hay, 1986), and co-ordination of pricing (Scherer and Ross, 1990) can be as significant as any positive outcome. The positive connotations of collaboration, however, seem to have led to an under-examination of negative outcomes in the empirical and theoretical literatures.

We believe that the study of collaboration requires a theoretical framework that can accommodate these three questions in a consistent and coherent manner. Understanding the relationships between antecedents, dynamics and outcomes is at least as important as predicting any single element. In this chapter, we propose an integrative theoretical framework that emphasizes the discursive aspects of collaboration. We argue that the dynamics of collaboration can be understood in terms of the negotiation of issues, interests and representation. We further conceptualize the outcomes of this negotiation in terms of the development of practices and rules that operate at both the level of the collaborative relationship and the broader institutional context. Finally, we argue that this broader institutional context provides the antecedents for collaboration: actors draw on the issues, interests, representations, practices and rules that constitute the institutional context to provide the resources for structuring collaboration.

Discourse and Collaboration

The term discourse has a range of meanings within social studies. As we use the term here, a discourse is a system of texts that brings an 'object' or set of objects into being (Parker, 1992: 5).[2] For example, the discourse of psychology brought into being a whole different understanding of madness, its causes, and its treatment. The unconscious appeared early on in this discourse, brought into being by a set of texts that allowed the unconscious to be discussed and examined, and behaviour to be interpreted based on its existence (Foucault, 1965). Similarly, another set of texts, the discourse around AIDS, produced a new social object that made sense of a set of symptoms and diseases that were previously thought to be unconnected. The medical and social discourse surrounding AIDS continues to encompass a massive struggle over the nature and appropriate response to this new object.

But the term discourse refers to more than simply a collection of texts; it also includes the discursive resources and practices that underlie texts and which allow their production, transmission and reception (Fairclough, 1992). Discursive activity is activity which acts to maintain or modify this discourse, the social structures related to it, or to enact a new discourse in a social situation in a significant way. This kind of discursive activity is of interest to social scientists as it is an important form of social practice; it is carried out between people, and has important social effects in that it is inextricably bound up in the production of social reality.

But discursive boundaries are not hermetic. Discourses draw on other discourses for resources and practices which can become part of a new discourse. For example, the eco-tourism discourse is particularly complex as it brings together discursive resources that are associated with the political, scientific, moral, and economic discourses. The discourse surrounding eco-tourism depends on a high degree of interdiscursivity to provide the many ways of talking and range of discursive resources available to the participants in the discourse.

From this perspective, the process underlying 'collaboration' is a discursive struggle between different groups of stakeholders each with access to different sets of resources. The struggle occurs through texts that construct the world in differing ways and that may be resisted or inverted through the construction, by competing groups, or other texts. The object of the struggle is to win a temporary equilibrium that privileges your own group and that exists until it is overwhelmed by the ambiguity produced by alternative texts. This sort of process occurs at many different levels in an organizational field and untangling this web is an important part of a discursive analysis of collaboration.

Concepts, Objects and Discourse

Underlying the above discussion is a strong argument for the active role of discourse in the creation of social reality: discourses do not mirror reality, they create ways of understanding the world; they do not reveal some hidden, pre-constituted reality, but rather provide subject positions, concepts and objects that actors use to fashion a social world. The idea that language has a role in the constitution of reality has, of course, become commonplace in a wide segment of social studies, primarily as a result of work in social constructionism and natural language philosophy (Wittgenstein, 1957; Winch, 1958; Berger and Luckmann, 1966). The idea that words divide up the world, and not the reverse, has been argued by a group of social theorists for decades. The influence of these ideas has also been widespread in organizational analysis. The theoretical position we are developing here is, therefore, an extension of ideas that are already current and well-understood in organizational analysis.

But what kinds of things are constituted in discourse? For our purposes here, it is useful to differentiate between two kinds of constructive effect: concepts and objects (Fairclough, 1992: 64; Parker, 1992: 6–8). Concepts are the set of categories, relationships and theories through which we understand the world and relate to one another. Concepts make up what Harré (1979) refers to as the expressive sphere: all of the conceptual ideas available to an actor in a social situation. From a discourse analysis point of view, concepts are all of the constructions that arise out of structured sets of texts and that exist solely in the realm of ideas. They are more or less contested, and are culturally and historically situated. They are the fundamental ideas that underlie our understandings and relations with one another. Concepts are historically contingent constructions that arise out of a discourse consisting of the texts produced, disseminated and interpreted by a set of actors in a social situation. Concepts depend on the ongoing construction of texts for meaning and they may therefore change dramatically over time and from social group to social group. Also, since the meaning of a concept is dependent on discourse, and since individual understandings of the world depend on these concepts, participation in the discourse is a political act as discursive acts that succeed in transforming concepts change the world as it is understood. Discursive acts that are intended to redefine concepts are attempts to fashion preferable social relations and depend for their success on the resources available to the actor producing the text.

The first important dimension of the discourse surrounding any collaboration is the ongoing struggle to define a collection of concepts sufficient to sustain the collaboration. These concepts may be drawn from other discourses around other collaborations within the field, or from more distant discourses that can be connected in some way to the situation at hand.

When concepts are brought into play to make sense of ongoing social relations or physical objects, then the discourse has constituted an object. Objects and concepts are obviously closely related. The primary difference is the fact that concepts exist only in the expressive order; they exist in the realm of ideas. Objects, on the other hand, are part of the practical order; they are real in the sense of existing in the material world. The concept of a tree exists in our minds as competent speakers of English. The tree in front of our building is an object; it is made as competent speakers of English. The tree in front of our building is an object; it is made sensible by the concept 'tree' and we can write about it using the same concept. But the tree itself has a certain existence outside the discourse that reveals it; it has an ontological reality beyond the discourse. It would continue to exist in a physical sense apart from the observer's experience of it (Bhaskar, 1978; Laclau and Mouffe, 1985).

The production of a collaborative relationship can therefore be thought of as a discursive accomplishment. Through the negotiation of various dimensions of collaboration, and through the importation of concepts from the organizational field, the members of a collaboration come to enough agreement about the nature of their activity that they can identify it as a collaborative relationship (i.e., a co-operative, non-market mediated, non-hierarchical relationship). It is an object constituted in discourse that can be used by members to work towards desired goals and the collaboration can act as an arena for the further negotiation of concepts and objects.

Dynamics of Collaboration

We believe it is possible to develop a view of collaboration that integrates the variety of disparate theoretical definitions and approaches that have developed in the literature. We believe that beneath the variety of activities associated with collaboration, a common discursive process is operating and, therefore, that a common theoretical framework can be developed for understanding the many kinds of collaboration that have been identified. All collaboration – defined as co-operative, non-market mediated, non-hierarchical, inter-organizational activity – requires the discursive negotiation of three important and interrelated questions: (i) what problem is the collaboration intended to address?; (ii) what interests should be represented in the collaboration?; and (iii) who should represent those interests? The answers to these three questions are mutually constitutive and form the framework for collaborative activity. Beginning with this view, it is clear that collaboration involves a political process of negotiation, and therefore a process of communication, around these three questions. The diverse literature on collaboration comes together around the complex social process through which these questions are negotiated and around the institutional frameworks that result. From a discursive perspective, the answers to these three questions are collaboratively-produced, discursive objects. Each of these objects requires the successful discursive use of some antecedent set of concepts and objects to bring it into being.

Issues

In the sense we use the term here, *an issue is an account produced by a participant in an organizational field that constructs the world as problematic and requiring action.* Issues are often contested by other participants who present contradictory, or at least opposing, views of the world in an attempt to reframe understandings and argue for alternative action. An agreement between actors on the existence of an issue within an organizational field provides the foundation for collaborative activity. But they are also the focus of extensive negotiation and conflict as actors struggle to manage understanding in order to shape the collaboration and the organizational field.

This definition has three important elements. First, issues are not naturally occurring, nor can they be non-problematically identified by actors within the collaboration nor by researchers looking in from outside. Issues are not laying about waiting to be correctly identified but are, instead, complex constructions of the world and brings with them calls for action (Blumer, 1971). Issues are accounts of 'objects' that exist in the organizational field. They exist as texts that draw on existing shared discursive resources to produce an account of objects and their arrangements in the organizational field. These accounts are negotiated over time and become more or less shared, and, if they are widely accepted, provide a foundation for action.

Secondly, issues are of critical importance as they provide an impetus for action. They are accounts that construct the organizational field in a problematic way that demands some sort of action by members of the field. It is at this point that the practical effects of collaborative activity are most strongly felt. The social construction of issues leads to demands for action on the part of the members of the field. If an arrangement of discursive objects – a state of affairs or potential state of affairs – is described as problematic, then it demands action. Actors may not agree on why a particular situation is problematic, but successfully gaining agreement that an issue exists leads to, at least, some consensus on the need for action.

Thirdly, collaborative issues are highly political. The fact that they lead to action ensures that they are contested and the focus of extensive discursive struggle as actors work to realize their goals and interests within the collaborative activity. The constructions of the world that are produced by actors are therefore not produced uninterestedly; they are not presented without reason. Actors see the world in a particular way and have personal goals for their participation in collaboration. These personal agendas appear in the way issues are perceived and in the way issues are constructed. Discourse, or perhaps more accurately meaning, is often highly political and this is certainly true of discursive activity within collaboration. The fact that collaboration requires some sense of intersection of purpose and requires the negotiation of mutual benefits and mutual responsibilities in the context of a co-operative venture ensures that the construction of issues will be a highly political, contentious, and sometimes divisive activity.

Interests

Within our framework, *interests provide assessable reasons for action*; to say that some practice or situation is in the interest of a person is to suggest that it benefits that person (Hindess, 1986). Our understanding of interests has three important elements. First, interests emerge out of the discursive processes that constitute the context in which collaboration occurs:

> Persons, as agents engaged in struggle, with strain over that which is constituted as arguable, according to the conditions of particular discursive processes, and will formulate their interests accordingly. It cannot be maintained that these interests are formulated outside the conditions of particular discursive practices and struggles, which a Marxian structuralist definition would seem to imply. (Clegg, 1989: 181)

Interests cannot stand outside the context in which they are situated. Organizations, institutions, and especially people, do not have 'interests' that are existentially independent of the context in which those interests are implicated: 'In other words, interests feature as elements of discursive availability' (Clegg, 1989: 181).

As elements of discourse, the concept of interests differs substantially from the psychological concept of 'motives'. 'Interests are effective, in the sense of having social consequences, as conceptions: they must be formulated if they are to be perceived, and if they are not formulated directly, then they must be reflected in reasons that are formulated' (Hindess, 1986: 118). While psychological motives are often attributed or inferred from behaviour, as in the notion of 'underlying motives', interests are only sensible in the context of a discourse in which they are articulated. Thus, the notion of an actor having 'real' or 'objective' interests is nonsensical from this perspective.

Secondly, a critical aspect of the role of interests in discourse is their assessability. To suggest that a practice is in someone's interest is to imply the ability to assess the benefits and costs of that practice with respect to that person. This is not to suggest that all collaborators go through some rational, conscious calculation of costs and benefits, but merely that the articulation of interests implies the possibility.

> The point is simply that [interests] are the result of some definite process employing particular conceptual means of specifying the actor's situation and possible changes within it. Interests are the product of assessment. They do not appear arbitrarily, out of nowhere, they are not structurally determined and they cannot be regarded as fixed or given properties of actors. (Hindess, 1986: 120)

Assessability is essential to collaboration because it provides a discursive mechanism to transcend individual motivations; without market or hierarchical mechanisms to rely on, collaborators require some method of assessing the costs and benefits of their participation.

The third important aspect of interest flows from the interaction of the first two. Competing accounts of social reality and competing methods of calculation render the assessment of actors' interests essentially indeterminate. Thus, as reasons for actions, interests are potentially political, conflictual and disputable. This is especially important because the formulation of interests is often done 'for' an individual or a group by others. Politicians describe the interests of their constituents as reasons for their policies and promises. Union leaders articulate the interests of their union members as reasons for their bargaining positions or strike mandates. Environmentalists trade on the interests of 'humanity' to justify the preservation of eco-systems or the protection of species. If the interests of all of these parties are disputable, then the actions they support are essentially contestable.

The politicality of interests, as theorized here, highlights an important departure from traditional sociological and political analysis. Traditional approaches assume that the validity of any interest is dependent on either its phenomenological association with an individual (e.g., Douglas, 1980) or its structural relationship to a social or economic position (e.g., Gramsci, 1971; Lukes, 1977). These approaches posit the existence of either subjective interests (in the case of phenomenology) or objective interests (in the case of structural analysis) associated with individuals or groups. However, if interests are discursive phenomena, serving as reasons for action, then they are inter-subjective, historical, local and strategic. Consequently, we take a position that is 'agnostic' (Callon, 1986) with respect to the validity of any claims based on interests. The validation or refutation of interests is not a central, or even sensible, aspect of our analysis. Rather, the focus of our analysis is on the role that interests play in the social negotiations around collaboration.

Representation

The question of representation in collaboration has traditionally been understood in terms of stakeholders: the 'organizations or individuals with a legitimate interest in the problem under consideration' (Gray and Hay, 1986: 96). More generally, *representation involves the discursive construction of actors and roles in a collaborative process.*

In the negotiations around collaboration, available concepts (e.g., 'industry association', 'commercial operator') are discursively attached to members of the collaboration to justify and explain their legitimate right to participate. According to Gray and Hay 'A significant step in defining the domain [of collaboration] is identifying who truly has a legitimate stake in the issues to be addressed. A stakeholder is viewed to have legitimate stake in the issues to be addressed. A stakeholder is viewed to have legitimacy when this individual or group is perceived by others to have the right and the capacity to participate' (1986: 96).

Gray and Hay suggest that some organizations gain legitimacy due to their power (capacity) based on expertise, or control of critical resources or processes. Others 'may hold little actual power but have the legitimate right to participate because they will be affected by the agreements reached' (Gray and Hay, 1986: 97). This implies a political relationship between the issues necessitating collaboration and the determination of legitimate stakeholders, where actors draw on issues (accounts of the world as problematic) to explain their role in the collaboration.

While Gray and Hay (1986) usefully highlight the discursive construction of actors' relationships to issues, the problem of representation also involves the discursive construction of relationships among actors and, indeed, the discursive construction of actors themselves. The legitimacy of an actor is not an assessment that can be made outside a context that includes other actors, as well as issues and interests. In negotiating roles in some collaborative activity, actors may successfully present themselves as important to the resolution of an issue and still remain excluded or marginal in the network of representation. For instance, cliques within the network of actors negotiating the domain and nature of the collaborative activity may work to exclude others in order to enforce a homogeneity of interests (reasons for action) with respect to an issue. In contrast, actors with seemingly marginal attachment to issues might be included where the goal of dominant actors is to ensure a heterogeneity of interests, as is seen in some governmental committees for example.

More fundamentally, collaboration can invoke the construction of social actors. Just as issues and interests are produced in communication, so too are actors as objects in discourse. This is, perhaps, most obvious in the case of organizations. In the social negotiation that surrounds collaboration, persons may find it strategically necessary to establish a collective identity with a discrete association to the issues and interests at hand. As some individuals or groups find themselves marginalized despite their self-perceived legitimacy (e.g., Cobb, 1993), for instance, they may work to re-present themselves as a collective agent with greater power and legitimacy. Because representation involves the negotiation of roles and status, individuals too may find themselves 'reinventing' their own identities with respect to the collaborative process. This is not a process of deception or guile, but simply an acknowledgement of the discursive nature of identity – social actors are not simply biological beings or collectives but include implicit or explicit relations to social context.

Outcomes and Antecedents of Collaboration

We deal with the questions of outcomes and antecedents together because the theoretical perspective we have adopted emphasizes the embeddedness and recursivity of social phenomena. An emphasis on the discursive aspects of collaboration leads us to the position that the negotiation of issues, interests, and representation both produces concepts and social objects and at the same time depends upon the utilization of sets of concepts and objects.

Outcomes

In this framework, outcomes refer to the social effects of actors' negotiations of issues, interests and representations. The negotiation of these discursive concepts and objects not only defines them, but can also affect the activities and relationships of actors in important material ways. These effects occur both within the collaborative relationship and in the broader institutional context in which it occurs.

Practices and rules

We conceptualize the outcomes of collaboration, whether in the collaboration or at the field level, in terms of two primary categories: practices and rules. By practices we mean not simply what people do, but the *patterns of action that become legitimated and institutionalized within some context*. In discursive terms, the establishment of a practice involves the construction of both a concept and an object. Practices involve concepts because they imply an understanding of a particular action as normal or legitimate. Practices also exist as an object – practices involve the attachment of some concept to a set of social relations and activities that are real in the sense of existing in the material world. The second type of collaborative outcome is the production of a rule. Whereas practices involve action, *rules express normalized understandings of legitimate behaviour* and, thus, exist strictly as concepts. These rules say nothing about the extent to which operators achieve a level of conformity or acceptance with respect to the guidelines. From an institutional perspective:

> Rules are classifications built into society as reciprocated typifications or interpretations. Such rules may be simply taken for granted or may be supported by public opinion or the force of law. (Meyer and Rowan, 1977: 341)

Consequently, rules involve only the construction and arrangement of concepts. Regardless of whether they are written down or exist only in oral communication, rules remain in the expressive sphere. Their link to the material world is in their relationship to practice. As rules are reciprocated, they affect the actions of participants in the collaboration and, if those actions become institutionalized, the rules effect practices.

Both practices and rules, as outcomes of collaboration, depend on the interaction of the dynamics of collaboration (the negotiation of issues, interests and representation) and the antecedents of collaboration. As collaborations form and dissolve, their 'success' is often measured in terms of the practices and rules they have produced, and this success, or failure, is attributed to either its dynamics or its antecedents.

Antecedents

Antecedents are the discursive resources which form the backdrop to any attempt to collaborate. Just as collaboration has an effect on the field of which it is a part, the field provides the initial set of objects, concepts, rules, and practices upon which the actors interested in collaborating can draw. In other words, collaboration never occurs in a social vacuum, and existing understandings which are brought by actors to a collaboration form the basis for the negotiation of the issues, interests and representation that underlies collaboration.

From a discursive perspective, the field can therefore play either an enabling or a constraining role. In some cases, the available resources will act to support collaborative activity. The nature of the organizational field is not only important in terms of the role it plays in supporting or undermining the collaboration, but also in the role it plays in privileging individual actors. The existing field provides the discursive resources from which individual actors construct their version of issues, interests and representation; that is, their versions of the world and their place in it. The field will always support some sets of issues, interests and representations more than others. Those that are not supported by existing understandings will have to work harder and have access to more resources in order to make up for the disparity in position created by the institutional structures of the field.

But this also points to the importance of the outcomes of collaboration discussed in the previous section. Successful collaborations will tend to structure the field in ways that provide the necessary resources for similar forms of collaboration to occur and for existing ones to continue. Over time, the issues, interests, and legitimate identities may become sedimented and increasingly hard to dislodge. Actors become able to see things in only one way, and to understand their role and identity in a limited fashion. These understandings then provide the antecedents for future collaborations and, over time, play an important role in the structuring of the field and other collaborations.

From our perspective, there is therefore no necessary antecedent or set of antecedents for collaboration (see McAllister, 1995; Smith et al., 1995). Instead, the nature of the discursive frame that allows collaboration is always an empirical question. The nature of the field may help or hinder the collaboration, and may privilege some actors at the expense of others, but this is always an empirical question and we can say little about the combination of antecedents and resources that produce a successful collaboration. Attempts to define some single element (e.g., trust) are therefore misguided and we should instead try to disentangle the role and dynamic between collaboration and the institutional field in which it occurs.

Conclusions

In this chapter, we have developed a theory of collaboration that focuses on the underlying dynamic that produces collaboration, and the relation of that dynamic to the institutional field in which it occurs. Our contribution is therefore a model of collaboration as a social process, embedded and growing out of an institutional field, with important ramifications for the ongoing development of the field and the meanings, practices and rules that characterize it.

Implications for research

The theory of organizational collaboration that we have developed has several important ramifications for research. First, our perspective highlights the embeddedness (Granovetter, 1985) of collaboration in wider institutional structures. We have referred to the connection between collaboration and the inter-organizational domain in which it occurs at several points in our discussion. But this connection between broad institutional structures and collaboration requires much more development and further empirical research. Based on our ongoing research in this area, it is clear that understanding the dynamics of collaboration, and in particular its antecedents and outcomes, requires an understanding of how broader institutional structures are produced, the role of collaboration in this production, and the way broader institutional structures are drawn upon to support collaboration. Conversely, it is equally clear that certain institutional structures can prevent collaboration and that this dynamic is equally important to a developed theory of collaboration. Future work in this area must therefore take the institutional field as its focus of attention (Wood and Gray, 1991) and study the range of collaboration that occurs across a field and the complex web of interrelationships that connect the various forms of collaboration.

Secondly, collaboration is a social accomplishment (Berger and Luckmann, 1966). It is highly discursive and depends on an ongoing process of discursive negotiation. Collaboration depends on the ongoing negotiation of meanings that allow sufficient agreement on the issues, interests and representation to allow the collaboration to move forward. Theoretical perspectives that fail to include an explicit theory of meaning and social construction are unable to consider this important aspect of collaboration. Similarly, empirical methodologies that ignore meaning and the necessity of developing common understandings are missing much of the process underlying collaboration.

Thirdly, the discursive perspective we have adopted includes an explicit connection to a nuanced idea of power (Parker, 1992). The focus on collaboration as a 'discursive struggle' highlights the need to understand the kinds of resources that make certain participants more successful in gaining support for their constructions of the world and thereby managing the collaboration. The critical discourse analysis literature (Fairclough, 1992) provides the necessary theoretical ideas to develop a more critical view of collaboration building on the theoretical framework developed in this chapter.

Fourthly, the discursive perspective we have adopted goes some way towards answering Zald's (1993) criticisms of organization studies. Zald argues that organization studies would benefit from a closer connection to the humanities. He argues that the concerns and subject of organization studies makes it as much a part of the humanities as a part of the social sciences. In terms of collaboration, the discursive perspective we have adopted provides some balance in theoretical perspectives with the more economistic perspective adopted by other researchers (Barney and Hesterley, 1996). Collaboration is about rational economic action, but it is also about social construction and the production of institutional structures. Discourse analysis, which began in the humanities and moved into the social sciences only fairly recently, provides a valuable addition to the more traditional methodologies used in organization studies.

Implications for practice

By implications for practice we mean implications for participants in collaborations and for consultants and other facilitators interested in assisting in the formation of collaborative groups. Understanding the highly discursive and negotiated nature of collaboration leads to three main implications for the practice of collaboration. First, the potential for collaboration lies not in trust or the existence of a shared problem, but rather in the ability of participants to negotiate a set of shared understandings of issues, interest and identities that provide a sufficient framework for concerted understanding and action. The existence of appropriate concepts and objects in the inter-organizational field is an important prerequisite of successful collaboration. For example, the development of SEMATECH depended on the pre-existing agreement that the Japanese posed a threat to the current market dominance (an object) and that collaborative activity was more effective at improving the technological competence of industry members than competition (a concept) (Browning et al., 1995).

Secondly, collaboration is a communicative process and the clear explication of the meanings of things should be the initial focus of collaborative activity. Tools from communication become the tools of collaboration and the development of collaborative practice begins with the development of communicative practice. All of the kinds of things that assist in the production of effective communication become part of the production of effective collaboration, including the recognition that communication is not occurring and that an agreement in some cases is very unlikely. Negotiation and mediation become the central activities for collaborators and facilitators respectively.

Thirdly, collaboration affects much more than just the 'issue' at hand. In modifying or creating objects and concepts it may have profound effects not foreseen by participants and, furthermore, the collaboration may have profound effects on groups not formally included in the collaboration. A discursive view of collaboration therefore highlights the importance of considering the ethical aspects of collaboration, particularly around the idea of representation. The profound effects of collaboration make fairness and openness important issues in a public policy sense.

Notes

1. Although Smith, Carroll and Ashford refer to 'intra- and interorganizational cooperation', they use the term 'interorganizational cooperation' in a manner equivalent to our use of organizational collaboration.
2. By text we mean any delimited phenomenon that can be interpreted (Phillips and Brown, 1993). While the texts interpreted in this study are limited to spoken language and documents, there is no necessity to limit the range of texts interpreted in this way.

References

Alter, C. (1990) 'An exploratory study of conflict and coordination in inter-organizational service delivery systems', *Academy of Management Journal*, 33: 478–502.

Alter, C. and Hage, J. (1993) *Organizations Working Together.* Newbury Park, CA: Sage.

Altheide, D.L. (1988) 'Mediating cutbacks in human services: A case study in the negotiated order', *The Sociological Quarterly*, 29 (3): 329–35.

Amara, R. (1990) 'New directions for innovation', *Futures*, 22 (2): 142–52.

Astley, W.G. (1984) 'Toward an appreciation of collective strategy', *Academy of Management Review*, 9 (3): 526–35.

Barley, S.R., Freeman, J. and Hybels, R.C. (1993) 'Strategic alliances in commercial biotechnology', in N. Nohria and R.G. Eccles (eds), *Network and Organizations: Structure, Form and Action.* Boston, MA: Harvard Business School. pp. 311–47.

Barney, J. and Hesterley, W. (1996) 'Organizational economics: understanding the relationship between organizations and economic analysis', in S. Clegg, C. Hardy and W. Nord (eds), *Handbook of Organization Studies.* London: Sage.

Berger, P. and Luckmann, T.L. (1966) *The Social Construction of Reality: a Treatise on the Sociology of Knowledge.* Garden City, NY: Doubleday.

Bhaskar, R. (1978) *A Realist Theory of Science.* Brighton: Harvester.

Blackford, M.G. and Kerr, K. (1994) *Business Enterprise in American History.* Boston, MA: Houghton Mifflin.

Blumer, H. (1971) 'Social problems as collective behavior', *Social Problems*, 19: 298–306.

Bresser, R.K. (1988) 'Matching collective and competitive strategies', *Strategic Management Journal*, 9: 375–85.

Bresser, R.K. and Harl, J.E. (1986) 'Collective strategy: vice or virtue?', *Academy of Management Review*, 11: 408–27.

Browning, L.D., Beyer, J.M. and Shetler, J.C. (1995) 'Building co-operation in a competitive industry: SEMATECH and the semiconductor industry', *Academy of Management Journal*, 38 (1): 113–51.

Buckley, P.J. and Casson, M. (1988) 'A theory of co-operation in international business', in F. Contractor and P. Lorange (eds), *Co-operative Strategies in International Business.* Lexington, MA: Lexington Books. pp. 31–54.

Byrne, J.A. (1993) 'The virtual corporation', *Business Week*, 8 February: 98–103.

Callon, M. (1986) 'Some elements of a sociology of translation: domestication of the scallops and the fishermen of St Brieuc Bay', in J. Law (ed.), *Power, Action and Belief: a New Sociology of Knowledge?* Sociological Review Monograph 32. London: Routledge and Kegan Paul. pp. 196–233.

Carney, M.G. (1987) 'The strategy and structure of collective action', *Organization Studies*, 8 (4): 341–62.

Clegg, S.R. (1989) *Frameworks of Power.* London: Sage.

Cobb, S. (1993) 'Empowerment and mediation: a narrative perspective', *Negotiation Journal*, July: 245–61.

Douglas, J. (1980) *Introduction to the Sociologies of Everyday Life.* Boston, MA: Allyn and Bacon.

Emery, F.E. and Trist, E.L. (1965) 'The causal texture of organisational environments', *Human Relations*, 18: 21–32.

Fairclough, N. (1992) *Discourse and Social Change.* Cambridge: Polity Press.

Foucault, M. (1965) *Madness and Civilization: a History of Insanity in the Age of Reason.* New York: Vintage Books.

Gomes-Casseres, B. (1994) 'Group versus group: how alliance networks compete', *Harvard Business Review*, 73 (July–August): 62–74.

Gramsci, A. (1971) *Selections from the Prison Notebooks.* New York: International.

Granovetter, M. (1985) 'Economic action and social structure: the problem of embeddedness', *American Journal of Sociology*, 91: 481–510.

Gray, B. (1989) *Collaborating: Finding Common Ground for Multiparty Problems.* San Francisco: Jossey-Bass.

Gray, B. and Hay, T.M. (1986) 'Political limits to interorganizational consensus and change', *Journal of Applied Behavioral Science*, 22 (2): 95–112.

Hardy, C. (1994) 'Underorganized interorganizational domains: the case of refugee systems', *Journal of Applied Behavioral Science*, 30 (3): 278–96.

Hardy, C. and Phillips, N. (1995) 'Overcoming illusions; combining trust and power'. Paper presented at the Second International Workshop on Multi-organizational Partnerships, University of Strathclyde, Glasgow.

Harré, R. (1979) *Social Being: a Theory for Social Psychology*. Oxford: Basil Blackwell.

Harrigan, K.R. (1985) *Strategies for Joint Ventures*. Lexington, MA: DC Heath/ Lexington Books.

Hennart, J.F. (1988) 'A transaction cost theory of equity joint ventures', *Strategic Management Journal*, 9 (4): 361–74.

Hennart, J.F. (1991) 'The transaction cost theory of joint ventures: an empirical study of Japanese subsidiaries in the United States', *Management Science*, 37 (4): 483–97.

Hill, Charles W.L. (1990) 'Cooperation, opportunism, and the invisible hand: implications for transaction cost theory', *Academy of Management Review*, 15: 500–13.

Hindess, B. (1986) '"Interests" in political analysis', in J. Law (ed.), *Power, Action and Belief: a New Sociology of Knowledge*? Sociology Review Monograph 32. London: Routledge and Kegan Paul. pp. 112–31.

Huxham, C. (ed.) (1995) *Creating Collaborative Advantage*. London: Sage.

Janis, I.L. (1972) *Victims of Groupthink*. Boston, MA: Houghton-Mifflin.

Kanter, R.M. (1990) 'When giants learn cooperative strategies', *Planning Review*, 18 (1): 15–25.

Koenig, C. and Thiétart, R.A. (1988) 'Managers, engineers and government: the emergence of the mutual organization in the European aerospace industry', *Technology in Society*, 19 (1): 45–70.

Kogut, B. (1988) 'Joint ventures: theoretical and empirical perspectives', *Strategic Management Journal*, 9: 319–32.

Kogut, B. (1991) 'Joint ventures and the option to expand and acquire', *Management Science*, 37: 19–33.

Laclau, E. and Mouffe, C. (1985) *Hegemony and Socialist Strategy*. London: Verso.

Lorenzoni, G. and Baden-Fuller, C. (1995) 'Creating a strategic center to manage a web of partners', *California Management Review*, 37 (3): 146–62.

Lukes, S. (1977) *Power: a Radical View*. Basingstoke: Macmillan.

McAllister, D.J. (1995) 'Affect- and cognition-based trust as foundations for interpersonal cooperation in organizations', *Academy of Management Journal*, 38 (1): 24–59.

McGuire, J.B. (1988) 'A dialectical analysis of interorganizational networks', *Journal of Management*, 14 (1): 109–24.

Meyer, J.W. and Rowan, B. (1977) 'Institutionalized organizations: formal structure as myth and ceremony', *American Journal of Sociology*, 83: 340–63.

Meyer, J.W. and Scott, W.R. (1983) *Organizational Environments: Ritual and Rationality*. Beverly Hills, CA: Sage.

Nathan, M.L. and Mitroff, I.I. (1991) 'The use of negotiated order theory as a tool for the analysis and development of an interorganizational field', *Journal of Applied Behavioral Science*, 27: 163–80.

Nohria, N. and Eccles, R.G. (eds) (1993) *Network and Organizations: Structure, Form and Action*. Boston, MA: Harvard Business School.

Ouchi, W.B. (1980) 'Markets, bureaucracies, and clans', *Administrative Science Quarterly*, 25: 129–41.

Parker, I. (1992) *Discourse Dynamics*. London: Routledge.

Pfeffer, J. and Salancik, G. (1978) *The External Control of Organizations*. New York: Harper and Row.

Phillips, N. and Brown, J. (1993) 'Analyzing communication in and around organizations: a critical hermeneutic approach', *The Academy of Management Journal*, 36 (6): 1547–76.

Powell, W.W. (1990) 'Neither market nor hierarchy: network forms of organization', in B.M. Staw and L.L. Cummings (eds), *Research in Organizational Behavior*. Greenwich, CT: JAI Press.

Powell, W.W. and Brantley, P. (1993) 'Competitive cooperation in biotechnology: learning through networks?', in N. Nohria and R.G. Eccles (eds), *Network and organizations: Structure, Form and Action*. Boston, MA: Harvard Business School. pp. 366–94.

Scherer, F.M. and Ross, D. (1990) *Industrial Market Structure and Economic Performance*. Boston, MA: Houghton Mifflin.

Smith, K.G., Carroll, S.J. and Ashford, S.J. (1995) 'Intra- and interorganizational cooperation: toward a research agenda', *Academy of Management Journal*, 38 (1): 7–23.

Strauss, A., Schatzman, L., Bucher, R., Ehrlich, D. and Satshin, M. (1963) 'The hospital and its negotiated order', in E. Friedson (ed.), *The Hospital in Modern Society*. Chicago: The Free Press. pp. 147–69.

Thorelli, H.B. (1986) 'Networks: between markets and hierarchies', *Strategic Management Journal*, 7: 37–51.

Trist, E. (1983) 'Referent organizations and the development of interorganizational domains', *Human Relations*, 36 (2): 269–84.

Tully, S. (1993) 'The modular corporation', *Fortune*, 8 February: 106–15.

Warren, R. (1967) 'The interorganisational field as a focus for investigation', *Administrative Science Quarterly*, 12: 396–419.

Warren, R., Rose, S. and Bergunder, A. (1974) *The Structure of Urban Reform*. Lexington, MA: DC Heath.

Williamson, O.E. (1975) *Markets and Hierarchies: Analysis and Antitrust Implications*. New York: The Free Press.

Williamson, O.E. (1985) *The Economic Institution of Capitalism*. New York: The Free Press.

Williamson, O.E. (1991) 'Comparative economic organization: the analysis of discrete structural alternatives', *Administrative Science Quarterly*, 31: 269–96.

Winch, P. (1958) *The Idea of a Social Science and its Relation to Philosophy*. London: Routledge and Kegan Paul.

Winkleman, M. (1993) 'The outsourcing source book', *Journal of Business Strategy*, 15 (3): 52–8.

Wittgenstein, L. (1957) *Philosophical Investigations*. Oxford: Blackwell.

Wood, D.J. and Gray, B. (1991) 'Toward a comprehensive theory of collaboration', *Journal of Applied Behavioural Science*, 27 (2): 139–62.

Zajac, E.J. and Olsen, C. (1993) 'From transaction cost to transactional value analysis: implications for the study of interorganizational strategies', *Journal of Management Studies*, 30: 130–46.

Zald, M.N. (1993) 'Organization studies as a scientific and humanistic enterprise: toward a reconceptualization of the foundations of the field', *Organization Science*, 4 (4): 513–28.

13 The Global Management of Professional Services: the Example of Accounting

Royston Greenwood, Teresa Rose, John L. Brown, David J. Cooper and Bob Hinings

Despite the antiquity of the international corporation 'surprisingly little academic research has focused on this complex and fast-changing field until recently' (Bartlett et al., 1990: 1). There is a particular shortage of empirical studies, partly because of the late interest shown in the operations of these corporations and partly their sheer complexity and geographical extension across space make access difficult. Most available studies suffer one or more of three shortcomings. First, the overwhelming majority are of manufacturing enterprises (e.g., Porter, 1986; Bartlett and Ghoshal, 1989; Johansson and Yip, 1994). And, although the differences between goods-production and service provision are well rehearsed (e.g., Schmenner, 1986; Giarini, 1987; Aharoni, 1993), little attention has been paid to whether the management and organization of global firms varies by type of industry. Particularly ignored are organizations that deliver professional business services, for example accounting, law, architectural, engineering and consulting services (Aharoni, 1993; Fladmore-Lindquist, 1993).

A second shortcoming is that more attention has been given to understanding issues of strategy (e.g., Porter, 1986; Morrison, 1990; Yip, 1992) than to issues of management and organization (Ghoshal and Westney, 1993). And yet, as Westney notes, 'it is easier to develop appropriate international business strategies than it is to build organizational systems to carry them out' (Ghoshal and Westney, 1993: 53). Hout, Porter and Rudden (1982: 29) similarly declare that organization, not strategy, is the 'Achilles Heel' of global firms. Studies that do focus on management and organization frequently equate organization with structure, in the tradition of Stopford and Wells (1972) and Franko (1976), and ignore or downplay decision processes and human resource practices that activate and give purpose to structural architecture. Studies using broader definitions (see Martinez and Jarillo, 1989, for a summary) mostly pre-date current debates on global strategy (see Johansson and Yip, 1994). Of the small number of studies that examine organizational arrangements in the wider sense (e.g., Egelhoff, 1984; Galbraith and Karanjian, 1986; Bartlett and Ghoshal, 1987, 1988, 1989, 1991; Prahalad and Doz, 1987), not one looks at professional service firms.

The third shortcoming is that most studies of international management fail to capture properly the temporal context of organizations (notable exceptions would include Bartlett and Ghoshal, 1989). Insufficient attention is given to the circumstances within which an organization is operating and to how those circumstances may be changing and impelling organizational adjustment. Instead, snapshots of organizational mechanisms are provided without proper analysis of the circumstances that influence their adoption and evolution. These usually ignored circumstances that include not only the 'administrative heritage' (Bartlett and Ghoshal, 1988, 1989) of the organization but also the history of the industry.

The purpose of the present chapter is to provide an account of how two of the world's largest and most successful accounting firms manage globally spread operations. Having done so, it will compare the arrangements of these firms with the models identified by Bartlett and Ghoshal (1989) as widely used in other industries. The discussion is set within a temporal context in order to understand why the two firms are managed as they are.

There have been several efforts to classify services (e.g., Sapir, 1982; Lovelock, 1983; Zeithaml et al., 1985; Schmenner, 1986), with accounting firms usually classified as professional business services. Business service firms are recognized as having characteristics different from services such as telecommunications and financial services (Aharoni, 1993). Even within professional business services, accounting has some unique characteristics. Our intent, therefore, is not to use accounting firms as cases from which broad, definitive generalizations may be attempted. On the contrary, we review the characteristics that define the accounting industry and then explore how two global firms manage within the parameters of those characteristics. Only having done so will we raise points of comparison and contrast with Bartlett and Ghoshal's observations on other industries, in order to push towards a theory of global strategic management.

There are three more sections to the chapter. The next section defines accounting firms as global organizations and describes the particular characteristics of the accounting industry. The third section analyses the current strategic management practices of two accounting firms. The following section compares the practices of accounting firms to the practices found in other industries. The comparison is based upon the organizational models put forward by Bartlett and Ghoshal (1989). Finally, we discuss the contribution of our findings for the development of a theory of global strategic management.

The case studies described below are of two of the world's largest accounting firms (see Table 13.1). Size alone, however, does not define a global organization (Perlmutter, 1969; Hout et al., 1982; Bartlett and Ghoshal, 1989; Morrison, 1990; Yip, 1992; Johansson and Yip, 1994). Perlmutter (1969), for example, emphasizes the importance of senior

TABLE 13.1   *Basic statistics of the 'Big Six' international accounting firms, 1997*

Firm	World-wide revenues (US$ millions)
Andersen Worldwide	11,300
Ernst & Young	9,100
KPMG	8,219
Coopers & Lybrand	7,500
Deloitte & Touche	7,400
Price Waterhouse	5,630

Source: Public Accounting Report (28 February 1998).

management's orientation, classifying firms as ethnocentric, polycentric or geocentric. Yip (1992) provides the most elaborate classification by identifying five dimensions, each on a continuum from a global to a 'multilocal' corporation:

1 Market participation: i.e., the range of markets and market shares (the more markets and the significance of market shares the more global the enterprise).
2 Products/services: i.e., the extent to which the firm provides the same or different products in different countries (globally standardized products indicate a global firm).
3 Location of value-adding activities: i.e., the location of functions in the value-added chain (the more that research, production and sales functions are located in several national markets, the more that firm is global).
4 Marketing: i.e., the extent to which a firm uses the same brand name and advertising across national markets (the greater the extent of brand marketing the more global is the firm).
5 Competitive moves: i.e., the extent to which a firm makes competitive moves in specific countries as part of a global strategy.

Organizations may be more global along some dimensions than others. In the case of the accounting industry, each of the 'Big Six' firms is global across at least four and possibly five dimensions. These firms have extensive operations around the world, provide a common range of largely standardized services, usually market themselves under a world-wide name and deliver value-adding activities in most markets.

Characteristics of the Accounting Industry

It is common in the literature to differentiate 'service' activity from 'goods' activity. Four characteristics of services are usually cited: their intangibility, heterogeneity, perishability, and the inseparability of production and consumption (Zeithaml et al., 1985). Services, however, are a heterogeneous category and professional business services, as a subcategory, has its own characteristics (Aharoni, 1993). Two features of professional business services generally, and this of the accounting industry specifically, might be expected to shape or constrain the strategic management arrangements of global players.

Professional service firms deal in knowledge, and hence are dependent on mobile employees

The core competence of a professional service firm (PSF) is the expertise and experience of its work force. The asset base is knowledge and the competitive advantage of the firm is its reputation (Zeithaml et al., 1990 Aharoni, 1993). Professional service firms are labour intensive with limited opportunities to obtain economies of scale from capital investment (Turley, 1994).[1] The importance of reputation is heightened by the inability of existing and potential clients to assess services in advance of consumption. Decisions on which firm to hire are thus made partly on the basis of perceived reputation, and partly on the personal rapport established between client and accountant. Knowledge-based organizations are thus deeply reliant upon highly mobile professional workers. As Starbuck (1992) notes, hierarchical and bureaucratic structures violate a sense of professional importance and desire for autonomy.

The knowledge competence of PSFs and their dependence upon mobile professionals create the essential managerial problematic of the PSF. On the one hand, the PSF has to secure sustained consistency of high-quality service across the firm in order to protect the firm's reputation; on the other hand, it has to retain its highly mobile professional work force (who constitute its knowledge stock) but who, as Starbuck reminds us (1992) are resistant to hierarchical and bureaucratic control mechanisms.

Production and marketing are inseparable, hence there is extensive geographic dispersion

Definitions of service activities usually report the inseparability of production and consumption. Much less noted in the service literature is the importance of the inseparability of production and marketing. In accounting firms, promotion of the firm's name can be undertaken but the real marketing effort is through the nurturing of relationships during and between engagements. To obtain business, accounting firms develop and sustain relationships with potential and existing clients. Partners that develop such relationships constitute the links connecting the firm with clients. Furthermore, because much audit and accounting work is repetitive, in the sense that there are repeat engagements, accountants have to be located near clients in order to nurture and retain client loyalty during and between engagements. The result is geographical dispersion, both within national firms but especially at the international level.

In the accounting firm, geographical dispersion means that there are offices in many locations, each office delivering production and marketing activities. That is, the firm is made up of self-sufficient, geographically dispersed units. The problem of geographical dispersion is particularly acute at the international level where the motivation is to service multinational clients. Unlike other global firms, where overseas expansion was deemed necessary to secure supplies of resources and raw materials, or to provide additional markets for production capabilities requiring stable and high demand (Bartlett et al., 1990), accounting firms first went overseas to service existing clients (Daniels et al., 1989; Cypert, 1991).[2] That is, accounting firms practice an unusual mode of isomorphism: wherever large clients located, accounting firms would follow (Daniels et al., 1989). As a consequence, accounting firms became very complex and globally dispersed.

Ernst & Young, for example, has over 66,000 people in over 680 cities located in over 125 countries. KPMG operates in 152 different countries; Price Waterhouse has offices in 119 countries; Arthur Andersen has 43,500 personnel in member firms, in 360 locations, in 76 countries. This dispersion is put into perspective by the figures for Pepsico, which operates in 45 countries, and Johnson & Johnson, which operates in 50 countries (*The Economist*, 1995). The extent of geographical dispersion, moreover, is increasing: Daniels et al. (1989) record that in 1985 the largest number of countries covered by an accounting firm was 97 (by Coopers & Lybrand). Peat Marwick Mitchell was in 82 countries and KMG Thomas McLintock in 55.

In summary, accounting firms (in common with professional business services generally) share a distinct set of work characteristics. First, the work is knowledge intensive and requires employment of highly trained professionals who are resistant to the use of bureaucratic control mechanisms. These professionals represent the asset stock of the accounting firm. The firm is dependent upon these workers. Knowledge workers are mobile assets, *and* could easily damage the reputation of a firm either by defection or by engaging in inappropriate behaviours (e.g., low quality service) while with the firm. Secondly, accounting work (more so than other professional business, e.g., management consulting) requires that the knowledge professional be located near the client and that he or she practise marketing and service delivery at one and the same time. In servicing multinational clients, therefore, accounting firms face the problem of co-ordinating the contributions of many professionals, in many countries, in order to provide seamless, world-wide service.

To understand how international accounting firms manage themselves we examined in considerable detail the practices of four firms, and in rather less detail the practices of the other two members of the 'Big Six'. Material from these firms was collected from 1989 to 1996, primarily through interviews with individuals in key managerial roles in the international firms, and in a number of national and local offices involved in international affairs. A total of 78 interviews was conducted. In several cases, second and third interviews were carried out in order to capture changes occurring over the seven-year-period. Interviews ranged from one to two hours in length. Interviews were usually conducted by two of the authors, and subsequent meetings held to compare notes. Convergence on observations and the key issues arising from the interview enhances the confidence of the findings. The interviews were transcribed. Interview material was supplemented with reports and numerous other documents (e.g., strategic plans, annual reports and directions, office procedure manuals, process reports). Nudist software (Richards and Richards, 1992) was used to facilitate the analytic process of both sources of data.

The focus of the interviews was twofold. First, we sought descriptive accounts of the orientations, organizational structures and decision processes of the 'Big Six' firms, so as to compare them with the organizational models proposed by Bartlett and Ghoshal (1989) as typically and widely used by industrial corporations. These organizational models are described more fully in the last section of the chapter. Essentially, the Bartlett and Ghoshal models represent combinations of responses to three broad questions, which, when applied to accounting firms, read as follows:

- What is the basic strategic orientation of these international firms?
- How far are the national firms relatively autonomous and self-sufficient organizational entities (i.e., what is the structural configuration of the firm)?
- How far does the international firm control the national firm and through what mechanisms?

These questions underlay the semi-structured interview schedule. Interviewees were asked to describe the organization as they understood it, and to describe their role within it. Attention focused upon obtaining an account of the basic structural configuration, and an understanding of how the configuration functioned. This latter understanding was achieved by placing particular attention upon critical processes: strategic planning (including investment decisions), budgeting and resource allocation, the appointment appraisal and compensation of partners, and the management of international clients (client management systems).

The second focus of the interview programme was also influenced by the work of Bartlett and Ghoshal. We were (and remain) persuaded of the importance given by these authors to the play of organizational history, or administrative heritage. Bartlett and Ghoshal rightly note that how organizations respond to international demands 'cannot be captured in a formula' (1988: 2). Organizations develop structure and practices that derive from, and which are consistent with, their 'administrative heritage', that is 'the company's existing configuration of assets, its traditional distribution of responsibility, and its historical norms, values, and management style' (1988: 3). The idea of administrative heritage resonates with Granovetter (1985) and Stinchcombe's (1965) notion of imprinting and the importance of decisions taken in the early years of an organization's history, and with Kimberly's (1987) stress upon organizational 'biographies'. The importance we attribute to history influenced our interviews, in which we asked questions on how and why current managerial arrangements had evolved and were evolving. This line of inquiry was supplemented by the availability of quasi-biographical accounts of the firms (e.g., Richards, 1981; Wise, 1981; Watt, 1982).

Writers who emphasize the importance of technology (i.e., the nature of the work done in an industry) would anticipate a single organizational model in any one industry, other things (e.g., size, ownership) being equal. Writers who acknowledge the importance of history, by contrast, would anticipate difference across firms in the same industry. In one sense, differences in histories means, as Kimberly puts it, that 'every organization is in some ways unique' (1987: 234). In fact, we found two distinct organizational models operating within the accounting industry, which we label the 'unitary' and the 'confederation/association' models. Only one of the models, corresponds, and even then in an adapted way, to the Bartlett and Ghoshal models. Below, the accounting models are described in some detail. For reasons of confidentiality the firms are referred to as Eastern Accounting and Western Accounting.

It is important to note that both Eastern Accounting and Western Accounting are constantly adapting their arrangements in order to anticipate and respond to evolving market circumstances. Organizational arrangements are not the product of a static set of tasks. Demands and opportunities unfold, sometimes in predictable and gradual ways, at other times in dramatic fashion. Any account of an industry's dominant organizational models is thus essentially an unfolding one. The descriptions here, of how the two accounting firms were organized and managed as of the middle of 1995, are essentially temporary accounts, perhaps already being superseded. It is also important to stress that our purpose is not to evaluate the two firms *vis-à-vis* one another, or with others in the industry. *Both* firms are *highly* successful.

The Case Studies

There are similarities and differences between the two case studies. Some of the similarities are taken for granted within the accounting industry, and it is only in comparison with other industries, where the corporation is the dominant organizational form, that the similarities become noticeable. Thus, both accounting firms share the characteristic of being partnerships; a governance arrangement which makes them different from other business forms in that ownership, management, and operations are fused

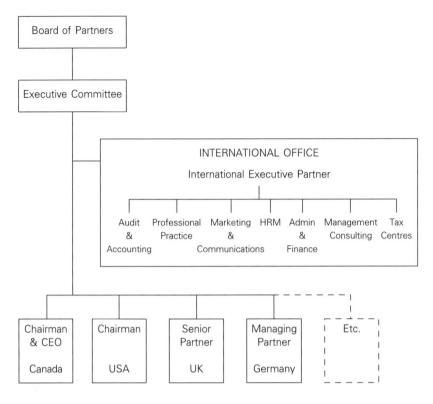

FIGURE 13.1   *International organizational structure: Eastern Accounting*

(Greenwood et al., 1990: 730). But, the partnership format can be operated in different ways.

The international structures of Eastern Accounting and Western Accounting are shown in Figures 13.1 and 13.2. In one sense, there is a similarity between the two structures, in that each is based upon the national firm, which is a self-sufficient unit, containing the full range of services and managerial functions. In short, both international firms comprise national firms, each with a full capability for operating autonomously. However, whereas in Eastern Accounting the focus is upon the national firm, in Western Accounting there is an attempt to de-emphasize the national firm as the operating unit.

Eastern Accounting is a confederation of national practices, a characteristic acknowledged by senior partners.[3] The arrangement is not regarded as a weakness (although some argue for a tilting of the balance between association and integration):

> The firm is very much a federation. I get annoyed when people call us a loose federation, because I don't think we are a loose federation. And frankly I think one of our strengths is that we are a federation.

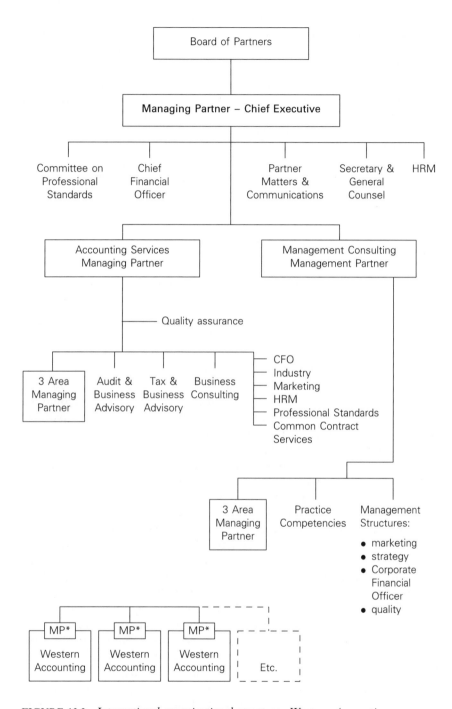

FIGURE 13.2 *International organizational structure: Western Accounting*

I believe that [Eastern] is the only global firm. . . . We have a strong global presence in each of the major markets of the world. We have common goals, common objectives, common values, common interests. But we are a strong federation of firms.

Yes, it is true that [Eastern] is a federation. This is, however, not a disadvantage or a weakness and certainly not a makeshift solution. This structure was created by a common conviction that the practice of our profession can be performed in France best by a Frenchman, in Italy by an Italian, in England by and Englishman, etc. etc.

Western Accounting, by contrast does not conceptualize itself as an aggregation of national firms. Instead, the firm is perceived as a unified entity (in Maister's (1985) terms it is a one-firm firm) operating in several countries:

In this firm there is lots of emphasis on integrated form: it's the only way we know how to operate.

Our firm does not operate as a franchise so to speak. We just don't lend our name out.

The organization cuts across the legal, country boundaries. You cannot run an international business on the basis of legal divisions.

The difference between the strategic orientations of the two firms is reflected in the governance mechanisms. In Western Accounting, admission to partnership is to the international partnership; in Eastern Accounting, admission is to the national partnership. In Western Accounting partners share in world-wide profits (i.e., the international firm is a revenue-sharing entity); in Eastern Accounting partners share in their national firm's profits (i.e., the international firm is a cost-sharing entity). Meetings of the partnership in Western Accounting are world-wide, not national; in Eastern Accounting each national partnership holds meetings, and the international meeting is of representatives of the national partnerships.

Emphasis in Western Accounting upon the firm as a unified entity is also shown in the low degree of differentiation between the country firms. This is hinted at in Figure 13.1, where Eastern Accounting uses different terms in different countries for the name of the firm itself, and for the heads of national firms. In contrast, Western Accounting has a common name and title in each country (Figure 13.3).[4] More significant differences between Eastern Accounting and Western Accounting are found in the approach to the management structures and process of each country. In Western Accounting a uniform managerial approach is used: in Eastern Accounting broader differences are tolerated. For example, there are differences within Eastern Accounting in terms of the use (or not) of regional structures within a national firm, the basis of partner appraisal and compensation, and the existence and the tightness of controls between national and local offices.

An interesting example of the contrasting philosophies is provided by the comment by one international partner in Western Accounting as to how he would evaluate, over time, the success or otherwise of a merger: 'Success, to me, means how much do they look alike to the rest of the organization.' An important means by which Western Accounting instils the concept of the firm as a single, unified firm is through its training and management development programmes. Both Eastern Accounting and Western Accounting spend considerable sums on training their professionals and have world-class facilities for doing so, recognizing the importance of training as a source of competitive advantage:

> Our continued support as a firm depends upon the quality of our people and their ongoing professional development throughout their careers. The quality of our training and management development is absolutely fundamental to our goal of remaining the leading accounting and consulting firm in the world.

And

> The way you can differentiate yourself is by the training. It can get better and can be superior over a sustained period of time. That's where we try to differentiate ourselves: we devote enormous resources to training.

There is, however, a noticeable difference between the two firms in the format and purpose of training. For Eastern Accounting, training traditionally has served a twofold purpose. First to standardize methodologies so that: (i) clients will receive a similar *standard* of service world-wide; and (ii) to ensure that services provided to international clients are seamlessly delivered despite national boundaries. Secondly, to maintain and improve the knowledge and skills of the work force, thus improving the asset stock of the firm. In other words, training and management development in Eastern Accounting are primarily cognitive activities intended to improve technical competence and develop standardized approaches. Turley captured this focus in his study of the impact of training upon accounting firms in Sweden:

> The effects of the international firms on training at the national level was also more indirect than direct. . . . One area where there did appear to be a considerable international impact on national practice was in the technical methods expected to be applied by staff. This was particularly true of the main service area of auditing. (Turley, 1994: 15)

Western Accounting also uses training to realize the advantages of technical standardization. But there is a rationale for Western Accounting's considerable investment in training, namely, to socialize its personnel into the values and norms of the firm, thus developing a deep-rooted commitment to the firm's organization and way of doing things. Training in Western Accounting is a vehicle for developing normative commitment to 'the firm'. One reason why Western Accounting has found it possible to develop a firm-wide culture is because its professionals progress through standardized training programmes, much of it delivered at the firm's world training centre. The training centre is seen as both 'a technology transfer point', and as a crucial mechanism for the dissemination of the firm's values:

> They're very tied to using the centre as the cultural glue that holds the place together. They're very conscious of trying to do that in such a way that it holds the individual nationalities together . . .

The role of the training centre as an instrument for achieving acculturation is deliberate. It incorporates a History Centre, which contains artifacts from the early days of the firm. Flags of all the country firms are displayed. Art objects from the country firms adorn the walls. Partners who teach at the centre are briefed on their role as transporters of the firm's values.[5] Intriguingly, a variety of disciplines are employed, including anthropology. There is now a deliberate attempt to understand the importance of the firm's culture and of how it can best be managed.

The importance attached within Western Accounting to centralized and standardized training as an instrument of acculturation is also found, but to a lesser degree. Especially in Europe, Eastern Accounting is developing courses aimed at strengthening 'our unity as a firm'. There is a process underway to rationalize and coordinate training programmes traditionally designed and delivered by each national firm. The difference between Eastern Accounting and Western Accounting, nevertheless, remains sharp. Mandatory training at the global level remains comparatively rare in Eastern Accounting. Instead, facilities are available to national firms and, essentially, are used voluntarily. Turley, commenting on the situation within Sweden, concluded that:

> In most cases, the majority of the training is developed and run *within* Sweden, but sometimes using basic material developed internationally. . . . In one case the interviewee described the use of the international firm's audit approach as just about *the only compulsory requirement* from being part of the firm. (Turley, 1994: 15, emphasis added)

The emphasis in Western Accounting upon world-wide standardization and integration, and the greater tolerance for heterogeneity of practice and style, is associated with differences in the structure and roles of the international headquarters. We use the term international headquarters, though it is not typically used by the accounting firms themselves. The term embraces two structures: the International Office, that is the full-time staff, and the international committees, used to oversee the international firm and to carry out many of its functions.

The International Office in Eastern Accounting is comparatively small (in staffing and budget) and has a decision-making style that is *primarily supportive and administrative*, rather than directive and authoritative. The international office has approximately 50 staff and a budget of $35 million (almost 0.5 per cent of world-wide revenues). Those inside the International Office recognize its primary role as that of assisting the international firm to develop a common level of service capability and of delivery to clients, not to promote a one-firm structure:

> The character of our head office is as supporter to the national firm.

> The term International Headquarter is something of a misnomer: it's a support for our federation.

A much more influential component of Eastern Accounting's international headquarter is the Executive Committee, to which the International Executive Partner (who heads the International Office) reports. The agenda of the Executive Committee embraces important issues, such as:

- Development of the global network: e.g., decisions on whether to open offices in new markets such as China or Eastern Europe, or whether to merge with a company not previously accessed by the firm.
- Development of client management systems: i.e., designing systems for managing the services provided to multinational clients. Thus, the roles and authority of lead partners (i.e., the head of a world-wide team handling a multinational client's account) would be established by the international firm. Issues of appropriate fees, the selection of local partners and their removal, would be considered relevant to the international firm. Servicing domestic clients would not.
- Development of new ideas and processes: i.e., research and analysis of new ideas and processes. For example, several firms are undertaking research into particular industries, in which they intend to develop and advertise distinctive expertise. The international firm facilitates (usually through lateral collective structures – see below) discussion and dissemination of analysis and policy proposals. Adoption of the ideas, however, would be a matter of national discretion.
- Risk management: accounting firms are struggling to manage the rash of litigation. Given the partnership mode of ownership, national practices are vulnerable to lawsuits in particular countries. The global firm would discuss policies for handling risk management, including self-insurance or alteration of the legal structure.
- Management of the firm's reputation.

Critically, however, the Executive Committee in Eastern Accounting has little formal authority to develop and enforce a global strategy. There are no systems providing the Executive Committee with detailed market and financial information on the performance of each national firm. Neither targets nor goals are set for the national firms. There is no international monitoring of national firm performance nor appraisal of each national firm's managing partner. Policies adopted by the international firm are implemented at the discretion of each national firm. As one senior international partner put it: 'We rely on the commitment of business units, i.e., the national practices.'

Turley, assessing the impact of six international firms upon their Swedish associates, described the role of the international centre thus:

> Interviewees often emphasized the level of decentralization and freedom of action that was present in the firm – freedom to manage the domestic organization in what they considered to be the appropriate way. There was little suggestion that by affiliating internationally local practitioners had surrendered much of their autonomy of action. All the firms had structures of committees and centralized coordination of certain areas of marketing practice or technical development, but little reference was made to formal effective accountability to these structures. They were seen primarily as facilitating and coordinating efforts rather than as authoritative management structures. (Turley, 1994: 14)

Ferner, Edwards and Sisson, studying one of the 'Big Six', reached the same conclusion:

> There was a small permanent international office whose job was primarily to develop and administer the policy decisions of the international committees, to collect data from national firms, and to provide support services to some of the weaker national partnerships; it in no way functioned as a corporate headquarters exercising strategic or financial control over the constituent partnerships. (Ferner et al., 1994: 12)

The constrained authority of the International Office and of the central committees in Eastern Accounting is reflected in two principles embodied in the governance structures of the firm, principles which emphasize the accountability of the international firm to the national firm (and not vice versa). First, most of the work carried out by the international firm is conducted through committees that embody the principle of territorial representation. For example, the Board of Partners comprised the 33 heads of the largest national firms, which produce 97 per cent of world-wide revenues. The Board elects its own Chairman, Vice Chairman and the Executive Committee, which has 11 members. Typically, the Executive Committee will include the heads of the largest national firms (e.g., the UK, the USA, the Netherlands, Germany and France). In other words, the most senior governing structure of the international firm are, *de facto*, directly accountable to the national practices by virtue of the representative structure of the Board and the Executive Committee. How far representatives act as representatives of national interests varies (both within and between accounting firms). However, there is always the potential, and in some instances the actuality, of members representing the national practice rather than the international firm.

A second governance principle within Eastern Accounting, which fixes accountability of the international firm to the national practices, is that international executive positions are usually for fixed terms (though renewable) and are often combined with other responsibilities. The chairmen of international committees are appointed for three years and continue to carry a client load. Members of the Executive Committee are national executive partners and are engaged at least as much, and probably more, in running their national firms than in running the international firm. Until recently, the only full-time executive positions were within the International Office, which services the committee structure. (From 1996, the Chief Executive became the full-time head of the international firm.)

There have been attempts in Eastern Accounting recently, to strengthen the commitment of the national firms to the strategies developed by the international Executive Committee. The senior management of the national firms has committed itself to implementing a global strategy aimed at positioning Eastern Accounting as 'The Advisory Firm'. Small committees of national managing partners are charged with monitoring the progress of each country in the implementation of the strategy. This development reflects a concern with the traditionally loose coupling between the international dimension of the firm and the national dimension. But even this development still primarily relies upon peer pressure, rather than overt, authoritative action. There have also been recent attempts in Eastern Accounting to strengthen the international client management system, the firm's system for ensuring quality service to global clients. This is best seen through the firm's application of the 'lead partner' concept:

> We have a lead partner concept within our whole firm world-wide. . . . The role of the lead *partner* being that of the person that maintains a relationship at the very highest level and who makes sure that the client obtains the best quality of services wherever the client goes globally.

> So we have a hierarchy, maybe if you image a Christmas tree where we have a lead partner at the top. His main role really is to keep the relationship going, to make sure that the best things are given to the client and then we have the engagement partner who is the partner who looks into the financials at the head office level – so we have a head office engagement partner, and then we have the respective lead partners all over the world servicing each location.

The lead person is not there as a technical person, but, instead, to maintain the relationship with the client. The lead partner has the prerogative to issue directives relating to the quality of service to clients in the various locations, to request that an engagement partner be changed if he or she believes it will enhance global service, and to negotiate fees on a global or regional basis, in order to maintain the client and the quality of service.

Despite these developments, the role of the International Office in Eastern Accounting contrasts with that of Western Accounting, which is much more clearly the strategic hub of the firm. Some senior managers within Western Accounting insist that there is no single headquarters, pointing out that the Chief Executive, and the heads of the two Business Units, reside in three different US cities. But it is difficult to deny the existence of a headquarters: over 1,100 staff work out of one centre, managing the activities of the world-wide firm.

Compared to Eastern Accounting, Western Accounting is tightly structured and places formal authority in a concentrated manner at the hierarchical apex of the firm. The distribution of power is clearly intended to favour the international firm, not the national firm. Explicit performance targets are set both for the world-wide firm and for each national firm, covering market share, revenues and net profits, in a manner not found in Eastern Accounting. These targets are monitored on an ongoing basis:

> each operating unit of the 75,000-person firm is wired into our central financial and operating system. And we in turn provide them with operating data on the 3rd or 4th day of each month.

The existence of such a financial information system illustrates how a single and consistent set of mechanisms permeates the organization, providing centralized knowledge of local performance and offering the possibility of making strategic adjustments across countries in the effort to sustain global results. Western Accounting not only has a more tightly structured and hierarchically arranged international organization than Eastern Accounting; in addition, its senior management team has the authority and is expected to act more assertively and decisively, to an extent unlikely to occur in the confederation model. As one world-wide partner openly acknowledged: '[Western Accounting] is a much more centralized organization than other accounting firms: all line managers report to [the CEO].' A senior executive of Western Accounting hinted at the authority of the hierarchy: 'Consensus is good but there are times when it slows you down. . . . The implementation of what we've decided will take some tough decisions.' And: 'There's a tremendous amount of management authority which is given to what we call the leadership group of the firm. . . . I really have a true global responsibility. . . . I have executive authority to commit the firm.'

Organizational structures, of course, are frameworks, whose usage can vary. Western Accounting, though exhibiting a hierarchical framework, uses that framework in a particular manner. Integral to Western Accounting are three values, which influence the exercise of formal authority:

- The notion of *stewardship*.
- The notion of a *meritocracy* of partners.
- An anxiety (or *angst*) of being the best.[6]

Stewardship, in the context of Western Accounting, refers to the commitment and desire to leave the firm as a stronger entity for the next generation of partners. Those in control of the firm constantly refer to Western Accounting not as something in which they are part owners, but as an organization for which they have temporary responsibility. One senior partner reflected on over two decades of management:

> Even more unique than our world-wide philosophy is this notion of stewardship. . . . The partners in this firm, for whatever the reason, believe that it was their responsibility to leave it in better shape, and they never measured what it cost them. And it cost them a lot of money to do it. But the next generation has always benefited, and there's always been a next generation. When we lose that formula, we'll lose our biggest competitive advantage.

The value of stewardship, we suggest in a moment, influences how decisions are made, constraining unilateral and essentially short-term decision-making. So, too, does the value of a meritocracy of partners, which emphasizes the importance of partners sharing responsibility for the performance of the firm. Specific indicators of this value include the practice of one man–one vote in partnership decisions (rather than voting by capital), the expectation that all partners world-wide will attend partnership meetings, the practice of partners sharing a world-wide pool of profits, and of partners starting out equally (every new partner starts off in exactly the same place . . .). This emphasis upon treating partners equally led one partner to suggest that: 'We're almost a socialist organization.'

The third value that appears important to us is not included in the firm's own statement of its core values, and it is something of a paradox or tension. Western Accounting, as with each of the 'Big Six' firms, aspires to be the pre-eminent firm. And, in many respects it profoundly believes itself to be the best and is proud of its achievements. Interview after interview reaffirmed that pride. But, there is an absence of complacency. On the contrary, there exists an anxiety, or angst, about becoming better. The firm exhibits tremendous self-confidence and, at the same time, an urgent concern to keep improving, stretching forwards. There is a dual-headed stamp of proud capability and yet a compulsion to improve, driven almost by insecurity. This angst is reflected in simple ways, one of which is the extensive parade of outside gurus and management thinkers invited to visit, advise and lecture to the firm. There is an impalpable desire to open the firm to new and challenging ideas and to promote learning. At the same firm, there is a concern with secrecy, retaining understanding of the firm's way of doing things so as to prevent competitors from copying the formula.[7] The importance of these three values is that, in concert, they provide an interesting paradox in the way that decisions could be, and are, made within Western Accounting's hierarchical structure. Formal hierarchy and tight control systems clearly exist. But the values of stewardship, meritocracy and the angst for improvement constrain and hold in check any tendency towards over-assertive leadership. We are suggesting that, while Western Accounting's formal structure provides considerable scope for authoritative leadership, the decision process is framed by the strong normative context of the organization. Leadership and sensitivity to the partnership, not the corporate basis of the firm. The authority of leadership is not unbounded but negotiated, held in check by the rooted values of the firm, and, should leadership overstep the tacit and presumed bounds of the negotiated authority, the partnership vehicle enables Western Accounting (as with other accounting firms) to remove its senior figures.[8] 'My partners', commented Western Accounting's chief executive, 'know that they could throw me out.'

We began by noticing an essential similarity between Eastern Accounting and Western Accounting, that is the partnership form of governance. We conclude by highlighting another distinctive similarity: the dense network of international committees and task forces (Ferner et al., 1994). This network is an extension of the theme underlying the partnership format, namely, the attempt to use collegial/clan (Ouchi, 1980) structures as alternatives to hierarchy. The number of committees, task forces and project teams in existence at any one time, in any of the large accounting firms, is difficult to gauge. Partners themselves found it hard to list them. Both firms, however, use a mosaic of lateral structures beyond the standing committees, both for the management of international assignments (especially management of multinational client engagements) and, significantly, as vehicles for organizational learning. Ideas and initiatives percolate through the extensive network of teams and committees, in which key figures learn of and disseminate ideas. Some appreciation of this emergent process is captured in the following quote:

> So we are on the road a lot because there are 10 or something groups and each one meets at least once and sometimes twice or three times a year, so we are hopping all around attending meetings. And there is a reason for that, too. People say, 'why would you go to all these meetings?' I will tell you now, it's because I am the information hub – that's where I got my information, that's why I know everyone who is a key person in any given industry or any given function anywhere in the world of importance. . . . So I know all these people first hand by attending these meetings and be attending these meetings I am kept up to date on what is happening in information technology or operations management or banking or manufacturing or whatever the steering group is.

Again:

> They said, there are some interesting things going on in the United States that are of interest to other countries . . . so why don't we give some money to them on a project basis to take what we are doing in the US and package it for international consumption and training and so forth.

One international partner, with a twinkle in his eye, when asked what he did, responded: 'My job? I sit on airplanes.' It is worth noting that the overwhelming majority (if not all) of the members of these teams are practising members of the firm, that is they are working on accounting engagements, tax or insolvency work, or on consulting assignments. In the parlance of the accounting firms, they have billable hours charged to the client. And, because they are involved with clients, they are sensitive to ideas and initiatives that surface in the committees, subcommittees and teams. These individuals are not merely 'hub's of information, but pushers of ideas. They are like bees, picking up ideas in one place, pollinating in another. The importance of lateral structures is explicitly reorganized by both Eastern Accounting and Western Accounting, and the role of the international headquarters is seen to include the promotion and harnessing of this activity: 'The key to our practice is networking – lots of little projects and collaborations. We aim to oil the wheels.'

The importance of lateral structures should not be underestimated; but their effectiveness should not be over drawn. There are potential weaknesses: 'What happens is, you can end up with some person running around the world collecting all this information. And if that person gets run over by a trolley in Moscow, it's gone.' There is, too, a (perhaps inevitable) looseness about which team, steering groups and committees exist from year to year, about their overlapping memberships and their points of discussion. The global accounting firm utilizes multiple criteria for dissecting its market setting: committees and teams are organized by industry, by service, by client, and by geography.

There appears, in one sense, to be almost a deliberate redundancy in the number of committees, subcommittees and project groups, and a deliberate overlap of membership. But the cost of this inefficiency, accounting firms believe, is balanced by the benefit of flexible and fluid organizational learning. It is from the interstices of this quilt-work of lateral relationships that new knowledge emerges and new opportunities become apparent. Both Eastern Accounting and Western Accounting use the lateral structure extensively. It represents the importance of collegial mechanisms for promoting co-operation within professional organizations, and for promoting the normative attachment of professionals to their organizations. In Western Accounting, the lateral structures complement more hierarchical arrangements; in Eastern Accounting they substitute for them.

Summary of the Two Accounting Models

The practices of Western Accounting and Eastern Accounting represent two distinct ways of managing the international operation of accounting firm. The models are summarized in Table 13.2, using the three questions derived from the work of Bartlett and Ghoshal as organizing themes. The Unitary Model is characterized by a strategic orientation that conceives the international firm as an integrated, global entity. The firm is built upon full-service, self-sufficient national units. The relationship between these

TABLE 13.2 *Characteristics of the unitary and confederation models*

The unitary model	The confederation model
1. What is the basic strategic orientation of these firms?	
• Is unicentric, emphasizing the international firm as a single entity operating in several countries.	• Is multi-centric, emphasizing the international firm as an association of strong, national firms.
2. How far are national subsidiaries autonomous and self-sufficient entities?	
• Promotes standard managerial and organizational arrangements across countries (combined with promotion of uniform standards of service).	• Accepts differences between national firms in their managerial and organizational arrangements (combined with promotion of uniform standards of service).
• Has full-service, self-sufficient national firms.	• Has full-service, self-sufficient national firms.
3. How far, and through which mechanisms, does the international centre control its subsidiaries?	
• Has a large authoritative, international office.	• Has a small international office with an administrative and service orientation.
• Has hierarchical and well developed information mechanisms converging on the international office: explicit targets are set for national firms.	• Has an absence and/or weak development of hierarchy and information mechanism at the international level.
• Emphasizes strong cultural development.	• Emphasizes collegial persuasion.
• Emphasizes lateral, collective structures.	• Emphasizes lateral, collective structures.
• Emphasizes centralized, standardized training, focused upon technical and behavioural socialization.	• Emphasizes training, often decentralized to national firms, focused on technical development.

national units and the international firm is clear, with explicit accountability to the international firm. This relationship resembles that between subsidiaries and parent company. The international firm achieves integration through a combination of three mechanisms: a *hierarchy of authority*, reinforced by explicit information systems that provide and monitor the market and financial performance of each national unit; a mosaic of overlapping *lateral structures* (culminating in the Board of Partners); and a strong *organizational culture*, deliberately managed through intensive training and development.

The Confederation Model is characterized by a strategic orientation that conceives of the firm as an association of full-service, self-national units. But it is recognized that some measure of integration is required to handle the requirements of multinational clients. The relationship between the international and national firms is not that of parent and subsidiaries. On the contrary, the international firm is an appendage to legally independent national firms. There is no parent firm. The degree of integration sought emphasizes two mechanisms: *training*, focused upon the promotion of consistent service methods, and *lateral structures* (culminating in the Board of Partners) supported by a small international administration. Decision-making is based upon discussion, negotiation and voluntary rather than mandatory adoption of international practices. Formal, hierarchical authority is avoided as a means of achieving international integration.

This section examines whether the accounting models are similar to, or different from those found in other industries. That is, we return to the starting point for the chapter assessing how far professional service firms utilize novel and distinctive organizational arrangements of nature of the work done (i.e., their technology).

The most useful discussion of how global firms manage their operations is provided by Bartlett and Ghoshal (1989) who, based upon detailed examination of nine companies, identified three organizational models.[9] The same authors describe a fourth model, which represents the direction in which several firms claim to be moving. The three models are:

- the multinational;
- the international; and
- the global.

Each model comprises a strategic mentality or *orientation*, a structural *configuration* (i.e., the extent to which assets, responsibilities and decision-making are centralized or decentralized) and a set of *control processes* linking the structural units.

In the multinational model, the strategic orientation sees the company as a portfolio of independent national businesses. Each unit maximizes the potential of the local environment. The structural configuration is that of the 'decentralized federation', characterized by a highly decentralized distribution of organizational assets and capabilities. The units have extensive operating independence and are responsible for the full range of managerial functions. Management processes are defined by simple financial controls overlaid on personal relationships and informal contracts (see Figure 13.3).

In the international model, the dominant strategic orientation sees subsidiary operations as appendages to the parent company, leveraging the resources and capabilities developed at headquarters. The structural configuration is a 'co-ordinated federation'. This model is characterized by retention of control at the centre through use of sophisticated management and of specialist corporate staffs. Information systems flow to the centre for analysis and action. The centre transfers knowledge and information to the subsidiaries (see Figure 13.4).

The strategic orientation of the global model conceives the world as a single, integrated market and the firm as one economic unit. The objective is thus to have tightly controlled subsidiaries. The structural configuration is that of a 'centralized hub' whereby assets, resources and responsibilities are centralized. The role of the overseas units is limited to the distribution of products or services produced in central locations. The subsidiary units

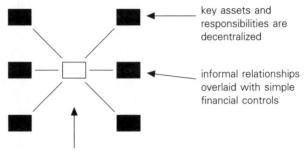

key assets and
responsibilities are
decentralized

informal relationships
overlaid with simple
financial controls

strategic orientation sees the company
as a portfolio of independent national
businesses

FIGURE 13.3 *The multinational model*

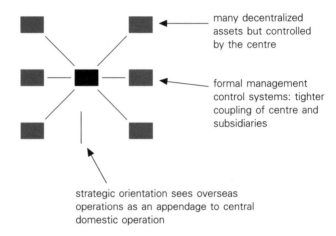

many decentralized
assets but controlled
by the centre

formal management
control systems: tighter
coupling of centre and
subsidiaries

strategic orientation sees overseas
operations as an appendage to central
domestic operation

FIGURE 13.4 *The international model*

assemble, sell and implement plans and policies derived at the centre. The
subsidiaries have no freedom to create new products or strategies. Knowledge is developed and retained at the centre (see Figure 13.5).

The three empirical models are summarized in Table 13.3, using the same
three questions as in Table 13.2. It is clear that neither Western Accounting
nor Eastern Accounting resemble the global model. The global model does
not have national organizations with a wide range of capabilities; on the
contrary, they are essentially sales outlets, with production and R&D
conducted elsewhere. Clearly, such an arrangement would be inappropriate
for accounting firms, not least because of the defining characteristic cited
earlier, i.e. namely, the inseparability of production and marketing. The
multinational and international models, however, bear some similarities to
the practices of Western Accounting and Eastern Accounting.

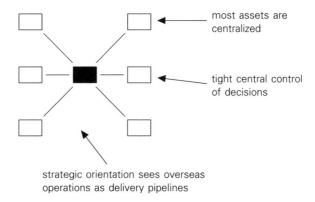

most assets are
centralized

tight central control
of decisions

strategic orientation sees overseas
operations as delivery pipelines

FIGURE 13.5 *The global model*

Western Accounting is nearest to the international model. There is a
close similarity of strategic orientation. Thus, national markets are in many
ways divisions of the international entity, although in Eastern Accounting
there may be the greater need to manage cross-border co-ordination
because of the needs of multinational clients. The structural configurations
of Western Accounting and the international model are essentially the
same. But, there are significant differences in the use made of particular
control processes. In the international model, the centre controls its
subsidiaries primarily through the imposition of standardized methods, and
the hierarchical application of financial and market targets underpinned by
salient information systems. In effect, the international model is integrated
through the use of bureaucratic structure.

Such emphasis upon bureaucratic structure would not fit easily with a
professional work force, hence the emphasis within Western Accounting
upon lateral collective structures and the distinctive pattern of acculturation. In other words, in many respects Western Accounting resembles the
international model – in particular, the strategic orientation and structural
configuration are very similar. But Western Accounting departs from the
international model in overlaying the bureaucratic control processes with
an array of lateral structures, and emphasizing normative values and
culture. This different mix of control patterns, we suggest, represents a
sensitivity to the nature of the work force.

Eastern Accounting is closer to the multinational than to the international model. There is a common emphasis upon the international
organization as a portfolio of self-sufficient and relatively autonomous
'businesses'. The strategic orientation within, however, has two features that
distinguish it from the multinational model. First, the multinational model
is unicentric, to the extent that there is a parent company and an originating
domestic market. There is a centre to the firm. Admittedly, the decentralized
federative structure, characteristic of the multinational model, has strong,

TABLE 13.3 *Three organizational models of global management (taken from Bartlett and Ghoshal (1989))*

Multinational model	International model	Global model
1 What is the basic strategic orientation?		
• National organizations are a portfolio of businesses owned by a parent company in a domestic market.	• National organizations are geographic divisions of an integrated firm.	• Markets are essentially global and serviced by integrated firm.
• National markets are seen as essentially discrete, with little overlap.	• National markets seen as relatively discrete, with overlap.	• National organizations are owned by parent company.
2 How far are national subsidiaries autonomous and self-sufficient entities?		
• National organizations are full-service and self-sufficient, capable of servicing the national market.	• National organizations are basically self-sufficient, but the parent company exports new technology and knowledge.	• National organizations are delivery pipelines for goods produced by centralized production facilities.
• National organizations are encouraged to use locally appropriate practices; hence, high differentiation is tolerated across the global company.	• Parent company establishes managerial and organizational arrangements, with some local adaption. Low differentiation.	• Low differentiation.
3 How far, and through which mechanisms, does the international centre control its subsidiaries?		
• Personal control overlaid with simple financial controls.	• Administrative (i.e., hierarchy and bureaucratic) controls, i.e., formal management planning systems providing tight parent–subsidiary linkages.	• Operational control, i.e., tight centralized control of decisions, resources and information. Use of hierarchy and bureaucratic structures.

quasi self-sufficient territorial divisions, but corporations of this form nevertheless have a legal centre usually associated with a home market. Multinational organizations, such as General Motors or Pepsico, typically can trace their history to a domestic market, but in the case of Eastern Accounting there are territorial centres and an evident lack of an originating home market: the firm is very much multi-centric in orientation. At Eastern Accounting there may be an official headquarters but that country is in no sense the home market. In fact, Eastern Accounting is very conscious of its origins as a non-Anglo-American firm, adamantly stressing its multiple of authority and power:

Eastern Accounting is not an Anglo-Saxon organization operating world-wide. Neither is it an organization dominated by Europeans. The fact is that Eastern Accounting is the first and only truly international accounting and consulting firm.

A second feature that distinguishes Eastern Accounting from the multi-national model is that although Eastern Accounting says that its national firms are largely autonomous (in terms of ownership and authority) and self-sufficient (in terms of functions covered), the firm recognizes the critical need for selective co-ordination between the firms, especially in the management of clients with operations spread over national borders and for purposes such as investment in new territories and products. This need for integration significantly qualifies national firms as a portfolio of independent businesses.

The differences in strategic orientation between Eastern Accounting and the multinational model are complemented by differences in structure. In particular, the multinational model recognizes the hierarchy as a significant means of securing co-ordination between the centre and the globally dispersed divisions. There may be emphasis upon personal relationships but there are, nevertheless, explicit financial controls and revenue expectations. Eastern Accounting, in contrast, because of the abbreviated international centre, does not stress hierarchy as a means of co-ordination and does not have clear financial controls. On the contrary, co-ordination is primarily secured through: (i) the network of committees and task forces, which, through overlapping memberships and regular, in infrequent, meetings, provides a loose and flexible form of co-ordination; and (ii) by training, to produce standardized practices. Even the management of multinational clients is done through teams, and these teams are run from several national firms (not from a single international headquarters). Such a range of committees and teams would not be found in the multinational model.

Discussion

Neither Eastern Accounting nor Western Accounting fully correspond to the models outlined by Bartlett and Ghoshal (1989). Western Accounting has similar features to the international model, but also has notable differences. At best, Western Accounting (hence our unitary model) could be classified as a variant of the international model. Eastern Accounting, by contrast, is sufficiently different to constitute a different model.

Taken together, the two accounting firms suggest that professional service firms – as exemplified by accounting firms – manage and organize themselves rather differently from industrial corporations. It is worth restating these differences:

- Emphasis upon *lateral, collective structures*, such as committees, teams and task forces, and the development of formal and personal *relationships* criss-crossing the organization. These lateral structures promote *collegial* control enshrined in the *partnership* mode of governance.
- Downplaying of hierarchy and bureaucratic structures. Eastern Accounting downplays the role of the hierarchy and lacks information and control systems. Western Accounting has an explicit hierarchy and developed information system but qualified them by intense processes of *acculturation*.
- Use of two key organization principles in the accounting firms (territorial representation: limited *management tenure*) that have no equivalence in the Bartlett and Ghoshal models. (In some ways, these are differences in the way that the structural framework is used rather than in the structure itself.)
- Heavy emphasis upon *training* as a vehicle for securing consistency of methods and behaviour. In Western Accounting, and to a lesser extent in Eastern Accounting, training is an instrument of acculturation. In both firms, it is a mechanism for improved international co-ordination.

The unitary and confederation models, in short, are distinctive because of the partnership mode of governance, the extensive use of lateral structure (such as committees, teams and task forces) and the emphasis upon training. These features are distinctive means of handling professionals within organizations. The same features have been found in large and small organizations and have simply been transplanted to the international arena. As such, to some extent the logic of structural-contingency theory, with its focus upon obtaining fit between organizational structures and an organization's task/technology, is supported. However that explanation does not go far enough: there remains the question of why there are *two* models in the same industry. Why do firms with similar tasks utilize different strategic orientations, structural configurations, and patterns of control processes? It is the existence of two models that raises the role of organizational history.

Administrative heritage, as defined by Bartlett and Ghoshal (1989), comprises the historical and structural factors (i.e., past ways of doing things, leadership, cultural values) that shape the 'strategic posture' of the firm and constrain its future direction. Though organizations are not akin to humans, with their genetic coding, they do have biographies (Kimberly, 1987) that contain initial imprints that become amplified (Granovetter, 1985). Decisions taken or not taken, actions pursued or avoided, converge to explain what is, and what might become. Early decisions become embedded in strategies, structures and processes, which then act to amplify the values and options of the original decisions. Organizations thus find it difficult to break from the traditions established in their youth.

In the case of the two accounting firms, the importance of early history is strongly shown in the implications of decisions within Western

Accounting to grow, so far as possible, from within, and to emphasize the concept of a single, unified firm, as compared to Eastern Accounting's preference to grow through mergers. Western Accounting, in other words, largely developed not through mergers between strong national firms, but through the opening of offices financed from internal revenues. Overseas offices were opened, often by using expatriates. Locally hired staff were centralized, trained, and socialized into Western Accounting's strong culture. This process of overseas expansion, financed and resourced from internal growth, inevitably made rapid growth difficult, and only in recent years has the firm altered its growth strategy. But an important consequence of Western Accounting's growth policy has been a greater homogeneity of perspectives, a clearer hierarchy world-wide, converging on the parent firm, and standardization of practices world-wide. That is, growth from within helped the development of strong co-ordination across national boundaries.

Eastern Accounting's history of growth is very different. Eastern Accounting grew through mergers of strong national firms. The historical process of growth shaped the configuration of power and thus the architecture of the firm's structures and systems. Growth via merger with and between national practices inevitably brought into the international firm considerable heterogeneity of perspectives. Furthermore, because these mergers were of large, national firms, each with an established market presence in their domestic jurisdictions, in many ways the national firm remained independent after the merger. For these firms, the primary competitive orientation of the international firm was, and remains, to develop a global network of offices capable of delivering seamless, quality service to global clients. But in developing that network the global firm has had to recognize that status and significance of the national firms. In short, because Eastern Accounting grew by multiple mergers (not from within a single entity) and it grew by mergers of equals, no strong centre has developed.

Organizational biographies not only help understand present circumstances but anticipate future directions. Opportunities available to one organization as present starting points appear less attractive and less viable to another. We see this happening in the accounting industry as firms evolve to cope with three types of pressure for tighter coupling:

- As more and more clients become multinational in scope, the demand increases for integration of single services (e.g., audit) delivered across national borders. Pricing policies, methodologies and selection of personnel have to be co-ordinated to win and implement engagements.
- The delivery of single bands of services in an integrated fashion is only the starting point of the international firm's strategy. A second and critical step is the capacity to deliver a spectrum of services (e.g., audit and tax consulting) in an integrated fashion. As the relative importance of audit revenues declines, firms use audits as entry points for other, higher value-added services.

- The third pressure for integration is somewhat different. Commodification of audit and accounting services has pushed accounting firms to develop specialized knowledge of particular industries, a development that requires harnessing skills and capabilities from around the world. The firm has to assemble expertise distributed world-wide, and take it to the client. Similarly, the firm has to co-ordinate investment efforts from several countries in order to achieve penetration of new territorial markets, or the development and widespread adoption of new services.

All accounting firms are aware of the need to meet pressures for better co-ordination world-wide. No partner, whom we interviewed, disputed the advantages of tighter, cross-border coupling. Eastern Accounting was acutely aware of the need to improve matters:

> We have to be able to react like a one-firm firm. Clients like . . . want one point of contact who can act authoritatively around the world.

> New emerging markets have to be acted upon swiftly, before the competition moves. The issue is whether we can access new ideas and best practices from within one country, and get them adopted effortlessly by other national firms.

Eastern Accounting has taken several steps to improve integration. These steps, however, do not include the strengthening of hierarchy, nor the imposing of bureaucratic control processes. There have been no steps to move Eastern Accounting closer towards Western Accounting's managerial arrangements, even though Western Accounting has been able to achieve much of the necessary integration. Instead, the changes in Eastern Accounting have built upon the firm's biographical format. Thus, Eastern Accounting has begun the introduction of changes. These include:

1 Strengthening the lead partner by giving responsibility to an individual for managing an international client's account. The lead partner has been given sufficient authority to lessen the need for cross-border negotiations and consensual decision-making, to speed up global responses, and to provide close attention to client needs. Implementation of this is not yet complete, and there are some indications that the concept is being undermined and may not be always effective in reconciling conflicts. But the concept builds upon the firm's existing emphasis upon lateral processes.
2 The same emphasis is observed at the strategic apex of the firm, where teams of senior partners have been struck to monitor and comment upon the extent to which individual national firms are implementing the international firm's strategy. Again, this process is an amplification of the emphasis upon peer pressure and collegial structures.
3 Greater emphasis upon the role of the chairman of the industry committees, in promoting the development of new products, the stalking of key new clients, and the provision of high-quality services to existing

multinational clients. Again, we see the emphasis upon the lateral structures.

4 Greater movement of personnel across borders, in a manner much more strategically disposed than hitherto. Partners may be moved to territories where they develop industry skills, or learn a new language. Partners located in countries serving a client's subsidiary company may relocate to spend time at the client's headquarters. This transfer of staff, clearly a potentially important way of strengthening international relationships, is voluntary, not mandatory, and involves agreement between national firms.

5 Broader recognition of training and the importance of acculturation. Eastern Accounting has traditionally emphasized the cognitive aspects of training, but increasingly forums for training are being used to deepen the cultural commitment of partners from different countries to the concept of Eastern Accounting as the firm.

These steps, taken by Eastern Accounting to develop tighter world-wide coupling, are consistent with the firm's traditional practice of de-emphasizing hierarchy and formal controls and thus illustrate how developments are extrapolations of previous themes and orientations.

In conclusion, the two case studies show the importance both of structural-contingency considerations and of biographical explanations, in understanding how organizations cope with global scope. The nature of the professional service firm work force, and the inability to separate production from marketing, produces a form of organization that emphasizes certain control processes over others. In developing theories of global strategic management, therefore, attention has to be paid to the nature of the work done and to characteristics of the work force. To date, rather more attention has focused upon the openness or otherwise of national markets and the availability or otherwise of technology of distribution and production economies of scale. There is a need to specify the nature of industry-based technological characteristics in order to understand better the generalizability of observations made from limited settings.

More attention should also be given to the biographical circumstances of particular organizations. Here we have identified one aspect of organizational history of particular relevance to international management, namely, the method of growth, that is whether through mergers or through internal expansion. How a firm grows, we have suggested, affects the distribution of power and authority within the international organization, and thus, subsequently, impacts upon the organization's strategic orientation, its structural configuration, and the choice of its control processes. These influences, once established, become amplified as the organization evolves. For this reason, a fuller understanding of how global organizations – whether partnerships of corporations – manage themselves, and why they do so as they do, requires sensitivity to the influence of biography with the parameters of technological imperatives.

Notes

1. This is still valid, although investment in information technology is providing a possible advantage to the larger international accounting firms.
2. The importance of mirroring clients' investments overseas is illustrated by the recent forays in China, Eastern Europe, and elsewhere (see Cooper, 1994).
3. Turley (1994: 14) provides a sharp illustration of the independence of the national firms by reminding us that they have the freedom to change their affiliation.
4. Only recently has Western Accounting departed from this practice.
5. Western Accounting have grown primarily through internal growth. One of the difficulties of growing via lateral hires is absorbing newcomers into the strong culture. As one partner put it, the difficulty is that we clubbed them with our culture.
6. Western Accounting has analysed itself and distilled what the firm perceives to be its seven values: quality service, quality people, meritocracy, one-firm approach, integrity, innovation, and stewardship. In highlighting stewardship, meritocracy, and the angst of being the best, we are reflecting our interpretation of how the culture appears to influence the manner of decision-making in the firm.
7. Resource-based theories of course, stress that sustained competitive advantage derives from non-imitable, unique resources (e.g., Barney, 1991; Grant, 1991). However, as Pfeffer (1994) has noted, managerial and organizational approaches are virtually impossible to mimic and replicate.
8. Johnson and Bird (1995) have raised similar ideas on the importance of strong cultures influencing managerial processes in accounting firms.
9. Bartlett and Ghoshal (1989) studied nine companies in some detail from three industries (branded packaged goods, consumer electronics and telecommunications). A further 63 were examined in less detail by questionnaire.

References

Aharoni, Y. (1993) *Coalitions and Competition: the Globalization of Professional Business Services.* New York: Routledge.

Arthur Anderson (1988) *A Vision of Grandeur.* London: Arthur Anderson & Co. Societè Cooperative.

Barney, J. (1991) 'Firm resources and sustained competitive advantage', *Journal of Management,* 17: 99–120.

Bartlett, C., Doz, Y. and Hedlund, G. (1990) 'Introduction', in C. Bartlett, Y. Doz and G. Hedlund (eds), *Managing the Global Firm.* London: Routledge.

Bartlett, C. and Ghoshal, S. (1987) 'Managing across borders: new organizational responses', *Sloan Management Review,* Fall: 43–53.

Bartlett, C. and Ghoshal, S. (1988) 'Organizing for worldwide effectiveness: the transnational solution', *California Management Review,* Fall 3 (1): 54–74.

Bartlett, C. and Ghoshal, S. (1989) *Managing across Borders: the Transnational Solution.* Boston, MA: Harvard Business School Press.

Bartlett, C. and Ghoshal, S. (1991) *Managing across Borders: the Transnational Solution.* London: London Business School.

Cooper, D. (1994) 'Globalization and nationalism in a multinational accounting firm: the case of opening new markets in Eastern Europe'. John V. Ratcliffe Memorial Lecture, The University of New South Wales School of Accounting.

Cooper, D.J., Hinings, B., Greenwood, R. and Brown, J.L. (1996) 'Sedimentation and transformation in organizational change: the case of Canadian law firms', *Organization Studies,* 17 (4): 623–47.

Cypert, S.A. (1991) *Following the Money – the Inside Story of Accounting's First Mega-Merger*. New York: AMACOM.

Daniels, P., Thrift, N. and Leyshon, A. (1989) 'Internationalisation of professional services: accountancy conglomerates', in P. Enderwick (ed.), *Multinational Service Firms*. London: Routledge. pp. 79–105.

Donaldson, L. (1995) *In Defence of Organization Theory. A Reply to the Critics*. Cambridge: Cambridge University Press.

Economist, The (1995) 'A survey of multinationals', 24 June.

Egelhoff, W.G. (1984) 'Strategy and structure in multinational corporations: a version of the Stopford and Wells model', *Strategic Management Journal*, 9: 1–14.

Ferner, A., Edwards, P. and Sisson, K. (1994) 'Coming unstuck? In search of the "corporate glue" in an international professional service firm'. Accepted for publication *Human Resource Management Journal*.

Fladmore-Lindquist, K. (1993) 'The impact of bargaining and negotiating on the globalisation of professional service firms', in J. Aharoni (ed.), *Coalitions and Competition: the Globalisation of Professional Business Services*. New York: Routledge. pp. 143–52.

Franko, L. (1976) 'The move toward a multi-divisional structure in European organizations', *Administrative Science Quarterly*, 19 (4): 493–506.

Galbraith, J.R. and Karanjian, R.R. (1986) 'Organizing to implement strategies of diversity and globalisation: the role of matrix designs', *Human Resource Management*, Spring: 37–54.

Ghoshal, S. and Westney, E. (1993) *Organizational Theory and the Multinational Corporation*. New York: St Martin's Press.

Giarini, D. (ed.) (1987) *The Emerging Service Economy*. Oxford: Pergamon Press.

Granovetter, M. (1985) 'Economic action and social structure: the problem of embeddedness', *American Journal of Sociology*, 91 (3): 481–510.

Grant, R. (1991) 'The resource-based theory of competitive advantage: implications for strategy formulation', *California Management Review*. Spring: 114–35.

Greenwood, R., Hinings, B. and Brown, J. (1990) 'P2 form strategic management: corporate practice in professional partnerships', *Academy of Management Journal*, 33 (4): 725–55.

Haveman, H.A. (1993) 'Follow the leader: mimetic isomorphism and entry into new markets', *Administrative Science Quarterly*, 38 (4): 564–92.

Hout, T., Porter, M.E. and Rudden, E. (1982) 'How global companies win out', *Harvard Business Review*, September–October: 98–108.

Johansson, J.K. and Yip, G.S. (1994) 'Exploiting globalisation potential: US and Japanese strategies', *Strategic Management Journal*, October: 579–601.

Johnson, G. and Bird, S. (1995) 'Strategic change in knowledge-based firms: learning from professionals'. Working chapter presented at the Conference on Change in Knowledge-based Organizations, University of Alberta, Edmonton, Canada, 19–21 May 1995.

Kimberly, J.R. (1987) 'The study or organizations: towards a biographical perspective', in J. Lorsch (ed.), *Handbook of Organizational Behaviour*. Englewood Cliffs, NJ: Prentice-Hall.

Lovelock, C. (1983) 'Classifying services to gain strategic marketing insights', *Journal of Marketing*, 9–20.

Maister, D. (1985) 'The one-firm firm', *Sloan Management Review*, Fall: 3–13.

Martinez, J. and Jarrillo, J. (1989) 'The evolution of research on co-ordination mechanisms in multinational corporations', *Journal of International Business Studies*, 20 (3): 489–514.

Morrison, A.J. (1990) *Strategies in Global Industries: How US Businesses Compete*. Westpoint, CT: Quorum Books.

Ouchi, W.G. (1980) 'Markets, bureaucracies and clans', *Administrative Science Quarterly*, 25: 129–41.

Perlmutter, H.V. (1969) 'The tortuous evolution of the multinational corporation', *Columbia Journal of World Business*, 4: 9–18.

Pfeffer, J. (1994) 'Competitive advantage through people', *California Management Review*, 36 (2): 9–28.

Porter, M.E. (1986) 'Competition in global industries: a conceptual framework', in Michael E. Porter (ed.), *Competition in Global Industries*. Boston, MA: Harvard University Press.

Prahalad, C. and Doz, Y (1987) *The Multinational Mission*. New York: The Free Press.

Public Accounting Deskbook (1996) Atlanta, GA: Stratford Publications.

Richards, A.B. (1981) *Touche Ross & Co., 1899–1981*. London: Touche Ross & Co.

Richards, L. and Richards, T. (1992) *Nudist: User Guide: Version 3.0*. APTOS, CA: Aladdin Systems Inc.

Sapir, A. (1982) 'Trade in service: policy issues for the eighties', *Columbia Journal of World Business*, 17 (3): 77–83.

Schmenner, R.W. (1986) 'How can service business survive and prosper', *Sloan Management Review*, Spring: 21–31.

Starbuck, W.H. (1992) 'Learning by knowledge-intensive firms', *Journal of Management Studies*, 29: 741–60.

Stinchcombe, A.L. (1965) 'Social structure and organizations', in J.G. March (ed.), *Handbook of Organizations*. Chicago: Rand McNally. pp. 142–93.

Stopford, J. and Wells, L. (1972) *Managing the Multinational Enterprise*. New York: Basic Books.

Turley, S. (1994) 'The theory of the international development of accounting firms'. Paper presented at *4th Maistricht Audit Research Symposium*, 24–25 October 1994.

Watt, L. (1982) *The First Seventy-five Years*. Toronto: Price Waterhouse.

Wise, T.A. (1981) *Peat Marwick Mitchell & Co: 85 years*. New York: Peat Marwick Mitchell & Co.

Yip, G. (1992) *Total Global Strategy. Managing for Worldwide Competitive Advantage*. Englewood Cliffs, NJ: Prentice-Hall.

Zeithaml, V.A., Parasuraman, A. and Berry, L. (1985) 'Problems and strategies in service marketing', *Journal of Marketing*, 49 (Spring): 33–46.

Zeithaml, V.A., Parasuraman, A. and Berry, L. (1990) *Delivering Quality Service: Balancing Customer Perceptions and Expectations*. New York: The Free Press.

Index

Torok, A., 112
Torraine, A., 209
Torslanda plant (Volvo), 189
Total Quality Control (TQC), 147
Total Quality Management (TQM), 9, 12, 13–14, 17–18, 22–32, 146, 163–75
Townley, B., 13, 60, 147
Toyoda, S., 180
Toyota, 128, 131, 177, 180–4, 193
training-related initiatives, 172–4
transnationals, 52–4
Treasury Department of the USA, 101
Trist, E.L., 248
Trompenars, F., 235, 236
Truman Doctrine, 38
trust, 75–7
Tugendhat, E., 230
Tully, S., 247
Turley, S., 268, 275, 276, 278
Turnbull, P., 132
Turner, B.S., 33
Tyson, S., 148

Uddevalla plant (Volvo), 135, 142, 187–9
Union of the Soviet Socialist Republics (USSR)/Soviet Union, 38, 39, 41, 48, 129
United Auto Workers (UAW), 40
United Kingdom (UK)/Britain, 48, 50, 53, 79, 135, 148, 149–50, 163–4, 179, 183, 278
United Mine Workers 40
United Nations, 92
United Nations Development Programme, 92
United States Armed Forces Institute (USAFI), 46
United States (USA), 7, 8, 9, 12–13, 30, 38, 39, 42, 43, 48, 50, 53, 79, 89, 103, 121, 125, 129, 132, 133, 135, 136, 148, 158, 179, 180–1, 183, 193, 278, 280
United Textile Workers, 40
universalism, 2, 6, 7–8, 12
Ure, A., 24
US Steel, 41
U-shaped cells, 131, 140

Values/value systems, 12, 14–15, 54–61, 72–80
Van der Ven, A., 19, 20, 33
Van Fleet, D.D., 56
Van Zon, H., 114
Varela, F., 202
Vice-Ministry of Regional Development (Mexico), 94
virtual organizations, 14, 190–192
Von Glaserfield, E., 165
Vurdubakis, T., 171

Walker, T., 22
Walton, R.E., 79, 156
Warner, M., 111, 122–3, 124, 149
Warren, E.K., 50, 56
Warren, R., 248
Warsaw Pact, 38
Waterman, J.A., 73
Waterman, R.H., 11, 21, 73
Watson, T.J., 79
Watt, L., 271
Webb, J., 142
Weber, M., 4, 13, 15, 29, 60, 178
Webster, F., 23, 199
Weick, K., 186–8, 196, 198
Weiner, M., 148
Wells, L., 266
Wells, P., 189, 190
Wemmerlöv, U., 129, 135
Western Accounting, 271–94
Western Electric Company, 205
Western Europe, 120, 125, 136
Westley, F., 186–8
Westney, E., 266
Wetzel, C.F., 22
Wheeler, B.O., 43–4, 48, 62
Whitley, R., 3
Whyte, W.F., 40, 50–1
Wickens, P., 147
Wiener, N., 203
Wiesenfeld, B., 70, 78
Wilkins, M., 53
Wilkinson, A., 166
Wilkinson, B., 10, 13, 25, 26, 27, 128, 133, 136, 142, 147, 149, 183
Williams, A., 148
Williams, J., 183
Williams, K., 9, 183
Williamson, O.E., 248